Relentless Pursuit

The Untold Story
of the U.S. 5th Air Force's 39th Fighter Squadron

For Dave Larkie with warm personal regards.
Ken Dooley

By Ken Dooley

Foreword by Dr. Patrick T. Conley, Historian Laureate of Rhode Island

Epilogue by J. William Middendorf, Former Secretary of the Navy

Pi Ken Production

Relentless Pursuit
The Untold Story of the U.S. 5th Air Force's 39th Fighter Squadron
All Rights Reserved.
Copyright © 2015 Ken Dooley and Pi Patel
v2.0

Cover Design: Mary Morgan Martin
Graphic Design: Peter Martin

PiKen Production

ISBN: 978-0-578-16542-4

PRINTED IN THE UNITED STATES OF AMERICA

So Nigh is grandeur to our dust

So Near to God is man,

When Duty whispers low, thou must

The Youth replies, I can!

Ralph Waldo Emerson

Books, plays, and screenplays

by Ken Dooley

MBA: Management by Auerbach

The Murder Trial of John Gordon

The Auerbach Dynasty

Ups and Downs

Bellevue Avenue

Empty Nesting

Kristallnacht in Cranston

Ghosts Over Providence

Good Stuff (Progressive Business Publications)

The Selling Advantage (Progressive Business Publications)

Table of Contents

Introduction

Combat in the Pacific Theater in World War II is usually associated with such epic and ferocious battles as Guadalcanal and Iwo Jima. Separating these tiny points of land was an endless expanse of water and occasional impenetrable jungle in the Western Pacific and the South China seas. Here, day after day for 4 years, battles were waged in the skies by skilled, dedicated, and astonishingly courageous pilots, many of them too young to be served in one of their hometown bars.

Wars, of course, have always been cruel destroyers of young men. As the sharp tip of the American spear, pilots of the American Fifth Air Force were charged with stopping the Japanese juggernaut advancing relentlessly down the island chains toward its goal of taking Australia out of the war.

Many died in dogfights, especially in the first year of the war when the planes they flew were inferior to the vaunted Japanese Zero. Many more died in the accidents and miscalculations that punctuated daily operations at the time. Overloaded with fuel, bombs, and ammunition, their planes flipped, crashed, and exploded while attempting takeoffs on jungle runways. Operating at the extreme range of their fuel capacity with primitive navigational aids, they were often lost without a trace. Attacking at low altitudes, even marginally effective Japanese antiaircraft fire brought them down. If shot down and captured, they were tortured and murdered by their Japanese captors.

So in the terrible complexities of human brutality, civilized standards gave way to impulsive savagery, as Japanese soldiers murdered helpless, sick, and unarmed POWs under what they described as *Bushido*, a Japanese word for the concept of chivalry as a way of life for Japanese samurai warriors. In the 1930s, the Japanese military changed the concept of Bushido and gave birth to the "Spirit Warriors" who murdered, raped, and committed crimes against humanity in the name of the emperor.

This book is about the bravery and experiences of the men of the 39th Fighter Squadron. It is about how they avidly joined, diligently trained, and faithfully, day after day, took part in missions, each of which had a significant probability of being their last. It is about how they remained staunchly committed to their military oaths, even when captured, tortured, and facing execution. Then, unlike other books about the Pacific air war, it traces the consequences of Japanese war crimes in the immediate postwar period.

Most significantly, we explore how justice was not meted out for those who had been captured and killed by the Japanese. Much has been written about the trials and convictions of the "Class A" war criminals, such as Generals Tojo and Homma. Less is known about the treatment of lower-level officers who extended the war by fanatically defending isolated island bases and inflicting ceremonial executions on helpless prisoners under their "Spirit Warrior" code.

At the war crimes trials held at Tokyo and Yokohama at the end of the war, these "warriors" became whining cowards arguing that they were only acting on the emperor's orders as they tortured and executed helpless prisoners of war.

Attorneys who defended them were not able to question Emperor Hirohito, the worst war criminal in the Far East—or even mention his name during the trials, under the orders of General Douglas MacArthur.

The young men of the 39th Fighter Squadron were thrust into a type of war never before encountered or even imagined. For these American boys, the war was conducted over a largely unmapped area with steaming jungles, glaciers, and towering thunderheads. They encountered new types of illnesses (malaria and dengue), a new type of civilian noncombatant (Stone Age men, women, and children), and a new type of enemy (barbarians with modern equipment).

They did not have books on tactics to study and remember. There were no old air battles to examine. It was all new. "Trial and error" was the only tactical lesson plan available. They were dumped into open areas and told to set up camp. These were unpopulated areas, most even unexplored. They fought the war with their brains, planes, and courage.

Not everything went well, particularly in the early days of the war when they faced an enemy with more experience and better aircraft. But the pilots of the 39th Fighter Squadron persevered and made it from Port Moresby, New Guinea, to Tokyo.

This is their story.

Ken Dooley
Newport, Rhode Island
April 2015

Foreword

This volume was inspired by the grisly, horrific death suffered by Lt. Robert Thorpe, a downed and doomed American pilot, at the hands of his Japanese captors. Although this atrocity occurred long ago on the other side of the world, for prolific author and playwright Ken Dooley it hit home. The Thorpe family of Cranston, Rhode Island, had been Dooley's neighbors and friends.

Lieutenant Thorpe met his fate stoically and heroically on a beach in New Guinea in May 1944. He was beaten, used for target practice, beheaded, and then his tormentors desecrated his lifeless body. Dooley, using the original court transcripts, describes the postwar trials of the sadistic naval officers who perpetrated this act. Three of those involved met more merciful deaths—two by suicide, the other by hanging. Four more were jailed for their crime.

The cold steel of battle nearly always pierces the thin veil of civility that masks human barbarism and brutality. This exposure of our primitive instincts is the great tragedy of war.

In the process of uncovering and relating the travails of Bob Thorpe, Dooley describes the litany of war crimes committed by the Japanese against military captives and civilian populations throughout East Asia. They rival those of Hitler. However, the focus on American prisoners of war discloses one irony—despite Germany's monstrous madness toward Jews, Russians, and Polish Catholic civilians, its treatment of American prisoners of war was far less barbarous than the actions of Japan. A sitcom like *Hogan's Heroes* is inconceivable in a Japanese concentration camp setting.

A far greater irony demonstrating the folly of war is that West Germany quickly became a leading American ally in Europe, and Japan, under the effective stewardship of General Douglas MacArthur, became America's most important East Asian ally after the fall of China to Communism in 1948—the year that five of the officers accused of murdering Bob Thorpe were tried and convicted.

Dooley's gripping and meticulously researched tale goes far beyond the tragic fate of Bob Thorpe. It is a detailed account of American airmen in a vital but somewhat neglected theater of the Pacific War—the East Indies (present-day Indonesia and Papua New Guinea). It not only relates their amazing exploits but also describes in minute detail the technology of the planes they flew, the terrain they traversed, and the daunting difficulties they encountered and overcame. Dooley not only learned aviation technology, he spanned the country to interview surviving pilots of Thorpe's unit (the 39th Fighter Squadron), and waded through thousands of pages of records generated by the war crimes courts.

As Rhode Island Historian Laureate, I am inclined to comment upon Rhode Island's earlier contacts with that area of the world where Bob Thorpe was assigned and met his dreadful demise.

Captain Robert Gray of Tiverton, the first American to circumnavigate the globe, sailed his ship *Columbia* just north of New Guinea on his triumphant 1790 voyage. This intrepid navigator took the same route again in 1792 on his second global circumnavigation after exploring America's northwest coast, and named its great river, the Columbia, in honor of his sturdy vessel.

Merchants from Rhode Island families such as the Browns and the Ives and other traders like Edward Carrington repeatedly dispatched their sailing vessels from Providence to the Dutch East Indies in the early nineteenth century. These ships, called East Indiamen, acquired sugar, spices, and large cargoes of coffee from Java and its surrounding islands. This trade returned profits to these entrepreneurs that earned them and their descendants places among Rhode Island's economic and social elite.

Commodore Matthew Calbraith Perry, a Newport native, visited Japan in 1853 and again in 1854 with his black-hulled fleet. He pressured that nation into accepting the Convention of Kanagawa, a consular treaty with the Empire of Japan, giving the United States access to the ports of Hakodata and Shimoda and opening that then feudal nation to Western influence. For the past 30 years the Newport chapter of the Japan-America Society has celebrated this achievement with a gala Black Ships Festival.

Brown University alumnus John Hay, as United States secretary of state, proclaimed an "Open Door Policy" for China in 1899, an ex parte pronouncement (which annoyed the European imperial powers and Japan) stating that all nations have equal trading rights and commercial opportunities in China.

For decades before and after World War II, the Catholic Columban Fathers, many of whom have retired to a home in Bristol, brought the message of Christianity to numerous Far Eastern countries.

These Rhode Islanders, native and adopted, were motivated either by fame, fortune, or faith. Thanks to Ken Dooley, another Rhode Islander, this one who was motivated by fearless patriotism, receives the recognition due to him. Though buried unceremoniously in the sands of a remote New Guinea beach, the exploits and the memory of Lt. Robert Thorpe are no longer buried beneath the sands of time. His life and his heroism have been duly noted for his posterity to acknowledge and admire.

Dr. Patrick T. Conley
Historian Laureate of Rhode Island

Dedication

For all the men of the 39th Fighter Squadron. You were, indeed, the greatest generation.

For Gill Thorpe for never giving up in his efforts to have his brother's remains buried with his parents.

For Mary Morgan Martin for her incredible research and photo restoration.

For Red Auerbach for teaching me that effort and teamwork will always overcome talent and statistics –always.

For Ed Satell for proving that less can be more when it comes to writing.

For Piyush Patell for his willingness to support worthy projects in India or the U.S.A.

For Gov. Lincoln Chafee, Sen. Jack Reed and Mayor Allan Fung for their efforts in honoring Lt. Robert E. Thorpe.

For Patrick T. Conley and J. William Middendorf for their incredible wisdom, advice and writing talent.

For Peter Martin for his motivation and "nerd" skills.

For Linne Haddock for her invaluable insights and knowledge of the history of the 39th Fighter Squadron.

For Margaret Satell for her superb copyediting.

For Sam Katz for fifty years of smiles.

For the two women in my life, my daughter, Alicia and my granddaughter, Sarah.

For Leo P. and Marion V. (Kenneally) Dooley, my mother and father, my sisters, Eileen and Peg, and my brothers Jack, Larry, Paul, Bill and Bob.

For my nephews, Scott, Jeff and Michael Dooley and my courageous nieces, Ann Brown and Kathy Ashley.

For Patricia Plourde, Wes Forcier, Herb and Chris Browne, Susan and Bill Hostnik, Wayne Muller, Margaret Coffee, Patti and John Concannon, Donald Von Statts, Bill Crofton, Dick Finnerty, Pieter Von Bennekom, Bil, Joan and Marion Kenneally, Jim and Curt Brown, Scott Molloy, Don Deignan, Matthew and Clifford Satell, Tom Schubert, Regina Lennox, Janet Stuart, Jen Erb, Nicole Riegl, Kerry Isberg, Christian Schappel, John Walston, Rich Henson, Renee Cocchi, Rick Wolff, Brian Zevnik, Steve Petrides, Paul and Marilyn Dunphy, Kevin O'Neill, Dick Bruno, Harry Cross, Stu Hobron, Ruth Nagle, Gary, Lois and Carl Lutender, Bob Klimek and Schuyler Jenks for always being there.

For my Newport support group: Angela Vars, Peg Murray, Francoise Pomfret, Gloria and Tony Cercena, Tim Cohane, Rick O'Neill and George Wardwell.

For all my colleagues at Progressive Business Publications

Chapter 1
Bob Thorpe's Last Flight

The slender 20-year-old knelt before the narrow trench soon to be his grave, exhausted, filthy, and clad only in a pair of blue shorts. He was in excruciating pain from bullet wounds in his legs administered as "target practice" by his captors. Imperial Japanese naval personnel gathered around, chattering and laughing. His executioner stood behind him, preparing the sword for his ceremonial beheading, much in the manner of the fanatical ISIS militants of our own day.

What was going through Bob Thorpe's mind in those last few moments before his death? The night before, May 27, 1944, he and 15 other pilots who would be taking part in the raid met for their preflight briefing at their airbase 300 miles to the south in Gusap, New Guinea. The target was the big Japanese airfield complex at Wewak. There was not much chance they would be intercepted by enemy aircraft since most of the Japanese planes were destroyed or damaged. But, as usual, there would be heavy ground fire.

As the pilots left the briefing talking quietly, each must have calculated his odds. It was a given that the most dangerous part of any of these missions was the takeoff. Their massive, 6-ton P-47s were powered by 2,000 horsepower radial engines. To carry the fuel to make the 600-mile round-trip flight, they needed an extra 400 gallons of gasoline in auxiliary fuel tanks slung beneath the wings, along with two 500-pound bombs. That weight, combined with hundreds of rounds of ammunition for their eight .50-caliber machine guns, made getting these massive machines off the ground over runways of metal sheets on spongy jungle earth a death-defying challenge. Planes that blew tires on the sharp edges of the metal sheets often flipped over and burst into flames, giving the pilots almost no chance to escape.

Once off the ground, the greatest danger they encountered was the weather. As the hot, humid air blowing in from the North Pacific Ocean reached the Owen Stanley Mountain Range that formed the central spine of the world's second-biggest island, it rushed up toward the 15,000-foot peaks, creating massive clouds and rainstorms. With compasses and wristwatches as their only navigational aids, pilots were easily lost in this turbulent murk. Disoriented, they ran out of fuel and crashed at sea or, worse yet, in the endless jungle. There were always searches but few rescues.

All of this faced those 16 pilots as they rolled out from under the mosquito netting covering their bunks at six the next morning, showered, ate breakfast, and piled into Jeeps for the half-mile ride to the airstrip.

The noise on the flight line was deafening as the huge engines roared to life. One by one the fighters taxied down the runway, gaining speed and taking off. Once in the air, they circled over Gusap until the entire 16-unit formation formed in four-abreast lines, climbed to 15,000 feet, and headed north along the Ruma River Valley toward the coast.

The river widens into a massive coastal marsh at its mouth. The formation banked west over the marsh and, dropping down to just over 1,000 feet, flew the last 150 miles to Wewak over the unbroken jungle canopy. There was less chance of the attackers being spotted over the jungle than over the coast, where the battered Japanese navy was still active. Just east of Wewak, the formation veered slightly south to avoid "sure-shot Charlie," a large caliber antiaircraft gun that had shot down several American planes.

The big Japanese base at Wewak was intended to block an Allied advance up the north New Guinea coast toward the Philippines. But after months of relentless air attacks, it was incapable of even providing its own air cover. Hundreds of wrecked Japanese planes lined its five airstrips.

Reaching the airfield complex, the first flight dropped to treetop level and began its attacks. Scores of 12.8-millimeter machine guns—the Japanese equivalent of the American .50-caliber—filled the air with metal. The American planes attacked from the east, using the morning sun to obscure the aim of the Japanese gunners.

"We attacked one-by-one, and the time over the field was only seconds," explains Lt. Jack Frost, who was on the mission when Thorpe was lost. "The first guy in is the safest. By the time the last guy made his run, all kinds of metal was coming up at him."

The field was already battered and smoking when Bob Thorpe, flying second wingman in the third flight, made his run. Damaged planes and a few buildings and vehicles were his strafing targets. When the formation finished the attack and reformed at 10,000 feet above the Wewak complex, there were just 15 planes. No one had seen Bob go down.

P-47 engines were notoriously tough, often returning to base with some of their 18 radial cylinders shot off. Ground fire must have penetrated crucial parts of Bob's engine. Unable to gain altitude, he banked out over the water and managed to maintain enough control to set the plane down in one piece. It sank immediately, but he was able to release his harness and scramble out of the cockpit. His inflatable raft went down with the plane, but a large log was floating nearby. He swam over to it and drifted in to the beach at Kairiru Island, just offshore from Wewak.

Something of a favorite today for surfers with a taste for the wild side, Kairiru is described in brochures as "an almost unbelievably picturesque setting, with the volcanic mountains rising out of the sea." On that May morning it was sweltering, and Bob Thorpe was parched with thirst after his ordeal of ditching the plane and swimming to shore. He also certainly had no illusions about what was in store for him at this point. Pilots downed in the jungle or the sea, unless they were quickly rescued, knew they were doomed if captured by the Japanese. Some pilots regarded the sidearms they carried as their tickets to instant oblivion. Whether or not Bob had considered that option, it was now moot since his pistol went down with his plane.

He was immediately captured by a patrol made up of "volunteers" from Formosa, under the command of Tobei Baba. Considered third-rate soldiers by the Japanese, these men were assigned only patrol and security duties. They apparently took him into custody without any violence or cruelty. He must have seen no point in resisting, and they understood that their commanders would want him brought in quickly for interrogation. Indeed, they probably regarded the capture as a stroke of luck. Delivering him physically intact and mentally coherent for interrogation would curry favor with their Japanese overlords.

Baba turned Thorpe over to Warrant Officer Naotada Fujihira of the 27th Special Base Force on Muschu Island. With two members of the Takasago Unit as guards, Fujihira tied a rope around Thorpe's hands and led him on the 6-mile journey, over rugged mountain trails, to the headquarters of his unit.

At one point they stopped to rest and Fujihira gave Thorpe water and a biscuit. The language barrier precluded any communication, but Thorpe may have felt some faintly reassuring sense of their common humanity at that point.

That ended when they reached headquarters. Thorpe was taken to an air raid shelter and tied to a post. Time passed as he waited for what was to come next. Inside headquarters 40 feet away, Admiral Kenro Sato, commanding officer of the 27th Special Base Force, was informed by Captain Kiyohisa Noto of the prisoner's capture. Sato's decision about Bob's fate was probably instantaneous, since he had just returned from Japan where all captured American flyers were considered war criminals and many were executed immediately.

Sato ordered Noto to interrogate the prisoner and extract any useful information. Commander Kaoru Okuma, who spoke some English, was given the assignment.

Testimony at the trial after the war indicated that the interrogation began in a relatively civilized manner. Asked where he was from in the United States, Thorpe told them about the Rhode Island town of Cranston "not far from Boston." He mentioned his parents and his younger brother and sister.

When the questions shifted to the military situation, however, he stubbornly stuck to the Geneva Convention requirement giving only name, rank, and serial number. As to the kind of plane he was flying, what base and squadron he was from, what the targets of the mission had been, he remained stonily silent. He did answer, however, when Okuma asked him who he thought would win the war. Thorpe replied that his country had too many resources to lose.

That infuriated Okuma, and he slapped the prisoner. By now, a dozen or more soldiers had arrived to witness the interrogation. Okuma turned to them and said that the prisoner had insulted the emperor and invited them to beat him. The scene turned savage. This was a group that had transitioned psychologically from dreams of triumph and control of the entire Pacific region to the grim reality of grinding defeat by overwhelming American military strength. It had been nearly 2 years since the Japanese Imperial Navy's catastrophic defeat in the Battle of Midway.

The triumphs at Pearl Harbor and in the Philippine campaigns were now distant and fading memories. Even large bases like Wewak were becoming strategically irrelevant, unable to adequately defend themselves, much less project power in their areas. Supply and communication lines were in tatters. Wewak's only remaining strategic significance was to block the Americans and Australians from taking control of New Guinea.

Under these circumstances, emperor worship was the only remaining unifying and motivating force for these men. That was certainly the motivation for hundreds of thousands of Japanese soldiers to sacrifice themselves fanatically in battle. What is so difficult to understand and impossible to forgive is how emperor worship could lead them to attack a prisoner tied to a post and beat him to a bloody pulp with fists and sticks.

The beating was still going on when Okuma left the scene to report the results of the interrogation to Noto. Okuma was ordered to execute Thorpe in any manner he chose. At 3 o'clock that afternoon, an execution party consisting of four officers—Kaoru Okuma, Tsunehiko Yamamoto, Naotada Fujihira, and Yutaka Odazawa, and about 20 enlisted men led Thorpe to a native cemetery where a shallow grave had already been dug.

Odazawa carried a sword, as it had been decided that Thorpe would be ceremonially beheaded, a procedure which, under the Bushido Code, was intended to bestow honor on a defeated military adversary. It was seen as some sort of ticket to paradise. But given the tattered state of the code, any ritual value of these executions was lost in their cruelty.

It was at this point that Okuma announced that the beheading was to be preceded by "target practice" by himself, Yamamoto, and Fujihira. Odazawa asked the officers to aim low so as not to compromise the victim with upper body wounds that would make beheading him difficult.

Fujihira fired first and missed, much to the amusement of the crowd. At his court-martial 4 years later, Fujihira claimed to have missed deliberately, because he felt compassion for Thorpe based on their travel together over the mountain trail. Yamamoto shouted in English that "I will now shoot you with my pistol," and Thorpe staggered slightly when the bullet hit his lower leg. Okuma shot next, and blood spurted from the prisoner's other leg. However, he remained standing.

Complete with its shooting gallery and raucous crowd, the execution site had taken on a carnival atmosphere. Odazawa ordered some of the enlisted men to drag the prisoner to the grave site as he filled a bottle with water. He offered it to the prisoner, then poured water on Thorpe's neck and on his heirloom samurai sword. Odazawa then performed an act as though it were from a play. He did it in a contemptuous manner and everyone laughed.

He said in Japanese, "I, Chief Petty Officer Odazawa, will now proceed to execute the prisoner." He pushed Thorpe into a kneeling position with his head bowed forward at the edge of the grave. Just before Odazawa beheaded him, Thorpe looked up and in a calm voice asked, "What time is it?"

Odazawa struck and Thorpe's body fell into the grave. CWO Waichi Ogawa, a medical technician, jumped into the grave, cut open Thorpe's chest with a knife, and removed an organ, probably his liver. As the late-afternoon sun set, soldiers filled in the grave. During the court-martial of the officers charged in Thorpe's execution, one of the accused drew a map showing the burial site. The court-martial records were sealed. For more than 60 years, Walter Thorpe was told that his son's remains were "unrecoverable."

During the war crimes trial in Yokohama in 1948, Kaoru Okuma, the man who made the decision to use the prisoner for target practice prior to the execution, described Thorpe's behavior throughout the ordeal as "magnificent."

Fifteen pilots assembled for a debriefing following the mission in which Thorpe was lost. Second Lt. James M. Robertson said, "Just as the first strafing run was started, I saw Thorpe, who was flying on my wing, peel off to make the pass. The airplane appeared to be okay."

1st Lt. Raymond Kramme conducted an aerial search for any sign of Thorpe's aircraft in the Wewak area the day of his disappearance. The results of his search were negative. Major Harris L. Denton also took off on a search mission but had to abort it when visibility dropped to zero. Denton said a search mission would be scheduled as soon as weather permitted, and he grounded the squadron.

Second Lt. Fred Tobi and Lt. Lew Lockhart ignored the order and flew an unauthorized mission to find Thorpe. They found no trace of him or his airplane.

Tobi had lost his brother in a plane crash in 1943, and Bob Thorpe had taken his brother's place. They had gone through flight training together, and Tobi remembered meeting Nora Thorpe, Bob's mother, during the graduation ceremony when they received their wings.

They shared the same tent at Gusap and flew many combat missions together. During an interview in 2007, Tobi was asked if he had ever contacted the Thorpe family to find out what happened to Bob. "I didn't know what happened to Bob until you just told me," Tobi said.

"You have to understand our thinking at the time. When a pilot went missing, we acted as if he had simply been transferred. Bob was my closest friend in the Air Corps. He was transferred out of the 39th, and that was it. War is hell. The scars are deep. Some losses are just too painful to think about."

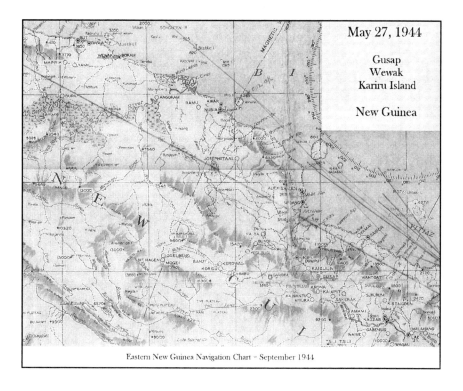

May 27, 1944

Gusap
Wewak
Kariru Island

New Guinea

Eastern New Guinea Navigation Chart – September 1944

Chapter 2
Meet the Thorpes

Walter Thorpe was never one to tell war stories, not that he did not have plenty to tell. A World War I Yankee Division artilleryman, he had been through some of the fiercest fighting and most grueling conditions in France. There were epic battles such as Meuse-Argonne and the Ardennes, where many of his friends were killed and wounded. Horses literally burst their hearts straining to pull the guns (until Walter and his battery mates stole sturdier mules from the French). There was always the filth and mud and terrible food.

"He never really said much about any of this," son Gill recalls now, some 90 years after his dad returned in the same woolen uniform he had worn going overseas 20 months earlier, a uniform he had to line with newspapers against the cold for two winters. "What he did tell us about was getting months of back pay just before boarding the ship and gambling all the way across. At one point in the crossing he was very wealthy. When they got to New York, someone else was."

Walter never gambled again. Even had he been so inclined, there really was not time. Within the next 3 years, he met and married Nora Gill, completed training as a pharmacist, and opened Thorpe's Pharmacy in his hometown of Cranston, Rhode Island, on the shores of Narragansett Bay.

The pharmacy was the kind of quasi-community center that thrived in so many towns in the years before the big national chains drove them out of business. There was the pharmaceutical area in the rear, counters for sundries in the center, and a 10-stool soda fountain up front where locals gathered to exchange their views on the great issues and events of the day. By the late 1930s, these had transitioned from the economic hardships of the Great Depression to the clashes in Europe and Asia that were to lead up to World War II.

Walter, whether filling a prescription or making up one of his renowned coffee milk shakes, made his views perfectly clear. He was adamantly opposed to the country entering another war. He had seen enough in France, and now he suffered the awful anxiety as a parent of a son of draft age.

Bob, born in 1923, was actually the Thorpes' second child. Richard, born in 1920, was a thriving 3-year old when an untended moving van rolled down a hill and crushed him to death in his playpen in the family's front yard. It was the kind of tragedy that no family ever really recovers from, and for Walter and Nora, the thought of losing Bob as well was more than they could bear. But, by 1940, Bob was a bright, adventuresome 17-year old, and they must have realized that if the country did go to war, the duty, challenge, and excitement of military service would be more than their son could resist.

Bob was an indifferent high school student. No one questioned his intelligence, but neither could anyone engage his interest in the subjects he was expected to study. He excelled, however, in anything that did interest him—mostly high activity pursuits like sailboat racing, fishing, and outdoor adventures with his Boy Scout troop. Scouting also seemed to bring out a commitment to civic responsibility. He spent time helping build camps, grading open space, and once disappeared from the family entirely for 3 days while fighting forest fires in Western Rhode Island.

"He was a sight when he got home," says his brother Gill, who was 8 years younger. "He was always skinny, but in his bedraggled clothes and covered with soot, he looked like a scarecrow."

Gill remembers Bob as a kind and caring older brother. "I think I was 6 when I got a Lionel train set for Christmas," he says. "I had no idea of how to set it up. So he did the whole thing for me, and then he let me run it first."

Another time when Gill was having trouble flying kites, he remembers the special pains Bob took to help him. "He'd bought some special material for making the frames. He glued on newspaper and attached the necessary string for the bow and bridle and showed me how to make the adjustments for the tail. That kite was the best. Every kid in the neighborhood wanted one. It lasted the whole season."

Bob's interests did not extend, however, to working at the pharmacy—much to his father's disappointment. It was very much a family operation, with Bob, sister Nancy, who was 4 years younger, and Gill helping out. Sweeping out in the evening was Gill's favorite chore since he was allowed to keep any change he found.

Walter had hoped that Bob would follow in his footsteps, becoming a pharmacist and eventually taking over the business. But Bob had no intention of doing so, and he worked there part time only reluctantly. Walter suggested that if Bob found the pharmacy so boring, perhaps he should try working in his uncle's machine shop. That lasted 1 day, and Bob was back working in the pharmacy.

The interests of father and son finally merged when Walter bought a pickup truck for making deliveries. In driving, Bob had found the combination of work and recreation that completely appealed to him.

"You would not believe how small that truck was," says Gill. "Two adults could just barely fit in the front. We kids would pile in the back. It was really cold in the winter."

Bob's range with the truck soon extended well beyond the Thorpe Pharmacy delivery area. By this time he'd discovered girls, and he regularly visited one in Southern Massachusetts. Often accompanied by a girlfriend, he would drive to Hillsgrove Airfield in Warwick.

By the late 1930s, U.S. military authorities realized they did not have a fighter plane capable of taking on enemy planes that were then lighting up the skies over Europe and China. The P-44 Rocket the U.S. had under development was clearly not in a class with the German Messerschmitt and the Japanese Mitsubishi. Something bigger, faster, and far better armed would be needed. In the inimitable American way, what designers at Republic Aviation came up with was in a class of its own. The P-47 Thunderbolt was the biggest, most powerful, and heavily armored fighter plane in the world.

What Bob Thorpe was watching at Hillsgrove were Thunderbolts being flown in and out on training missions from Republic's fields on Long Island. In this day of jumbo jets, it is hard to imagine the impression these planes must have made on him. A Thunderbolt weighed over 12,000 pounds, 4,000 pounds heavier than any existing single-engine fighter. To achieve the required speed and climbing performance, the designers used a 2,000 horsepower, 18-cylinder radial engine. Since the conventional three-bladed propeller could not utilize all this power, a four-bladed propeller 12 feet in diameter was needed. Early models were to achieve speeds of 412 miles an hour and later models over 470.

What Bob could not understand or appreciate gazing through the chain-link fence was the extraordinary engineering that had gone into the plane's development. For the powerful engine to operate efficiently, a supercharged duct system was needed to provide the least interrupted airflow. This supercharger was built into the rear fuselage, with a big intake for the air mounted under the engine together with the oil coolers. Exhaust gases were piped separately to the turbine and expelled through a waste gate in the bottom of the fuselage. Ducted air was fed to the centrifugal impeller and returned to the engine under pressure.

All of this precise and complex design, moreover, was to prove extremely rugged. Although Bob was to be a tragic exception, Thunderbolt pilots grew accustomed to returning home in badly shot-up airplanes. Self-sealing fuel tanks kept the fuel from burning and exploding when hit—a notorious weakness of the vaunted Japanese Zero. The cockpit was heavily armored to protect the pilot from all directions. The massive engine could keep turning even when cylinders had been shot off. One Thunderbolt survived after losing a 4-foot section off one wing.

Watching these marvels roar in and out over Narragansett Bay, Bob recognized his calling if not his destiny. Graduating from high school in June 1942, he went on a crash course to gain the weight he needed to enlist in the U.S. Army Air Corps. "He only weighed 125 pounds when he graduated, and he had to gain 10 pounds to be inducted," says Gill. "He drank Dad's coffee milk shakes with malted milk powder and ate bananas every day. He also wore heavy clothing to the weigh-in. And he made it."

After basic training at Fort Devens, Massachusetts, Bob was sent for air cadet training at Dorr Field in Florida. Dorr was one of five separate training fields supporting flight training at Carlstrom Field, where the Embry Riddle Academy operated a contract flight training school.

Named for Stephen Dorr, a pilot killed in a midair collision in 1917, Dorr had been used to train World War I pilots, then closed until 1941. With a 5,300-foot runway and the nearly perfect flying weather in the southwest Florida area, Dorr was an ideal training facility.

Bob described his training in great detail in his weekly letters to his mother, which unfortunately have been lost. But we get a vivid picture of what the air cadets went through from the letters, diaries, and even some published works by fellow trainees. Flight training progressed through the three phases of Primary, Basic, and Advanced.

Primary was clearly intended to weed out those cadets who had been selected for flight training but who had no chance of completing it. William Rogers, who went through training at about the same time as Bob and who wound up in the same squadron in the Pacific Theater, recalls that in the first two flights on the Stearman biplane trainers, the instructor flew and the cadet went along for the ride.

The first flight on the Stearman PT-17 was fun. This Primary Trainer had 250 hp, a low-wing biplane with fixed landing gear. With the blue-green waters of the Gulf of Mexico stretching out to the west and the lush semitropical Florida interior to the east, it was a short and easy orientation for the majority who had never been off the ground before.

The second flight was altogether different. "That one separated the men from the boys," Fred Tobi recalls. "The instructor wrings out the plane in acrobatics with the poor student hanging on for dear life. He gets sick and messes up the side of the plane. Now I know why the student gets the backseat."

Tobi's descriptions evoke the mind-set of the instructors. All were civilians, although one of them, an instructor by the name of Richard Litchfield, had flown with the Eagle Squadron in the Battle of Britain. There was another instructor by the name of James Reilly who was quite good, according to Fred Tobi, who went through flight training with Thorpe and was later stationed with him at Gusap Air Force Base in New Guinea.

The instructors had a few months to turn complete novices into fighter pilots capable of surviving and winning air battles against German and Japanese pilots, many with years of combat experience. Any slacking off in demanding the highest standards of performance would be no kindness. It could be a death sentence.

"It was a rude awakening to discover that it took tedious practice to learn to do even the simplest maneuvers," Rogers found when he got to take the controls. And it was all with the instructor's "malevolent voice" constantly "beating on my ears" in the one-way Gosport, a rubber tube fitted to the trainees' helmet that the instructor spoke, or yelled, into: "Take your goddamn foot off that rudder! Keep your fucking nose up! Quit beating the stick. Let the damn thing fly itself! It can fly itself better than you can!"

On average, more than half of the class would "wash out" during Primary and Advanced training. Jack Frost, another fellow trainee, remembers a lot of good-natured harassment by instructors. "In general, if the trainee wasn't going to make it, he'd get a lot of sympathetic treatment preparing him for other duties," Frost says.

"On the other hand," Frost continues, "if the trainee was a hot shot, he might be visited with a variety of harassments, such as the instructor overriding the controls to see how he'd react. Some were treated with the 'Gosport dosage.' That is, the instructor would stick his end of the funnel into the wind stream. That blast was sure to get the trainee's attention."

Tobi recalls that the grueling routine left little time for socializing. "Everyone was too busy to worry about morale," Fred says. "But the facilities at Dorr were pretty good. It was more like a motel than a barracks. There were six cadets in double bunker beds, laid out nicely, a swimming pool, and a PX. The town of Arcadia wasn't much, but we didn't have time to go there anyway."

On May 2, 1943, Bob and Fred's class of cadets was transferred to Bainbridge (Georgia) Air Force Base, where they found a radical change in military atmosphere. "We arrived by train in the middle of the night," says Fred, "and it was like being back in the service again." The commanding officer was known as the "Whip."

Under the Whip's strict regimentation, they had intense instruction, learning how weather conditions affected flying, something that would become especially crucial when they reached New Guinea. They advanced to flight training with the AT-6 (Advanced Trainer). With retractable gear and a 450-horsepower engine, this was the most maneuverable airplane the cadets had flown. Although they weren't allowed to fly them, cadets also sat in the P-39 and the P-47.

Tobi liked the P-39 because of its looks, but, in fact, it was one of the worst planes during World War II. "The Russians liked it because it had a cannon that could knock out German tanks," he says, "but there were lots of mechanical problems. As for the P-47, he thought it was too big and heavy. Bob, however, loved the P-47 because of his early days watching it take off and land in RI."

Minus the cadets who had washed out at Bainbridge, the class moved on to Marianna (Florida) Air Force Base on July 2, 1943, where they entered the Advanced Phase of their training. Here, they continued to fly the AT-6 as they learned techniques of strafing, bombing, and dogfighting.

It was at Marianna that they were asked to list their choices of flight assignments: transports, fighters, or bombers. Fred listed his selection in just that order, but Bob made fighters his first choice. Both were selected for fighters, and while they waited to be sent to the Venice (Florida) Air Force Base for P-47 training, they caught up on some other skills that the rushed pilot training schedule hadn't left much time for.

One was mastering the .45-caliber pistol, the pilot's personal sidearm. Fred qualified as a marksman, but Bob achieved sharpshooter status. "That was so typical," Fred recalls. "Bob was a quiet, reserved New Englander, but he worked with total determination at everything he did. He became one of the best pilots in the class."

As he advanced through flight training to the P-47, Bob was constantly building up his physical strength as well as his knowledge and skills. There was good reason for the size and weight requirements the army had for its pilots. The force required to operate the mechanical controls of the fighter planes of the period was substantial. The P-47, particularly, could demand the strength of a wrestler. The big engine and enormous propeller exerted so much torque that an airplane could flip over on takeoff if the pilot did not have the arm strength to hold it back. Many did not, and they were killed. Bob did special exercises all through flight training to build up his arms and wrists.

On August 30, 1943, Bob graduated from flight training and was commissioned a second lieutenant, with his mother attending the ceremony in Florida. Tobi recalls meeting Bob's mother and watching as she proudly pinned the wings on her son's uniform.

In September of 1943, Bob was granted a 10-day leave to await assignment overseas. When he got home, he found his parents were delighted with his accomplishment. Walter suggested that Bob go to Europe and fly a P-51.

"No, Dad," Bob replied. "The war in Europe will be over soon. I'm going to the Pacific." Young Gill was most impressed with Bob's dress uniform. "Gabardine trousers, shiny brown shoes, starched khaki shirt with a brown olive tie, and his officer bars," Gill remembers. "Wow, my big brother!"

There were visits with family and friends at home and at the pharmacy, and soon the leave was over. Gill went with Bob to the train station.

"I have vivid memories of that," Gill says. "It was a beautiful day. Bob and I were standing outside, and some soldiers came by and saluted him. He returned the salutes, but then he took me to a less exposed area, and the saluting stopped."

The train arrived. Bob boarded and waved good-bye. Gill would never see him again.

Chapter 3
The Threat to Australia

The Australians had relied upon the British forces in Malaya, the base in Singapore, and the British Eastern Fleet to hold the Japanese enemy from their shores in any invasion attempt. They had sent troops, ships, and airplanes to Malaya before the Japanese attack on Pearl Harbor on December 7, 1941.

The means available to the Australians for the defense of their country were extremely limited. By late 1941, Australia, a country of about 7 million people, had already been at war for 2 years, joining England in the fight against the Germans and Italians.

Its home defenses were in a desperate state. Most of the 163 combat aircraft it had in the Pacific were lost when the Japanese struck in Malaya. The ground forces were not much better off, with virtually no trained soldiers left in Australia. An organized reserve of about 50,000 men, the Volunteer Defense Corps (VDC), was made up principally of veterans of World War I. The VDC used whatever weapons were at hand, including shotguns and antiquated hunting pieces.

The Australian Chiefs of Staff faced the problem of how to use their inadequate forces in its defense. To begin with, they had to decide whether to make the principal defense effort in Australia or in the Northeast Area, including New Guinea.

They came to the conclusion that, with untrained, ill-equipped troops, a critical lack of aircraft, and insufficient naval forces, an effective defense of the forward bases, especially the one at Rabaul, New Britain, was out of the question. They decided that no reinforcements be sent to Rabaul, a fine seaport at the northwest tip of New Britain.

The garrison at Port Moresby, the territorial capital of New Guinea, was increased to a brigade because Australian strategists felt it had a better chance of survival due to its more favorable geographical location. Its strength, with the arrival of the promised reinforcements in January 1942, was 3,000 men, but the troops were only partially trained, and the garrison was without fighter planes.

On Jan. 22, 1942, the main body of a Japanese invasion convoy arrived off of Rabaul and began landing at Karavia and Simpson Harbor. The Australians, who had only mortars, machine guns, and rifles, resisted stoutly and continued to fight through the night and early morning. Some of the Australian troops held their positions and fought to the death, even after being ordered to withdraw.

Many of the fleeing Australians were caught and massacred, but 400 of them escaped and lived to fight again. With the fall of Rabaul, the forward defense of the Northeast Area crumbled. All that was left of it was the garrison at Port Moresby, the troops in the Bulolo Valley, and a handful of commandos in the Admiralties.

On February 14, 1942, the campaign in Malaya came to an end with the surrender of Singapore when 64,000 troops, their guns, and equipment were surrendered to the Japanese, in what Winston Churchill called "the worst disaster and greatest capitulation of British history." The Japanese, by this time, had invaded Borneo and the Celebes, taken Amboina, and landed in Sumatra. On Feb. 19, they bombed Darwin, Australia, into rubble.

Because of Australia's vast area, its 12,000-mile coastline, and the slowness and general inadequacy of road and rail communications, a local defense of the country's most vital areas was adopted.

The main concentration of forces was in the Brisbane-Newcastle-Sydney-Melbourne area, the industrial and agricultural heart of Australia. Smaller forces were deployed in South Australia, Western Australia, and Tasmania, and independent garrisons were established at Darwin, Townsville, Cairus, and Thursday Island. The Australian military decided it had no choice but to make the fight for Australia in Australia itself.

The strategy changed abruptly after General Douglas MacArthur arrived in Australia on March 16, 1942. When General MacArthur took charge of Australia's defense, a great feeling of relief swept across the country.

Almost immediately, MacArthur decided that the key to Australia's defense lay not on the mainland but in New Guinea. The strategic principle he conceived at the time was that the successful defense of Australia required that the battle "be waged on outer perimeter territories rather than within the territory to be defended." As events turned out, both the defense and the offense pivoted on Port Moresby, New Guinea.

MacArthur did not realize how much he had to contend with when he came to Australia. There were countless cross currents and dangerous shoals in Australia's political waters, but he managed to steer clear of them.

Australia was in chaos. There was confusion everywhere, among the government, the army, and the people. A spirit of despair and defeatism seemed to contaminate the air. Political squabbling took precedence over consideration of the danger to the nation. Politicians seemed more interested in enhancing their own reputations than they were in saving the country from invasion.

Some insisted that all Australian troops be recalled immediately from Africa to defend the homeland. Others wanted only part of them brought home. Some agreed that the troops should remain in Africa, but would not permit the militia to leave Australia to fight. MacArthur induced all warring factions to get together and present a united front to the enemy. He had to cope with a political situation with one hand while trying to whip up an offensive against the Japanese with the other.

His first step was to request the American Joint Chiefs of Staff to provide additional air and sea power for the defense of Port Moresby, including several aircraft carriers and at least 675 land-based aircraft. In turning down his request, General George Marshall told MacArthur that the Joint Chiefs of Staff had decided to maintain a strong defensive position in the Pacific, while it built up forces in the United Kingdom for an early offensive against Germany.

In a personal letter to MacArthur, President Franklin D. Roosevelt wrote that he found it difficult to get away from the fact that the armies of the USSR were "killing more Axis personnel than all the other Allies combined." The message was clear—General MacArthur would have to make the best with what he already had.

With his limited resources, MacArthur also realized he was racing against time. The Japanese already had the Philippines, Sumatra, Java, Borneo, New Britain, New Ireland, and many small islands in the Dutch East Indies. New Guinea stood between them and the invasion of Australia.

The odds were heavily stacked against a successful campaign in New Guinea. When MacArthur began plotting his strategy, the Japanese had five divisions in the Philippines, four in the Mandated Pacific Islands, eight in Java, twelve in Malaya and Burma, and two in New Guinea. They had complete air superiority everywhere and absolute control of the seas in the Far-Western Pacific.

If the Japanese captured Port Moresby, they could have their navy and Air Corps there, on the south coast of New Guinea, with only a short span of water separating them from Northern Australia. From that port, they could have bombed Australian cities at will, blockaded its ports, cut the lifeline to the United States, and slowly starved it into subjection.

So imminent was the danger when MacArthur took charge that the Australians had a plan of defense calling for ceding much of Northern Australia to the Japanese and making a fight for the richer regions of the south.

If MacArthur lost New Guinea, the Air Corps would have been rendered impotent. He would have had no close base from which to launch his own offensive. Consider the situation confronting him when he landed in Australia. The Japanese had swept into China where their forces soon became hopelessly bogged down in a war of attrition that they could not win. However, elsewhere, they were much more successful. They had swarmed through Malaya and Burma and captured what had once been regarded as impregnable—Singapore.

They had most of the Philippines and lost no time in adding Sumatra, Java, Borneo, Celebs, New Britain, New Ireland, and many small islands in the Dutch East Indies to Hirohito's imperial realm. They had poured down in an avalanche into the Solomons and only New Guinea stood between them and the projected conquest of Australia.

The reinforcement of Port Moresby was no easy matter. Its supply line from Australia across the Gulf of Papua was exposed to enemy action. Its port facilities were inadequate, and the two existing airfields were small and poorly built. Plans were developed immediately to improve existing airfields. Three new airfields were to be built which, when completed, would permit the rapid staging of all types of aircraft in Port Moresby. The improvements would make it possible for the air force to provide cover for Torres Strait and the supply line to Port Moresby, while improving offensive and defensive operations.

Elsewhere, the Axis forces were also triumphant. Everybody was crying for American help, and the American Joint Chiefs of Staff had to decide where to allot resources for the most immediate and pressing needs. Unfortunately for MacArthur, the urgency for help in the Atlantic seemed greater than in the Pacific.

MacArthur had a handful of Australian troops in New Guinea, a few thousand raw, untried Americans on the mainland, and a tiny combined Australian and American Air Corps. The Japanese were aware that MacArthur didn't have enough transports to move an army large enough to do them any harm. So MacArthur turned to a small band of American airmen and used them as his navy.

Under the command of General George C. Kenney, these young bomber and pursuit pilots sought out and sank Japanese warships and transports, bombed enemy strongholds, and blasted Japan's dreaded Zeros out of the skies. When the Japanese tried to land on the beaches of New Guinea, it was these pilots who sank their landing barges, strafed and bombed their transports and escorting warships, cut their lines of communication, and joined Australian and American infantry to crush Japan's bid for mastery of the Southwest Pacific.

The fight for New Guinea started with the Air Corps and culminated with a glorious victory at Buna. Many of these pilots had very few hours of flying time when sent on their first mission. They went up against seasoned Japanese pilots who knew the tricks of aerial warfare. They had to learn the hard way—in combat with seasoned enemy fighters who knew every trick of aerial warfare. Many didn't live long enough to learn at all. Our P-40s and P-39s were not as maneuverable or as capable of fighting at high altitudes as the Japanese Zero.

The Air Corps even flew the infantry from Australia to Port Moresby, and then across the perilous Owen Stanley Mountain Range to the scene of action. All the pilots were young. Some were quite serious, but they were talkative and cheerful and always ready for a fight or a party. Nothing daunted them. They didn't care whether they faced a suicidal low-bombing mission, a battle against overwhelming odds with Zeros, a crash landing, or a long trek through the jungles.

New Guinea was a harsh place to fight a war, with 750,000 square miles seething with mosquitoes, flies, gnats, and hundreds of other crawling creatures. There were fetid swamps and forests of kunai grass, which cut human skin like a razor. Everything mildewed from the incessant heat and moisture, leading to trench foot and jungle fungus.

Before the war, the western part of New Guinea was under Dutch control, while the eastern half was administered by Australia. The southeastern part of the island was called Papua, the most densely populated part of New Guinea. This is where Port Moresby, the island's major settlement, was located.

Further inland, on both sides of the Owen Stanley Mountain Range, lay thousands of square miles of uncharted territory, filled with fierce, aboriginal people who ate their enemies and sometimes each other. Downed pilots parachuted into great danger, with some of them still listed as missing more than 70 years after the war ended.

New Guinea is truly a land where time stands still. In November of 1961, 16 years after World War II ended, Michael Rockefeller, son of future Vice President Nelson Rockefeller, disappeared during an expedition in New Guinea. Headhunting and cannibalism were still prevalent in the area where his boat was swamped and overturned. Although his cause of death is still listed as "unknown," a group of tribal elders admitted to killing and eating Rockefeller after he swam to shore. His body was never found, and he was declared legally dead in 1964.

Darwin, Australia

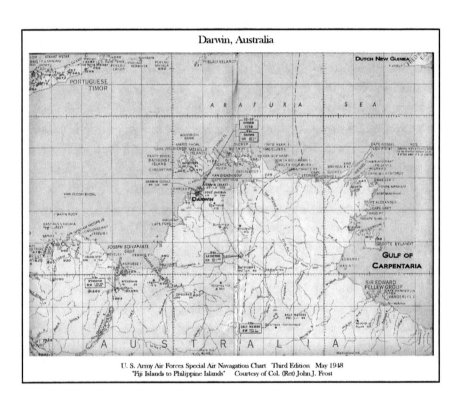

U. S. Army Air Forces Special Air Navagation Chart   Third Edition   May 1948
"Fiji Islands to Philippine Islands"   Courtesy of Col. (Ret) John J. Frost

Chapter 4
The Battle of the Coral Sea

On May 1, 1942, a powerful Japanese fleet steamed toward Port Moresby on the south coast of New Guinea. Capture of this critical Allied base would solidify the defensive perimeter of the enormous empire Japan had conquered since bombing Pearl Harbor less than 5 months before that put its air force within bombing range of northern Australia. The U.S. Navy was aware of the Japanese plan because of its success in breaking the Japanese naval code that was to result in its great victory over the Japanese a month later at Midway. At the time, U.S. naval forces were believed to be too far away to stop the Port Moresby attack.

That evening at a U.S. airfield in Townsville, Australia, pilots of a squadron of P-39 fighter planes, the only military aircraft available, were being briefed on their mission the next morning by General Bernard Harris. They were to attack the Japanese invasion fleet by skipping bombs along the surface at the ships. Calculating the distance to the target, one pilot pointed out that they would not have fuel enough to get back. "Who said anything about getting back?" General Harris replied. He described a plan in which pilots would ditch as they ran out of fuel, hopefully to be picked up by amphibian airplanes.

General Harris's briefing reveals the harrowing state of Allied defenses in those early days of the war. These American pilots would have been sacrificed, much as the Japanese Kamikaze pilots would be, 3 years later off Okinawa. Fortunately, the U.S. fleet arrived in time to inflict serious enough damage on the invasion fleet to make the mission unnecessary. In what became known as the Battle of the Coral Sea, it marked the first sea battle in which no surface ships exchanged fire or even came within sight of each other and all damage was inflicted by carrier aircraft.

Three cruises of the Allied Naval Force, the *Australia*, the *Chicago*, and the *Hobart*, under Rear Adm. J. G. Grace, were sent to the Coral Sea to reinforce the U.S. Pacific Fleet. After strikes at Lae-Salamaua on March 10, the carrier *Yorktown* had remained in the Coral Sea. It was rejoined there by the *Lexington* and the combined force—two carriers, seven heavy cruisers, a light cruiser, thirteen destroyers, two oilers, and a seaplane tender were placed under the command of Rear Admiral Frank Fletcher.

Just before noon on May 6, 1942, search planes from the *Yorktown* discovered the enemy carrier *Shokaku* off of Misima Island. Planes from the *Lexington* and the *Yorktown* heavily damaged the *Shokaku* and sank a light cruiser escorting it. During the ensuing battle, the *Lexington* and the *Yorktown* were damaged and the Japanese carrier *Zuikaku* lost most of its planes.

Admiral Inouye, in charge of the Japanese forces, broke off the engagement and withdrew to the north. Meanwhile, the *Lexington* developed uncontrollable gasoline fires and had to be abandoned and sunk. Although the Allies had suffered heavier losses than the Japanese, the fact that the invasion of Port Moresby had to be abandoned was seen as a victory.

American code breakers intercepted a message from General Horii, head of Imperial General Headquarters, stating that the invasion of Port Moresby would have to be temporarily postponed because of the action at the Coral Sea. Any celebration of the postponement was diminished by Horii's threat that the invasion would take place in July.

The Coral Sea was the 300-mile-wide moat separating the Australian population from this terrifying enemy, and the most effective force guarding this moat was the American Fifth Air Force, which had been established in Australia on September 3, 1942. The Fifth was led by Major General George C. Kenney, who had arrived in Brisbane in late July and revealed his leadership style by firing the entire air command staff after a quick tour of bases in Queensland. He had asked approval of General Douglas MacArthur to get rid of "deadwood" and received the theater commander's enthusiastic approval.

The 52-year-old Kenney was an aggressive leader. A fighter pilot himself in World War I, with two "kills" to his credit, he had been sent to France in early 1940 with the temporary rank of lieutenant colonel, as assistant military attaché for air. His mission was to observe Allied air operations during the early stages of World War II. As a result of his observations, he recommended many important changes to Army Air Corps equipment and tactics, including upgrading armament from .30 caliber- to .50-caliber machine guns and installing leak-proof fuel tanks.

Kenney's frank reports on the superiority of the German Luftwaffe were frowned upon by much of the Army Air Corps brass, however, and he was sent back to a desk job in the States. But superior leadership was not to be suppressed for long in the rapid buildup to war, and he was sent to Brisbane, Australia, as MacArthur's air chief.

Initially, there was a brief clash with MacArthur's chief of staff, General Richard Sutherland. After some initial disagreements over air strategy and tactics, Kenney reportedly presented Sutherland with a sheet of paper, blank except for a dot in the center. "The dot is what you know about air strategy," Kenney told him. "The rest is what I know."

Kenney won that argument, but he had to have been disheartened by the planes available to his airmen for turning back the Japanese juggernaut. For an admirer of the incomparable German Messerschmitt, the American P-39 was a bad joke. A poor performer at high altitudes, the only faint positive was that by the time American pilots had managed to reach combat altitude, the attacking Japanese planes would usually have done their damage and left.

The Fifth consisted of eight bomber groups and three fighter groups at the time Kenney took command. The 39th first three commanders (Allen R. Springer, William R. Clingerman, and Marvin McNickle) as well as many of the key enlisted men came from the long established 94th Pursuit Squadron. Initially, the 39th was equipped with a few Seversky P-35s and AT-6s. In early 1941, the squadron received some P-40s, but they were quickly replaced with Bell P-39 Airacobras.

The 39th did not have an insignia, and a designer at Bell Aircraft came up with the "Cobra in the Clouds" emblem, soon to become the official emblem of the 39th Fighter Squadron. Checking out pilots in the new fighter was given top priority. It started in early 1941, with a gunnery camp at Oscoda, Michigan, followed by war maneuvers all over the South-western United States. These exercises involved working with army, navy, and marine units, both on the ground and in the air, while operating under rough field conditions. This period would prove to be excellent prepara-tion for the air war the 39th would encounter in the skies of New Guinea.

When these maneuvers ended, the 39th flew to its new base at Baer Field, Fort Wayne, Indiana, with most of the men arriving on December 6, 1941. The next day, December 7, Pearl Harbor was attacked and the United States was at war. The squadron was ordered to deploy, and on Dec. 8, the 39th left for the West Coast. Led by Flight Leader Lt. Robert Faurot, the 39th landed at March Field, Riverside, California. A small group of 39th mechanics, traveling in trucks stocked with spare parts, was assigned to follow the squadron's route across the country.

At March Field, .50-caliber machine-gun ammunition was loaded in their nose guns and a few coastal patrols were flown. Lt. Charles King recalls an incident during a training flight, led by Lieutenant Faurot. "We were snaking down the canyon under clouds that obscured the cliff tops on either side. The clouds lifted a bit so the flight could clear some huge power lines spanning the canyon. Later, some of the pilots questioned why Lieutenant Faurot would take inexperienced pilots through a canyon in bad weather. Faurot had learned a great deal about flying in adverse weather as an American volunteer with the RAF in Europe. When flying missions in New Guinea, pilots of the 39th would soon come to realize what adverse weather was all about."

In mid-January 1942, the 39th Squadron was ordered to pack and pre-pare to deploy to a secret tropical overseas destination via San Francisco. Capt. Marvin McNickle, CO of the 39th, was reassigned and 2nd Lt. Frank R. Royal succeeded him. The 39th consisted of about a dozen officers and 80 enlisted personal. The squadron traveled by train to San Francisco, and then boarded the USS *Ancon*, a transport ship that had been used in the banana trade between the East Coast and Central America.

After arriving in Brisbane, Australia, in April 1942, Royal assumed responsibility for about 100 men with nothing more than what they were wearing or had in their duffle bags. Constantly talking with Australian officers and civilians, Royal explained that his squadron needed trucks, Jeeps, all manner of transportation, tents, a field kitchen, and food supplies. After signing contracts worth tens of thousands of dollars, a senior Australian officer expressed amazement that a second lieutenant had so much authority.

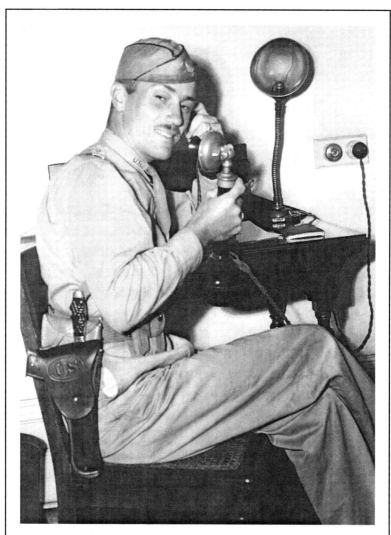

**2nd Lt. Francis R. Royal, Commanding Officer
39th Fighter Squadron, 35th Fighter Group, 5th AF
1942**

Royal told his officers to round up some enlisted men, go down to the docks, and bring home what the squadron needed to become an effective fighting force. No requisition or paperwork was supplied. It worked. Soon, crews were assembling airplanes at Amberly Field, test flights were flown, and the squadron was beginning to take shape and resemble a fighter squadron.

New pilots were assigned to bring the squadron to full strength. Most of the new pilots were just out of flight school, but a few were combat veterans. Lt. Gene Wahl and Lt. Frank Atkins were experienced P-40 pilots who had seen action at Java. Another experienced pilot, Lt. Richard Suehr, was on his way to join the 39th when the engine in his P-40 quit, and he had to crash-land in an Australian jungle. Slogging through wet jungle for 10 days, he stumbled upon a railroad track and was picked up by a passing train.

The young pilot's legs were infected and black, and doctors concluded that gangrene had set in and amputation was needed to save his life. When informed of the decision, Suehr pulled out his .45 pistol and held the hospital staff at bay, screaming, "Nobody is going to cut off my legs!" When news of the standoff reached U.S. Headquarters, a plane was sent to evacuate him to a hospital in Brisbane. It was determined that the dye from his wet dress socks had caused the blackness that resulted in the gangrene diagnosis. He made a full recovery and was flying planes for the 39th a month later.

Another addition to the 39th was Lt. Bob McMahon, a P-40 pilot who had engaged attacking Zeros over Darwin. McMahon suffered a gunshot wound to his leg after his P-40 was shot to pieces by attacking Zeroes. The wound may have saved his life, since few American pilots survived those Darwin aerial battles against a more experienced enemy flying faster, more maneuverable planes.

The 39th camped at Ascot Race Track where they flight-tested P-39s and P-40s. Later, the squadron moved to Woodstock, Queensland, to train for combat, primarily with the P-39. The plane was designed around a gun, and what had been intended as a major combat advantage resulted in severe performance deficiencies.

"American Pursuit Squadron shown above at a Michigan aerodrome was first in world to be equipped with fighters with tricycle landing gear. In this model of the Bell Airacobra, armament - cannon and machine guns - is mounted in the nose. Allison liquid cooled engine of more than 1000 hp is located behind the pilot. Tricycle landing gear, which provides greater safety for take-off and landings, retracts in flight. This type has clocked 385 mph. A similar model, made for RAF, incorporates armor, self-sealing tanks, two fuselage, four wing mounted guns."

39th Pursuit Squadron, 31st Pursuit Group, Selfridge Field, Michigan
1941

Standing at left: Squadron Commander, Capt. Marvin McNickle. Building at left is a base hanger, the next building is post headquarters with the enlisted barracks in between. At the far right is Officers' Row.

The gun was a 37 mm T9-cannon to be fired through the center of the propeller hub for optimum accuracy and stability when firing. Since the plane's primary mission was interception of enemy bombers, H. M. Poyer, designer for project leader Robert Woods, was impressed by the power of this weapon and pushed for its incorporation. This recommendation was unusual, because fighters had previously been designed around an engine, not a weapon system.

Although the T9-cannon was devastating when it worked, it had limited ammunition, a low rate of fire, and was prone to jamming. Far worse problems resulted from having to position the engine behind the cockpit so the cannon could be accommodated in the plane's nose.

The midengine placement arrangement did make possible the P-39's smooth and streamlined nose profile, achieving the "beautiful airplane" many pilots admired. The downside was that the plane needed a turbo-supercharger to operate efficiently in the thin air at high altitudes. The supercharger had to be cooled, which created drag and reduced speed.

To lessen this drag and increase speed, the supercharger was enclosed within the plane, and, in the very tight interior space, there was no internal space left over for the turbo. As arguments over drag and speed continued, the decision was made to go into production with the P-39 without the turbocharger.

Bell's true motivation for reconfiguring the plane has been argued for decades. The darkest assertion is that the company did not have an active production program and was desperate for cash flow. Whatever the reason, the production P-39 retained a single-stage, single-speed supercharger allowing an optimum altitude of only about 18,000–20,000 feet. The cure for the drag problem turned out to be worse than the drag itself.

To make matters even worse for pilots of the 39th, all of whom had trained in the States on the P-39, the planes assigned to them when they got to Australia were nearly worn-out castoffs from the Royal Australian Air Force.

All of these problems and limitations figured prominently when some pilots of the 39th were sent on temporary duty to Port Moresby, New Guinea, to fly combat missions with an experienced combat squadron. The plan was for 39th pilots to learn good combat tactics from the more experienced pilots to learn how to deal with their highly experienced enemy.

The advanced echelon of the 39th operated from 12-Mile Drome, a fighter strip that had been made by scraping off the kunai grass, also known as "razor grass," because the rough leaf edges could cut skin deeply. After the Construction Battalion engineers had smoothed the ground, PSP (pierced steel plate) was laid and the strip became operational.

Here are excerpts from the 39th Combat Diary for the first days of combat duty:

May 16, 1942

> *Lts. Green, Adkins, Lynch, Wahl, and Carey, the first of our squadron to participate in combat activities in New Guinea, arrived on the evening of May 16 and immediately reported for duty.*

May 17, 1942

> *Interception, Lt. Green leading. Flight of 4 in 2 ship elements took off on an intercept mission. When at an alti-*

tude of 11,000 ft., a flight of 5 Zeros were sighted at the same level, 90 degrees left flying in a luffberry. Our flight maneuvered for position and attacked head-on. The enemy executed an Immelmann, giving them a position to the rear of our A/C and attempted pursuit. The result of the engagement was nil.

May 18, 1942

Interception. Lts. Lynch and Wahl went on a mission of interception, climbing to 22,000 feet. The enemy was sighted 80 degrees left at the same level. 30 bombers in two "V" formations and 15 Zero fighters in luffberry. Our pilots dived out of the sun at 4 E/A. This action was observed late by the enemy and they attempted to turn into the attacking formation. The main enemy force continued on their course. Each pilot made contact and scored hits on the enemy. Enemy casualties, 2 Zeros probable.

May 20, 1942

Interception. Lt. Lynch downs two Zeros.

May 26, 1942

Lts. Adkins, Wahl, and Lynch each down a Zero.

At this time, the 39th Squadron's advanced echelon score was six Zeros shot down and the main body of the squadron had not yet left Australia. The remainder of the squadron left Australia on June 1, aboard a Dutch freighter, and arrived in Port Moresby 2 days later. The squadron moved into a camp named Virgin Lane. The squadron also flew their P-39s from nearby 14-Mile Drome, which was much like the 12-Mile Drome in that one end of the strip ended on the bank of the Laloki River while the other end of the strip turned into a swamp. Both strips were short, but pending the development of adequate bomber strips, they were even pressed into service by a B-26 bomber squadron, and then later by a B-25 bomber squadron.

This early in the war, the enemy forces enjoyed air supremacy and could bomb the Port Moresby port facilities and American airfields at any time of day or night, while suffering only minor losses. Flights of enemy bombers, sometimes in formations numbering up to 100 planes, attacked constantly.

The problem of these American fighters achieving combat altitude before attacking planes arrived over their targets was lessened somewhat by the network of coast watchers the Australians had stationed along the New Guinea north coast. The defenders now had up to 15 minutes warning of an impending attack.

As soon as the warning arrived, the P-39s would take off in a mad scramble, heading out to sea as they strained to reach 20,000 feet, the usual altitude of enemy bombers. It took 30 minutes for the P-39s to reach engagement elevation and return to Port Moresby to confront the enemy. By that time, the bombers had usually completed their mission and were on their way home. It was frustrating that the P-39 climbed so slowly and was so limited in its high altitude performance.

Although the Americans were not yet effective in fending off bomber attacks, they did manage to engage some of the escorting Zeros. They could not maneuver with the Zeros, but they did manage to use their higher diving speed and those devastating cannons when they did not jam. With the main body of the squadron now in the combat zone, the 39th escorted bombers in attacks on Lae and Salamaura on the far side of the island.

The combat diary entry for June 9 states that three B-17s, five B-25s, and eleven B-26s were to take off at designated intervals to attack Lae, which was being used to refuel enemy aircraft. The 39th's assignment was to meet and protect the bombers.

In the engagements between P-39s and Zeros, in the early days of the war, the sides were about even with some 80 losses each. The major difference was that when a Zero went down, the pilot was usually lost as well. Since the fighting was over the Port Moresby area, the American pilots survived to fight again, often the following day.

Some of these survival stories were legendary. Lt. Gene Rehrer was about to engage a flight of Zeros when his engine stalled because of an interruption in fuel flow from the external tank. While he was trying to get the engine restarted, the Zeros caught up with him and shot his plane full of holes, setting his engine on fire. Another American pilot reported that Rehrer's plane went down in flames and he didn't see the pilot bail out.

But there was a chute. With his engine burning behind him, and Japanese bullets still hitting the plane, he pulled his emergency door release lever. The P-39 did not have the conventional sliding canopy like most fighters. There were doors on either side, like those on a car. With the doors gone, a pilot in this emergency situation was expected to roll out of the seat onto the wing where the air stream would sweep him away and clear of the plane. But Rehrer's doors stuck, and he banged them with his knees and elbows to no avail.

Desperate, with the engine fire growing hotter behind him, he released his seat belt in an effort to have a better shot at opening one of the doors. But the plane suddenly flipped and went into a flat, inverted spin. Now he was crammed against the top of the cockpit. He was helpless until the plane flipped again, flinging him out in midair.

So now he was clear of the plane, but it occurred to him that when he released his seat belt, he might also have released his parachute harness. He reached for his chest to where the parachute "D" ring should have been and found it! He pulled the ring—but the chute didn't open.

"That probably saved my life," he said later. "I was up around 17,000 feet, and the Japs would have had plenty of time to use me for target practice if the chute had opened immediately."

With his chute still trailing, he plummeted through the overcast to about 2,000 feet when it did open. His arm had tangled in the shroud lines, severely wrenching his shoulder when the chute opened. He plunged into the jungle trees, coming to an abrupt halt about 6 feet off the ground. In an effort to get to the coast and helpful natives, Gene struck out downhill and found a stream. He fashioned a raft and floated by crocodiles sunning themselves on the banks. Tense days went by as he fought his way through the jungle. Some friendly natives found him and brought him to their village. A week later, he rode into the 39th camp in an Aussie truck. Two days later, he was flying missions again.

After encountering some enemy fire, Lt. Richard Rauch's engine failed, and he was forced to bail out in a dive doing above 400 mph at an altitude of 10,000 feet. After passing through several clouds, he was happy to see that he would land in a clearance. His joy was short-lived, however, because he went up to his neck in muddy and slimy water. He was forced to crawl on his knees over the grassy swamp, spending the night battling mosquitos and trying to sleep on a small ridge in the area.

Eluding the swamp, Rauch next met the jungle and after hours of hacking and hiking he came upon the Venapa River. He fashioned a raft of logs, tying them together with grass. Numerous logjams broke up his raft until he finally straddled a log, riding downstream while dodging more jams and crocodiles. Exhausted, he finally approached the mouth of the river where natives spied him and came to his rescue. Here he received food and rest before getting in a small boat that brought him back to Port Moresby. He was flying missions 3 days later.

The Combat Diary reports that Zeros crossed on the American side of the Owen Stanley Range looking for a fight. Lieutenant Royal saw one of his planes go down during the dogfight. The pilot, Lt. Frank Angier, bailed out, and he was being targeted by two Zeros as he fell to earth. Royal dove in front of one of the Zeros, and his plane was hit with machine-gun fire. The other Zero followed Angier all the way down, struggling to get a clear shot.

Four passes were made at Lieutenant Angier while he floated in his chute. He survived by swinging from side to side and "climbing" the parachute shroud lines like a monkey. When he hit the ground, Angier got out of the chute harness and scampered into the bushes just as the Zero blasted the ground where he landed. He struggled through the jungle for 3 days, always with the uncomfortable feeling he was being watched. On the third day, natives appeared with an Australian plantation owner. They had seen his parachute land, but they were not sure if he was friend or enemy. He was taken in and returned to the 39th.

The combat challenges were complicated and intensified by the problems of living in an equatorial climate. Port Moresby was only 125 miles below the equator. "It stank of rot and mold," remembers Royal. "The smell permeated everything. I don't know what the temperatures were, but it was hot all night and even hotter during the day, and with the tropical humidity, life was nearly unbearable."

There was an epidemic of dysentery almost immediately after the 39th arrived at Port Moresby and after that, the fungal sores and itches started. The men seldom wore anything more than shorts, and there was one bush that would "set their skin on fire" just by walking by it. "Jungle crud and crotch rot started a weeping, itching mess in the moist areas of the underarms and crotch," he says. "This was mostly treated with gentian violet, and we all looked like clowns."

The problem became so serious that Dr. Baluss, the flight surgeon, took action. He ordered trucks to haul all of the "sick call" guys to a sandy beach with clear, warm tropical waters lapping at its shore. Squadron members were ordered into the water for a good soak. This therapy worked miracles, according to Royal.

Malaria also took its toll. At first, the pilots were given a quinine tablet each day for protection, but this precaution caused a constant buzzing in the ears. They were switched to an antipybrine tablet. That stopped the buzzing, but everyone turned a peculiar shade of yellow.

Most did adjust to the climate, however, and, with frequent R&R tours to Sydney where the squadron kept an apartment, morale stayed reasonably high. Everyone knew what they really needed were better airplanes, and those planes soon arrived. In August of 1942, pilots of the 39th Squadron were sent back to Townsville, Australia, to be equipped with the new P-38 Lightning, an airplane that promised to be better than the P-39 in the air war with the Japanese.

Route of the Cobra

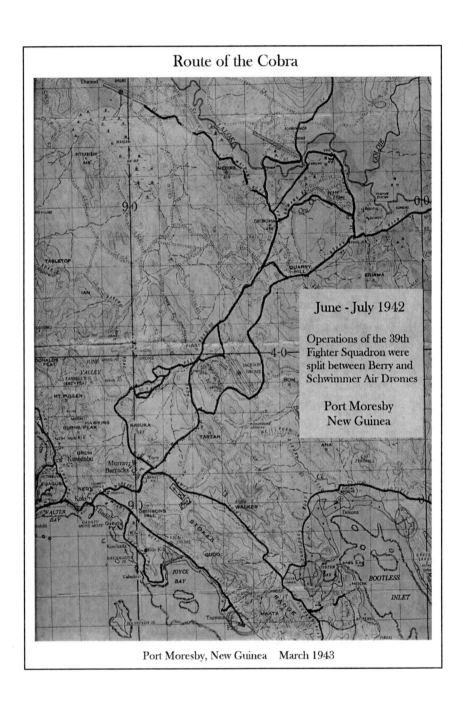

June - July 1942

Operations of the 39th Fighter Squadron were split between Berry and Schwimmer Air Dromes

Port Moresby
New Guinea

Port Moresby, New Guinea   March 1943

Chapter 5
The P-38 Arrives

In June and July 1942, the 39th Fighter Squadron lost several planes to enemy action, but in every case the pilot survived. Some were injured, many had harrowing tales to tell, but all lived to fly and fight again. Was it luck? It seemed that something, some force, had been protecting these pilots.

On August 4, 1942, a tragic accident called into question any thinking about Divine Providence. Squadron Commander Jack W. Berry remained in New Guinea with a skeleton crew of ground people as the rest of the squadron returned to Australia to be equipped with the P-38 Lightning. Berry was a flying commander who led by example and took part in all of the early missions. He had won the respect and confidence of all 39th personnel. As the 39th's first combat period ended in late July 1942, Berry was proud of its performance and, in the eyes of his men, he had done well as a leader.

When not on duty, Berry was a friendly, open person who mixed easily with all ranks. He could be firm and positive when appropriate. On one occasion, a big ex-college football player had too much to drink and was picking on one of the smaller pilots. Berry told him to stop, and he was immediately invited to go outside with the drunk. The football player was a lot bigger than Berry, but he was knocked out with one punch. It turns out that Berry had been a champion boxer in college.

An excellent pilot, Berry was always looking for better ways for his squadron to do its job. The Fifth Air Force, under General Kenney, was pushing all squadrons to improve skip bombing techniques and capabilities, so Berry was experimenting with different bombs and fuses.

Major Jack W. Berry

The harbor of Port Moresby was almost entirely surrounded by a coral reef lying just a few feet under water. Entrance was through a narrow, tricky reef, a passage that few ships tried to make in peacetime, except in clear daylight. Shortly after World War I, a large tourist liner grounded on the reef near the passage and, after a long and costly attempt was made to float her, was abandoned. Her great rusting hulk was the first sight to greet American soldiers as they steamed to Port Moresby in their transports.

That old ship was also the first thing spotted by the Jap bombing crews as they flew out of Rabaul in 1942 and began bombing Port Moresby. From several thousand feet in the air, she looked like another troop transport poking through the reef, where defensive maneuvering was out of the question. She also looked nice to the Americans, since she took bombs that might have destroyed the nearby barracks, airfields, and supply ships standing at the docks. Half filled with sand, there she proudly and defiantly stood, living up to her nickname of "Old Unsinkable."

Later when the Fifth Air Force began ruling the skies in New Guinea, the ship served as a perfect practice target. Day after day, pilots flew practice runs over her, sharpening their skill at bombing and strafing. It was against "Old Unsinkable's" rugged hull that General Kenney's fliers perfected their lethal invention—skip bombing, a technique that destroyed a convoy of Japanese ships during the Battle of the Bismarck Sea.

On Aug. 4, 1942, while practicing skip bombing against "Old Unsinkable," Berry was killed when a bomb prematurely exploded under his plane at a low level. This was a great loss to the 39th and to the Air Corps. Those who served under him and flew with him in combat remember Major Berry as a good man and a courageous leader.

After Berry's death, 1st Lt. Frank Royal was again named interim commander and started the squadron's transition into the new P-38 Lightning. As before with the P-39s, the squadron had crews at Amberly Field, Brisbane, receiving the airplane parts from the ships and assembling them in preparation for flight-testing. After test flights, the new planes were flown north to Antil Plains, near Townsville, Australia, where the squadron was busy teaching former P-39 pilots to fly the new twin-engine powerhouse.

P-38 Lightning Under a Stormy Sky

Design of the Lightning began in early 1937 in response to an Air Corps request for a twin-engine, high-altitude "interceptor" having "the tactical mission of interception and attack of hostile aircraft at high altitudes." Airacobra designs, which got underway at about the same time, lacked the high-altitude capability of the Lightnings. As a result, the Airacobra had a weak high-altitude combat performance record in the early days of the war.

The word *interceptor* was used as a way to bypass an Air Corps requirement that pursuit aircraft carry no more than 500 pounds of armament, including ammunition, and be restricted to single-seat aircraft with one engine. The Lightning design team decided on a minimum of 1,000 pounds of armament, a maximum airspeed of at least 360 mph, and the ability to climb to 20,000 feet within 6 minutes. This was the toughest set of specifications that had ever been devised for a fighter plane.

The design team considered a range of twin-engine configurations, eventually deciding on twin booms to accommodate the tail assembly, engines, and turbo-superchargers, with a central nacelle for the pilot and armament. The only other designs like it at that time were two German planes. In 1941, an RAF pilot shot down a Lightning, having mistaken it for a German-made Focke-Wulf.

A range of armaments was considered, with the designers eventually settling in June 1941 on a configuration of four .50-caliber machine guns and one 20-mm cannon, all concentrated in the nose of the aircraft.

Most other U.S. aircraft at the time used wing-mounted guns with trajectories set up to crisscross at one or more points in a convergence zone. Nose-mounted guns had the strong advantage of not being limited in their effectiveness to pattern convergence. The Lightning's straight-ahead firing enabled the pilot to hit targets at 1,000 yards. With convergence firing, the pilots had to pick a distance of 100 or 250 yards, depending on the angles of the wing-mounted guns. With any target closer or farther away, the fire would still be converging or spreading ineffectively.

The straight-ahead configuration was further enhanced by a devastating rate of fire. The cannon shot at a rate of 650 rounds per minute and the four machine guns at 860. This combined rate of fire was over 1,500 rpm with every sixth projectile a 20-mm shell. The duration of sustained firing for the 20-mm cannon and .50-caliber machine guns was approximately 14 seconds and 35 seconds, respectively.

Production of the thoroughly tested and approved design began at the Lockheed plant in Burbank, California, in February 1937. By September 1941, 65 Lightnings were ready for service, with many more on the way for the USAAF, the RAF, and the Free French Air Force operating from England.

Twenty-five of these planes were sent to Townville, Australia, in 1942 where, in mid-August, the 39th Fighter Squadron had been transferred from Port Moresby, to train on the Lightnings. "We can only guess why the 39th was chosen to be the first squadron in the Pacific Theater to be equipped with the big, powerful P-38 Lightning," recalls Colonel Frank Royal, a second lieutenant at the time and the squadron's interim commander. "Surely one factor must have been that the 39th had enthusiastically engaged the enemy for the 2½ months with P-39s and had not lost even one pilot in enemy action."

Pilots and ground crews were enthralled with their new plane, but the introductory training did not go without a hitch. One plane, attempting to take off, suddenly lost power and crashed, but the pilot survived. The problem, they discovered, was that it had run out of fuel due to a defect in the otherwise invaluable self-sealing fuel tanks. These tanks were made of a thick outer layer of hard rubber and fabric and a thin hard rubber inner layer.

Between these layers was a soft rubber layer specially formulated to swell instantly when penetrated by a bullet or shell fragment. Any small crack in the inner hard rubber layer would allow the soft rubber to expand and seemingly fill the tank. So the fuel gauge would register full on what could be an essentially empty tank. Inspections revealed that many tanks were defective in this way, and new tanks were flown in from the States.

Their arrival took several days. "There were nearly 1,000 screws that had to be removed from each tank, and then, of course, replaced by new tanks," says Royal. "It took all of us, pilots working alongside mechanics and crew chiefs, to complete the job," he recalls. One pilot complained in his diary about blistering his hands on the screwdriver handle.

Berry Drome
39th FS, 35th FG, 5th AF
Port Moresby, New Guinea
1942

Lieutenant Frank R. Royal inspecting the
damage to the wing of his P-39.

"We had never even seen a P-38 when we joined the 39th Fighter Squadron in Brisbane, Australia, in December 1942," Lt. Lew Lockhart said in an interview in 2010. "All of our training had been with the P-39. Since none of us had any twin-engine training, we were put on a train headed north to Charters Towers in North Queensville. When the train stopped in the middle of nowhere, we got off and walked to the engine to see what the trouble was. We found the crew drawing water from the boiler. That was our introduction to morning and afternoon tea.

"When we began flying the P-38, we ran into problems with the local farmers who claimed we caused their chickens to stop laying eggs, because we buzzed their farms," Lockhart said.

The transition into the new airplane was helped considerably by the influx of new pilots from the States who had trained in the P-38. The fresh P-38 pilots helped the old P-39 pilots learn to fly the big twin-engine bird. In turn, the old combat-hardened pilots taught the new pilots how to win in the deadly art of aerial combat with the enemy. Trained P-38 mechanics also were assigned to the 39th, which greatly helped in the transition.

When orders arrived on September 15, 1942, for the squadron to return to Port Moresby, only half of the Lightnings were ready, but off they went. "It was piecemeal," notes Royal. "Only a few planes at a time flew up to Laloki (aka 14-Mile Drome) where the landing strip had been lengthened for the new, bigger fighters."

By September 1942, the strategic situation in New Guinea had changed. Having failed to make a seaborne landing after the Battle of the Coral Sea, the Japanese switched to attacking Port Moresby overland, pushing down the Kakoda Track, over the Owen Stanley Range. The Australians recalled troops from North Africa, and, in some of the war's most brutal fighting, stopped them 20 miles short of Moresby.

The Japanese overland campaign required an enormous resupply effort with shipping arriving at Lae and Buna. Meanwhile, Australian and American pilots were disrupting Japanese efforts with daily bombing attacks. Swarms of Japanese fighters rose to attack the bombers, providing the 39th and other fighter squadrons with unprecedented opportunities for air-to-air combat. This had become the era of the dogfight in the Southwest Pacific, a fight Lightnings had been built to win.

On December 27, 1942, 12 Lightings of the 39th Squadron met the enemy and were tested in combat. The results, according to Royal, were "fantastic." Advised of "bandits in the vicinity," 12 Lightnings in three four-plane flights sighted a swarm of enemy planes, including eight Val dive-bombers and about 30 Zeros and Oscars.

The first flight was led by Capt. Thomas Lynch and included Lt. Richard Bong, Lt. John Mangas, and Lt. Kenneth Sparks. Lynch, Bong, and Sparks each shot down a Zero and a dive-bomber, and Mangas got an Oscar. The second flight shot down three Zeros and the third flight destroyed three Zeros.

"The total for the day was 13 enemy aircraft destroyed and none of ours brought home so much as a bullet hole," says Royal. "Squadron morale and pride, already high, went through the roof. After months of struggling with the inadequate Airacobra, the squadron finally had a weapon with which to blast the enemy out of the sky and take control of airspace over New Guinea. With a bit of warning, our planes could be up there ready for the Japs as they came in. This turned the whole war around for us."

It was during this battle that Lt. Richard Bong, who became the leading ace in the Pacific War, shot down his first enemy plane. Here is his description of his first victory:

"The date of my initiation into the art of battling Japs in the air was December 27, 1942. Ever since the start of the Buna campaign, we had been running routine four-ship fighter patrols over the battle area, and we had done a good job with every air melee that turned up. Lt. Col. Tom Lynch was flight leader, and I was on his wing. Lt. Kenneth Sparks, one of the hottest younger pilots in the squadron, was leading the second element with Lt. Dick Mangus on his wing. We took off just before noon, and Lynch led us up to about 23,000 feet. He always liked to start trouble from a high altitude, because it made him the master of the situation.

"We crossed the Owen Stanley Mountains of New Guinea, and we were just coming into the area we were supposed to cover when the ground station at Buna crackled over the radio with news that about 40 enemy planes were in the area. That sounded like the start of something, and Lynch called for a check on the Nips' altitude. 'Look for them at about 13,000 feet,' the ground station radioed back. Eight other P-38s from the 39th were sent to join us.

"We didn't have any trouble finding the Japs—they were right below us, and they had already decided we weren't exactly friends. I'm not sure they knew definitely what we were though. They hadn't see our P-38s in combat yet. Lynch didn't give them any time to consider the matter either. He took us down in a really screaming dive, and we let go of our belly tanks on the way down. Mine didn't want to come off, but what I couldn't do automatically, the wind pressure took care of.

"It was a major problem trying to stay with Lynch. I finally gave up and concentrated on a war of my own. There were Zeros all over the place and a flock of dive-bombers underneath them. We came tearing down and went through the Nips for our first pass. I tried to remember everything I had ever learned about keeping calm, aiming right, watching my flight leader, and not letting the enemy pull any countertactics that might end up with one of them on my tail.

"Maybe I was trying too hard to remember. The first four I shot at was a total waste of lead. I didn't hit a thing, and if a barn had been there, I would probably have missed that, too. About all I succeeded in doing was to scare one Jap off of Lynch's tail. There were too many Nips for too few Lightnings right about then. Finally, I gave myself a mental kick in the ribs and decided I'd better make some contribution besides conspicuous flubbing of the interception club.

"It was somewhere between 12:10 and 12:15 p.m. that I finally got into the groove. While I was getting the Nip off Lynch's tail, another one parked himself on mine. We were at about 10,000 feet, and I decided my best move would be to dive in a hurry. That's how I got my first Nip. As I leveled off about 2 inches above the shortest tree in the Buna area, there was a Jap dive-bomber sitting right ahead of me. It was a perfect setup and one even I couldn't miss. I gave him a short burst, and he blew higher than a kite. I wasn't feeling any too bad about that, so I wanted to enjoy it for a minute or two. He—or rather what was left of him—splashed into the water off Sanananda Point.

"I pulled up in a vertical turn and ran into my second Jap. Out of the corner of my eye, I saw a Zero in a vertical turn that put him right in the line of my fire. I started shooting an impressive assemblage of .50-caliber dynamite, and it takes a lot more than a Zero to get through a solid burst of it in one piece. That particular Zero expired right in the middle of my sights, and he never fired a single shot at me. He just rolled onto his back and went straight down. That's the best position I can think of for a Jap—going straight down with maybe a little explosion to hurry him along.

"By this time I was beginning to think combat was a lot easier than everyone seemed to suppose. I swung around and got back into the main brawl again, convinced I could take on the whole crowd if I had to. I got in a good series of hits on another Zero, but I never saw what happened to him. Then I chased after a Jap dive-bomber, but in the middle of that, my ammunition gave out.

"Lynch got us together to go home, and I noticed that Sparks was missing. I looked all over for him. Finally, I saw a P-38 landing on the Bobodura strip. It was Sparks, and he was okay. Well, that was combat number one. I felt like I had been through a washing machine with the accent on the wringer, and my mouth didn't feel normal again until the next combat we had, which was 3 days later. But with the first one behind me, I thought the future looked pretty bright for the squadron and me, too. As it turned out, it was."

An elated George Kenney sent the following letter to General "Hap" Arnold a few weeks after the air battle:

Dear General Arnold:

As a matter of interest, I am enclosing the reports of a recent air battle with Japanese fighters and bombers a couple of weeks ago. This was the first time the P-38 had ever been in combat in this theater. An analysis of these pilots' reports, written a few minutes after landing, show 12, definite, three probables, one possible, and results unobserved in six cases. Final returns to date confirmed: 15 enemy aircraft destroyed.

We had 12 P-38s in the show. One of them made a forced landing with a shot-up engine. The airplane is repairable. The rest came home. No casualties. This batch of Japs came from New Britain, and I expect that some of them, in addition to the 15, never got back. The boys did pretty well for their first combat, although they opened fire too far away and did entirely too much dog-fighting. They learned a lot, however, and will do better next time. Right now, the morale in that squadron is so high it almost scares you.

The Jap weaknesses and our real hope for victory is in the air. His fleet and his army can hold their own in any league, but he simply cannot train airmen to compare with ours in a hurry. His original highly trained crews were superb, but they are dead. His new crews cannot fly in bad weather, his night efforts are piddling, and his combat skill is low.

Our hurriedly trained youngsters are outflying and outshooting him at every encounter. All he has left is sheer guts. We wipe out a large percentage of his raiding squadrons, but he keeps coming.

Sincerely,
George Kenney, Commanding General
Allied Air Forces
Southwest Pacific Area

Chapter 6
Gaining Air Supremacy

With early warnings from the Australian coast watchers, pilots of the 39th no longer had to scramble and fly out to sea before engaging the enemy. The planes were up and ready to engage the enemy before critical target areas were damaged. In early January 1943, the enemy successfully reinforced its troops at Lae, a naval and air base on the northeast New Guinea coast. Army Air Corps bombers conducted round the clock missions in an effort to destroy them, with pilots of the 39th flying cover for many of these missions.

After a year of frustration—albeit valiant frustration—with outdated and outclassed planes, the squadron suddenly achieved superiority in the skies with the arrival of the P-38 Lightning.

It was the daily strafing by the 39th and other members of the 35th Fighter Group between August and October 1942, which led directly to the Allied recapture of the Kokoda Trail. Australian soldiers reported that the Japanese dead, piled high on the trail, could not be seen from the air.

The Allies began an all-out offensive on September 25, 1942, pushing the enemy deeper into New Guinea's Owen Stanley Mountains. On October 2, the Australians recaptured Menari, a mountain hamlet 46 miles north of Port Moresby.

Meanwhile, Airacobras, Flying Fortresses and P-38s from the 39th Fighter Squadron attacked enemy bases at Salamura and Buna on the east coast of New Guinea and hammered the mountain trail the Japanese used to move supplies to the front.

A special target was the Wairopi Bridge that spanned the Kumasi River. It was a strategic target, since it was the only means the Japanese could use to move heavy material across the rain-swollen Kumasi River. Among the pilots who participated in those attacks were Lt. Bill Nolan and Lt. James Miller, who both flew P-39s.

Miller became lost in weather on one of the missions and was reported missing. He ran out of gas and bailed out at 2,000 feet. After cutting his way through the jungle and reaching shore, he was picked up by an Australian plantation owner and taken to the native village of Hula. He spotted a wrecked P-40 and, with the help of some natives, got it into flying condition a few days later.

Meanwhile, Nolan and three other pilots went looking for Miller and spotted his crashed plane with its wing tips and tail sheared off. The plane was lying about 15 yards from the shore of the beach. The searchers also sighted the other P-40 with a man, thought to be Miller, standing on a wing. A number of natives were gathered around the plane, which appeared to be in flying condition.

When the searchers returned to base, arrangements were made to bring Miller back. Before a rescue team was dispatched, a P-40 approached 7-Mile Drome, circled, and made a perfect landing. Out stepped Miller who reached into the cockpit and helped out a small native boy. "He is my parachute," Miller said. Without a parachute to sit on, Miller had found he could not see out of the P-40. He asked a native boy to volunteer to be his "parachute." By sitting on the boy in the cockpit, he got sufficient height to see out of the plane.

On January 8, 1943, while escorting bombers over Lae, pilots of the 39th Fighter Squadron shot down seven Japanese planes, but one P-38, flown by Lt. John Mangas, was reported missing. It was not until after the war that the real story of his loss emerged, told by members of a B-17 bomber crew he saved that day. The crippled bomber was under attack by a flight of Zeros when Lieutenant Mangas dove in, guns blazing.

Lieutenant Mangas was credited with two "probable" as he made pass after pass, allowing the bomber to escape further damage. When last seen, his engine was smoking as his plane came under withering fire from enemy fighters. It is not known whether he crashed over land or water, so there is little hope that any remains will be found. He died a hero in the eyes of that bomber crew, a crew that survived because John Mangas gave his life in their behalf.

Rabaul was a primary bombing target during that period, and these missions were the toughest of all for pilots of the 39th, because there were so many miles of ocean to cross and so many Zeros rising to fight them when they arrived. Moreover, the harbor and airfields were surrounded by hundreds of antiaircraft guns. Lightnings flew from Port Moresby over the Owen Stanley Range to the island of Kiriwina in the Bismarck Sea, where they refueled and waited for the bombers to arrive. They would take off, escort the bombers to Rabaul, and defend them during their bombing runs. They were not cleared to head for home until all of the bomb runs were completed.

On Nov. 1, 1943, U.S. Marines landed in Empress Augusta Bay on the island of Bougainville, bringing American forces to the upper region of the Solomon Islands. A Japanese force of cruisers and destroyers sent to annihilate the marines was intercepted by an American cruiser-destroyer force, which sank an enemy light cruiser and a destroyer.

On Nov. 2, B-25s, escorted by P-38s from the 39th and 80th Fighter Squadrons, a total of 78 planes, attacked Rabaul. They were intercepted by 112 Zeros. Rabaul's air defenses, under the overall command of Rear Adm. Jinichi Kusaka, included three carrier groups.

The declining caliber of Japanese fighter pilots—after so many losses over the past year—was not in evidence that day. The carrier pilots were some of the most experienced and skillful in the war. Warrant Officer Kazuo Sugino from the carrier *Zuikaku*'s air group was credited with shooting down three American planes. *Shokaku*'s carrier group included Warrant Officer Kenji Okabe, who scored seven victories in one day during the Battle of the Coral Sea.

From the light carrier *Zuiho,* Ensign Yoshio Fukui downed a B-25, but then he was shot down. Fukui survived with a burned foot and insisted on returning to action. The loss of nine B-25s and nine P-38s earned the day the "Bloody Tuesday" label in Fifth Air Force annals, but the Japanese suffered an identical 18 planes destroyed or damaged, in addition to bomb damage to Rabaul's ground installations.

As the P-38s battled the Zeros overhead, the B-25s bombed ships in the harbor. The citation for Major Henry Wilkens, a B-25 pilot killed that day and awarded the Medal of Honor for "conspicuous gallantry and intrepidity above and beyond the call of duty" described his action that day:

> *"His airplane was hit almost immediately, the right wing damaged, and control rendered extremely difficult. Although he could have withdrawn, he held fast and led his squadron into the attack. He strafed a group of small harbor vessels, and then, at low level, attacked an enemy destroyer. His 1,000-pound bomb struck squarely amidships, causing the vessel to explode. Although antiaircraft fire from this vessel had seriously damaged his left vertical stabilizer, he refused to deviate from the course. From below-masthead height he attacked a transport, scoring a hit which engulfed the ship in flames. Bombs expended, he began to withdraw his squadron. A heavy cruiser barred the path. Unhesitatingly, to neutralize the cruiser's guns and attract its fire, he went in for a strafing run. His damaged stabilizer was completely shot off and the plane crashed."*

Five days later in another attack on Rabaul, the 39th lost two more planes and their pilots. The 12-plane flight took off from Dobadura to escort B-24s on a bombing mission. Battling Zeros, Major George Prentice shot one down, but the Zeros got Lieutenant Round who "seemed to disappear in midair" and Lt. Alphonse Quinones, who managed to bail out. Quinones's chute was seen to drift into the Rabaul Harbor, and a small Japanese boat set out to get him.

As a Japanese POW, he was not given much chance of survival. He, along with some 80 other American POWs, was imprisoned at Rabaul. Living conditions and food were awful, and tropical diseases raged throughout the prisoner community. For 2 years in this wretched situation, he found strength in his unwavering Roman Catholic faith.

Quinones nursed and comforted his fellow prisoners and gave them Last Rites as best he could. Other Catholics in the group joined him in prayer, and he took the lead and held prayer groups every evening. Some other non-Catholic POWs joined his group and found comfort. So it went until the end of the war when they were released and sent home.

Back at Port Moresby, Quinones's comrades assumed he had been killed, and, as with other deaths, they stoically packed away his personal belongings and quietly went on with the terrible business of waging war. It was not until years later that the 39th Fighter Squadron Association learned what had really happened to Alphonse Quinones.

He had returned home in broken health but opted to stay in the military. In 1949, he was sent to Fort Lewis, Washington, where Colonel Charles King was commander of fighter operations—the same Colonel King, then a captain, who had been commander of the 39th and the flight leader on the mission when Quinones was shot down.

King was checking over a list of in-coming personnel, and the name Quinones jumped out at him. "Where is this man?" he asked his secretary.

"He's sitting in the waiting room waiting to talk with you," she said.

The survival of Quinones and the other POWs may have had something to do with Rabaul being bypassed in the Allied advance toward the Philippines and eventually Japan. Japanese captors usually slaughtered prisoners to keep them from describing their inhumane treatment.

Meanwhile, in New Guinea, Allied engineers built new landing strips north of the Owen Stanley Mountain Range at Bena, Marilinan, Dumput, Dobadu, and Tsili Tsili. The Tsili Tsili strip was assigned to the 39th's sister squadrons, the 40th and 41st. These squadrons were still flying the short-ranged P-39 Airacobras, and their new base allowed them to take part in the air battles over Lae. Control of this deep-water port was essential in the development of the huge, flat Markham Valley into a forward-most bomber base.

During this time, the 39th FS was kept busy escorting C-47 transport planes to Wau, a landlocked and precariously defended Australian base that could be supplied only by air.

Schwimmer Drome
39th FS, 35th FG, 5th AF
Port Moresby, New Guinea
1943

Charles W. King, Thomas J. Lynch, and Charles P. Sullivan standing in front of the pilot board showing the day's flight assignments.

Japanese General Okabe, a skillful tactician, managed to get his 1,200-man force through trackless jungle to attack the 700-man Australian garrison by surprise. Bad weather had closed the airfield to transport planes, and the Australians were nearly out of ammunition when the weather cleared. Planes arrived with supplies and reinforcements, and the Japanese were defeated in hand-to-hand combat.

By autumn, the Japanese ground forces had withdrawn to the Lae and Buna areas, but regular traffic of C-47s into Wau was still required to keep the base supplied and bad weather often kept the planes from landing. Indeed, weather was always the most serious hazard to all aircraft flying over New Guinea. It was quite normal, especially in the afternoon, for enormous thunderheads to develop over the Owen Stanley Mountain Range. With virtually all combat missions flying over the range to the far side of the island, pilots often had to push through very heavy weather to get home, and some never made it.

On July 16, 1943, four 39th FS pilots—Denton, Morgan, Andrews, and Steele—were assigned to escort a photo reconnaissance plane on a mission to Madang. Known as "Photo Joes," the reconnaissance planes were P-38s specially adapted for these missions. To accommodate the photography equipment and assure maximum getaway speed, these planes had been stripped of armor plate, guns, and ammunition. Usually, other fighters escorted them.

When this mission over Madang was completed, the Photo Joe pilot leaned on his throttles and took off for home. The escort planes were unable to keep up and, as they approached the mountains, they flew into a storm. Denton and Andrews managed to get back to Port Moresby, but Morgan and Steele were missing.

There was good and bad news in the Combat Diary for July 19, 1943, which read:

> *The good news for today is the return of Lieutenant Morgan. He had crash-landed on the beach about 40 miles up the coast from Kerema. The natives took good care of him and a Tiger Moth, a light plane, picked him up. The bad news is that Lieutenant Steele remains missing.*

Steele was never found and was declared legally dead after the war.

Over time, pilots developed methods of dealing with this weather challenge. Lt. Stanley Andrews marked his time, speed, heading, and altitude as he passed over the north New Guinea coast, enabling him to calculate when he should arrive over the south coast. When he reached that time, he throttled back and dropped down through the clouds until he could see the ocean. If his altitude was high enough, he would clear the 12,000-foot peaks of the range and come down over the ocean somewhere near Port Moresby. He then took a compass heading that would take him to the 14-Mile Drome.

The 39th FS pilots said the most nerve-racking part of this kind of navigation occurred when getting down to the last 300 feet with the sea still not in sight. If a heavy fog was close to sea level, it was possible to be in the water before seeing it.

The truly epic story of disappearance and survival during this period involved Captain Charles Sullivan, who took part in a 16-plane sweep of Wewak and Boram on September 20, 1943. After the sweep, "Sully" had disappeared, and no one remembered seeing him go down. A check of the various airstrips in range of the operation turned up no information about Sully's whereabouts.

Planes went out to search for him in the Ramu Valley when weather permitted with no results. Any time pilots flew a mission in the vicinity of the area in which Sully went down, they looked for him. Then, on October 14, word came in that Sully was all right and that he was "coming in."

The October 19 Combat Diary reads:

> *There were no missions today, but there was plenty of excitement. Captain Sullivan, who had been missing since September 20, returned to camp and had a thrilling story to tell about his 24 days in the jungle before reaching an Aussie forward outpost.*

Everyone wanted to know how he had survived in the jungle for weeks, so the whole squadron assembled to hear Sully's story.

"Wracked with fever and looking very worn, Sully sat up front with a couple of our officers and related his story of survival," says Royal. "Those of us attending spent most of an hour awestruck and with mouths agape. His was a one-of-a-kind story of surviving against extremely high odds."

Chapter 7
The Battle of Bismarck Sea

The pilots of the 39th had lived something of a charmed, though uncomfortable, life in their initial deployment at Port Moresby. Although some 80 of their planes had been lost, all of them managed to crash-land or parachute to safety. Often, they flew again the following day.

But with the arrival of the Lightning, they had a far better aircraft flying with far greater range into far greater danger. They were no longer only providing air cover for Port Moresby. Now they were escorting bombers that were attacking Japanese bases and battling a still highly effective Japanese air force.

The risks rose rapidly as the Japanese sought to recover from defeats at Guadalcanal, the Kokoda Track, and Buna-Gona, and to counter an expected Allied counteroffensive in New Guinea and the Solomons. The Allied aim was to capture the main Japanese base at Rabaul and clear the way for the eventual reconquest of the Philippines. Desperate to prevent that, the Japanese were determined to send convoys from Rabaul to reinforce their bases on the north coast of New Guinea.

Code breakers' reports of this plan greatly disturbed General Douglas MacArthur, and he directed General Kenney to prepare an air offensive against the Japanese convoys. Kenney ordered that flying hours be cut back to allow for a large strike and moved as many aircraft as possible to the captured airfields around Dobodura, where they would not be subject to the vagaries of weather over the Owen Stanley Range. On February 26, 1943, he flew to Port Moresby to inspect fighter and bomber units in the area and made plans to attack the Japanese convoy in the Vitiaz Strait.

An enemy task force of five troop transports left Rabaul bound for Lae carrying some 3,000 troops from Major General Toru Okabe's 51st Division. Allied aircraft spotted and attacked that convoy, which was shielded by low clouds and Japanese fighters. The Allies shot down 69 Japanese aircraft while losing only 10 of their own. This was the action in which the 39th's Richard Bong achieved ace status when he shot down three planes.

An Australian bomber sank the transport *Nichiryu Maru*. Although enemy destroyers rescued 739 of the 1,100 troops on board, the ship took down with it most of the expedition's critical supplies. Another transport was so badly damaged by B-25s that it had to be beached. The rest of that convoy succeeded in reaching Lae on January 7 and landing its troops. But this was all for naught since the Japanese were defeated in the Battle of Wau.

The new Japanese plan to move 7,300 soldiers from Rabaul to Lae was acknowledged to be risky because of the growing Allied air power in the area. Japanese planners predicted losses of four out of eight transports and between 30 and 40 aircraft, and gave the operation only a 50-50 chance of success.

The decision was made to take that risk, however, because if the troops landed at the alternative and far safer destination of Madang instead of Lae, they faced a march of more than 140 miles through swamps, mountains, and jungle terrain without roads. Three naval and two army fighter groups assigned to protect the convoy were augmented by 18 fighters from the aircraft carrier *Zuiho*.

Signs of the preparations for this convoy were almost immediately detected by Allied reconnaissance flights. On February 7, 1943, a Japanese floatplane of the type normally used for antisubmarine patrols was sighted, prompting General Kenney to order more reconnaissance patrols over Rabaul. On February 14, 1943, aerial photographs showed 79 vessels in the port, including 45 merchant ships and six transports. Another convoy was clearly being organized, but the destination was unknown.

On February 16, 1943, code breakers in Australia and Washington decrypted a message showing that the Japanese intended to land convoys at Lae and Wewak. A few days later, another decrypted coded message showed that a 16-ship convoy was expected to reach Lae on March 5, 1943.

The first Lae reinforcement convoy hugged the south coast of New Britain, making it easier for the Japanese to provide air cover. However, being close to the airfields made it possible for the Allied air forces to attack both the convoy and the airfields at the same time.

The route the Japanese chose for the second convoy was along the north coast. They believed this route would have two advantages. First, Allied planes would have to travel much farther in interdict it, and they would have to fly over Japanese air bases on New Britain. Second, the route might deceive the Allies into thinking that the destination was actually Madang.

There was a major disadvantage for the Japanese. In the final leg of the voyage, the convoy would have to pass through the restricted waters of the Vitiaz Strait. Worse yet, because of the decoded messages, General Kenney knew their plans.

Moving at 7 knots, the convoy was not detected for several days because of two tropical storms that struck the Solomon and Bismarck seas between February 27 and March 1, 1943. At about 3 p.m. on March 1, 1943, a patrolling B-24 Liberator heavy bomber spotted the convoy. Eight B-17s sent to the location failed to find the ships.

The morning of March 3, 1943, dawned bright and clear, and at about 11 a.m., Private Tatsue Machida of the 115th Regiment's Headquarters signal company was on the deck of the transport *Oigawa-Muru* listening to an inspirational briefing by Lieutenant Noboro Hashimoto. Powerful Japanese air force units were attacking the Allied airfields at Port Moresby, the lieutenant told the men, so the threat of air attack on their task force was over.

As the lieutenant spoke, he must have noticed there was no sense of reassurance or renewed confidence in the men's faces. They were staring at the sky behind him where a formation of large planes—B-17s and B-24s above and B-25s and RAAF Beaufighters below—came into view.

"He kept talking heedlessly, and I wished he would stop," Machida remembers. When the lieutenant did stop, the men fled below deck to follow orders about preparing to abandon ship, if necessary. It would be necessary. The attacking formation that was about to sink the *Oigawa-Muru,* seven other troop ships, and four of the eight escorting destroyers, was the Fifth Air Force's solution to earlier tactics that had failed to interdict Japanese supply lines at sea.

In January 1943, the Fifth had flown more than 400 sorties against a previous troop landing and managed only to sink two ships and damage three. Group Captain Bill Garing, an RAAF officer on Kenney's staff, came up with the revised tactics. Garing had just returned from the fighting in Europe where he had witnessed the success of Allied planes attacking convoys from different altitudes and directions. Why not try that here?

Douglas A-20 Havoc light bombers were modified by installing four .50-caliber machine guns in their noses, and two 450-gallon fuel tanks were added, giving the aircraft more range. An attempt was made to create a longer-range attack aircraft by doing the same thing to a B-25 medium bomber, but that proved to be more difficult.

Even with lead ballast in the tail, this aircraft became nose heavy, and the vibrations caused by firing the machine guns were enough to make rivets pop out. But when tail guns and belly turrets were removed, since they would be of little use when the aircraft was flying low, the B-25 also became an effective part of the low-level attack force, which would include intensive strafing, skip bombing, and mast-height bombing.

The B-17 and B-24 heavy bombers approached well above these low-level attack planes. Above them were the P-38 Lightnings from the 39th and other fighter squadrons searching for whatever Japanese air cover would arrive to attempt to fend off the attack. Leading the 39th's fighters was Captain Robert Faurot, who would not survive this battle.

At dawn on March 3, 1943, RAAF bombers attacked Japanese airfields at Lae to reduce their ability to provide support for the convoy. At about 10 a.m., a Liberator found the convoy, and an hour later the Allied air forces arrived in strength. Attacking with 1,000 pound bombs, B-17s sank one ship carrying 1,200 troops and damaged two others. They also destroyed eight Japanese fighters and damaged 13 others. Two destroyers picked up 950 survivors and, running at high speed, managed to get them to Lae.

Captain Robert L. Faurot

1st Lt. Hoyt A. Eason

1st Lt. Fred B. Shifflet

At 10 a.m. the following day, a force of 90 Allied planes swept in over the convoy. B-17s bombing at 7,000 feet forced the ships to disperse, reducing their concentrated antiaircraft fire. It was during this action that the crew of a crippled B-17 bailed out and Zeros strafed them as they descended and after they hit the water. Lightnings from the 39th Fighter Squadron flown by Faurot, Hoyt Eason, and Fred Shifflett attacked the Zeros, shooting down five of them, but then were shot down themselves.

Fred Shifflet was one of the few American pilots able to get his plane off the ground during the attack on Pearl Harbor. He was unable to engage the enemy, because his plane was hit by friendly fire, and he had to make a dead-stick landing.

"Little clear information is available as to just what took place," says Frank Royal, "but Bob McMahon, flying in another flight that day, reported that he saw Faurot's flight diving to rescue a damaged bomber that had dropped out of formation and was being swarmed by Zeros. As Faurot was diving, McMahon spotted a flight of Zeros converging on him and radioed a warning. Faurot responded, 'Got 'em.'"

Then McMahon saw another flight of Zeros tracking Faurot's flight from a better angle and shouted another warning. At that moment, McMahon came under attack and had to take evasive action himself. Afterward, he did not remember getting a response from Faurot. When he finally cleared his tail, McMahon could see three P-38s smoking and spinning down.

Another 39th FS pilot on the mission, Jack Jones, reported that Zeros were everywhere as he dove into the melee. He soon found himself down low over the ocean, out of ammunition and low on fuel. So he turned toward home. Ahead of him he saw a P-38 land in the ocean. The pilot got out and started swimming for the nearby shore. He thought it might have been Hoyt Eason. Lieutenant Eason was never found and was listed as killed in action on March 4, 1943.

Bombing and strafing attacks continued on the convoy for the next 3 days, leaving all but four of the ships sunk. Japanese destroyers managed to carry 1,200 of the surviving troops to Lae and 2,700 back to Rabaul.

On March 4, 1943, Private Machida had been on a life raft for 48 hours, the *Oigawa-Muru* having been sunk early in the battle. He reported that when the Allied planes made their strafing runs, the only protection was to jump into the water until the aircraft had passed, and then climb back in. "This was repeated many times, and each time we used up valuable strength," he said.

General Kenney ordered Allied patrol boats and aircraft to attack Japanese rescue vessels, as well as the survivors from the sunken vessels swimming or floating in the sea. He justified his order on the grounds that rescued servicemen would have landed at their military destination and promptly returned to active service. These orders violated the Hague Convention of 1907, which banned the killing of shipwreck survivors under any circumstances.

For the next several days, American and Australian airmen returned to the sight of the battle, systematically prowling the seas in search of Japanese survivors. Certainly, some aircrew were motivated by revenge, but most felt that military necessity justified their actions. As a coup de grâce, Kenney called these missions "mopping-up" operations. A March

20, 1943, secret report proudly proclaimed, "The slaughter continued till nightfall. If any survivors were permitted to slip by our strafing aircraft, they were a minimum of 30 miles from land, in water thickly infested by man-eating sharks." Time after time, aircrew reported messages similar to the following: "Sighted, barge consisting of 200 survivors. Have finished attack. No survivors."

All eight transports and four of the escorting destroyers were sunk. Out of 6,900 troops only about 1,200 made it to Lae. Another 2,700 were rescued by destroyers and submarines and returned to Rabaul. The Japanese made no further attempts to reinforce Lae by ship, hindering their efforts to stop Allied offensives in New Guinea.

Kenney's chief of staff, Maj. Gen. Don Wilson, insisted that the Japanese "set the pace for 'no quarter' procedures" after an incident involving the only Allied bomber lost in the battle. During the initial assault on the morning of March 3, bullets penetrated the wing and radio compartment of the B-17 piloted by Lt. Woodrow Moore. Fire engulfed the plane, and it went into a steep dive. Before the plane disintegrated, seven of the nine-man crew bailed out, but Japanese fighters strafed the airmen as they drifted to the sea 6,000 below.

The consequences of the Bismarck Sea Battle reverberated all the way to the Imperial Palace in Tokyo. Grand strategy had called for the movement of 100,000 troops to bolster Japanese defenses on the north coast of New Guinea. Without the intervention of a single Allied naval ship, Allied planes had bombed and strafed the convoy out of existence. What, the emperor demanded, was Admiral Isoroku Yamamoto going to do about that?!

The admiral's proposed solution was Operation I-Go, a massive aerial campaign against Allied naval and land bases, but mainly against airfields to stop the rapid buildup of Allied air forces in the theater. The operation would involve a series of aerial strikes on U.S. bases at Port Moresby and Milne Bay on New Guinea and on Guadalcanal and other bases in the Solomon Island chain.

When he arrived at Rabaul on April 3, 1943, Yamamoto had 86 fighter planes, 27 dive-bombers, and 72 bombers available for the operation from the land-based Eleventh Air Fleet. He added 96 fighters and 65 dive-bombers from the Japanese Third Fleet, which included carriers *Zuikaku,* *Zuiho, Junyo,* and *Hiyo.*

Initially, the strategy had been to concentrate efforts on New Guinea, but instead, Yamamoto launched the first attack at Guadalcanal. Intent on luring U.S. fighters into a one-sided battle, a swarm of 58 Zeros attacked shipping just off the island. U.S. planes rose to meet the challenge, but the outcome was not what Yamamoto had hoped for. The Zeros did manage to shoot down six U.S. planes, but they lost 18 of their own.

Undeterred, on April 7, 1943, Yamamoto sent 67 dive-bombers and 110 Zeros, the largest concentration of Japanese air power since Pearl Harbor, to attack the Allied ships in Savo Sound, north of Guadalcanal. Japanese reconnaissance that morning had reported a concentration of a dozen warships and a number of transports in the sound. When Yamamoto's air fleet reached the area, most of the ships—having received advanced warning from coast watchers—had left. So 76 U.S. fighters from Henderson Field scrambled and reached attack altitude before the Japanese arrived at 3 p.m. Some of the enemy dive-bombers managed to sink the U.S. destroyer *Aaron Ward* and the New Zealand corvette HMNZS *Moa.*

In the battle above the ships, the Japanese lost 12 dive-bombers and nine Zeros at a cost of seven Allied planes. Failure to catch the concentration of Allied ships at Savo did not bother Yamamoto. His target was the Allied air arm, and postaction reports he received greatly exaggerated U.S. losses, while minimizing those of his own air force. Yamamoto turned his attention to Allied bases on New Guinea.

On April 11, 1943, 22 dive-bombers and 72 Zeros attacked shipping in Oro Bay, southeast of Buna. The dive-bombers sank one merchant ship and forced another to beach, but, in the air battle above the bay, six Zeros were destroyed without accounting for a single Allied plane.

The next day, in the biggest air raid yet carried out in the South Pacific, Yamamoto sent 131 fighters and 43 medium bombers to attack shipping and airfields at Port Moresby. Among the U.S. fighters intercepting them were eight P-38s from the 39th FS led by Maj. Tom Lynch and another eight led be Capt. Charles Gallup.

Gallup shot down a Zeke for his sixth kill, and Lt. Richard "Snuffy"

Smith shot down a bomber for the third of his seven kills. Another bomber crashed after Lt. Dick Suehr shot it down for his fifth kill. Suehr was the pilot who held off doctors in an Australian hospital with his .45 when they wanted to amputate his legs. Lt. Grover Fanning flew into a heavily escorted formation of bombers and shot down two of them. He destroyed an Oscar a few minutes later and accounted for nine kills in his time with the 39th.

A flight report by P-38 pilot Danny Roberts, flying with the 80th FS, captures the action of this battle:

"I took off at 1210 hour and climbed at full power. Reached 20,000 feet at 1235 and flew up-sun and very close to a cloud formation, reaching 25,000 feet. Eighteen to 20 dive-bombers were sighted at 1240 hours directly ahead of us, about 8,000 feet below. They made a wide circle above a thin overcast at about 19,000 feet and went into a string formation headed down for ships 10 to 15 miles away. We dove hard after them once we had dropped our auxiliary tanks, and I gave instructions to attack— 'This is our meat!'

"My first burst at about 17,000 feet caught a bomber. It lost pieces of a wing as I passed very close overhead. The second half of the enemy formation seemed to split wide open and disbursed without attacking. However, the first attack had apparently scored a hit on one of our vessels that was smoking badly.

"At this point, three enemy planes flew under me. A sharp turn downward set me in a position for a good burst, which I fired at one of them at 5,500 feet. A part of its right wing was lost and the dive-bomber immediately made a violent turn, apparently out of control, and headed for the sea, smoking as it went. The plane was seen to strike the sea. My No. 3 man then passed under me, with dive-bombers in front of him and fighters on his tail. I dove toward the water to help him, by which time he had destroyed the plane in front of him. It burst into flames and hit the water."

Returning to base, Roberts claimed two dive-bombers, his third and fourth kills. He would go on to become a Fifth Air Force legend, accounting for 10 more kills before losing his life in a collision with a squadron mate on Nov. 9, 1943.

Captain Charles W. King
39th FS, 35th FG, 5th AF
Schwimmer Air Drome, Port Moresby, New Guinea
January 1943

On April 14, 1943, a large formation of twin-engine bombers and Zeros from Rabaul and dive-bombers and Zeros from Japanese carriers, a total of 188 planes, appeared at 11 a.m. over Milne Bay. Rising to meet them were pilots from the 39th, including Lts. Dick Bong and William Sells. Bong shot down two of the bombers, and his wingman, Sells, got another. Sells was killed that day when, attempting to land his badly damaged plane, he pulled up, stalled, and then crashed.

On April 16, 1943, Yamamoto ended Operation I-Go believing his staff's exaggerated reports that 175 Allied planes had been destroyed—seven times the actual number of 25—and that the Allied air buildup had been halted.

The failure of Operation I-Go was compounded later that month when American code breakers intercepted a message that Admiral Yamamoto would be flying from Rabaul to Balalae Airfield on the morning of April 18, 1943. When informed of the message, American President Franklin D.

Roosevelt ordered Secretary of Navy Frank Knox to "Get Yamamoto." Roosevelt had never forgiven Yamamoto for being the architect of the attack on Pearl Harbor. Ironically, Yamamoto had warned Japanese military leaders before the attack that if a war with America lasted more than 1 year, Japan would lose.

Admiral Nimitz authorized a mission to intercept Yamamoto's plane and shoot it down. Yamamoto's plane left Rabaul as scheduled on April 18, 1943, and 16 Lightnings intercepted it over Bougainville and shot it down. His body was found in the jungle, and doctors determined that he had been killed by gunfire from one of the attacking planes. Yamamoto died having been right about two things: the effectiveness of aircraft carriers in long-range naval attacks and that Japan would lose a drawn-out struggle with the United States.

39th FS pilots who participated in the Battle of the Bismarck Sea[1]

March 2, 1943

Only mission of the day—16 pilots take off at 0745 hrs.

Major George W. Prentice	Lt. Kenneth G. Sparks
Lt. Lloyd P. Shipley	Lt. Paul M. Stanch
Capt. Robert L. Faurot	Lt. John C. Dunbar
Lt. Charles P. Sullivan	Lt. Robert H. Baker
Capt. Thomas J. Lynch	Lt. John J. Rogers
Capt. Charles W. King	Lt. Edward W. Randall
Capt. Curran L. Jones	Lt. Wilmot R. Marlatt
Lt. Harris L. Denton	Lt. James D. Walters

---

1 Per the 39th FS Squadron Diary

March 3, 1943

First mission of the day—16 pilots take off at 0850 hrs.

Major George W. Prentice Capt. Charles W. King	Lt. Paul M. Stanch Lt. Ralph C. Bills
Capt. Robert L. Faurot (MIA) Lt. Hoyt A. Eason (MIA)	Lt. Fred B. Shifflet (MIA) Lt. Henry H. Turick
Capt. Thomas J. Lynch Lt. Benjamin Widmann	Lt. Richard E. Smith Lt. John H. Lane
Capt. Curran L. Jones Lt. Charles P. Sullivan	Lt. Stanley O. Andrews Lt. Edward C. Flood

Second mission of the day—11 pilots take off at 1330 hrs.

Capt. Thomas J. Lynch Lt. Kenneth G. Sparks	Lt. John J. Rogers Lt. Lloyd P. Shipley
Capt. Curran L. Jones Lt. Robert H. Baker	Lt. Lloyd P. Shipley Lt. Edward W. Randall
Capt. Charles W. King Lt. Harris L. Denton	Lt. Wilmot R. Marlatt Lt. Lee. C. Haigler

March 4, 1943

Only mission of the day—12 pilots take off at 1110 hrs.

Major George W. Prentice Lt. Paul M. Stanch	Lt. John C. Dunbar Lt. Edward C. Flood
Lt. Charles P. Sullivan Lt. Benjamin Widmann	Lt. James D. Walters Lt. Ralph C. Bills
Lt. Kenneth G. Sparks Lt. John H. Lane	Lt. Richard E. Smith Lt. Robert H. Baker

March 5, 1943

Final Bismarck Sea Mission—8 pilots take off at 1140 hrs.

Capt. Charles W. King	Capt. Thomas J. Lynch
Lt. Lee. C. Haigler	Lt. Lloyd P. Shipley
Lt. John J. Rogers	Lt. Edward C. Flood
Lt. Harris L. Denton	Lt. James D. Baker

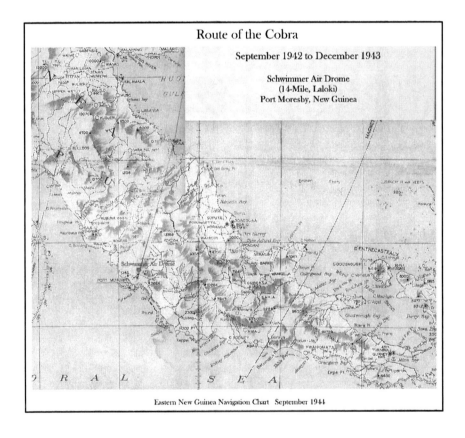

Route of the Cobra

September 1942 to December 1943

Schwimmer Air Drome
(14-Mile, Laloki)
Port Moresby, New Guinea

Eastern New Guinea Navigation Chart September 1944

Chapter 8
The Flying Circus
(Lynch and Bong)

Richard Bong had just turned 22 at the time of the Battle of Bismarck Sea when he achieved "Ace" status. During the month that Bong remained with the 39th, he and Lt. Col. Tom Lynch, the "old man" of the squadron at 25, became good friends. Lynch, who would account for 17 Japanese kills, was a perfect match for Bong. Somewhat more mature and less flamboyant, he was Bong's equal in flying skills and courage.

Bong and Lynch had just returned from leave in the United States and were assigned to desk jobs at Fifth Headquarters in February 1943. After a few weeks of administrative duties, they became bored and asked to be returned to flying status. They were given permission to fly on any missions they wanted and thus, the "Flying Circus" was born.

The son of Swedish immigrants, Bong grew up on a farm near the small town of Poplar, Wisconsin, where he did well in high school, helped on the farm, and pursued many interests as a teenager. He starred on the school's baseball, basketball, and hockey teams, played clarinet in the school band, and sang in the church choir. He enjoyed fishing and hunting and became a good shot. Like many boys of his era, he developed an interest in aviation at a young age and became an avid builder of model planes.

In 1938, he enrolled in the Civilian Pilot training program while a freshman at Superior State Teachers College. He also took private flying lessons before enlisting in the Army Air Corps Aviation Cadet Program in 1941.

During fighter pilot training at Luke Field near Phoenix, Arizona, where he learned to master the AT-6 training plane, one instructor said Bong was the finest natural pilot he ever met. There was no way he could keep the trainee off his tail, even though Bong was flying the slow AT-6. In January 1942, just after Pearl Harbor, he was assigned to Luke Field to teach gunnery to the new pilots.

After a few months, he got the chance to train on the P-38 at Hamilton Field, San Francisco. It was here that he first attracted the attention of General George Kenney.

There is a famous story about Bong "high-hatting" all over San Francisco Bay, flying under the bridges, buzzing Market Street, and blowing wash off clotheslines. When a harried housewife complained, Kenney called Bong on the carpet and told him,

> *Monday morning you check this address out in Oakland, and if the woman has any washing to be hung out on the line, you do it for her. Then you hang around being useful—mowing the lawn or something—and when the clothes are dry, take them off the line and bring them into the house. And don't drop any of them on the ground or you will have to wash them all over again. I want this*

woman to think we are good for something else besides
annoying people. Now get out of here before I get mad
and change my mind. That's all!

Clearly, General Kenney recognized Bong's flying skills as well as his rambunctious attitude, because when he became Fifth Air Force commander, Bong was one of the pilots he selected to come with him to the Pacific. Initially assigned to the 9th Fighter Squadron, he was waiting in Australia for Lightnings to be delivered. When the 39th got the Lightnings first, he was temporarily reassigned to them.

Short, round-faced, boyish, and always smiling, Bong did not look like a ferocious fighter pilot. Of the small group of trained Lightning pilots who arrived in Australia together, it was suggested that he was the least likely to succeed when pitted against the enemy. The crew chief of the plane Bong was assigned certainly had that opinion.

"That li'l son-of-a-bitch ain't gonna do nothing," the chief predicted. "He'll just waste fuel and put wear and tear on the plane." But returning from the mission on December 29, Bong did a superlow buzz job of and pulled up after making two beautiful aileron rolls.

The crew chief was still unimpressed. "He's just playing," he muttered. But with the plane back in the revetment and the canopy open, Bong was busy filling out the action report, Form One. "How'd you do?" the Jeep driver who pulled in to pick him up shouted, and Bong held up two fingers and smiled.

Thomas Lynch was a Boy Scout at Saint Lawrence Parish in Catasauqua, Pennsylvania, advancing to become an Eagle Scout. After high school, he enrolled at the University of Pittsburgh, majoring in chemical engineering. He joined the ROTC program and was elected a member of the Scabbard and Blade Society, an honorary military group.

In June 1940, Lynch entered the U.S. Army Air Corps and was selected for flight training. By 1941, he was a part of the 39th Pursuit Squadron at Selfridge Field, engaging in maneuvers flying the P-39 Airacobra during the summer and fall. He was among the handful of pilots that left the United States aboard the USS *Ancon* bound for Australia in January 1942.

In Brisbane, pilots and ground personnel began assembling and testing the airplanes coming off the ships. Pilots had to be checked out in flying the planes, and ground crews had to be trained in maintenance and repair. It was not until June 1, 1942, that the squadron was ready to take on combat duty.

Aces of the 39th Fighter Squadron
Schwimmer Drome, Port Moresby, New Guinea
39th FS, 35th FG, 5th AF
May 1943

With Captain Lynch's P-38 #10, are:

Front row - L to R: Capt. Charles P. Sullivan; Capt. Thomas J. Lynch, Squadron Commander; and 1st Lt. Kenneth G. Sparks.

Back row - L to R: Capt. Richard C. Suehr; 1st Lt. John H. Lane; and 1st Lt. Stanley O. Andrews.

A select group of 39th Squadron pilots were sent on temporary duty to New Guinea in May1942, to gain experience before the main body of the squadron arrived. Lt. Tom Lynch and Lt. Ralph Carey were in good company as they flew up to Port Moresby, New Guinea.

The official 39th Squadron Combat diary records that Lynch and Carey were accompanied by Lt. Donald Green, who had been flying Spitfires in defense of England with the remnants of the Polish Air Force prior to Pearl Harbor. Lt. Frank Adkins and Lt. Gene Wahl had been flying P-40 Warhawks against the Japanese over Java. These five men arrived at Port Moresby on the evening of May 16. Contact with the enemy was immediate.

The Combat Diary records:

17 May 1030 hrs Interception. Lt. Green Leading. Flight of 4 in 2 ship elements took off on intercept mission. When at altitude of 11,000 ft 5 Zeros were sighted at the same level 90-deg. left, flying in Luffberry. Our flight maneuvered for position and attacked head-on. Enemy executed an Immelmann giving them a position to the rear of our A/C and attempted pursuit. The result of the engagement was nil. Enemy aircraft had cowlings painted red.

18 May 0940 hrs Interception. Lts. Wahl and Lynch went on mission of interception climbing to 22,000 ft. The enemy was sighted 80 deg. left, at same level—30 bombers in two V formations and 15 Zeros flying in Luffberry. Our pilots dived out of the sun at 4 Zeros. This action was observed late by the enemy, and they attempted to turn into the attacking formation. The main enemy force continued on their course. Each pilot made contact and scored hits on the enemy.

Enemy casualties = 2 Zeros probable; our casualties = nil.

Comments: 4 escorting fighters remained in Luffberry below the main body of bombers.

20 May 0755 hrs Interception. Lts. Wahl, Lynch, Adkins, flying in 5 ship flight in cooperation with 35th Sqdn., 8th Grp., intercepted 6 Zeros at 15,000 ft. When first sighted enemy was 45 deg. left, at same level. The attack executed was head-on and observed by enemy who were flying in loose echelon. Lynch reported hits on an enemy aircraft, but no result determined. After attack enemy aircraft pulled around on our planes' tails and our pilots dived away. Lt. Wahl and Adkins reported no results.

Enemy casualties = 2 Zeros damaged.

Our casualties = Lynch's plane was shot up, but he landed safely. Lt. Carey bailed out of the plane and was injured when he hit the ground.

Comments: Lt. Atkins = "Could have done better with a truck. It's more maneuverable and will go higher." Lt. Wahl = "Could have done damn good with an altitude ship."

It was immediately clear they faced a more experienced enemy with more maneuverable airplanes. Lynch proved to be an excellent pilot and was quick to learn the tactics needed to defeat these experienced Japanese pilots.

After another 2 months of combat duty, the 39th Squadron was selected to be the first squadron in the Pacific to be equipped with P-38 Lightnings. After a period of familiarization and shakedown flights in Australia, the 39th FS moved up to Port Moresby and joined the war. Now they had the "altitude ship" that Lieutenant Wahl said they needed.

Aces were being made while the Japanese pilots took a beating. Tom Lynch came into his own with this airplane and soon became an experienced leader and brilliant tactician. When Major George W. Prentice was taken from the 39th FS to form the new 475th Fighter Group, Capt. Tom Lynch was tapped to command the 39th.

Under his hand the squadron continued to excel and build an enviable record. By March 1943, the 39th FS was the top-ranked squadron in the Pacific with well over 100 kills on its scoreboard.

In December 1942, Lieutenant Bong was assigned to the 39th FS while his 9th FS waited to be equipped with P-38s. On Dec. 2, the P-38 was tested in battle for the first time.

Bong was flying Captain Lynch's wing that day.

The 39th Combat Diary:

27 Dec. '42. Our first patrol patrolled Buna beginning at 1145 hrs. At 1210 hrs Capt. Lynch and his Red Flight consisting of Lts. Bong, Sparks, and Mangas were warned of "Bandits" in the near vicinity. When locating the enemy planes (they were) 20 or 30 Zekes and Oscars with 7 or 8 Val Dive-Bombers. Capt. Lynch led his flight of only 4 planes in to attack the enemy of approximately 35 airplanes. During the combat his flight claimed 7 victories. Capt. Lynch = 2 Oscars; Lt. Bong = 1 Zeke and 1 Val; Lt. Mangas = 1 Oscar; and Lt. Sparks = 1 Zeke and 1 Val.

During all this ensuing combat, White Flight, led by Lt. Eason, was on the way and got there in time to add more victories to the squadron's record. Lts. Eason, Andrews, Flood, and Widman dived on the enemy and Lt. Eason bagged 2 Zekes; Lt. Andrews = 1 Zeke; Lts. Flood and Widman claimed no victories.

Yellow Flight was led by Lt. Gallup, and with him were Lt. Bills, Planck, and Denton. While at 20,000 ft., Yellow Flight was preparing to attack the enemy below and was dived upon by two flights of Zekes—the first of 4 and the second of 6 planes. In the ensuing combat, Lt. Gallup claimed 1 Zeke certain; Lt. Bills = 1 Zeke certain; Lt. Planck = 1 Zeke certain; Lt. Denton = 1 Zeke possible. All of these planes returned home except Lt. Sparks,

who had to land at Dobadura. All pilots are safe and un-
harmed. 13 planes to our credit. Pretty good hunting.

So this was the beginning of the combat career of Lieutenant Bong, who would go on to become the Ace of Aces, the top-scoring Allied fighter pilot in all theaters of World War II. Tom Lynch and Dick Bong quickly became close friends. Later, each of them was relieved of duty within their respective squadrons and assigned to Headquarters Squadron, where they were given carte blanche to initiate their own combat flights, joining other squadrons on their assignments or splitting off and making fighter sweeps of their choice. It was on one of those sweeps that tragedy struck on March 8, 1944. Bong tells the story in his own words:

"Tom and I were up on a routine sweep above Tadji when we came across three Nip 'luggers' flubbing around in the water off the coast. It looked perfect for a strafing pass, and it appeared as if there were fuel barrels on the ships' decks. Tom led us down, and we must have been doing a good 300 miles per hour.

"I didn't see any kind of ack-ack, and the run was easy. We were only going to make one pass. I was following Tom, and when we pulled up, I suddenly noticed his right propeller fly off and his engine started smoking. Tom made for the nearest shore, and just as he approached it, he bailed out. Almost right away, his plane exploded. And that's the last time I saw him.

"I had been hit, too, and landed at Gusap, home of the 39th Fighter Squadron. My own plane was riddled with small caliber bullets. The best I could figure out was that one of those luggers must have been a flak ship providing protection for the rest of the convoy. Losing Tom was just about the worst single blow I ever took while flying combat in the Southwest Pacific. He was not only a good pilot and a good friend but an ideal fighting teammate. Tom had been made lieutenant colonel only a day before, and we'd had a promotion party that night. Tom was gone, but he had cost the Japs 20 of their fighters and bombers before they were able to get him."

It seemed appropriate that Dick Bong passed the devastating news of Lynch's death to members of the 39th directly, rather than having them learn of the loss "via the grapevine." Tom Lynch was beloved by all members of the 39th, and the news of his death devastated the squadron.

During his tour in the Pacific, Bong went on to achieve 27 kills, one more than the iconic Eddie Rickenbacker in World War I. By now, at age 23, he had been promoted to major.

When Rickenbacker heard about it, he sent a message of congratulations reading, "Just received the good news that you are the first one to break my record in World War I by bringing down 27 planes in combat, as well as your promotion, so justly deserved. I hasten to offer my sincere congratulations with the hope that you will double or triple this number. But in trying, use the same calculating techniques that have brought you results to date, for we will need your kind back home after this war is over. My promise of a case of Scotch still holds. So be on the lookout for it." General Kenney also sent Bong a case of champagne.

Word that liquor was being supplied to the famous, clean-cut, young pilot caused a mild uproar in certain circles. In response, General MacArthur sent two cases of Coca-Cola with the message: "I understand you prefer this type of refreshment to others. You thoroughly deserve to have the kind you want. The Army Air Forces are proud of you and your splendid record. Congratulations!" When word of this reached other squadrons, those pilots let it be known that they would be glad to take Bong's unwanted booze off his hands.

Bong returned to the Southwest Pacific on September 10, 1944, reporting to General Kenney at Hollandia. Bong's latest HQ assignment was "advanced gunnery instructor," and while allowed to go on combat missions, he had orders to only defend himself and not seek out the enemy. Apparently the enemy sought him out because he scored another 13 kills to reach the remarkable total of 40.

The following paragraph is quoted from the Dick Bong article at the National Aviation Hall of Fame:

> *Bong described combat flying as fun and a great game that made life interesting. Some pilots were only concerned with their scores, almost to the point of recklessness. Bong relished in the actual flying of combat, not*

how many enemy aircraft he could shoot down. Bong of-
ten referred to his gunnery skills as being lousy, perhaps
the worst in the Army Air Force, and this was after break-
ing Eddie Rickenbacker's record of 26 kills! However, his
skills were very adequate, and estimates were that he
had a 91 percent hit rate. Bong also knew how to get the
most from the aircraft he was flying. He loved flying the
P-38, and many pilots who flew with him commented on
his mastery of it. He was not a flashy pilot, and knew
the limitations of the P-38 and never pushed it beyond.
His analytical nature was valuable when flying combat,
and he always analyzed the situation before going in with
guns firing. Most importantly, he felt no shame in break-
ing off an engagement when the odds turned against him.

After Bong scored his 40th victory, General Kenney sent him home,
this time for good. He was America's "Ace of Aces," with 40 aerial victories, 200 combat missions, and over 500 combat hours behind him.

After a lengthy public relations trip, he returned to Wisconsin and
married on February 10, 1945. After the California honeymoon, he went
to work at Wright Field as a test pilot, helping to develop the Lockheed
P-80 Shooting Star. He studied jet propulsion theory and boned up on the
engineering details of the new plane for 2 months before getting a chance
to fly one. After being checked out in the P-80, he flew it 11 times that
summer.

On August 6, 1945, while half a world away, the *Enola Gay* dropped
the bomb on Hiroshima, Bong stepped into an airplane for the last time.
His P-80 malfunctioned just after takeoff. While he bailed out, he never
had a chance as he was too close to the ground. After surviving 2 years
of combat flying, Richard Ira Bong met his end while on a routine testing
flight.

Chapter 9
Faith, Determination and a Bit of Irish Luck

Charles Peter Sullivan was born in Eureka, Illinois, on July 31, 1915. In February 1941, after graduating from Northwestern University with a degree in business administration, he enlisted in the Army Air Corps Flying Cadet program. He learned to fly at the Spartan School in Tulsa, Oklahoma, Randolph Field in San Antonio, Texas, and at Brooks Field in Brooks, Texas. Upon receiving his commission and pinning on his silver wings at Brooks Field on September 21, 1941, 2nd Lieutenant Sullivan was transferred to Mitchell Field, New York. In January 1942, he was shipped to Australia and assigned to fly P-39s in combat with the 35th Fighter Group's 39th Fighter Squadron.

While flying a P-400 fighter (a P-39 export variant) near Port Moresby on June 17, 1942, Sullivan scored his first aerial victory, a Japanese bomber. But it wasn't until after the 39th Fighter Squadron transitioned to P-38s that Sullivan began his steady climb to ace status: He downed a Ki-43 near Gasmata, New Britain, on January 6, 1943; a Zero over Lae on March 3, 1943; a Zero probable over Huon Gulf on March 4; a Betty near Port Moresby on April 12; and, finally, a Ki-43 near Lae on July 26, 1943.

On September 20, 1943, he was flying one of 16 39th Fighter Squadron P-38s that were escorting V Bomber Command B-24s on a raid against the Japanese base at Wewak. He was leading a four-plane flight. South of Wewak, flying at 24,000 feet, his plane developed engine trouble, and he tried to return to Port Moresby. Here is his dramatic story, told in his own words.

After I left the formation, I had not gone far before the engine began running fine—so I turned back to rejoin my squadron. Then I looked into my rearview mirror and saw an unmistakable image: a Japanese fighter in firing position. He was so close I didn't bother to look over my shoulder, and I didn't have time to be afraid!

Instinctively, I shoved the P-38 into a violent dive, dropping my auxiliary line tanks as I went. It was then that I felt the shudder of bullets striking my plane. He had bit my left engine, which began spraying oil that started a smoky fire. I raced for the clouds below at speeds of nearly 500 miles per hour. The plane shuddered and shook from the strain. I looked back. I was pulling away from the Japanese fighter, but he was still stalking me. Oil began to spray on my windshield, obscuring my vision. I thought about parachuting right then, but instead, I cut off the flaming engine and feathered the propeller, which stopped the fan and turned the blades so they would cut through the air with minimum drag. The fire in the left engine went out, and my windshield cleared—but the stalker was still with me.

At about 3,000 feet, I entered fleecy clouds, but the clouds had gaps between them. I sailed through the first cloud, emerging into the clear, and saw that the stalker was still there. I went into a second cloud, then out into the clear air again. The stalker was still trailing me. To make matters worse, I was beginning to lose my precious dive speed now that I was on one engine. The third cloud loomed up. I needed to vary the program, or eventually he would nail me. So, while in the third cloud, I put my plane in a spiral and came out underneath the cloud, then flew beneath it for some time.

While I was in the third cloud, I thought about how clever it would be of me if I could circle around behind the stalker and shoot him down. But wisdom said, "What if you miscalculate and come out right in front of him?" Wisdom won! I quickly dismissed that idea. When I came into the clear again my pursuer was nowhere in sight. I had eluded him! Or perhaps he was low on gas and had turned for home.

I had radioed my squadron that I was hit and on fire, but the fire was now out and I was on a course for Port Moresby at 3,000 feet. But there were complications. With my left engine cut off, I had lost my plane's only generator, causing my batteries to give out. As a result, I lost radio contact with Port Moresby. I berated Lockheed and the Army Air Forces for not spending a little more money in order to put a generator on the right engine, too. For want of a nail . . .

As soon as I was certain I had lost the stalker, I began to think about the long flight home—at least 2 more hours in the air—and the necessity of climbing to at least 7,000 feet to get through a pass in the mountains. But this was not to be. The right engine began heating up, and white smoke was soon trailing from it—most likely because of a Prestone leak in the coolant radiator. I decided to try the left engine again. Somehow I got it cranked up and running, so I feathered the right engine and shut it down. I flew for about 5 minutes before the left engine began to smoke again. So, with black smoke streaming from the left engine and white smoke streaming from the right, I decided I must either make a forced landing or bail out.

I had been flying over tall trees for some time and did not wish to parachute, as I had friends who had parachuted and landed in tall trees, with the result that they sustained everything from broken legs to broken backs. I elected to set the plane down if I could. I was at the end of the road! Both engines were dead, the props were feathered, and I was sinking rapidly. As I lined up on an open area, I jettisoned the canopy, pulled down my goggles, and rode it in at about 130 miles per hour. The P-38 acted like a giant lawn mower, cutting off small trees, kunai grass, and brush.

I came to a screeching, sizzling halt. The engines sounded as if they would explode. In landing, I had hit my head on something in the cockpit; it split my cloth flying helmet and gave me a deep head wound. With blood pouring from my head, I thought I was mortally wounded, but the shock spared me some severe pain. It was only a scalp wound, which I quickly bound up. My right elbow was also hurt, but not seriously. I grabbed my parachute, survival pack, and the one-man raft in the seat. I was still wearing my Mae West inflatable life vest. I took off with hardly a backward glance, for I feared the Japanese might have seen me come down and because the engines were so hot they might explode or start a fire.

I went down at high noon about 5 degrees, 30 minutes south of the equator. The air was stifling, and the silence oppressive in the kunai grass, which stood 10 to 12 feet tall. A few moments earlier, I had been sailing along at about 180 to 200 miles per hour. Now I was on the ground, feeling lonely, and sensing that I had been thrust back 500 years in time. Home was nearly 400 miles away. To the west were mountains, which I hoped to cross to an outpost mission and air strip named Bena Bena.

It took me 3 or 4 hours to slice my way through the tall, swaying grass to the shelter of some trees, a distance of probably no more than 700 yards. I tried cutting the kunai with my machete, but it was futile, so I highstepped and fell forward time and time again. I finally reached the trees and shade, but I was exhausted. I found a bit of a clearing, where I cut up my parachute to make a tent and hammock of silk. Such luxury!

The first night in the jungle was terrifying because of the strange noises and shrieks of birds and small animals. It later rained almost every night starting about 1600 hours, but I was spared that first night, the only night of my travels that it did not rain. I stayed the second day among the trees, peering out frequently toward my plane, which I could not see.

At the time, the Fifth Air Force's air-sea rescue efforts were meager, to say the least, especially in the interior of New Guinea. Rescue efforts on my behalf probably consisted in their entirety of instructions to all pilots: "Look for Sully somewhere down in the jungle." Indeed, they did look for me the next day—from about 25,000 feet, then went home and reported, "No sign of Sully." The following day the instructions were, "Don't forget about Sully; he's out there someplace." Flying once again at 25,000 feet, they did not see me. On the third day, the talk went to, "Too bad about ole Sully." And that's the way it actually happened!

I watched for rescue planes all day from below my canopy of trees. Then I ventured out to see what was around me. Water, which I had needed badly the previous afternoon, was hardly 75 yards from where I slept. It was so welcome! I filled my faithful little emergency drinking can (about one-plot capacity) and ate some of my chocolate bar. I was still a bit jumpy and watched closely for Japanese troops or natives.

I wasn't really frightened, but the jungle was new to me, so I felt I could not take chances. I was very lonely, but full of hope, and I wanted to get somewhere before my head injury gave me trouble. I put sulfa powder on the wound, which I bandaged with my field dressing.

I slept rather well the second night, but I frequently awoke to check noises. The moon was on the wane but still quite large.

On the third day, I decided I was gaining nothing staying where I was. I thought of my trip ahead and optimistically concluded I could be home in 4 or 5 days. Little did I comprehend the power of the jungle and the difficulties that lay ahead!

I hid the remnants of my parachute at the edge of the kunai grass and covered or otherwise obliterated most of my camp markings. Wisely or unwisely, I did not spread my chute above the top of the kunai—I reasoned that the Japanese had as much chance of seeing it as my friends did. I felt that I was truly on my own, because I didn't think the friendlies could pluck me out of the woods.

I gathered my possessions—the tent, the hammock, the one-man raft, took a heading of 135 degrees for Port Moresby, and bravely set off. When I crossed my drinking stream, I took off all my clothes and shoes to wade across the 12-foot wide, 4-foot deep run. On the other side, I dressed back up in my long-sleeved khaki shirt, long khaki trousers, woolen socks, ankle-top GI shoes, and cloth flying helmet. Then I took up my course of 135 degrees again. The going was much easier here than in the thick kunai grass; it was all trees, thickets, and some grass.

At about 0900 hours, I heard a radial-engine plane. I thought it was a Japanese fighter, which were mostly radial-engine aircraft, but it turned out to be an American single-engine A-24 dive-bomber, with a crew of a pilot and observer or gunner. I tried in vain to start a fire in the damp underbrush. I searched for my matches in my waterproof container, and came up with a good, old farmer-type match. But the kunai grass was too wet. Frantically, I searched for tracer ammunition for my trusty Colt .45-caliber automatic pistol. The A-24 was then only a quarter of a mile from me, flying at about 100 feet. It was so close, I could see the pilot and the observer, who had his canopy rolled forward in order to see better. Moments later, the A-24 was gone—out of sight. It was disappointing, but not overwhelmingly so. After all, this was only my third day down. So I struggled on.

The path was hard, but I found some trees that had been chopped down some time before. This greatly encouraged me. The path led to an abandoned grass hut—an exciting discovery! My thoughts raced from one idea to another. Was this just a way station for a native hunting party? When had people last been here? I found some discarded fish bones, but it did not appear that anyone had been in the hut for some time. I continued on, crossed another small stream, and then came to another shelter on the bank of another stream. I crossed this stream and continued along the path, which was marked by crocodile footprints.

Losing the trail where wild pigs had rooted up the path, I returned to the last stream, set up my hammock, cleared an area, and retired for the night. I always retired at sundown, because the dangers of wandering about in the dark jungle were apparent to me. It began to rain about midnight, and the downpour continued all night. I was drenched and rose frequently to exercise by simulating skipping rope and shadowboxing until I was warm, then I went back to sleep. What an uncomfortable night it was.

I suspected there was a river nearby, so I elected to leave my hammock, Mae West, one-man raft, and box of .45-caliber ammunition at my camp while I searched for the river. I intended to come back and retrieve the heavy stuff. I blazed a trail as I went along, breaking off small branches and cutting into the bark of trees to leave marks. I found the river, but when I tried to retrace my steps to my camp, I became lost, confused, and bewildered. I could not recognize my trail-blazing effort.

The jungle closed in on me oppressively. I panicked. I wanted to run blindly away—anywhere—just run and run. It was a terrible, fearsome feeling that I had never experienced before or since. Somehow, however, faith and reason prevailed. I knelt down and prayed earnestly, "Mary, conceived without sin, pray for us who have recourse to thee. Never was it known that anyone who sought your help or intercession was left unaided."

Mary was listening and interceded with God. I stood up, now calm and confident. I resolved to take a compass course, which I believed would take me back to the river. I did not deviate from the course. In about 20 minutes, I was back at the riverbank, but it was not the same spot here I had first come upon the river. The jungle had won. I was not about to try to find my heavy equipment.

Now my problem was getting across the river without my Mae West life vest or the raft. Undaunted, I looked for trees with which to build a raft. I began to flail at small trees with my 12-inch machete, but the trees were tough, and the job was arduous. I gave up that idea and began collecting limbs and logs from along the riverbank. I tied seven or eight logs together with parachute cord and confidently set sail. It was not to be.

The logs were soaked through and the raft would not fully support me, so I just lay on it, half in and half out of the water. I drifted with the current, kicking my feet for a little extra stability. All seemed to be going well; at least I was still afloat. Then I came to a bend in the river where the current quickened, and I was swept against a muddy bank about 4 feet above the water level. The swift current swung my raft around, and it hit me in the back. I lost the raft and, like the proverbial drowning man, I frantically grasped for anything around. I kept my pistol in my right hand and above the water all the time I was flailing. Then, Providence came to my aid! I saw a vine hanging down from the side of the bank, grabbed it, and steadied myself. The makeshift raft floated merrily on, disappearing downriver.

I surveyed my precarious position. I was in deep water, in the current, but the swift part of the current was narrow. I realized that if I shoved off from the bank, I would cross the swift current and soon be in shallow water. This I did, and after reaching the shallow, pebbly shore, I decided to wash my clothes. I had had enough for one day, so I prepared for night. Beneath a huge tree only a few feet from the river, I fashioned a little shelter, using sticks to support huge banana leaves that served as my roof. Then I booby-trapped my little area, using parachute cord as a cordon, hoping that any intruder would trip over my alarm system and awaken me.

Branching into my river was a beautiful mountain stream, which I planned to explore the next day. Bridging the juncture of the river and the stream was a fallen tree, which I believed was used by the natives to cross the river. It rained most of the night, but my tree and banana leaf roof shelter served me quite well. I was tired and slept soundly!

I awoke, ate the last square of my chocolate bar, looked to the east, and got ready to start up the mountain stream. There was a sandbank on the left of the stream that extended for a short distance and appeared to lend itself to easy walking. As I approached the sandbank, I was startled to see a solitary human footprint in the sand. Just one footprint. I looked on either side of the print for another footprint. There was none. It was baffling. I thought of when Robinson Crusoe discovered his man Friday's footprint in the sand.

The footprint was pointing up the mountain stream. In the distance I detected a clearing on the side of the mountain. We had been told that the natives girdled a tree near the base, so the tree would eventually die and fall over. It was in such clearings that the natives planted their gardens. The mountain stream seemed to lead in the direction of the clearing—hopefully, a garden tended by friendly natives.

We had had good luck with the coastal natives in the Port Moresby area. Indeed, natives had helped several of my comrades in the 39th Fighter Squadron back to our camp after being shot down. So up the middle of the sparkling stream I proceeded. The stream varied from knee to waist deep. The bottom was rocky and uneven, but I never fell.

After proceeding up the stream for about an hour, I began to shout periodically in the hope of attracting the attention of the "friendlies." About 0900, movement on the right bank caught my attention. I stopped dead in my tracks. Gradually, the figure of a man appeared from behind the tree cover. He had a weapon, a spear or bow and arrow, which he lowered. I felt he had drawn a bead on me from behind his cover.

I raised my hand and waved, smiled, and tried to appear very friendly. Under such circumstances I could be *very* friendly, but at the same time, my right hand moved ever so close to my trusty .45, which was holstered on my right hip.

I advanced very cautiously, gun hand at the ready, smiling, and trying constantly to appear relaxed and friendly. I reached the bank, which was about 3 or 4 feet above the water. The native extended his hand and helped me up the bank. We went back into the trees a few feet, where on the ground lay a freshly killed wild pig. Nearby was a young native woman. My host indicated that I should sit down, which I did, and he proceeded to dress his pig.

He laid the pig on its back and chopped it open through the chest cavity with a stone ax. I noticed the woman had a bunch of ripe bananas in a fiber bag. I indicated by munching actions that I was hungry, and I pointed to her bananas. My host indicated to her to give me some bananas, and she gave me two or three, which were delicious. She was very shy and giggled a little, but my host was stern and businesslike as he continued with his task. I was fascinated when he sopped up blood from the pig's chest cavity with spongy leaves, and then squeezed the blood into a 3- or 4-inch diameter bamboo tube. I was to see more of the bamboo tube later.

Soon, the dressing of the pig was complete, and it was obvious we were ready to depart the area. I then saw New Guinea chivalry at its best. My host—I was to learn later that his name was Tootaroo—loaded the pig on the shoulders of his mate, gathered his spear, bow and arrows, and headed for the stream.

Very shortly we were at the bank of the stream. Tootaroo took the pig from the woman's back, and she got down into the water. Then Tootaroo loaded the pig on her back again. Next, he got down into the water, and I followed. We walked downstream for about 15 minutes before coming to a path on the left side, where the bank was almost level with the water. Tootaroo and his mate started up the path, and I began to follow at a tactful and respectful distance.

Suddenly, Tootaroo turned to me and pointed emphatically back down the stream whence I came. I protested and indicated by my motions that I wished to continue with them. He shook his head angrily and again pointed downstream. By sign language it came out: "Go back downstream." I said, "No, I go with you," and he replied, "No, you don't." To this I responded, "Yes, I do!" After a couple of these exchanges, he simply turned away and started up the path. I hesitated, then followed. I expected him to turn on me again, but he did not, though it was obvious he did not want me to come along.

Quietly, we plodded on for perhaps 30 minutes before Tootaroo stopped and began to shout as if to warn someone ahead that he was bringing a stranger home for dinner. My heart sank. What should I do? I considered my options: either leave them and go back to the known loneliness of the jungle, or continue with them to an unknown but at least human company. I reasoned that if I left them, they would still know I was out there, some-place. The thought of more food and what I hoped were friendly natives won the debate. Apprehensively, I followed.

Shortly, we arrived at a small, level clearing. There were old campfire remains and a strange-looking stick placed in the fork of a short vertical stick that was stuck upright into the ground. Tootaroo started a fire and cooked some pig meat in a cylindrical earthen vessel. He later placed some whole bananas in the ashes and baked them. In about a half hour, my feast was ready. Bananas have never tasted so good. Meantime, I was aware that little dark faces were beginning to appear from behind the bushes and foliage. Soon the faces materialized into bodies of men, women, and children. They approached me cautiously.

Still on my best behavior, I smiled and did nothing to excite them. They were curious about all my possessions and poked at my pockets. One youth was particularly curious and wanted to see everything in my pockets, which were loaded with compasses, parachute cord, ammunition, and a small can. The can was similar to a sardine can and had contained my field bandage. The bandage was now wrapped about my head and tied under my chin. I had my cloth flying helmet, split in the crash landing, perched on my head with my flying goggles still attached.

I sensed that the curious boy was a little retarded, but he looked happy, and his companions appeared most tolerant of him. I must have been a bedraggled-looking curiosity. More and more natives began to appear and disappear, seeming to bring back a whole new audience each time. Twice, men, who were obviously chiefs, arrived to look me over from a comfort-able distance.

The chiefs wore beaded bands around their foreheads and all the men appeared to have little sticks in their noses and ears. The men's hair was different from the bushy hairstyle of the Port Moresby-area natives; it was twisted into many small, tight braids. Each time a chief or newcomer arrived or left, I was frightened. For all I knew, they would bring Japanese soldiers.

The afternoon passed this way. I was the new sideshow in town. During the early part of the afternoon, I tried to determine the meaning of the strange sticks, the campfire remains and a small shelter that was open on all sides. It was obvious someone had camped here before. I pointed to the shelter, fire, and sticks and, by sign language, questioned the natives.

One man held up three fingers and pointed to me, as if to say that three men like me had been there. I made signs: did they go that way (toward suspected Japanese-held areas), or did they go that way (toward Australian- or American-held territory)? The native pointed down at the ground! Now there was a discomfiting thought: the three like me had not left the area; they had died—or had been killed!

As twilight approached, the audience, never more than 10 at a time, had dwindled to five or six people. By implicit invitation, I accompanied Tootaroo, his mate, and several others into a nearby area containing two thatch-covered huts. I concluded that they did not consider me a threat, so were taking me in for the night.

It was an interesting family affair. Actually, I believe these were two families of three men in all, including one chief, Tootaroo, and a new acquaintance named Sego, plus two women—Tootaroo's mate, Sego's mate, and three or four children. The other natives I had seen during the day apparently lived elsewhere.

The women prepared dinner: more pig, yams baked in the ashes, and lima-type beans cooked in blood. They also got out the bamboo tube that contained the blood from the dead pig's chest cavity. After putting some herbs or leaves in, they held the tube over the open fire. Presently, when the mixture was bubbling nicely they proceeded to take the contents into their hands and ate it with great gusto. As we sat around the campfire circle, I was served food on a huge banana leaf. Occasionally, a dog tried to run through the circle to get a morsel of food.

Eventually, we arrived at names for the major players. I explained I was Charlie, which they thought was pretty funny. Tootaroo was the native I had found with the pig, Sego was another young man with a mate and a boy of 5 or 6, and the chief was either Lulawai or "Headman."

It was a pleasant, lighthearted, jovial evening. After dinner, we were joined by other natives from the area. I tried to explain my presence among them. I simulated a plane (a "balus" in their language) flying high in the sky with engine sputtering, then crashing to the ground. I made signs to show me crashing forward in the cockpit and injuring my head. Strangely enough, my story got through, except, to my dismay, they all laughed when I pointed to my head. Then one native took over and retold my story in his native tongue, accompanied by appropriate gestures. Again, they all laughed at the crash landing and my injured head. Perhaps they laughed in relief that the mighty flying "balus" was indeed vulnerable.

They had a pet emu or cassowary, which was cute but nonetheless a pest. It circled the group around the fire, came up behind me, and began pecking my back. I tolerantly pushed it away a couple of times, but it was persistent. So I backhanded it with my right hand, knocking it back a bit. My hosts loved that; they laughed merrily. Everything seemed so congenial and friendly.

When it became dark, the women and children went inside a rectangular thatched hut while the men remained near the fire with me. At length they gave me a small hollow log to sleep in, or on. It was about 4 feet long, and wide enough for even a very heavyset person. I lay near the fire in my log, with my right hand placed comfortingly near my holstered .45. I was alert for any strange behavior or action, but it became apparent to me I had nothing to fear.

Occasionally, during the night, one or another of the men stirred and replenished the fire. It was obvious that they had to keep the fire burning. I suspect they started fires by friction or sparks from stones. I awoke each time the fire preserver got up to tend the fire.

The night passed without incident. At dawn, the small village began to stir. It appeared that Sego's mate, their son, and Headman were planning to travel. Perhaps I wanted to go with them? I made signs about departing, hoping to convey the idea that I wished for a plan or route to go home. They seemed to get the idea and mentioned several places or names of people. I copied these on the back of my map. There were such names as Masaro, Lowy Kowy, and Bena Bena.

I tried to write the words phonetically, then repeated them back to Sego. I had heard of Bena Bena, which I knew was somewhere across the mountain range from my suspected location. It occurred to me that a relay system to get me home could be arranged. The names I had been given were locations or contacts along the way. This sounded encouraging, for earlier that morning I had had the sinking feeling that I would not be able to escape the area and perhaps would have to spend the rest of my life in the jungle wilds. That was a sobering thought, but the more we exchanged signs, the more hopeful I became.

Not wishing to waste time, I signed, "We go." Strangely enough, they were ready also, so we turned to leave the village. I suspected then that Sego, his family, and Headman were actually returning to their own village, located some distance away. Before we left, I gave Tootaroo the small field-dressing can as a farewell gift. He received it stoically. *Not too impressed,* I thought.

Shortly after we left Tootaroo's home, we began a rather arduous climb. I thought I was in fair shape but began to tire. At one point, about an hour after starting out, Headman approached me and signed that he wanted my big machete knife. I thought he was leaving us for good and simply desired a souvenir, so I shook my head "No!" He disappeared into the trees, but he returned in about 20 minutes with freshly cut stalks of sugarcane, which we sucked on for a time. It was delicious and refreshing. I felt a bit of remorse at not giving him the knife to cut the cane for all of us.

We started on again, and in about another hour we all stopped when Sego pointed out a small pitfall in the path that had been covered with light branches and leaves. It appeared to be a security measure for a nearby village. Thoughtfully, they detoured me around it, and shortly we stopped again as they shouted a warning to unseen natives that they were bringing in a stranger.

In a few minutes, we arrived at the top of a lightly forested ridge. It was about noon and a most pleasant day, sunny and nice. A few locals came out to look me over, and the overall atmosphere was relaxed. When we arrived in the village, Sego cooked some food, which was unremarkable in comparison to the feast I had the night before.

It seemed to be a lazy day. I decided to rest, perhaps share another meal with them, and depart early in the morning for that faraway place called Port Moresby. The villagers left me alone, except for Sego's little son, an alert and happy child. I tried to amuse him as best I could as I took off my shirt so I could better enjoy the pleasant sunshine. I also cleaned my .45. At Tootaroo's village, I had made signs for something with which to wipe my gun, and my idea got through. I had been rewarded with fibers impregnated with lard or some other grease, which I now used. I was constantly amazed and pleased at how effective sign language could be when you really worked at it.

I was enjoying myself, but my idyllic afternoon came to an abrupt end. Sego came and led me to meet two new natives, and it was as if a cool wind and dark clouds permeated the scene. Suddenly, I had a sense of impending danger. However, I tried to seem confident and cheerful as by sign language indicated how I hoped to be relayed over the hills to friendly territory.

The obvious leader of these two visitors was named Aidee, but Aidee's partner did not give his name, so I named him "Grinning One" or "Grinny." Facetiously, I thought he had cut cards early in the afternoon for my knife and won. I did not like his attitude and distrusted both of them.

Standing toe to toe in the clearing, Sego and Aidee had a violent argument. Finally, Aidee grabbed two spears and thrust them violently into the ground as he appeared to read Sego the riot act. And Sego obviously acquiesced to whatever Aidee wanted of him. I was standing nearby throughout the argument, and I felt compelled to say something to ease the tension. In what I hoped was a lighthearted manner, I said, "What is the matter, Sego, did you take his spears?" Of course, I knew that the natives did not understand my words or care about my opinion. I was later to conclude that my ultimate fate was the subject of the argument, that Sego had tried to defend me . . . and lost. Sego appeared crestfallen as we all turned away from the scene of the argument.

As twilight approached, the waning moon came out, and the villagers began to prepare dinner. Gone was the hospitality and friendliness of the previous village. I wandered about, but no one asked me to eat with them, not even Sego. I walked up to one family campfire and made signs of eating. I was no longer hungry, but I wanted to see whether they would give me food. They handed me something, but did not ask me to sit down on the ground with them. I wandered away, not knowing what to do.

Aidee and Grinny suddenly appeared beside me and started a small fire. Nearby was a thatched roof hut with a very small doorway. As I sat down near the fire, facing the rising moon, Aidee and Grinny took up positions on the other side of the fire and stared at me without showing any emotion. I felt was being stalked!

To show my nonchalance, I sang every popular and college song I could think of. I was determined not to show fear or undue concern. Earlier in the day, Aidee had conveyed the idea that he had been to the coast, and he did seem to be a worldlier person than the others. As we sat around this fire, he pointed to the moon and indicated that I perhaps had arrived at the wrong time of the month and that perhaps he regretted it had worked out this way. These were only impressions, but the feeling that there was an impending threat was definitely there.

After I had exhausted my song repertoire, I suppose Aidee thought it was time to move on with his plan. He and Grinny rose and slowly approached me. They sat down on either side of me, so close that they brushed my sides. This was too close and threatening for me, so I immediately stood up. I believe they were about to attempt to overcome me. As I cast about for an idea to ease the tension or provide them with reason to leave, I again noted the nearby hut and crawled through the doorway, taking with me a little grass mat the natives had given me. I crouched just inside the doorway, hoping they would go away, but this was not to be.

Aidee and Grinny approached the doorway and Aidee reached inside to tug at my shoulder, a clear suggestion that I come out. Thinking that perhaps Aidee was simply envious of my attentions to Sego and his little boy, I stepped outside. Immediately, several natives, including Aidee and Grinny, closed in around me. They were carrying spears, bows, and arrows.

Without anyone actually jabbing me with a spear, I was prodded, not too subtly, along a path that led up a small incline. Soon we reached a circular hut—the execution chamber? Above the doorway I could make out in the dim light a stick device that reminded me of the stick symbol I had seen the day before at the edge of Tootaroo's village. This symbol was a forked stick embedded in the ground with another stick placed across the fork. Whatever it was, I took it as a disturbing sign.

My escorts gestured that I go into the hut. I didn't see any alternative, so I bent down and entered. Four natives followed me in. One carried a firebrand and an empty—but ominous-looking—bamboo blood tube. My heart sank a little lower, as all signs were most foreboding. I felt maneuvered, but no course of action came to mind. Hoping against hope that things would get better, I continued to play their game. The native with the firebrand started a small fire in the middle of the hut and another native handed me the grass mat again, suggesting, by signs, that I lie down and sleep, to which I replied aloud, "I always sleep sitting up." Simply responding aloud made me more confident, although I knew they understood little beyond what I could convey by means of my limited sign language.

I was about 6 feet from the door, wary, and sitting on my mat with my back against the wall. I realized I was in a very vulnerable position. If a melee ensued, they might block the door to prevent my escape, even if I shot some of them. When I pressed my hands against the bamboo wall at my back, I realized I could not easily break through it.

The room began to fill with smoke, as there was no ceiling opening. Seizing on this situation, I began to cough and wave my arms to indicate the smoke was too much for me. A native stood up and began tearing a hole in the roof to let out excess smoke. *Now or never,* I thought, as this had created the diversion I needed.

From a crouching position, I bolted for the opening and came out of the hut just in front of the doorway. As I came out, I pulled my .45 automatic from its holster and chambered a round. The hammer was back, and the .45 was ready to fire. Then I slipped the safety switch on and dropped the .45 back in its holster.

As I stood and waited for their next move, more natives appeared, so I elected not to make a run for it. Those in the hut followed me out, bringing the bamboo tube and the firebrand with them. Once again, by common consent, we moved down the path away from my "execution chamber" to a rectangular hut with a porch extension that was open on three sides. There we stopped. I was escorted inside and again given my grass mat along with a firm indication to lie down. I took the mat and sat down, facing the interior of the enclosure with my back vulnerable to the outside darkness.

The men stacked their bows, arrows, and spears against a post and started up the fire. Once again, we eyed each other as we all sat on the ground. Some of the men decided to smoke or chew betel nut. They made some square motions with their arms, as if to say, "See, I have nothing to harm you with." They wanted me to see that they weren't making any overt moves. I let them smoke and chew. Most of the men who chewed took betel nut with some lime from a small gourd. They put a little lime on some betel leaves, chewed up a bit of betel nut, and then spit it out in one hand. After looking at the mess, they would put the betel nut combination back in their mouths. The headman had a little fiber bag that contained a broken mirror. I suppose that made him the kingpin. He chewed with great dignity. After chewing for a while, he would reach into his bag and pull out the mirror. Then he would stick the mess out on his tongue and look at it to see if it was the right consistency or color. Because he had a mirror he did not have to spit the betel mess into his hand.

Sego and his little boy were inside, too. The boy's job was to keep the fire going. It might have been sort of an initiation ritual for him. The boy was only about 6 years old and was clearly there against his wishes. He kept crying. Suddenly, Aidee took a brand from the floor and stuck it right on the child's face. The little boy stopped crying and kept up the fire real well after that. That didn't make me like Aidee any better.

The contingent inside the hut included Sego, his son, Grinny, Aidee, the Headman, and a lookout who sat in the back of the hut. I could hear other natives rustling around outside the hut. I was afraid that if we sat there long enough, someone on the outside might strike me with a spear. If I could manage to move to the doorway of the hut, they would all be in front of me. I got up slowly, walked slowly toward the entrance, and sort of stooped over sideways by the doorway. I then took a firebrand and sort of flashed it in back of me to make sure that there was no one in back of the hut. My move placed all of them in front of me, so I was at least temporarily in command. Just to be sure, I took out my .45 and placed it across my right thigh.

We sat there from about 2000 hours to about 2200. I threatened them with the strength of the Fifth Air Force: "The balus will come and boom-boom the hell out of your villages." But that didn't seem to bother them, though they did shrink down and repeat, "boom-boom!" a few times. They didn't like the idea, but I guess they didn't really think the air force was going to get there.

Next, I thought I'd try a little religion on them, thinking that the missionaries might have contacted them. Since I was convinced they were going to kill me, I didn't see any reason not to be frank about it. So I said, "God wouldn't want you to kill me." I think I spoke pretty convincingly. Aidee, who apparently had been out to the coast, muttered a word that sounded something like "Lord." But after I had gotten all through, Aidee said, "No savvy talk." I answered, "You savvy this gun, don't you?" and shook the .45 right in his face. I sat there for over an hour with my gun trained on Aidee. The whole time, I snapped the safety on an off *click, click, click* to be sure he got the message. But this guy remained cool as a cucumber.

After a while, the home team began to get a little anxious. The headman got up and sort of stretched, as if to show that he was tired. Then he walked toward me, indicating that he wanted to go behind me into the hut. It was pretty obvious that if he went back there I would have two fronts to cover. He got real close to me and motioned again that he wanted to go inside. I swung the .45 around on him and shouted, "Sit down!" Well, he withered right down beside me, clearly frightened.

This standoff had been going on for hours. I was thinking, I'm in command—temporarily. If I can just get them in close, in sort of a semicircle, they won't shoot through their own people. I didn't know how I was going to get out of the hut, but I didn't want them to shoot me before I did. The headman played right into my hands. He crouched right down beside me, which made Grinny unhappy. I thought that Grinny was showing some fear, so I reached out with my left hand and motioned for him to come in a little closer to protect me on the right. But before he did, he looked at Aidee, who was sitting right in the middle, sort of headon to me. Aidee blinked his eyes. I think that meant, *Yeah, go ahead and humor him.*

Grinny moved a little closer but kept looking over his shoulder. He was sort of a sassy little guy, and I didn't like the way he grinned. So, with the gun in my right hand, I grabbed him by a shoulder with my left hand and sort of yanked him. The poor guy probably thought I was going to shoot him in the back because he was really scared.

At this point, I established a priority list of how I was going to take care of them. They all understood "Number One." I said, "Aidee, I get you, number one. Grinny, I get you, number two. Headman, I get you, number three." I didn't go to number four, because I didn't think it would last that long. Then I waved the .45 and described what it would do to them. Aidee sort of believed it. It all sounded rather grim, but I had to keep talking to try to make the point. Aidee was the only one who had not shown a bit of fear, but his team had not shown much initiative.

Next, I motioned for Aidee to move to a position right in front of me. He was close enough that I could touch him with my left hand. I signaled, "Come in a little closer." He rose slightly and sat without moving forward. "No! Closer!" I said. I then reached out a little farther and motioned him in closer. I guess he thought I was off balance, for he came right out of his crouching position and lunged at me like a tiger. He threw me against the wall, but I came to my feet naturally. I had the gun in my right hand, but he grabbed both my wrists and pinned me back briefly. Somehow, I forced the gun down and shot him from a distance of about 6 inches— right through the chest. The shot blasted him clear across the room.

A split-second later, the headman came at me from the left side. If he and Aidee had timed it a little better, they might have had me. The headman came in from my left and went for both my wrists. He got my left wrist and grappled for my right. I pulled my gun back and shot him in the chest from my left side, *WHAM! WHAM!* Two shots, one to Aidee and one to the headman, in the space of 2 seconds. It was practically all over. My grim prediction was almost true. I got number one, Aidee, skipped number two, Grinny, and got number three, the headman. I still remember it like it was yesterday. I can picture the dull glow from the fire, my smoking .45, and me standing there in a crouched position, like it was Custer's Last Stand

I thought they would come after me in waves, but they didn't. Instead, they ran off like a bunch of scalded dogs and left me alone. The headman staggered outside and died. I then realized that no one was left in the hut but me. I ran out to the left as fast as I could, in the same direction as the staggering headman, and cut back and made an end run, like in football. I ran full tilt to the left, then back to the center, and then I tripped in the tall grass. This probably saved my life, because if I had not fallen, I would have been still running. I slithered down into a little depression.

Back at the village, the natives had lighted torches and were screaming and shouting. I could hear them answering from all the neighboring villages. I seemed to be surrounded by their war whoops. When the torches were lit, they started to come up the hill. After they found the two men I had shot, they had a mourning ceremony. They beat on the ground and wailed, sobbed, and shouted for about an hour. It was terrible to just lie there on the ground and listen. The mourning ceremony went on and on. I could see their shadows.

Although I am usually optimistic, I couldn't see how I would possibly get out of there alive. As I lay there motionless with the .45 in my right hand and a fresh clip with six bullets in my left hand, I pondered the chances of my leaving alive. I knew the natives would not be kind to me after I had killed two prominent members of their tribe.

I prayed some more. "Dear Virgin Mary, never was it known that anyone who sought thy help or intercession was left unaided. Inspired with that hope and confidence, I ask your intercession with God the Father, God the Son, and God the Holy Spirit." I prayed the Hail Mary, which ends with "Holy Mary, Mother of God, pray for us sinners now and at the hour of our death." The chilling thought hit me: *"Now and at the hour of our death"* had become one and the same for me!

What could I do? Should I save the last bullet for myself—a permanent solution to a temporary problem? I agonized over this decision. My faith and upbringing had taught me that suicide was wrong and the cowardly way out. But I dreaded torture. Then I remembered somewhere in scripture it was said that God will not permit a person to be tempted beyond his will or capability to resist, and that even Christ was tempted. So I decided not to save the last bullet for myself, but to continue to fight to the end or escape alive. It was comforting when I realized I had weathered that trial of temptation.

After about an hour, the mourning ceremony stopped and the natives went down into the lower end of the camp. Everything got real quiet. No fires, no voices, nothing. It was as still as death. A little hope trickled through my veins, but at about 0200 the natives came alive again. Up the hill they strode, with torches held high. This time, the light seemed to penetrate my little hideout, and I thought surely they would see me. But they didn't. They went through the mourning ceremony again, beating sticks on the ground, and all of that.

From the shadows, I spotted the figure of a woman coming toward me. It seemed as if she had guessed where I was. She walked straight toward me, closer and closer. I couldn't bring myself to shoot her, so I thought I would shoot at the ground, get up, and run. She got closer. Now about 2 or 3 feet from me. I could have reached out, stretched a little, and touched her toes. She stood right over me, sobbing and wailing her heart out. After what seemed an eternity, she turned and walked back to the camp.

By 0400, everything became very quiet again. It was totally dark . . . no fires, no moon. Dawn was coming, and I knew I had to get out before first light. With a great deal of fear and trepidation, I stood up, fully expecting to become a human pincushion. But nothing happened, so I took a couple of steps while thinking perhaps they wanted a moving target. Still nothing happened. Then I really began to feel that I might get out of there after all. I tiptoed across an open area and climbed over a couple of little stone walls. I made up my mind to head for Port Moresby.

I had two compasses. One was a luminous compass that I could read at night. Having two compasses was a great consolation, because you get to where you don't trust one compass. I ran the gauntlet, past two open huts, but nothing happened. After I got by those, I went down a path. It was beginning to get light now. As I looked down the valley, I could see that a couple of natives were hunting. I immediately withdrew off the path, but as I did I stepped on a twig. It snapped, and the sound reverberated like a shot across the valley.

The two hunters just froze in their tracks, like a couple of hunting dogs on point. They just stared at the spot at which they had heard the noise. They couldn't see me, but they had me pinpointed. Then one of them dropped out of sight. I knew I had to get out of there quickly, because they were going to either circle around to investigate or go back to the village to get help. I pulled off the path and took off my shoes, because I felt they had betrayed me by the noise of stepping on the twigs. I hung them around my neck and started crawling.

I crawled all morning. I was in such a desperate frame of mind that I hid my shoes under some bushes because they were making a clumping sound. I put them in there neatly, like I was putting them in a closet or under a bed, as if I might come back for them later. I was determined to make it difficult for the natives to follow me. I would crawl for 3 minutes and listen for 2 minutes, then crawl again. I did this for about 2 hours. I figured that if they were getting close, I would hear them during my rest interval.

I got to a tiny mountain brook which was clogged with bushes and fallen trees and had several waterfalls. Remembering Boy Scout training and lore, I walked in the water to hide my tracks. About midmorning, I reached a rushing mountain stream. It took me about a half hour to decide where to cross it so as not to leave footprints on the banks. After I crossed the stream, I took off, almost running to get away from the area. My feet felt like they were cut to ribbons. I put my sulfanilamide powder from my jungle kit on them to keep them from getting infected.

When it seemed certain that I had gotten safely away, I stopped to build a shelter. I rested there for a couple of days, then moved on, built another shelter, and rested again. I went on this way for about 3 weeks, and by then I was getting pretty weary. One time I built a big fire, hoping that someone from my squadron was still looking for me. I gathered a huge pile of logs and started a fire that burned all night, like a prairie fire. It must have burned off about half of New Guinea. In fact, at one point, I had to get down in a ditch to get away from the fire. The next day I had to walk through miles of burned stubble.

One day, I saw a shadow on the path, and then noticed a figure coming toward me. It was a native woman. As soon as she spotted me, she started running away like a deer. I took off after her, but she left me in the dust. I spent a very uncomfortable night in an abandoned hut. I'm sure the natives were also uncomfortable that night, knowing I was out there.

One of my few possessions was my toothbrush, which was a great consolation. I brushed my teeth, but didn't have much to eat. I had a pamphlet that told about native foods, but it had gotten wet and the ink ran all over it, so I couldn't read it. However, I did eat some papayas and small bananas. By then, I had been barefoot for about 3 weeks. But I put on my socks every night, because the insects drove me wild. Without my cloth helmet, mosquito head net, flying gloves, and socks I would have been in terrible shape.

One of my favorite respites each day was to climb a hill and try to figure out where I was. I wanted to get up into the mountains, but every time I got to the top of one mountain, there was just another mountain, another valley, and another mountain ahead. Finally, I left the mountains and went back down into the plains. On my way down, while contemplating the panorama and the beauties of New Guinea, I saw a glimmer of light a few miles away. It turned out to be a reflection from a small, conical hill. I walked toward it, and late in the afternoon I was able to see some human figures up there. I didn't think they were natives, but I couldn't tell if they were Japanese, Americans, or Aussies.

I was so desperate by this time that I thought, even if they were Japanese, I might sneak into their camp at night and steal food. The next day I homed in on the camp. I saw someone wearing an Aussie hat, but even that didn't convince me. Maybe one of those tricky Japanese was wearing an Aussie hat. I sneaked up closer and closer until I was about 30 feet from them. It was like playing hide-and-seek, where you come out from hiding and jump up to scare the seeker. I was so close to them that it was almost embarrassing to jump out and say, "Here I am!"

Finally, I came out from behind a tree and saw that they were indeed Aussies who had come down from their fortification for lunch. I just stood there and tried to think of something clever to say, but the only thing I could think of was, "Well, here's another one of those bloody Yanks." The Aussies didn't say anything; they just looked at me in disbelief. It was kind of awkward. Later, I learned that 2 weeks earlier, in a skirmish with the Japanese, they had lost a second lieutenant who was about my size and had the same color hair. That was why they were so surprised to see me. I was all bandaged up and looked so much like their lieutenant that they thought I was him, come back from the dead.

The Aussie soldiers gave me some food but warned me not to eat too much or I'd get sick. Well, I did eat too much, and I did get real sick. However, after 3 weeks of not eating, you can't really eat too much. The Aussies had a radio and asked if I wanted to send a message. Of course I wanted to let my squadron and the Fifth Air Force know that I was safe. I composed a very concise message: "Captain Sullivan, 39th Fighter Squadron, arrived at this point. Injury slight. Please advise."

The next morning, there came a reply: "Captain Sullivan will proceed on when able." Some callous, headquarters type must have composed that thoughtless message, because no one in the 39th Fighter Squadron would have been so inconsiderate. I thought, *To hell with them; I'll stay here for the rest of the war; I'll never go back!* Then I decided that I had better return.

The Aussies offered to send a native back with me across the mountains. I thought it over and quickly decided against the plan. They also suggested I might go with one of their patrols, which was planning to cross the river, although there was some danger of running into the Japanese. I decided that I had had enough of the natives and that I would go with the Aussies.

I was with the Aussie patrol, in their camp, for 2 days. I felt guilty about eating their food, because everything they had came in on their backs. They had no air drops whatever, but had lugged all of their food and supplies over the mountains.

The first night out we saw a big fire. The Aussies thought it might be the Japanese, who would sometimes advance behind the cover of a big fire. As the fire came toward us, I was afraid I had really jumped from the frying pan into the fire, but it was much better to be with 20 other guys than to be out there by myself. The threat did not materialize. I don't know who started the fire.

The Aussies were awfully nice to me. They even carried my .45, which had become too heavy for me. They realized I was very weak. A couple of big Aussies on either side of me helped me along. Although they had said we wouldn't go too far, we walked about 15 or 20 miles a day. Eventually, we got across the big river and soon arrived at a camp where there was a small observation plane. We had been walking for 2 days.

The pilot, Lieutenant Frederick, who wore glider wings, said to me, "Captain, I will save you a big walk if you'll get into my little airplane. We'll fly to another airstrip." I agreed and got in. It was a tandem arrangement, so I sat in the front and Lieutenant Frederick sat behind me.

We didn't have any parachutes, and the plane didn't run very well. "It always runs better in the air," Frederick said. *Famous last words,* I thought. Somehow, we took off and flew for a bit. When we got up to about 1,500 feet, he asked if I wanted to fly. I said I would like to try. But when I took control, it felt like I was holding it up in the air with my bare hands, so I gave it back to him. Soon after that, I saw that while the throttle was advancing and advancing, the engine wasn't reacting. Then Frederick announced, "I think we have to turn back." But as he turned it back in a big chandelle, the plane began to lose power. We had been flying over some real tall trees for a long time and I knew firsthand what tall trees could do if you had to crash-land. Fortunately, the trees thinned out, and the pilot made a pretty good crash landing in an open area. But the plane had fixed gear, so when it bit the grass, it flipped over on its back.

I was hanging upside down by my seat belt. So I just pulled the buckle and fell about 4 feet to the ground. Frederick was very solicitous. "Are you all right? Thank God! I'm glad it wasn't the general." It turned out he had been flying an Aussie general around. I fired off three shots—the international emergency signal—waited, fired another three shots, and waited again. Nothing happened, so we walked back to camp. The next day a C-47 transport plane picked me up at Dumpu airstrip. I spent a night in Nadzab, and the next day, October 20, I was flown home to 14-Mile Drome, near Port Moresby, where a glorious welcome was put on by my squadron. I was back from a 30-day mission!

During the welcome, one dear friend said, "I knew you would make it. Oh yeah, I'll bring back your razor in the morning." I was on cloud nine. I sent a cablegram to my beloved wife, Mareelee, advising her to pay back the insurance money. Ironically, as I learned later, one insurance agent had indeed tried to begin payoff procedures, but Mareelee politely threw him out! I sent a wire to my dear friend Captain Tommy Lynch, who was on leave in the States: "Bring back my boots, you vulture." Tom had taken my favorite flying boots home with him. Tom was killed later, so I never got my boots back.

Malaria struck me, which deprived me of following up on a suggestion made by one of the Fifth Air Force generals that I lead a revenge mission against the natives. Actually, my plan was simply to drop supplies to my Aussie commando friends and cause the natives no further harm. I was to direct the mission from a B-25 covered by four P-40 fighters.

Before I left Brisbane, Australia, for the States, I was advised that General Douglas MacArthur wished to see me and possibly decorate me. My weakened condition and the questionable condition of my uniforms motivated me to decline.

After arriving home, I spent Thanksgiving with Mareelee and our families. Following welcome rest and recuperation, I was assigned to a replacement-training unit in Santa Maria, California, to teach combat skills in my favorite airplane, the P-38. I was even able to give Mareelee a piggyback ride in a P-38. She literally rode on my shoulders.

Charlie Sullivan remained in the service and retired after nearly 30 years of active duty with the rank of colonel in 1968. In1973, he added "O" to the family name. In September 1993, he learned that a pair of Australian aviation enthusiasts had located, almost to the day, the remains of the P-38 he crash-landed in the middle of nowhere a half-century earlier.

Chapter 10
An Odyssey of Youth

Lt. George Edwin Morgan flew with the 39th Fighter Squadron during its New Guinea days—from March 1943 until May 1944.

Born in Columbus, Alabama, to Jay L. and Stella F. Morgan, on November 15, 1920, George joined two older siblings, brother Jay L. Jr., and sister Eva C. The family moved to Memphis, Tennessee, where George attended Humes High School and sports dominated his activities. He graduated from Memphis State College in 1941.

During George's time in the South Pacific, he joined his brother, Jay—assigned to Weather Central, U.S. Army's Fifth Air Force, in Port Moresby, and met his future wife, 1st Lt. Mary L. Scott, U.S. Army Nurse Corps, U.S. Army 105th General Hospital, in Gatton, Australia.

Born in Sauk Centre, Minnesota, to Roy L. and Mary C. Scott, on June 27, 1918, Mary Louise Scott would become the eldest of three children, with both James "Jim" W. and Elizabeth "Betty," her junior.

When Dooley first began his research for this book in 2007, he received the following letter from Mary Morgan Martin, daughter of George Morgan and Mary Scott.

February 11, 2008

Dear Ken,

The military history of my parents actually began with my grandfather, Lt. Col. Roy L. Scott.

While with the Minnesota National Guard, my grandfather was ordered to active duty February 10, 1942, and assigned to Headquarters, 217th Coast Artillery (AA) Regiment as the executive officer. When the regiment moved to Camp Haan, California, the whole family relocated, to include my mother, Mary L. Scott.

On May 1, 1941, having begun nursing training in Minnesota, she joined the U.S. Army Nurse Corps for a 1-year period of training and was assigned to the 155th Station Hospital, Camp Roberts, California. Nearing the completion of her nurse's training, Mary volunteered for overseas duty.

Meanwhile, in Memphis, Tennessee, my dad, George E. Morgan, signed up for the Army Air Corps in October 1941, and was called to duty by the end of December.

I am thrilled that you are writing a book about the 39th FS and will be more than happy to help you in any way that I can.

I have photographs, documents, and many letters that my parents wrote to each other when my mother was an American nurse in Australia and my father was a pilot with the 39th Fighter Squadron.

Best wishes in your new endeavor.

Mary Morgan Martin

YOUTH 1943

More grief than joy we've known
But if we found
One hidden murmur in a sea of sound
If we have seen one star unknown before
And wept for peace, yet learned to laugh in war;
If we who wanted all
Did not disdain
To seek great things in small
And strength in pain—
Then we have justified
Our silent oath.
We have not lived in vain.

—Written by an unknown nurse in the Southwest Pacific

November 28, 1941

George Morgan received notice to report to the Aviation Cadet Examining Board at the Municipal Airport in Nashville, Tennessee, for his physical examination for aviation cadet on December 3rd, 1941. Successfully passing the examination, he enlisted in the Army Air Corps as an air cadet on December 27th and reported to Kelly Field, Texas.

Kelly Field, San Antonio, Texas—
7th Squadron, Flight C, Pilot Replacement Center

Fortunately, A/C George E. Morgan wrote the following diary entries during his early training.

December 31, 1941

It is 4:30 p.m., and we are off until 10 o'clock tomorrow night, but we can't leave the post. They keep us moving every minute of the day. The Replacement Center is about 2 miles from Kelly Field proper. We get up about 45 min. before the sun comes up, and it's pitch-dark. Eat breakfast, then clean up the barracks, drill and physical training until 11 a.m., eat dinner at 12, go to class at 1 p.m., get out at 4 p.m. Parade from 4:30 until 6:30, eat supper at 7 After supper, we are off until 8, when we are confined to quarters and lights out at 10:00. The food here is the best one could get. The way things are divided is: 9 squadrons with each squadron divided into four flights (A, B, C, D) and each flight has 4 elements. There are about 1,800 cadets here. We got our uniforms yesterday. Everything's the best. Every building here is new. Our ground school is Military Discipline, Duties of Officers, and Math. The math is primary math. I don't think I will have much trouble with it. A colonel's wife is organizing a Cadets Club for us (where we will get a clubroom at one of the hotels) and give dances for us. There is going to be a Tea Dance for us Sunday night in town. We are going to be here until about the 21st of January, and then we will go to some primary flying school.

January 13, 1942

They have us going to lectures at night as well as during the day. We had gas drill today. We just used smoke, but we had to wear our gas masks just the same. You ought to see how we have to make our beds. It takes about 15 min. to fix it up in the morning. We also have to sweep every day and dust. Have to mop 3 to 4 times a week. Got paid $30 on Monday for my December wages, but they took out $14 for certain expenses. We won't have any taken out from now on._

January 24, 1942

We start flying Monday. It won't seem as hard after we get started. We were issued our flying suits and other flying gear yesterday. Our upperclassmen are really rough on us, but most of them are swell guys. Our upperclassmen will be here for four more weeks, then we will be the up-perclassmen—thank goodness. I am the meteorologist of our barrack. I have to go outside as soon as I get dressed and find out the wind direction and velocity, the ceiling and visibility, temperature and dew point. I just guess at most of it because it is still about an hour before sunup. We are getting used to the routine, so it is not as hard as it was.

February 1, 1942

We will be here for 8 more weeks, then I don't know where we will be sent. This school is the toughest in the United States. In the Gulf Coast area, it has the highest percent of washouts, and the highest percentage of course comple-tion with receipt of commissions. We have one minute to get undressed and get in bed at night, and we have to get up the moment the bugle sounds in the morning. I wake up about 5:30 every morning and lie in bed until 5:50 when we have to get up. We will get 95 hours of ground school and 60 hours of flying while we are here. That is 50 hours less of ground school but the same amount of flying as the upperclassmen have received. They are not relaxing on flying qualifications at all.

February 7, 1942

I soloed this week. I was the second one to solo, the first one to solo had 5 hours and 30 minutes, and I soloed in 5 hours and 38 minutes. Now I have 9 hours and 36 minutes. The food here is better than that at Kelly Field. We have all the milk, tea, or coffee we want. The food is served cafeteria-style and we can get as many helpings as we want. The upperclassmen are letting up a lot. This week passed a lot quicker than the first. We get up at 5:40, clean up, and eat. We are on the flying line from 7:45 until about 12:00. Eat at 12:15, then ground school from 1:00 until 5:00. Fall out at 5:15 for retreat. Eat at 5:45. Then we have freedom of PX until 6:55. Study hall from 7:15 until 9:15. In bed at 9:30. My instructors told me not to worry any about washing out, just to keep going like I am and I will be OK.

February 23, 1942

This coming week we fly all morning, go to school in the afternoon, and then study hall at night. We are flying from an hour and a half to three hours every day. Our ground school consists of Engines, Theory of Flight, and Physical Ed. This coming week we are going to have navigation, I think. I am now an upperclassman. Our "Dodos" (underclassmen) will be in some time tomorrow afternoon. It's been nice around here with our upper class gone. They went to San Angelo, Texas, for their basic training. Our dance Friday night for the upperclassmen was really nice. We had it in Oklahoma City in one of the hotel ballrooms. I have passed all the ground school exams we have had—we've had five so far, and my flying instructor seems to think I am doing all right. I imagine we will be leaving here in about 4 or five weeks for basic training, somewhere. We won't know until about 5 days before we are to leave just where we will be going.

March 4, 1942

We have received some nice compliments on our class (42-G). Captain Waters, Commandant of Cadet, told the "dodos" that our class is the best that he has had in here in over a year. We got paid Saturday, and after taking out for the pictures, watchband and crash bracelet combination, and $20 worth of PX coupon books, I still got $61. That was pay for about a month and a half. I am letting them hold $50 of it. I can get it any time I want it. I am still passing all my ground school exams, and I think we are through with the hardest ones (I hope). I have 37 hours of flying now.

Air Cadet Basic Flying School, Enid, Oklahoma— Basic Air Cadet Training

Many of the young cadets would gain experience, slowly gain rank and standing, and become leaders. Other died in fiery crashes during training, while the majority simply washed out and ended up in the infantry. A few, like George Morgan, were quickly recognized as natural pilots.

April 5, 1942

We arrived here last Sunday morning and started flying Tuesday. These planes are really swell. They are the Vultee BT-13 and BT-15 basic trainers with 450 HP motors. We do all our flying from the front seat. I like it much better than in the back. These planes are closed by use of a sliding hatch. They have more controls and instruments than I knew existed. There are so many gadgets to work, it seems impossible at first. While here, we get day and night cross-country flights, formation flying, and instrument flying. Here we have two cadets in each room. It

makes it much easier to study or write. We will be here 8
more weeks before going to advanced. There we will get
about 9 more weeks training. That will make it about the
first of August when I get my commission.

After volunteering for foreign service and being selected, 2nd Lt.
Mary L. Scott was assigned to the newly formed U.S. Army 105th General Hospital at Fort Lewis, Washington, arriving there on April 30, 1942.

From across California, other nurses, including Patricia (Patty) M.
Knapp, Eileen (Fitzie) Fitzgerald, and Edna (Buckey) F. Buckley were arriving. Reporting in as well were the experienced physicians from the Harvard Medical School in Boston, Massachusetts.

The 105th (also known as the "Harvard Unit") was in the process of being organized, assembled, and equipped for the trip overseas—destination still unknown.

On that same day, George was at the Air Cadet Basic Flying School, in Enid, Oklahoma.

April 30, 1942

I started formation flying yesterday. It is really fun. I had
my parachute on for four hours today and didn't get a
single chance to take it off. First period I flew solo, sec-
ond period I had instrument flying, and third period I had
another solo ship. We start night flying next week.

On May 1, 1942, nurses who had joined the U.S. Army Nurse Corps
back in 1941 for an expected 1-year period of training suddenly found themselves "locked-in" military service for the duration of the war. Then on May 7, 1942, the entire 105th (approximately 5,000 personnel and all the equipment and supplies to fully equip a complete hospital) traveled by truck and train to their point of embarkation—San Francisco, California. Arriving in San Francisco on May 8, the unit personnel continued their preparation for overseas duty. On May 18, personnel of the 105th and the 155th Station Hospital boarded their ship. The USS *West Point* and all

aboard set sail for the Southwest Pacific the following day, May 19, 1942. Due to her high speed, the former luxury ilner sailed alone without escort. Meanwhile, George is continuing his air cadet training at Enid, Oklahoma.

May 26, 1942

Dear Mom,

I am going to Victoria Field, Texas, for pursuit. We finished up flying last week, and ground school today. Myself and four others didn't have to take the final exam in meteorology because we had an average of over 90 in the course. We leave here Sunday or Monday and have to be there Tuesday. My instructor here graduated from Victoria, and he says it's a swell place.

Love,

George

Nearing their destination on June 2, 1942, the USS *West Point* was diverted from docking at Sydney and sent to Melbourne, Australia. Japanese midget submarines had penetrated the Sydney Harbor defenses, causing casualties and damage. Docked at Melbourne, the personnel and equipment of the 105th debarked on the 4th of June and began their move by truck and train north to Queensland—a journey of 1,300 miles. Back in the States, George has moved to Texas.

Foster Field, Victoria, TX, Class 42-G— Advanced Air Cadet Training

June 3, 1942

We arrived here at Foster Field yesterday and we are treated practically the same as officers, except for the sa-

luting. It's the best place we have been in yet. We love the place already. We get up in the morning anytime between 6 and 7. When we get through in the afternoon, about 4 o'clock, we can go into town and go swimming until 9:30. I ordered my officer's uniform yesterday. We have to order them now so they will be ready by the time we graduate. I ordered $190 worth and still need about $25 more. They allow us $150 for them, then we have to pay for the rest. I will just about have enough saved to pay for the rest when we graduate about the 1st of August. They will charge them if we want to. I've learned an officer's credit is about the best in the country. We start flying tomorrow. They say the AT-6s here are about the best ever made. Later on, we will spend about a week on an island in the Gulf getting gunnery practice. They say it's just like a week's vacation with swimming and fishing in the Gulf.

By June 14, the nurses of the 105th are at Stuartholme in Brisbane, Australia, for staging and billeting while awaiting the preliminary preparation of their permanent hospital site; and the Foster Field men of Class 42-G are still in Texas receiving their advanced air cadet training.

July 3, 1942

We have been finishing up ground school, and we've had plenty of work to do. I had two notebooks to fix, one in Aircraft Identification and another in Naval Identification. It took about ten hours of work on each of them, and we had to do them in our spare moments. It took almost two weeks to get them done. We leave for Matagorda Island tomorrow for gunnery training. It will be a nice trip for the Fourth. The island is not but a few miles from here, but they say it really is a swell place to spend about a week. Most all of our flying now is formation. It really is fun. We have our last class in ground school in a few minutes.

While George was spending his days and nights on Matagorda Island just off the coast of Texas in the Gulf of Mexico, the 105th in Australia is preparing to move again.

The following is paraphrased from *Two Years Down Under*, the official unit diary of the U.S. Army 105th General Hospital—"In June, a group of officers and men had been sent ahead to work on detached service with the 153rd Station Hospital.

"Arriving on March 15, 1942, it is the first U.S. hospital to arrive in Australia and was located on the grounds of the Gatton Agricultural College. The 153rd was subsequently transferred to Port Moresby, New Guinea; and on July 14, 1942, the whole 105th organization boarded trucks and moved to the former site of the 153rd located near Gatton, Australia.

"The journey of many thousands of miles was finally over and the U.S. Army 105th General Hospital was ready to begin operations." Back at Foster Field, George noted:

July 15, 1942

Wednesday morning. We got back from the Matagorda Island Monday afternoon. We had a swell time except for the mosquitoes. We went swimming about twice a day. I learned more about flying down there than I thought possible. Some days we flew five and six hours. While there, each of us fired about sixteen hundred rounds of ammunition. My score was one of the best, and one day I was high score man in ground gunnery (that's shooting at stationary targets on the ground, after diving about 800 ft. in the plane). I am afraid I will be made an instructor here at this field. If I have to be an instructor I hope it's here, but I don't want it. We are through with ground school so all we have now is flying. We fly this afternoon and tonight. I tried on my uniforms yesterday, and they fit perfectly. We get them a couple of days before we graduate.

July 24, 1942

I have really been lucky. I was one of twelve picked for twin-engine training. We will be sent to the "Fourth Interceptor Command" to fly P-38s. The P-38 is one of the fastest pursuit ships in the world. It is a single-seater, twin-motored ship with a top speed of over 400 MPH. I have a major for an instructor in the twin-engine ship. We need the twin-engine time so we will be able to step right in the P-38 and be ready to go at our next assignment. All this besides the regular flying I have to do in the AT-6. We graduate the morning of August 5th.

HEADQUARTERS, FOSTER FIELD, VICTORIA, TEXAS,
OFFICE OF THE COMMANDING OFFICER,
August 4, 1942,

SPECIAL ORDERS NO. 189 EXTRACT 4. The following named Aviation Cadets, Aviation Cadet Detachment, this station, are discharged this date to accept appointments as 2nd Lieutenants, AAF, Res. August 5, 1942. DP the following 2nd Lieutenants, Air Res, are ordered to AD, August 5, 1942; they are assigned and WP to station indicated. Date of Rank August 5, 1942.

4th AIR FORCE, PAINE FIELD, WASHINGTON - TEN (10) DAYS DS AUTHORIZED

CHARLES A. GRICE, 1807 Forrest Ave, Nashville, Tenn.
GEORGE E. MORGAN, 1808 N. Parkway, Memphis, Tenn.

George and Charles left Foster Field on August 6th and traveled together as far as Nashville where Charles spent his leave with his family and George traveled on to Memphis to be with his. Joining up again at George's home in Memphis, the two men traveled by train to Paine Field, Everett, Washington.

330th Fighter Squadron, 329th Fighter Group, 4th AAF

Port Moresby, New Guinea
39th FS, 35th FG, 5th AF
July 30, 1943

"These four pursuit pilots were decorated during an evening presentation ceremony. Left to right: 1st Lt. Richard T. Cella, N.Y., N.Y., Air Medal; 1st Lt. John C. Dunbar, Braddock, Pa., Distinguished Flying Cross; 1st Lt. Lee C. Haigler, Austin, Texas, Distinguished Flying Cross; 1st Lt. George E. Morgan, Memphis, Tennessee, Air Medal."

August 16, 1942

Sunday, we reported in yesterday and everything is swell. This country is really beautiful. We can see the mountains to the east and Puget Sound is only a mile or so from the field. The trip out was nice. We went by Glacier Park Hotel which was really nice. The climate is perfect. In the morning one needs a jacket, but during the day it's not needed. We are living in the Officers Barracks. We have someone that makes our beds and cleans up the room. The eats at the Officers Mess are good, and our Club Rooms are real nice. I ran into an old friend from Memphis, Hugh Muse, yesterday, and we had a long talk, but I didn't get in the squadron he's in.

AIR BASE HEADQUARTERS, Paine Field, Everett, Wash. August 17, 1942.

SPECIAL ORDERS NO. 220.

12. Effective this date the following are assigned to the 329th Fighter Gp: 2nd LT GEORGE E. MORGAN
2nd Lt CHARLES F. ROWSEY
2nd Lt RICHARD M. TANSING
2nd Lt WILLIAM W. ANDERSON JR
2nd Lt WALTER C. BAKER JR
2nd Lt GENE DUNCAN
2nd Lt JOHN L. EHLINGER
2nd Lt EUGENE I. MCGUIRE
2nd Lt ARTHUR L. PEREGOY

330th FS to Grand Central Air Terminal, Glendale, CA— September 7, 1942

September 14, 1942

We really have a nice setup here. The field is inside the city limits of Glendale and only a mile or so from the middle of town. Our squadron is the only one at this field. Our quarters will be an old country club building with a swimming pool and tennis courts in the back. The P-38s we will be flying are newer and better than the ones we have been flying. Hugh Muse and I followed the coastline route down. We stayed in Portland one night and San Francisco another. We went sightseeing last night. We spent some time in Hollywood and Los Angeles and rode through Beverly Hills as well some other part of L.A. I believe this will be one of the nicest places I have been stationed.

September 30, 1942

We have to be down on the flying line every other morning to stand alert or fly patrol, and we are usually here until eight at night. I am getting where I really feel at home in the P-38s, and I like them more every time I fly them. We have received some very good reports on the 38s in action. I flew the patrol out to Catalina again tonight and have to stand the alert in the morning beginning at five-thirty and lasting until noon, then I will get the next twenty-four hours off. Next week some of us are going over to a gunnery range about a hundred miles north of here for two or three days to get some gunnery practice. I had the other night off so a couple of us went down to Hollywood and saw Ken Murray's stage show Blackouts of 1942. *Marie Wilson had a leading part in the show with Ken Murray, and they were both very good and funny. I've also gone to Grauman's Chinese Theater to see* Panama Hattie. *The theater is really beautiful. This is about the nicest setup anyone could have. I never thought I would get a free trip to California, and when I did get it, it was right in the middle of all the things I have always heard about. (Charles A.) Grice and I went to the Palladium last night to hear Jimmy Dorsey's band. It is the nicest place for dancing I have ever seen. Judy Garland and Mickey Rooney were there, and you should have seen those two jitterbug. Everyone stopped dancing to watch. Milton Beryl, Rags Ragland, Tommy Dorsey, and a number of others were there. I have never been anywhere where people were nicer than they are here. I feel embarrassed to have to turn down so many offers for dinner. I could eat out every night if I had the time. The USO has been very nice to us. For our lounge room down on the flying line, they got us a couple of couches (one can be made into a bed for those that have to stay there all night), a yard swing, a couple of soft chairs, a couple of tables, a reading lamp, and a radio, also a number of good books.*

October 7, 1942

Official Statement—Took off from Grand Central Air Terminal at 1600 o'clock for a routine formation training flight. About 1700 o'clock, while in formation, my left motor began to cut out, and then run intermittently. I switched gas tanks to reserve, but it did no good. With the motor giving more drag than thrust, I feathered the propeller. In the meantime, I had gotten into the clouds and thick haze, and I was unable to locate the field here at Grand Central Air Terminal. I then flew out toward the ocean, and upon finding a hole in the overcast, I set the plane down in the ocean about three-quarters of a mile offshore of El Segundo where I was picked up by a fishing boat.

1st Lt. John D. Monahan writes: "I was circling the field at about 3,500 feet prior to landing with a 4-ship flight. Went out to make my final turn and approach into the field to peel off and land. The second element leader, Lt. Morgan, went straight-ahead toward the ocean. I thought maybe the controller had sent us on a vector, and he was the only one who received it. I followed him, and as I was about to catch up with him, he turned toward me and headed inland. I turned and passed him. He kept on turning and headed again for the ocean. I did not know he was in trouble at this time. I followed him, and he was letting down. I am pretty sure I saw his left engine feathered. We followed him to about 1,500 feet. He let down thru fairly bad weather, but I could see the water so figured he was going to set down. I returned to the field with my 3-ship flight and landed. I was unable to establish radio contact with Lt. Morgan."

Statement of Accident Classification Committee—"It is the opinion of the Committee that engine failure occurred due to refusal of the fuel system to function properly, caused principally by faulty carburation. Since the generator is operated by the left engine on subject aircraft and this engine was the one that failed, the electrical system would have ceased to operate possibly within less than one hour, causing instrument and propeller failure on the right engine. In general, the conclusion drawn by this committee in view of the pilot's limited experience and time on this type of aircraft is that he took the best course of action under the circumstances."

October 23, 1942

Our squadron is short of qualified pilots so we are having to stand nearly all the alerts and fly the patrols. We have been flying also the last few nights. I haven't been back to my barracks since early yesterday morning. There are only four ships in a patrol but sometimes as many as ten of us take off on a scramble. I had to land a P-38 out in the ocean about two weeks ago, and a fishing boat picked me up about fifteen minutes later. The plane sank within a few minutes, but the life preserver we have to wear held me up fine. Confidentially, I enjoyed the swim. All I got was a scratch on my nose, but it couldn't be seen two days later. Everyone congratulated me on the good job I did, and I was cleared of all blame. I now have close to sixty-five hours flying time in the P-38. I still think it's the best plane flying. I think Grice and I are leaving for Alaska in

a few days, but we don't know for sure. We probably won't
be up there but for about six months. I think I am going to
like it up there. I am tired of staying in one place.

SECRET By authority of CG IV Fighter Command Oct 24/42, HA
IV F COMD, Oakland, Calif. Oct 23/42, Special Order No. 295,
paragraph 2: Following named 2 LTS, AC, reld fr asgmt to orgns
indicated, and asgd to perm sta outside the continental limits of
the United States, Shipment No. OGF-705-B (temperate climate)
and will proceed without delay to the San Francisco Port of Embarkation, Ft Mason, Calif, reporting upon arrival the Transportation Representative, Ft Mason, Calif, for transportation by first
available United States Army transport or commercial steamship
to destination. <u>329th FG, perm sta March Fld, Calif, temp sta Glendale, Calif</u>

WILLIAM W. ANDERSON
JOSEPH E. FOREST
CHARLES A. GRICE
JOHN L. EHLINGER
EUGENE I. MCGUIRE
RICHARD M. TANSING
ARTHUR L. PEREGOY
CHARLES F. ROWSEY
GEORGE E. MORGAN
WALTER C. BAKER
JOHN K. PARKANSKY
GENE DUNCAN

Trav fr present sta to San Francisco Port of Embarkation, Ft Mason, Calif, will be by rail, Govt auto, priv convey, mil ap, or by
comm. ap and is neces for the accomplishment of an emergency
war mission. If trav by comm. ap, excess baggage not to exceed
140 lbs.

While awaiting transportation to destination, the above named O
will report to CO, Flight Section, Fourth AF, Hangar No. 5, Hamilton Fld, Calif, for flight training, until notification that transportation is available, at which time they will proceed without delay to
destination, reporting upon arrival to CG, thereat, for duty.

Ea of the above named O will comply with prov of AAF Memo 25-9, re immunization against diseases, and will have physical inspection as prescribed by par 14, AR 40-100. Ea O will be equipped for extended field service in semitropical climate—.45 cal pistol and holster, gas mask, steel helmet and liner, first aid kit, mosquito bar, and parachute. Personal baggage will be marked with O's name, c/o Port Transportation Officer, San Francisco Port of Embarkation, Ft Mason, Calif. Relatives and friends will not accompany the above name O to Port of Embarkation or join them prior to sailing.

In lieu of subs a flat per diem of $6 auth while trav on official business and for period of temp duty at San Francisco Port of Embarkation, including all delays incident to embarkation, in accordance with existing law and regulations.

Orders, dated Oct 17/42. By comd of
Brig Gen KEPNER: RUSSELL V. RITCHEY, Lt Col, AC, Adj.

Hotel St. Francis, Union Square, San Francisco

San Francisco was strictly blacked out at night and incoming pilots were warned to do everything during the day and rest at night. Rumors were also rampant, since no final orders had been issued concerning final destinations. Most of the pilots of the 39th hoped to be sent to the Pacific, as George Morgan suggests in this letter to his mother:

October 30, 1942

Dear Mom,

I'm in San Francisco. Thought I was going to Alaska, but I'm not. Maybe I will get to see Jay. Grice and (Charles F.) Rowsey, my roommate at Paine Field, are also along with some others going my way. We are staying together here at the hotel while we are waiting. Wait is all we have to do now as we have already checked out all our equipment and had our express baggage taken care of. We get six dollars a day living expense besides our regular pay, but here at this hotel we need it. I have plenty of money with me, mostly in traveler's checks. Sure am glad I am going to where I think I am. We all think we're lucky.

Love,

George

Western Union Telegram, 7 November 1942, 5:09 P.M.

"MRS. JAY L. MORGAN, OFF TO VISIT JAY = LOVE, G E MORGAN"

Handwritten note to self: *"Left Hamilton AAF, California, November 17, 1942, at 0345 hrs.; Arrive Hickam AAF, Hawaii, November 17, 1942, at 1300 hrs.; leave Hickam AAF, Hawaii, 1942, at 2145 hrs."*

HEADQUARTERS, FIFTH AIR FORCE, APO 923, 15 November 1942, Special Orders No. 71, paragraphs 7: Pertaining to the following named O, AC unasgd, then at Brisbane, Qld, to the 370th Serv Sq, Brisbane, and placing them on DS at Amberley Fld, Qld.

2nd Lt WILLIAM W. ANDERSON JR
2nd Lt CHARLES A. GRICE
2nd Lt GEORGE E. MORGAN
2nd Lt CHARLES F. ROWSEY
2nd Lt RICHARD M. TANSING

HEADQUARTERS, FIFTH AIR FORCE, APO 923, 18 November 1942, Special Orders No. 74, paragraph 6: Pertaining to the following named O, AC unasgd, then at Amberley Fld, Brisbane, Qld, to the 370th Serv Sq, Amberley Fld.

2nd Lt WALTER C. BAKER JR

Schwimmer Drome
39th FS, 35th FG, 5th AF
Port Moresby, New Guinea
March 1943

Sgt. Jay L. Morgan, Weather Central, and
2nd Lt George E. Morgan standing beneath
one of the squadron's P-38s.

2nd Lt GENE DUNCAN
2nd Lt JOHN L. EHLINGER
2nd Lt JOSEPH E. FOREST
2nd Lt EUGENE I. McGUIRE
2nd Lt JOHN K. PARKANSKY
2nd Lt ARTHUR L. PEREGOY

RAAF Amberley Field, Ipswich, Australia— 17th FS (Provisional), 49th FG, Fifth AAF

November 21, 1942

> *Things I've seen and done since joining the Air Corps couldn't be duplicated for thousands of dollars. Trip over was wonderful. The trip over alone repaid for the things I had to go through as a cadet. The country over here is nice but about twenty years behind the States in every way. Haven't found out where Jay is yet, but I hope to soon.*

HEADQUARTERS, FIFTH AIR FORCE, APO 923, 27 November 1942, Special Orders No. 83, paragraph 6 and 10: VOCG Nov 13, 1942, assigning the following named O, AC unasgd, to the 370th Serv Sq, Brisbane, placing them on DS at Amerley Fld, Brisbane, Qld, in connection with the P-38 training program, and authorizing them a flat per diem of $6 in lieu of actual and necessary expenses.

2nd Lt WILLIAM W. ANDERSON JR
2nd Lt CHARLES A. GRICE
2nd Lt GEORGE E. MORGAN
2nd Lt CHARLES F. ROWSEY ,
2nd Lt RICHARD M. TANSING,
2nd Lt WALTER C. BAKER JR
2nd Lt GENE DUNCAN
2nd Lt JOHN L. EHLINGER,
2ndLt JOSEPH E. FOREST
2nd Lt EUGENE I. McGUIRE ,
2nd Lt JOHN K. PARKANSKY,
2nd Lt. ARTHUR L. PEREGOY

370th Service Squadron, Amberley Field, Australia, APO 710— P-38 Training Program

On Thanksgiving weekend, 1942, George, with fellow pilots, came out to the 105th General Hospital to a dance. When George saw Mary he asked Patty Knapp, an army nurse soon to be married to Captain Jack C. Mankin, if she would introduce him to Mary.

She did, and they danced many dances together. Several days later, George called Mary and asked if she would come to a picnic the following Sunday that the pilots were planning. She said yes.

Gatton, Australia
U.S. Army 105th General Hospital
December 1942

"Off to Adventure"

2nd Lts. Eileen (Fitz, Fitzie) Fitzgerald, Mary (Scottie) Scott, and Patricia (Patty) Mankin.

On Sunday, some of the pilots came over on an army bus and picked up some of the nurses for the picnic. George came walking down the street—he had on suntan trousers, a white T-shirt, and a suntan baseball cap on the back of his head.

Mary saw him and thought, *I like what I see—he's cute!* The picnic was a big success. They had dug a pit and barbequed. They also had a barrel of beer and played softball. Great fun was had.

Mary and George dated until he left Amberley Field.

December 28, 1942

Dear Mom,

Some of us in the squadron go with some American nurses and we all had a party Christmas Eve. I've been going with one of them about a month now and we have had some picnics whenever a bunch of us could get the day off. We usually get a lamb and barbeque it ourselves. All the nurses are a swell bunch of girls, and we are lucky to have them to go with. I have been feeling fine since being over here. Haven't had a cold or anything like it.

Love,

George

HEADQUARTERS "V" FIGHTER COMMAND, APO 929, 17 January 1943, Special Orders No. 12, Paragraph 7: The following named O are, of this date reld fr asgt to the V Fighter Comd, Maple, are reld fr atchd to the 370th Serv Sq, Charters Towers, Qld, are asgd to the 370th Serv Sq and will report to the Co thereof for duty.

2nd Lt WILLIAM W. ANDERSON JR
2nd Lt WALTER C. BAKER JR

2nd Lt GENE DUNCAN
2nd Lt JOHN L. EHLINGER
2nd Lt JOSEPH E. FOREST
2nd Lt CHARLES A. GRICE
2nd Lt EUGENE L. McGUIRE
2nd Lt GEORGE E. MORGAN
2nd Lt JOHN K. PARKANSKY
2nd Lt ARTHUR L. PEREGOY
2nd Lt RICHARD M. TANSING

370th Service Squadron, Charters Towers, Queensland, Australia

January 17, 1943

Dear Mary,

Still in Australia and still haven't received any mail. Found out where Jay is. Ran into one of the boys he came across with and had a nice talk. Jay is doing a good job, much rougher than what I'm doing. Food here is really swell, about the best I've seen in the army. We have about everything we need except cigarettes which are rationed. This life seems to agree with me—I'm getting fat. Up to about 173 pounds.

Love,

George

January 25, 1943

Dear Mary,

I hit the "jackpot" today. I received twelve let-ters, some from people I never expected to hear from. Received your letter yesterday. You asked if this is a good deal here. Some might think so, but I don't. I'm tired of fooling around and want to get on with it. About all we do at night is go to the club. When I tried to write that first letter to you, there was a big bull session going on, and I couldn't write a line without stopping. Now Perry has started talking, and I'm having trouble again. I haven't seen John Price yet, but Carl Rauch is here. It seems odd to see all the new faces instead of the old bunch. Perry and myself are still planning on having a big time if and when we get a few days off. Hope you and "Fitz" will be able to get some time off. Perry and Grice now want to go to a show here so I had better run.

Love,

George

February 14, 1943

Dear Mary,

Here it is Valentine's Day, and I don't have a card to send. Speaking of cards, I am just beginning to receive birthday and Christmas cards. I also received a batch of letters written last October and sent to my last post in the States. We had a squadron picnic the other day—how I wished you were here. Rauch, Andy (William W. Anderson), Perry, and myself did all the work. We had a swell place to swim so we would barbeque a while, and then swim a while. Nice sunburns were had by all. Our *bunch is where we said we would be (Charters Towers), but all the older boys except Rauch have moved on. Tell everyone "Hello" for me.*

Love,

George

Mary's father, Lt. Col. Roy L. Scott, wrote to Mary after she let him know about the leave in Australia. He also shared his plan about running for the U.S. Congress after the war is over.

Cold Bay, Alaska

February 15, 1943

Dear Mary,

Received your letter of January 20 today. I thank God you are where you can have some good times. God knows this is tough enough no matter where you are. All any of us want is to get it over and go home. Used to be all pepped up over promotion but am over that idea. I am always in command of something, and that is enough. I know, dear, that when you tell me of your good times, there is a hell of a lot of work back of it. Thanks for the pictures. Sure looks funny to see the trees in the pictures. Had forgotten what a tree looks like. Hear that they are sending some nurses here. God pity them. When this is all over, everyone in this mess must organize to help get each one back into civilian life. That is going to be a big job. I am going to be elected to Congress and when I get there, I'm going to make one speech and tell them what I think and what we will do for these men and women of ours who have given so much of their young lives. Doesn't make too much difference to me because I'm an old man and have lived a full life, but for you kids, it's hell.

All my love,

Dad.

I don't think I care to be
A person of great fame
I just want to win this war
And start for home again,
I'm tired of wearing uniforms
And roguish khaki lids,
I just want to get back home
And raise a million kids.

—Written by an unknown nurse in the Southwest Pacific

February 16, 1943

Dear Mary,

Not a thing has happened since I last wrote. Discovered I'm not good at blackjack. I just lost five pounds and quit. Perry is winning all the money. My brother came to see me the other day, and we had a big time talking over old times. He looks the best I've ever seen him. Be good and have a good time.

Love,

George

U.S. Army 105th General Hospital
Gatton, Australia
December 25, 1942

2nd Lts. Mary L. Scott and George E.
Morgan, 17th FS (P), 49th FG, 5th AF,
RAAF Amberley Field enjoying Christmas
in the warmth of an early summer day.

17th STATION HOSPITAL, Office of the Mess Officer, APO #710, 16 February 1943: NAME—GEORGE E. MORGAN, ORGANIZATION 370th Ser. Sq. For subsistence in hospital: From 3 Feb. to 16 Feb. 1943, 13 days @ 6/2 Total L 4/0/2 The foregoing bill was paid this date. (Dengue Fever).

HEADQUARTERS V FIGHTER COMMAND, APO 929, 20 February, 1943, Special Orders No. 39, Paragraph 3: The following named O are, off this date reld fr asgd to the 370th Serv Sq, APO 710, are asgd to the 35th Fighter Gp, APO 929 and WP MOCA or by rail, reporting upon arrival the CO thereof for duty. $6 per diem is auth for travel.

2nd Lt WILLIAM W. ANDERSON
2nd Lt GENE DUNCAN
2nd Lt JOSEPH E. FOREST
2nd Lt EUGENE I. McGUIRE
2nd Lt JOHN K. PARKANSKY
2nd Lt RICHARD M. TANSING
2nd Lt WALTER C. BAKER
2nd Lt JOHN L. EHLINGER
2nd Lt CHARLES A. GRICE
2nd Lt GEORGE E. MORGAN
2nd Lt ARTHUR L. PEREGOY

17th STATION HOSPITAL, Office of the Registrar, APO 710, 27 February 1943, SUBJECT: Hospitalization of Patient, TO: The Commanding Officer, 370th Serv Sq. (sep) AC, APO 710

1. In compliance with par. 7 (3), AR 40-590, report that the following named patient was this date, discharged to duty from this hospital and directed to report to his organization for duty:

   a. Morgan, George E. 2nd Lt 370th Serv Sq (sep) AC
   b. 19 February 1943 to 27 February 1943
   c. Line of Duty: Yes
   d. Illness or injury was not due to patient's own misconduct. (Dengue Fever)

HEADQUARTERS THIRTY-FIFTH FIGHTER GROUP, UNITED STATES ARMY AIR FORCES, APO NO. 929, 2 March 1943, Special Orders No. 12, Paragraph 3: Having been assigned to this Head-quarters per par. 3, SO #39, Hq. 5th Fighter Command, dated 20 February, 1943, the following named officers are further assigned to the 39th Fighter Squadron, as of same date.

2nd Lt Gene DUNCAN
2nd Lt Joseph E. FOREST
2nd Lt Eugene I. McGUIRE
2nd Lt Richard M. TANSING
2nd Lt Walter C. BAKER
2nd Lt John L. EHLINGER
2nd Lt Charles A. GRICE
2nd Lt George E. MORGAN
2nd Lt Arthur L. PEREGOY

39th FS, 35th FG, Fifth AAF, 14 Mile Strip, Port Moresby, New Guinea, APO 929 - 4

March 3–5, 1943

> *Battle of the Bismarck Sea—"The Fifth Air Force achieved a spectacular victory over the Japanese in the last few days. The convoy was absolutely destroyed. It is a victory for air power over sea power without precedent." Three men of the 39th Fighter Squadron were lost in the battle—Capt. Robert L. Faurot, 1st Lt. Hoyt A. Eason, and 1st Lt. Fred B. Shifflet.*

March 4, 1943

Nine new pilots arrived from the mainland today.

March 5, 1943

Dear Mom,

Haven't seen Jay since I arrived but will look him up in the next day or so. Grice and I are still together and will probably stay together. Really has been swell that we could stay in the same outfits. This outfit we are in now is really swell, the fellows are as nice as they can be. This outfit is one that anyone can be proud to be in. I really feel good. Every night I'm just tired enough to get to sleep easy, and I have a nice air mattress to sleep on. We are more comfortable than we were.

Love,

George

Somewhere in New Guinea

March 5, 1943

Dear Mary,

I guess you are angry with me because I haven't written more often, but just remember—when I don't write to you, I don't write to anyone. Perry and myself are still together as is the rest of our bunch. I saw John "Jump" O'Neill and some of the other old boys today. It was really nice to see them. We have things very nice here, nicer than where we were. My biggest pride is a nice air mattress. I finally found my baggage, and I'm sending you a little P-38 pin I had packed. If you don't like it or don't want it, please send it back as there is quite a demand for them here. I am afraid to wear the "loud" socks you girls knitted so I am going to let Perry wear his first.

George

George and the rest of his "bunch"—the nine pilots that came into the squadron together—are receiving flight training from the older boys of the squadron.

March 13, 1943

Dear Mary,

Today I received your letters written on the 13th and 22nd of February. It was the first mail I've received up here. Please, in your next letter, don't write about food. I can't stand it. It will probably be 3 months before I can get leave and a decent meal. My waistline has really been cut down. We don't ask the enlisted men to do any of our work because they have plenty of their own to do. That means we get plenty of exercise. I have been catching on the softball team we have, and was I sore the first day I played. We have a fairly good team but we never get a chance to practice. I still have that quart of rum you gave me for Christmas. I'm saving it for a special occasion. I will let you know when I drink it. When I did go to the hospital, I was glad I did even though it was nothing serious. I now appreciate nurses—even if they are American girls!! Really, I don't think I could have enjoyed myself more while I was down there. What I am trying to say is, just being with you was fun for me. I only hope you miss me half as much as I do you.

Love,

George

My life consists of bully beef,
Soggy clothes and wiggly teeth,
Gunshot wounds and jungle rot,
And days that are so bloomin' hot
That even hell compared to this
Would seem a simple life of bliss

—Written by an unknown nurse in the Southwest Pacific

On March 16, 1943, George completed his first combat mission with the 39th escorting transports to Wau.

Somewhere in New Guinea

March 18, 1943

Dear Mary,

Right now, Anderson and Grice are in a black-jack game—probably losing. Everyone else is either reading, writing, or listening to the Victrola, and some are just "shooting the bull," as usual. We played softball this afternoon and won by 1 point. You would be surprised by how nice we have things here. Of, course, it took a lot of hard work, but it is worth it. We all have blisters on our hands, but the work really helps the waistline, and we all need it. Perry got Fitz's letter today, and he was very glad to receive it.

Love,

George

March 23, 1943, Major George W. Prentice made an important announcement, that today was his last day as commander of the 39th Fighter Squadron. He is being succeeded by Capt. Thomas J. Lynch.

March 28, 1943

Dear Mary,

I spent the other night over with "Jump" O'Neill and Jack. We really talked over old times. I see you have heard the good news about "Jump" (a kill). I know Bucky is proud of him. We had some pictures taken of our bunch which will probably appear in the newspapers and news reels down there, but this was just recently.

Love,

George

With the main body of the squadron now in the combat zone, the 39th often escorted bombers on attacks on Lae, which was being used to refuel enemy aircraft attacking from the Japanese strongholds of Wewak and Rabaul.

April 4, 1943

Dear Mom,

Have been up here (New Guinea) a little over a month and beginning to feel like an old veteran. Have been doing a lot of flying, and I like it more every time I go up. Jay came over the other night, and we were going to a show, but it rained. Had a nice talk tho. He never looked better. He's darn proud of his three stripes. See him every other day or so. Really like my work; it was worth all I went through to finally reach here. I enjoy being and seeing news in the making. I've saved almost a thousand dollars in the last 5 months and spent less than $25 a month.

Mary writes to me at least once a week. Hope to see her if I do get a leave. She really is a swell kid.

Love,

George

April 9, 1943

Dear Mary,

I'm saving the rum for the day I do as well as Jack or Jump. I heard Rauch got down there on leave, is that right? If he did, I really envy him. We had a nice show here tonight. It was George Washington Slept Here, with Jack Benny and Ann Sheridan. It was good except we couldn't hear the first reel, and it rained so hard at the end of the second that we had to leave. Perry, Grice, Jay, and myself had today off so we went sightseeing. We went to just one place (Rouna Falls) and had fun. It was almost like a picnic. Tell your dad that I would be very happy to swap him some trees for a few chunks of ice.

Love,

George

George's combat missions for the rest of March and early April were uneventful escorts for the transports—DC-3s—to Wau and A-20 attack bombers to Finschhafen.

April 12, 1943

Today was an exciting one. During the morning numerous calls were received from 4ES requesting all planes available be kept gassed and ready to go. From 9 o'clock on things were expected to come. A jap recon came over. At 0935 an order to scramble was received and 6 P-38s took off, all that were available. At 10 o'clock Capt. Lynch took off with a 4-ship flight and at that time the enemy was expected in 5 minutes. Capt. Lynch and his flight were taking off just as the enemy formation came into view. At 1008 Capt. Gallup took off as the bombers were overhead. The enemy formation consisted of approximately 45 medium bombers and approximately 60 fighters. At about 1015 or 1020 the raid had commenced. This field was bombed however no damage was done to our aircraft or personnel. The other end of the field, the dispersal area for B-25s, was bombed, along with 12-mile strip. The enemy also hit 5-mile strip and Kila strip or in the vicinity of Kila. Capt. Sullivan made a pass at a formation of about 9 enemy bombers, and his attack was seen by all of us on the ground. He fired on 2 enemy bombers, one of which fell out of formation, losing altitude and smoking. It was destroyed. Lt. Smith destroyed one enemy bomber in the vicinity of Kokoda. Lt. Suehr destroyed one enemy bomber near Mt. Chamberlain. Capt. Gallup destroyed one Zeke fighter near 17-mile hospital, Lt. Clymer destroyed one Zeke about 40 miles E. of Moresby. Our pilots shot down 5 for certain on this day. Capt. Lynch's flight was unable to contact the enemy. This was the 106th raid on Moresby. In comparison to the enemy's scale of effort the damage was slight.

April 17, 1943

Dear Mary,

It seems "Pudge" is my nickname. My sister started it when I was about 2 years old. Perry heard my brother call me that, and now he is using it. As for weight, I have lost about 10 pounds since leaving down there. What is this Perry told me about you being head nurse in your ward? I am very glad for you but don't come up with any silver bars ahead of me!! Yes, we also have to pay income tax the same as anyone else. Tell Fitz and everyone "Hello" for me.

Love,

George

George's missions for the rest of April consisted of an intercept mission to Buna with no enemy sightings and four uneventful escort missions to Wau for the DC-3 transports.

Dear Mom,

May 2, 1943

Haven't seen Jay since last Sunday, and then for only a few minutes. He's been studying for some exams. This work of mine is not very hard, but the hours are long. I am keeping a form of a diary about my work. We have a Victrola down here and about 18 records. The Victrola is one of the small winding types, and it's usually going all the time. We have "Stardust," "What to Do," "Practice Makes Perfect," and others of the same type. We have a few "jazz" records, too.

Love,

George

May 2, 1943

Dear Mary,

Your package arrived today, and I was just as happy as a young boy with his first long pants. I believe you have someone up here to tell you what I needed. I needed the matches more than anything; I had only three boxes left and no prospects of getting more. We get some candy, but none like you sent. With my new "loud" socks, I am the best dressed man here. Perry is writing Fitz and every 2 minutes he asks me whether he can write certain things or not, just as if I know. Thank you again for the package.

Love,

George

May 5, 1943

There was no flying today because of the bad weather. The rain came down almost all day long. The opening of the new Officers Club took place tonight.

May 9, 1943

Dear Mary,

We had a big party a few nights ago to cele-brate the opening of our new Officers Club we built. Just about everyone went home on instruments through about 6 inches of mud. You can imagine what happened. I must confess, I was in as bad a shape as anyone else, but I, at least, found my own tent and that is more than some can say. Since that night, I have sworn off getting drunk and intend to stick to it.

May 18, 1943

There was no flying today. The continuation of "Over The Hump Week" was the only thing taking place. It was Open House at our camp. Also, the enlisted men received their decorations.

May 23, 1943

Early this morning, Capt. Suehr, Lts. Marlatt, Bartlett, and McClure took off and headed for the States. Quite a lucky break?

May 25, 1943

Dear Mary,

I hope you know that if it was possible, both Perry and I would be there on the date you suggested, but as things seem now, it will be the middle of July before we can get leave. The last couple of days, we, the boys in the tent, have been fixing our little home up on stilts. It's been a lot of work but is worth it. Our tent is up on

top of a hill giving us a good view and a wonderful breeze. We are sleeping in it tonight for
the first time. Outside of working on the tent, I
haven't been doing much except working. I saw
Ice Escapades at the local cinema last night. It
was enjoyed very much by us up here, especially the hula-hula scene. I hope to see the picture,
Air Force soon. I understand it is very good. As
always,

Love,

George

May 30, 1943

Lt. Cella had a "crack up" this evening. He was injured just slightly,
but the plane is a washout. Lt. Cella will be out again in the morning.

May 31, 1943

Dear Mom,

Plans I had for my leave have gone to pieces.
Perry and I both went with some nurses down
south (Australia). We all had our leaves arranged for the same time. Now, Perry and I
have had our leaves delayed, and they can't
delay theirs! Didn't do much today, just fooled
around my tent, fixing this and that. We've
fixed our tent up on stilts and raised the floor
(which we stole) about 5 feet off the ground. It
makes everything so much cleaner.

Love,

George

The May missions for George were "fighter cover for bombers and strafers on a strike mission" to Arawe, New Britain; local—Port Moresby—interception with unidentified aircraft spotted at 23,000 feet but no contact; an escort for DC-3 transports and two offensive fighter sweeps all to Wau and Bulolo; and another local intercept without any enemy sightings.

June 1, 1943

Dear Mom,

We stole a wooden floor for our tent which is about 5 feet above the ground with a frame about another 5 feet above that to keep the tent from sagging. It's on top of a hill with a great view and breeze. We have the cutest lizards here. There was one about 3 feet long (and I mean 3 feet) playing (or stalking) a few feet from our tent this morning. I saw one the other day that was about 5 to 5½ feet long. We also have a "wallaby" (baby kangaroo) that lives nearby. It must weigh about 35 to 40 pounds. There are also rock pythons in the area. Jay is now less than a quarter of a mile from me, but I still don't get to see him but a couple of times a week. I tried to call him tonight but couldn't get him.

Love,

George

HEADQUARTERS 35th IGHTER GROUP, UNITED STATES ARMY AIR FORCE, APO #929, 3 June, 1943, Special Orders No. 32, Paragraph 6: The following named officers are relieved from assignment to organizations indicated opposite their name and further assigned to Headquarters, 35th Fighter

Group, and appointed Asst. Group Operations Officers (Principal Duty).

2nd Lt. Gene DUNCAN, 39tht Fighter Squadron
2nd Lt. George E. MORGAN, 39th Fighter Squadron
2nd Lt. John K. PARKANSKY, 39th Fighter Squadron
2nd Lt. Richard M. TANSING, 39th Fighter Squadron

June 4, 1943

Dear Mary,

You should get this letter upon your return from leave so I hope you had a good time. One of the boys who has just returned from where you mentioned (Southport, Australia) has informed us of what we have missed. If I hadn't had so many disappointments before it would be enough to make me sick. Three months ago I arrived where I am now (New Guinea). It's the longest I have been in any one place in almost a year and a half so it's beginning to seem like home. You know, Butch and the fellows can't understand why I don't want to go way down south (Sydney). In fact, they can't even understand a guy just having fun by being with a special person. Good night, Mary, I am looking forward to seeing you more than you can possibly imagine.

Love,

George

HEADQUARTERS 105th GENERAL HOSPITAL, APO 923, 9 June 1943, SPECIAL ORDERS NO. 159 EXTRACT

4. Following O, ANC, this Hq are granted lv of abs of seven (7) days effect this date. Address while on lv will be San Soucci Hotel, Southport, Qld.
2nd Lt. MARY L. SCOTT ANC
2nd Lt. EILEEN FITZGERALD ANC

June 9, 1943

Dear Mary,

Give Patty my congratulations. I suspected it but wasn't sure. I had asked Jack, but he would never give an answer either way. I saw the picture, Somewhere I'll Find You tonight and what a picture! What are they trying to do, build up our morale or tear it down! I saw Palm Beach Story a couple of nights ago and it was the same as the one tonight. It's only a few minutes before "lights out," and I want to get this in the mail so it will be waiting for you when you return.

Love,

George

HEADQUARTERS, FIFTH AIR FORCE, APO 925, 14 June, 1943, General Orders No. 119, Section III

AWARDS OF THE AIR MEDAL: By direction of the President, under the provisions of Executive Order No. 9150, May 11, 1942, as amended by Executive Order No. 9242-A, September 11, 1942. Air Medals are awarded to the following named officers:

GEORGE E. MORGAN, 0662970, Second Lieutenant, 39th Fighter Squadron, 35th Fighter Group, Air Corps, United States Army. For operational flight missions from March 8, 1943, to May 1, 1943. The citation is as follows:

For meritorious achievement while participating in twenty-five operational flight missions in the Southwest Pacific Area during which hostile contact was probable and expected. These operations included escorting bombers and transport aircraft, interception and attack missions, and patrol and reconnaissance flights. In the course of these operations, strafing and bombing attacks were made from dangerously low altitudes, destroying and damaging enemy installations and equipment.

June 18, 1943

Dear Mary,

If I am not mistaken, you and "Fitzy" should have returned from your leave today. I hope you had the good time you hoped for. My brother was over this morning, and we took some more pictures, but we are having trouble getting prints made. Except for the show, Stage Door Canteen, I haven't seen any more good ones since I last wrote. I hope to see Casablanca in the near future.

Have you seen Holiday Inn yet? It's up here now, and I hope to see it again. We have some good books here, but I don't recommend them for children. One is The Autobiography of Box Car Annie. It's hard to believe all that is claimed happened to one woman. Another book I have just finished is Wild Is the River about New Orleans during the Civil War. It's a swell book but a bit crude in spots. I finally received my "pinks" and shirts from down south (Australia). Anderson will be down that way soon, and he is going to leave them with Mrs. Field (head of housekeeping, 105th) to be cleaned and pressed. Tomorrow night I hope to get a chance to see London By Night and The Amazing Mrs. Holiday. It's nearly time for lights out so had best close.

Love,

George

June 25, 1943, George Morgan received the Air Medal from Lieutenant General George Kenney as described in a letter to George's mother:

Mrs. Stella Morgan,

Memphis, Tennessee

My Dear Mrs. Morgan:

Recently your son, Lt. George E. Morgan, was decorated with the Air Medal.

It was an award made in recognition of his courageous service to his Combat Organization, his fellow American airmen, his country, his home, and to you.

He was cited for meritorious achievement while participating in aerial flights in the Southwest Pacific area from March 8 to May 1, 1943.

He took part in more than 25 operational flight missions during which hostile contact was probable and expected. These flights included interception missions against enemy fighters and bombing planes and aided considerably in the recent successes in this theater.

Almost every hour of every day your son and the sons of other American mothers are doing just such things as that here in the Southwest Pacific.

Theirs is a very real and very tangible contribution to victory and to peace.

I would like to tell you how genuinely proud I am to have men such as your son in my command, and how gratified I am to know that Americans with such courage and resourcefulness are fighting our country's battle against the aggressor nations.

You, Mrs. Morgan, have every reason to share that pride and gratification.

Very sincerely,

George Kenney

June 25, 1943

We have some of the worst skin infections and irritations. One of them I tangled with this afternoon. There is a certain type of caterpillar that gets in one's clothes (while they are lying around) and will leave them infected. When the cloth comes in contact with the skin, it immediately starts to itch with welts about the size of silver dollars. Within 30 minutes, the itch is over. It's nothing serious, just inconvenient as hell. One of the sayings around here is you can tell how long a guy has been in New Guinea by how much he scratches himself. The other day, on my day off, Jay and I were together most of the afternoon. We both had some business near the same place so we spent the afternoon getting things out of the way. Didn't get back to camp until time for supper. Found some ink for my pen without having to go up to my tent. It's a nice walk uphill. This is the pen I bought about 14 months ago, a Parker 51, while at basic. Thought I lost it the other day. Grice had borrowed it, and it scared me to death. One just can't get fountain pens over here.

HEADQUARTERS, FIFTH AIR FORCE, APO 925, 27 June, 1943; Special Orders No. 178, 19. Announcement is made of the temp promotion of the following named O to the gr indicated in the AUS (AC) with rank fr date of this order.

2nd Lt. to 1st Lt.

DUNCAN, GENE,
MORGAN, GEORGE E.,
PARKANSKY, JOHN K.,
TANSING, RICHARD M.

By command of Lieutenant General KENNEY

HEADQUARTERS THIRTY-FIFTH FIGHTER GROUP, UNITED STATES ARMY AIR FORCES, APO No. 929, 1 July, 1943. Special Orders No. 38.

(Paragraph 3): The following named officers are relieved from assignment to Hq. 35th Fighter Group and further assigned to organizations indicated opposite their names:

1st Lt. Gene DUNCAN
39th Fighter Squadron

1st Lt. George E. MORGAN
39th Fighter Squadron

1st Lt. John K. PARKANSKY

39th Fighter Squadron

1st Lt. Richard M. TANSING
39th Fighter Squadron

(Paragraph 4): With the concurrence of the CG, Fifth Air Force, APO 925, and per VOCG, Fifth Fighter Command, APO 929, the following named officers, Air Corps, organizations as indicated are granted seven (7) days leave of absence exclusive of travel time to and from APO 927, effective on or about 3 July, 1943:

1st Lt. George E. MORGAN
39th Fighter Squadron

During the month of June, George flew two missions to Bena Bena escorting DC-3s. On one of the missions, they were recalled when reaching Mt. Yule due to enemy aircraft—dive-bombers with fighter escort—in the Wau area. No contact was made with the enemy. Six additional missions were to the Wau-Bulolo area patrolling ahead of the transports and returning with the last group. A supply mission escorting B-25s to and over Guadagasal was aborted at the rendezvous point when the bombers failed to show and could not be contacted by radio. His final mission for the month was a patrol over the "entire area of Lae, Salamaua, Bulolo, Wau, and the Ramu and Markham valleys without any enemy sightings."

July 1, 1943

Dear Mom,

I just found out a few minutes ago that I have been promoted to a first lieutenant. I have been expecting it, but I was surprised just the same. My gold bars were just about worn out, so I am darn glad to get the silver ones. Jay was over last night, and we went to the show.

*I will have to call him up and tell him the good
news.*

Love,

George

Lt. Col. Roy L. Scott, Mary's father, who was stationed in Cold Bay,
Alaska, wrote frequently to her during the war.

July 3, 1943

Dear Mary,

*Received your letter of May 13 today. Must
have gone around the world getting here. So
you are blue and lonesome. Well, dear, that is
the way most of us are. I had a bad spell of it
a while ago but found a remedy for it. I read a
story of a man who was in prison for 15 years.
Most of the men with that long a sentence go
crazy. He was asked why he had not, and he
explained it this way. Those who went crazy
thought from day to day of the 15 years and
how long it was. But the ones who lived each
day and did not think of how long they were to
be there came through all O.K. So I have tried
it, and it works. Try it out, little girl, and see if
it doesn't help. Things look good and have hopes
that it won't last much longer. Am still in the
hospital with this damn arthritis but expect to
get out soon. This is a good place to save money. Have saved $3,000 this year I've been here.
I wasn't going to tell mother but your brother,
Jim, gave it away so I sent it to her. I have
$1,000 marked for a trip when this is all over.
How about it—do you want to go with us? It*

will all be on land. I don't ever want to get on a boat again after I get back. Suppose Jim is getting married this month. Wish I could be there for it. Received a picture of Betty. Has been so long since I have seen her that it is hard for me to recognize her. Keep your chin up and it will soon be over.

Dad

Dear God
Please give me peace of mind
And in my work please let me find
Some kind of consolation,
I guess I've put up quite a bluff,
I thought I really had the stuff
To help them save our nation,
But now I find that I was blind,
and fully understand,
Without your help I cannot do
The many things they want me to
—and I need your helping hand.

—Written by an unknown nurse in the Southwest Pacific

This letter to her father was the first indication that a relationship was developing between Mary and George.

Dear Dad,

George came down on leave on July 3rd. He came to Gatton to spend his leave with me. The doctors let George have a room in their barracks. I was working, but I did get one day off while George was here which we spent in Ipswich. When I got off duty each day, we spent time together—bike riding, picnics, time in the nurse's reception lounge. If there was a dance, we danced.

Mary

In a letter to his mother, George makes mention meeting "an American nurse who loves to dance."

July 14, 1943

Dear Mom,

My leave to Brisbane was really swell. Ate steak and eggs practically every meal. Sometimes I couldn't get eggs so I just ate steak and chips (potatoes). Went to a number of dances and visited a number of Officers Clubs. Just about everywhere I went there were some fellows I knew so I always had company. Dated an American nurse and she loves to dance, so we got along very nice. I brought back a lot of old magazines, but new to us. Most of them were Pix, a magazine very much like Look. Also brought some sheets back, the best I could buy. The sheet I have is almost ratted to pieces. In a way I am glad to be back. With so much going on I don't want to miss any of it. Kind of exciting at times. I haven't shot any Japs down so far, but it hasn't been because I haven't tried. Grice and I are no longer together. He has gone to another outfit. It makes the first time in over a year we haven't been together.

Love,

George

A new all P-38 fighter group was being developed—the 475th activated at RAF Amberley Field in Australia, on May 14, 1943—and experienced fighter pilots from within the Fifth AF were being recruited.

From the 39th Fighter Squadron went John L. Ehlinger, Eugene I. Mc-
Guire, Arthur "Perry" L. Peregoy, Charles A. Grice, John K. Parkansky,
and William S. Jeakle. So, too, did George's good friend, Jack C. Mankin.

These men of the newly formed 475th remained at Amberley Field not
far from Mary, Patty, Fitzie, and Buckie of the 105th until mid-August.

July 14, 1943

Dear Mary,

*Here I am, home again. I really had a wonderful
time, even though you couldn't get any days off.
My luggage nearly broke my back before I finally reached my tent. The records came through
without a crack. I got to rest today, but tomorrow it's back to work. The tent is really lonely
without Perry and Grice, and what a mess they
left. I was folding their blankets (they left their
beds the way they got out of them) trying to
clean up the place, and I got that damn caterpillar itch I told you about all over my arms. I
pity whoever slept on them last. At present, everyone is reading the magazines I brought back.
I took it easy today, slept late (I had no one to
wake me), cleaned up the tent, and then slept
some more. There's not much more to write except to tell you how much I enjoyed my leave.
Tell Perry and the rest of the gang "Hello" for
me.*

Love,

George.

It was after George returned from his July leave that he crash-landed and was reported as missing in action. He developed engine trouble during a mission and had to land on a remote beach. Fortunately, he was not injured and was taken in by a missionary couple. He was located after 3 days.

July 16, 1943

Four planes took off here (Schwimmer) at 1355. It was an escort mission for the 8th Photo Squadron to Madang. Lieutenants Denton, Morgan, Andrews and Steele were the pilots. When arriving at the target, Lieutenant Morgan left the formation and is unaccounted for as yet. The other three proceeded with the mission. They had much trouble in locating Moresby area because of the weather. Lieutenant Andrews landed at 30 Mile. Lieutenant Denton landed at 17 Mile, and Lieutenant (James F.) Steele is also unaccounted for. Lieutenant Andrews landed at 30 Mile at 1730 and Denton landed at 17 Mile 1835.

July 17, 1943

Lieutenants Morgan and Steele are still unaccounted for.

July 18, 1943

Still no information as to the location of Morgan and Steele.

July 19, 1943

The good news for today was the returning of Lieutenant Morgan. He had crash-landed on the beach about 40 miles up the coast from Kerema. The natives took good care of him and the "Tiger Moth" picked him up. Lieutenant Morgan was still in the best of health. Lieutenant Steele is still missing.

Piloting the "Tiger Moth," a De Havilland DH82, was Flight Sergeant Flannery of the RAAF No. 1 Rescue and Communication Flight, commanded by Squadron Leader Alexander "Jerry" A. Pentland—an Australian ace of World War 1. Lieutenant James F. Steele was later reported as killed in action.

Mary had been told George was missing before word came that he was found. He wrote to her at his first opportunity.

July 20, 1943

Dear Mary,

I am sorry I haven't written sooner, but it hasn't been possible. I had quite an experience a few days ago, but everything came out OK. You might have heard why but if you haven't, you'll just have to take my word for it.

My experiences in the last few days are hard to believe. I didn't have any hardships as Rauch did, but I don't want to go through it again.

I sent Mom a cablegram so she would know I am in the best of health and I am all right. She'll have to wait until I get home for the details. My brother, Jay, came over yesterday to see me, and we had a nice talk. It was the first time he had seen me since I was down there with you. He had been slightly worried about me.

There is a radio program coming in from the

States that's pretty good. Glen Miller was on a few minutes ago and Ginny Simms before.

I wish you would thank Capt. (John J.) Kneisel and Maj. (John H.) Harrison for me for being so nice while I was down there with you. They are two swell guys.

For now as always,

Love,

George.

From his letters to both his mother and to Mary, it was obvious he could not tell them about the crash due to censorship of the outgoing mail. Before receiving George's letters, his parents learned something had happened when a telegram arrived from George telling them to "ignore all reports—am well and safe." A few days later, they received an official telegram stating George was missing in action.

July 21, 1943

Dear Mom,

Had an interesting day at work today. I took part in a darn good fight. Although I shot at plenty of them, I didn't shoot any down myself, but I saw others that did. Went to church last Sunday under very unusual circumstances. I was staying with some missionaries. A middle-aged couple from Samoa had charge of the place. At church, I was the only white person. There were about a hundred natives. The women had only grass skirts on, and the men had cloth skirts. The missionary couple from Samoa wore regular clothes. I was their "guest" for about 3 days, and they really treated me wonderfully.

Love,

George

And to Mary . . .

July 22 1943

Dear Mary,

Those 3 days I was a "guest" of a couple of missionaries weren't bad at all, but I don't want to go through it again. Yesterday, I was in a nice fight, but I wasn't lucky enough to get one. Although we got off to a bad start, we did OK before it was over. Tell Perry he should have been here, I know he would have enjoyed it. I have a good chance of getting some pictures for you. I'm almost certain—don't say what you are thinking—my leave will come sometime in October, so be careful when you go on night duty. I understand Perry and the others are being kept pretty busy. Our work is picking up, too, so time seems to be passing fast. I will close for now. Don't work too hard.

Love,

George

July 23, 1943

Today's action brought the squadron's enemy planes destroyed to 109.

WESTERN UNION—1943 Jul 23 AM 9 02

NLT MRS. JAY L. MORGAN = AM WELL AND SAFE IGNORE ALL REPORTS LOVE = GEORGE MORGAN

Postal Telegraph— GOVT = WMU WASHINGTON DC JULY 24 118P

= MRS STELLA S. MORGAN = I REGRET TO INFORM YOU THAT THE COMMANDING GENERAL SOUTHWEST PACIFIC AREA RE-PORTS YOUR SON FIRST LIEUTENANT GEORGE E MORGAN MISSING IN ACTION SINCE SIXTEEN JULY IF FURTHER DETAILS OR OTHER INFORMATION OF HIS STATUS ARE RECEIVED YOU WILL BE PROMPTLY NOTIFIED = ULIO THE ADJUTANT GENER-AL 133P =

George's family later learned the details of this episode from a letter his mother received from his friend's wife, Patricia Mankin.

Dear Mrs. Morgan,

George's little episode of being listed as missing was a picnic to him—and to him only according to the way we felt. He had a bit of motor trouble and landed on a sandy beach. It is rumored that the missionary and his wife took exceptionally good care of him. The wife fed him roast duck, let him sleep in her feather bed, and even went as far as to draw hot baths for him. Needless to say, the boys all have that particular spot marked on their maps.

Patricia

By July 23, 1943, the combat diary of the 39th states that the squadron had downed 109 Japanese planes, the highest kill score to date in the Pacific war and, at the time, the highest score for all American units in the European theater as well.

July 24, 1943

Dear Mom,

Had some interesting experiences this past week. Had Jay worried for a couple of days, but everything came out OK. I came damn close to getting a Jap the other day, but I wasn't fast enough. Got some good hits on him and before I could make another pass another kid knocked him down. We really gave them hell, and we didn't have anyone get hurt, but that's nothing unusual. This outfit's record is tops over here, and we think in all the U.S. Army Forces. We passed the hundred mark last week. It's an out-fit anyone would be proud to be in.

Love,

George

Lieutenant Morgan's friend Gene McGuire stopped before going on leave in Australia. George asked him to hand deliver a letter to Mary.

July 24, 1943

Dear Mary,

(Eugene I.) McGuire came in this afternoon, so I am going to send this letter down by him. In a way, I envy those guys down there, but I am satisfied with this outfit. I had hoped you wouldn't hear of my "little" experience until you knew I was all right. It was the closest call I have ever had. When I had my motor cut out, I was directly over Madang. I had to fly almost 2½ hours on single engine before it started to

get dark. Near the place I crash-landed was a mission run by a middle-aged couple from Samoa. As you heard, they treated me very well. I couldn't make it all the way back here because of the weather. There were four of us that started out and one of the fellows, Lt. (James F.) Steele was lost in the weather, and we haven't heard from him since. The weather has been very bad for the last 2 weeks, and it's always a problem of where to land returning from a mission. We have been getting darn good food recently, and when we return from a mission, the Red Cross sends Cokes (one each) for the ones flying. Have you started knitting my red socks yet? Red is easy to keep up with, but I will have to watch the natives. Be good and I will keep on trying to be the oldest pilot—

Love,

George

WAR DEPARTMENT, U.S. ARMY AIR FORCES, REPORT OF AIR-CRAFT ACCIDENT, July 30, 1943

1. The Accident Classification Committee, 35th Fighter Group, met to consider the accident of Lt. Morgan. Verbal statements were received from Major Lynch, Commanding Officer, and Lt. Cella, Engineering Officer, 39th Fighter Squadron.

2. Lt. Morgan states that while over Madang at 25,000 feet, pulling 34 inches of manifold pressure, the left engine commenced to backfire, at which time by throttling back to 20 inches of manifold pressure the backfire was only occasional, at 15 to 20 second intervals. After 15 minutes of this type operation, continuous backfiring necessitated feathering of left propeller, at which time the belly tanks were dropped. En route to home base, heavy

weather conditions were encountered making it impossible to get through. Because of coming darkness crash landing was made upon an island sandbar.

a. Major Lynch and Lt. Cella concur in the above.

3. The left ignition harness probably failed causing the backfiring of left engine which probably broke loose pieces from the intercooler which eventually blocked the carburetor intake scoop and choked the engine until it stopped.

4. No recommendations.

July 30, 1943

Dear Mary,

This is another short note to you by special messenger. I wrote you a regular letter last night. I will try not to repeat here too much I said earlier. I was over where "Jump" is day before yesterday. I didn't have time to go over to the camp where he was as we had a mission to fly right away, but I did get to talk to him over the phone. I thought we would come back that night, and I planned to stay with him. He didn't know I was all right until he received my call. The last he had heard about me was while he was down there (Amberley Field) and you know what that was. He told me about the debate regarding what to tell you. How did they go about it when they did decide? I didn't fly today because they had a board meeting on my crash landing. I didn't get any blame at all. I told them what happened and Major (Thomas J.) Lynch told them it was impossible for me to

*get back because of the bad weather. I don't
know if I told you, but they tried to call us and
tell us all to bail out. I couldn't hear it because
I had to turn my radio off to conserve the battery (ask Perry about that). Lt. Steele, who is
still missing, apparently didn't hear it either.
We are hoping he will still walk back. I'm not
kidding now but after flying around on one engine for 2 hours and crash landing, I was really
tired that night. I like the way things are now.
We are flying every other day. I wouldn't mind
if we only had one day off in three. We are
having the worst weather we have had since I
have been up here, but because we are contact-
ing the Japs more often, it makes flying more
interesting. Our squadron had 109 Jap planes
to its credit. "Jump's" outfit (9th FS, 49th FG) is
ahead of us now but we were the first to break
a hundred. We had our decoration formation
tonight. I got the air medal officially. I took
it off as soon as the formation broke up. I will
wait until I get home to wear it. I will say good
night for now.*

Love,

George

During the month and on a mission to Kamantum, George and fellow pilots sighted other P-38s and P-40s attacking 15 enemy aircraft and
joined the fight. George claimed "0" and thus, was unable to open his
bottle of rum upon his return to base.

George's other missions for the month of July were two missions escorting transports to Bena Bena and Garoka with George and Lt. Lee
Haigler returning early on the second mission due to "left engine difficul-

ties" and landing at 7 Mile. Both aircraft returned to 14 Mile (Schwimmer) the next day.

August 4, 1943

At 1330, 16 P-38s were scrambled on an interception at Marilinan and a fighter sweep over Markham River. Lt. Rothgeb in No. 10 crashed when both his engines cut out in landing at 1340. Rothgeb was able to get out of the burning plane but was burned on his face and hands. He was immediately removed to the hospital. Because of the damage to the runway on Rothgeb's crash, the planes were ordered to land at 7 Mile and await repairs to our field.

August 9, 1943

Dear Mary,

I am sorry to hear your father is ill. I hope everything works out OK for him. I imagine the cold up there is worse than the heat is here. Being from the South, I am fairly use to the heat. As for Grice's story about the "hot bath, feather bed, and roast duck" (he forgot to mention the roast English pheasant), I deny it. The bed was just an ordinary mattress. I don't remember what I ate, but it was probably chicken. It just goes to show you how stories change. If you insist, I will ask the guys to stop referring to you as "Morgan's girl." After all, you do have your reputation to think of. If you see any lightweight leather gloves, I wish you would get them for me. They would have to be lightweight or I couldn't use them. I think you know what I want them for. My hands nearly froze today as

well as my feet, but the "loud" socks I have help.
I saw a good cowboy picture tonight—Valley of
the Sun. As usual, I am looking for a letter.

Love,

George.

In a letter to his father, George referred to the transfer of his brother, Jay, who had left Port Moresby the previous month. He also explained that any rumors about his drinking too much were unfounded. He mentions that Eva, his sister, had worked as a volunteer for the Red Cross during the war.

August 11, 1943

Dear Dad,

Haven't heard from Jay since he moved. I've
done more work since returning from leave
than in the preceding 2 months. I've sent home
about $1,850. In about a year, I should have a
couple thousand more put away. I think mother
has the idea from someone that I drink a lot. I
don't. I've only been really drunk once. She has
been referring to it quite a bit lately. I know it
shouldn't, but it does make me mad sometimes. I
guess she doesn't realize we use real bullets over
here. Eva is still working with the Red Cross at
home, and the Red Cross does some good work
for us over here.

Love,

George

The 475th Fighter Group began the move to New Guinea—starting at Port Moresby. George wrote to Mary. Except for training missions the 39th had a quiet month.

August 12, 1943

Hello, Darling,

Thank you for the one red sock, the picture of us, and the book to keep it in, the first lieutenant bars, and the flints for my lighter. Guess which one I like the best? The picture, of course. I saw Perry and McGuire last night and Jack the night before last. Perry and I had a nice long talk. Guess what the favorite topic was? (Andrew K.) Kish and (Edward C.) Flood told me about meeting you. They said you all were having quite a party. Perry has something of Fitz's. To be one of the gang, I think I should have something of yours. How about one of your insignias? Think you can spare one? I'm pretty sure I will get down there sometime this month so I hope you can avoid night duty this time. Not much news from this way so I will close by saying there is someone up here that misses you.

Love,

George

The 40th and 41st Squadrons moved to Tsili Tsili. The 39th remained at Nadzab.

August 16, 1943

Hello, Mary,

OK, so you won't send me any pictures! You had better hide your album then because I will probably make a "raid" on it if given the chance. By the way, that native that takes care of my tent likes to read your letters, too—she's an Oxford graduate. What were some of the other stories Perry told? Do you realize that Andy, Jack, and now Perry have all worn the pair of pinks that fit me, and I have only worn the pair that don't! There "ain't" no justice! I guess Perry needed clothes as bad as I did when he first arrived. I am afraid Perry wasn't telling the truth about the native cleaning up the tent. We don't need anyone since we spend so little time there. From what the fellows said, I guess the rumor is still going around that I slept on a feather bed. Again, I deny it. It was on just an ordinary bed.

I hope to see you soon and please have the beer on ice.

Love,

George

August 17, 1943

The mission today was a 16-ship escort mission combined with the P-38s of five other squadrons, escorting B-25s to Wewak on a bombing and strafing mission. When arriving at target the enemy was taken by surprise and heavy damage was done to grounded aircraft and some personnel. There was no fighter opposition as was expected and probably caused by the surprise attack. This mission was considered a very successful mission and was done without loss to any of our aircraft, either bomber or fighter.

Mary received a letter from her brother, 1st Sgt. James W. Scott, telling her about his recent marriage.

Berkeley, Calif.

August 17, 1943

Dear Mary,

I'm going to attempt to tell you about my wedding to Ethel (Ethel M. Fraser, daughter of Alex D. and Elizabeth C. Fraser). I arrived in Sauk Centre, Saturday, July 17th, and Mother, Betty, and I drove to Grafton, North Dakota. Tuesday morning, Ethel and I went down to the courthouse to get the marriage license and the county judge wasn't going to issue it because I had my blood test taken in California. We finally convinced him it was perfectly legal, and he issued the license. The wedding was held that afternoon in the Episcopal Church right next to the Fraser's house. About 4:30, Ethel changed into her traveling clothes and just as she came out, our friends grabbed us and put us into a two-wheeled trailer they had decorated. The trailer (and Ethel and I) was hitched to a car and we were hauled all over town followed by a bunch of cars all honking their horns. We felt awfully foolish, but it was actually fun. I suppose Mother has written you and told you that Dad is coming back to the States. She is just tickled pink. I'll close for now.

Love,

Jim

HEADQUARTERS THIRTY-FIFTH FIGHTER GROUP, UNITED STATES ARMY AIR FORCES, APO No. 929, 11 August 1943. Special Orders No. 47: With the concurrence of the CG, Fifth Air Force, APO 925, and per VOCG, V Fighter Command, APO 929, the following named officers, Air Corps, 39th Fighter Squadron, are granted seven (7) days leave of absence, exclusive of travel time to and from APO 927, effective on or about 18 August 1943:

1st LIEUT. WILLIAM W. ANDERSON JR.
1st LIEUT. JOSEPH F. FOREST
1st LIEUT. GEORGE E. MORGAN

The August missions for George were primarily for the purpose of escorting transports to Bena Bena, Garoka, Bulldog, Marilinan, Mt. Hagen, Wau, Bulolo, and Tsili Tsili. B-25s were escorted to Madang, Finschhafen, and Wald Bay.

At the last two locations, the P-38 pilots, to include George, also assisted the B-25s in their missions of barge hunting. Two B-17s of the 8th Photo Squadron were escorted to and from the south coast area of New Britain.

On a day following the surprise attack on Wewak, B-24s were escorted in their attack on the area. These missions were uneventful.

September 3, 1943

16 pilots took off at 0715 this morning to escort transports to Tsili Tsili. Major Lynch, Captain King, and Lts. Mettler, Clymer, Salmon, Anderson, Walters, Hollabaugh, Bills, Tansing, Rogers, Vining, Dunbar, Morgan, Randall, and Dorsey. All of the planes and pilots remained at Tsili Tsili and remained on the ground alert the rest of this day and staying there overnight.

September 4, 1943

The 18 of our planes at Tsili Tsili were scrambled three times today. The third time they met the enemy (over Malahang). The only certain victory was two for Major Lynch. Lt. Dorsey is missing from this mission, and all of the other planes returned back there at the home base.

The transport missions of September 3rd and 4th were in preparation for the paratroop landings near Lae scheduled for September 5th. The escorting P-38s of the 39th remained at Tsili Tsili with the transports and paratroopers for the purpose of protecting them from an air attack by the enemy.

September 5, 1943

Major Lynch led the flight of 16 P-38s covering the transports to Lae. Takeoff time was at 0850, and the landing time was at 1150. The target area was covered from 1020 to 1030 at about 2,000 feet. There were no enemy aircraft (encountered) on this mission and the operation was carried out as planned without any air resistance at all. Major Lynch, Lt. Tansing, Smith, and Shipley all returned early due to mechanical failures.

September 6, 1943

Dear Mary,

This will be a short note. Short because I am as tired as I have ever been. I want you to know that I haven't written before because I haven't had the chance. You have read what has been going on around here, I know, and that explains it. I see Jack almost every day now. Mary, if I promise to write a long letter the first chance I get, will you understand this short note? I hope so. I have to work again in the morning, so the way it is—I just have to go to bed. Until later then—as always,

Love,

George

September 20, 1943

16 P-38s took off at 0745 to complete a fighter sweep (at 28,000 ft.) over Wewak and Boram, prior to the run of the bombers. The pilots were Capts. King, Sullivan, and Stanch, and Lts. Morgan, Rogers, Anderson, Prentice, Walters, Haigler, Tansing, Smith, Lockhart, Dunbar, Cella, Kish, and Duncan. Lt. Morgan returned at 0825, left turbo out; Lt. Cella at 1135, engines cutting out. Due to the weather, planes landed at different places, Tsili Tsili, Dobodura, 7 Mile, and 30 Mile. Later, all planes returned to our base except the two at 7 Mile, which remained there overnight. Capt. Sullivan could not be located at any strip and has been reported as missing. Word has been received that Major Lynch is to return to the States, possibly leaving tomorrow.

September 20, 1943

Dear Mary,

I received three wonderful letters today. Now I can tell Jack I have heard from one of the mob. As you know, I see him at least once a day as his bunch is eating their meals with us. We had the show Human Comedy tonight, and I am all wet with mud added. As tonight was the only chance we will have to see it, we went, although it was raining. Andy and I had a blanket over our shoulders, but the rain soon soaked through. It poured down for part of the show, but no one left. I have been wearing the red socks, and they fit fine, no kidding, and they feel wonderful when it really gets cold. I haven't opened the rum yet—but from the looks of things, I will have plenty of chances. Take care of yourself and have a good time for both of us.

As always—

Love,

George

September 22, 1943

14 P-38s took off at 0628 for Dobodura. At 0920, the planes took off from Dobodura to patrol (shipping) over Finschhafen (at 10,000 ft.). The pilots were Capts. King and Stanch, Lts. Morgan, Randall, Anderson, Prentice, Smith, Forest, Andrews, Duncan, Baker, Kramme, Kish, and Tansing. At 1245, about 30 miles SE of Finschhafen, a number of Zekes and Oscars intercepted the flights. In the fight, seven Japs were destroyed, one probable, and two damaged. Capt. King has one destroyed and one probable; Capt. Stanch has two certain; Lt. Anderson one certain; Lt. Smith one certain and one damaged; Lt. Kramme one certain; Lt. Forest one certain; and Lt. Morgan one damaged. Lt. Forest is missing from the fight. It is believed that Lt. Forest crashed into a Zeke, tearing off part of his wing and crashed in the water. Lt. Dunbar and Rogers took off at 1315 to search the Ramu Valley for Capt. Sullivan.

POSTAL TELEGRAPH—GOVT = WASHINGTON, DC—1943 Sep 22 PM 7

MRS STELLA S. MORGAN = I AM PLEASED TO INFORM YOU THAT THE COMMANDING GENERAL SOUTHWEST PACIFIC AREA RE-PORTS YOUR SON FIRST LIEUTENANT GEORGE E MORGAN WHO WAS PREVIOUSLY REPORTED MISSING SINCE SIXTEEN JULY RE-TURNED TO DUTY NINETEEN JULY = ULIO THE ADJUTANT GEN-ERAL

September 25, 1943

Lt. Rogers made a search mission for Captain Sullivan but no good luck.

September 26, 1943

Dear Mary,

I have been in two fights. First, when the Aussies landed at Lae—was plenty rough. I almost didn't live up to my motto. We lost (Harry N.) Dorsey in that fight. The second, when they landed at Finschhafen, was a damn good fight. I lost my roommate (Joseph E.) Forest. He rammed a Zero and never got out of his plane. I saw both when they got it. Capt. Sully is also missing, but there are possibilities of him walking back. The mission today made my seventy-fifth. Now I am a "senior birdsman" or something. I have gotten so I never fly without the gloves. Now I don't get my hands scratched up, and more important, they are warm. It doesn't make any difference what I wear, my feet still get cold. They nearly froze today. As you probably know, things are get-

ting rough here. Perry can tell you about it. He is staying in the tent with us tonight—in his old place. It's really nice to have him around again. We went to a show earlier called The Flacon's Brother—not bad. I am writing this on the table with the Victrola. Every time it is cranked, I have to stop writing. I put in 4½ hours today and tomorrow it will be worse or longer anyway. Andy is yelling at me to go to bed and since it is late, maybe I'd better. Take care. As always.

Love,

George

With the exception of a few eventful missions, escort duty again prevailed for George during September. Transports were escorted to Tsili Tsili, B-24s to Wewak, and B-25s to Madang, Bogadjim, Wewak, and Mt. Hagen.

On October 12, 1943, 17 pilots of the 39th FS and one pilot from 35th FG escorted B-24s to attack enemy shipping in Simpson Harbor at Rabaul, New Britain. Captains King and Stanch, Lieutenants Cella, Shipley, Mettler, Larson, Rogers, Round, Denton, Vining, Flood, Rothgeb, Dunbar, Duncan, Clymer, Lockhart, Morgan, and Major Gallup took off at 0640 landing at Kiriwina to refuel.

Taking off again, they made their rendezvous with the bombers. All then proceeded to the target where the bombers dropped their bombs over the harbor. Flying at 25,000 to 30,000 feet, the results were unobserved by the squadron.

All the planes flew directly back to their base after escorting the bombers back to within 50 miles of Buna. Lieutenants Round, Vining, and Clymer returned early due to various aircraft malfunctions.

The remaining 15 planes returned at 1430. The four P-38s that had remained overnight at Dobodura also participated in the Rabaul attack.

This flight led by Lieutenant Andrews with Lieutenants Prentice, Smith, and Anderson, escorted B-25s to Rapopo Air Strip at Rabaul.

Lieutenant Prentice was forced to return to Dobodura shortly after takeoff because of mechanical difficulties. This flight left Dobodura at 0800, refueled at Kiriwina, and took off again for Rabaul.

The three planes completed their mission and returned to our base at 1400. Lieutenant Prentice returned from Dobodura late in the day.

October 14, 1943

There was very good word received today that Captain Sullivan was all right and that he was coming in. Capt. Sullivan has been missing since September 20th.

October 19, 1943

Captain Sullivan who had been missing since Sept. 20th returned to camp and had a thrilling story to tell about his 24 days in the jungle before reaching an Aussie camp.

October 29, 1943

The first mission was an escort for the B-24s to Rabaul. We had 14 ships, and they engaged the enemy with Captain King shooting down two enemy aircraft, Lt. Prentice getting one. Vining and Lockhart got a probable each, and Morgan getting a damaged one. Their takeoff time from here was 0700. They landed at Kiriwina to and from the target. Captain King and Prentice landed at Dobodura, Anderson at Kiriwina, and then back to Dobodura, and Lockhart landed at Kiriwina with one engine feathered. The plane lost all the oil out, and not from enemy action.

October 30, 1943

Dear Mary,

Yesterday was a hell of a day. I got wet (sweat) about 8:30 a.m. and could not put on dry clothes until after supper. Coming home in the afternoon, we had to get so high that my clothes started to freeze. In the morning, although we were all working, Perry, Grice, and myself got together. Perry and Grice didn't get wet, but that didn't stop them from kidding me. I couldn't have gotten wetter if I had gone in swimming with all my clothes on. The work we've been doing isn't the easiest on our nerves. Our bunch out of the old "17th" (Amberley Field 1942) is taking a beating, isn't it? It used to be that whenever I went over to the other side (other side of the Owen Stanley Mountains, i.e., Dobodura), I would see a bunch of them. I saw Ralph the other day. He has changed a lot—he seems to be worrying a hell of a lot. T. D. and Lidstrum were two of his closest friends. Parkansky stayed up in the tent last night. We are going to start charging rent. We supply clothes, towels, soap, shirts, mosquito net, bed (with air mattress), and cigarettes. It cost "Parky" a quart of whisky to settle his "debt." Really though, we enjoy having the fellows stay with us. About 3 days ago, I received a letter from you that was written while you were on night duty—the first night. You mentioned that the next day began your third year in the army. In case you are wondering, the letter was written April 30th. It must have gone the long way around. I bet Pat and Jack have been having a big time. Jack didn't tell me the big news, but I understand what you meant. What do you mean that you and Fitz are really sweating this out? I bet Pat is the least concerned of the three. You should have seen the bunch of us that got together for a few minutes the other day. There was "Jump," Ralph, Perry, Grice, (John L.) Ehlinger, Anderson, and myself standing around talking. It wasn't about women (for once) as at that moment we were just sweating. You would not have known us for the conversation. I have seen the show The More the Merrier. I know what you mean about it being hard on the morale. I think it was one of the best pictures I've seen in a long time.

Love,

George

George participated in three additional missions escorting B-24s to Rabaul. On one of the missions, he returned early after landing at Kiriwina due to supercharger trouble. The other two Rabaul missions were cancelled due to weather. An interception mission to Dobodura and an escort mission for transports to Gusap were completed. No enemy sightings.

November 5, 1943

Captain Sullivan checked out in a 38 today. This is the first time he has been up since his stay in the jungle. (He had to pump his wheels down.)

November 7, 1943

13 planes escorted the B-24s to Rabaul (at 23,000 ft.). They took off from Dobodura. Lt. Prentice claims one enemy plane probably destroyed. That is all the claims we make, but the Japs (got) Quinones and probably Round. Quinones was seen to bail out over enemy territory, but Round seemed to disappear in midair. All the rest of the planes returned to Dobodura.

HEADQUARTERS, FIFTH AIR FORCE, APO 925, 8 November 1943. General Orders No. 264. II.

AWARDS OF THE DISTINGUISHED FLYING CROSS.
By direction of the President, under the provisions of the Act of Congress approved 2 July 1926 (Bulletin 8, W.D., 1926), a Distinguished Flying Cross is awarded by the Commanding General, Fifth Air Force, to the following named officers:

First Lieutenant GEORGE E. MORGAN (0662970), 39th Fighter Squadron, 35th Fighter Group, Air Corps, United States Army. For operational flight missions from 4 May 1943 to 26 September 1943. Home address: Mrs. Stella S. Morgan (Mother), 1808 N. Parkway, Memphis, Tennessee.

The citation is as follows:
For heroism in flight and exceptional and outstanding accomplishment in the face of great danger above and beyond the line of duty. These operations consisted of over fifty missions including escorting bombers and transport aircraft, interception and attack missions, and patrol and reconnaissance flights. In the course of these operations, strafing and bombing attacks were made from dangerously low altitudes, destroying and damaging enemy installations and equipment.

George's next leave was in November 1943. On November 8, George and Mary got to spend a day at the beach at Southport.

November 13, 1943

Lt. Andrews and Haigler were escorting a F5 to Rabaul this morning (t/o 0905). The mission was incomplete be-

cause of the bad weather and Lt. Haigler hasn't been heard from since.

George wrote this letter shortly after being appointed as a squadron leader. He continued in missions against Wewak and escorting bombers to and from Rabaul.

November 15, 1943

Dear Mom,

Saw Jay while on leave. He has been running around more—just what he needs. Today's my birthday. It makes about 3 days over a year I have been in this part of the world. This leave was great. I spent most of my time near a wonderful beach. We had a cottage so we didn't have to do anything we didn't like. Spent most of the time in bathing suits. It's been a long time since I enjoyed anything as much. The beach was better than any I have ever seen. There are so many fellows that have come over since I have that I am beginning to feel like an old "vet." As far as experience goes, I am now one of the old boys.

Love,

George

George wrote to Mary reflecting his unhappiness about the 39th FS losing the P-38s to the P-47s.

November 17, 1943

Dear Mary,

I am not in a good mood tonight. I don't know when I have felt worse. You remember what I told you when Anderson and I went out to see you. You keep on wearing that P-38 pin anyway. It will always be my true love, no matter what. I know you must know how I feel. I can't seem to write. I think you understand why. You could cut the "gloom" around here with a knife. Thanks, Darling, for a wonderful leave.

As always,

Love

George

Nurses Quarters
U.S. Army 105th General Hospital, Gatton Australia
November 9, 1943

1st Lt. George E. Morgan and 2nd Lt. Mary L. Scott outside her quarters following a chicken dinner prepared for George by Fitz, Patty, and Mary.

Chapter 11
Japan Goes on the Defensive

The success of the Fifth Air Force in the Battle of the Bismarck Sea dealt a fatal blow to the Japanese in New Guinea. Unable to reinforce and supply troops in the region, the Japanese were put on the defensive.

Pilots from the 39th, including Captain George Morgan, continued to bomb, strafe, and make life miserable for Japanese units at Wewak and Rabaul. As one of the more experienced pilots in the squadron, George Morgan helped train the new pilots in the art of air war.

November 19, 1943

Thirteen P-38s were flown to Dobodura to be transferred to the 475th Fighter Group. The pilots were Major King, Captain Denton, and Lieutenants Cella, Morgan, Kish, Andrews, Smith, Widmann, Randall, Duncan, Rogers, and Walters.

The *Post Record*, Australia's Biggest American Newspaper—November 19, 1943 (Official unit newsletter of the U.S. Army 105th General Hospital)—"What a wonderful thing a woman's hair. By it you may keep track of her social life. For example, Mary Scott: Now her hair is pulled back in a knot; last week her tresses cascaded triumphantly on her shoulders."

November 20, 1943

We received our first P-47 today. We got one from the 35th Fighter Squadron.

> *November 20, 1943*
>
> *Dear Mary,*
>
> *I am in a better mood than the other night. It's something we can do nothing about, so it's no use going around with a long face. I sat through the show Sing Your Troubles Away last night in a downpour. Although I had a raincoat, I would have been as well off without one. I haven't done anything useful since I got back—play cards and read most of the time. I don't know what it is, but I just can't sit down and write like I used to. I dropped in to see Perry and Grice yesterday, but they were both out, so, of course, I didn't get to talk to any of them. Jack should know about Patty going home. I told a friend of his to tell him. It seems as if I am back in school again with all the stuff we have to read and learn because of this change we are making. I'm going to close now, I'm the Officer of the Day tonight, and the lights will be out before I finish my rounds.*
>
> *Take care—*
>
> *Love,*
>
> *George*

November 21, 1943

Our last two P-38s were flown to Dobodura today. We also got two more 47s from the 35th Squadron, making our total of three airplanes today. Several of the pilots checked out in them today.

> *November 26, 1943*
>
> *Dear Mary,*
>
> *I hope you had as good a dinner yesterday as we did. Ours was about the best I have eaten in the army. Perry stayed with me the other night, and "Jump" came by to see me before he left, but I was just getting ready to take off when he drove up. Take care of yourself for me and here's hoping for more fun next year.*
>
> *Love,*
>
> *George*

November 27, 1943

About all we are still doing is checking out in the 47s.

November 29, 1943

Still quiet!

November 30, 1943

We got three more 47s today to make the total of six now. The pilots are still checking out in the 47s.

December 1, 1943

One more 47 today. Lt. Baker returned from down south and tells us that Lt. Hollabaugh went into a spin in his 47 while taking off at Eagle Farm. He was burned bad. The other pilots that are here are still doing the checking out in the 47s.

> *December 1, 1943*
>
> *Hello, Dear,*
>
> *You should see Anderson today—complaining on the same subject we all are. I received your letter of November 20th today. The article in the "scandal sheet" (105th newsletter) is cute but, of course, I do not understand.*
>
> *Love,*
>
> *George*

December 2, 1943

The training program is still underway.

December 2, 1943

Have been taking things easy the last couple of weeks. Have been sleeping until around ten nearly every morning. Probably be working hard again soon. A notice came out on the bulletin board the other day that said I have been awarded the Distinguished Flying Cross. It's being given to me for having made 50 combat missions in excess of the 25 for which I was given the Air Medal. I have 96 combat missions. The older boys have between 160 and 200. I am not flying the P-38 anymore. I am flying the P-47 (Thunderbolt). I don't think I will ever fly a plane that I will like as much as I did the 38. I felt more at home in the 38 than I do in my tent. In my opinion, it is the world's best fighter plane. Our Thanksgiving dinner was tops. Turkey with all the trimmings. It really was the best possible.

December 3, 1943

Dear Mary,

Jack is here so I will write this before he leaves. I loved the pictures you sent of us at Southport. Do you think we can go again? Don't be surprised if I should get back down there around the first of January; it's not impossible. The name I have thought up for this airplane I am now flying expresses what I really think of it—"The One-Holer." Truthfully, it's no comparison to my favorite airplane. We are doing practically no flying, just an hour or less a day in the new planes. We haven't had a single combat mission since I returned. I hate to think of flying combat in these crates. When we move is anyone's guess. It will probably be as soon as we get enough planes. Take care of yourself and think of me.

Love,

George

December 4, 1943

39th Fighter Squadron Training Program was still in full swing today.

December 5, 1943

Darling,

We have been doing very little work, and it makes the time go by much slower. Maybe I just miss being down there with you. Things are all messed up regarding leaves so nothing at this time is certain. Major Lynch has been over to see us tonight. From some of the things I have heard, I'm not sure just how bad I want to get back to the States. From the latest "dope" we've heard, I needn't worry about it until July.

Love,

George

December 6, 1943

Dear Mary,

Perry told me he would be here tomorrow, but now I find out he is leaving in the morning. He can explain the circumstances. My pictures turned out very well. Perry was going to bring the negatives down to you so you could have prints made for yourself, but the way things are I will bring them. One of my favorites is the one I took when we were sitting on the concrete pipe down the road from the railroad station. We are still in the same place and will probably remain for some time. The 47s aren't too bad, but doesn't compare to the 38s. The mosquitos are about to eat me up so I better close.

As ever—

Love,

George

A Combat Squadron of P-47 Thunderbolts
39th FS, 35th FG, 5th AAF
Over the Markham Valley, New Guinea
July 28, 1944

Leading the squadron, Capt. Leland P. Vining is followed by flight leaders Capt. William L. Urquhart, Capt. Wayne P. Rothgeb, and Capt. Lewis Lockhart. Following the squadron and flight leaders are Lts. Robert A. Mittlestadt, Richard L. Ross, Kenneth M. Dunn, Howard G. Newmann, Carl A. Rymer, James C. Steele, Robert Rohrs, Marcus Trout, Robert W. Querns, Forrest E. Lynn, Frederick G. Tobi, and James J. Querns.

This photograph was taken from a Douglas P-70 Nighthawk flown by the 39th FS Squadron Commander, Captain Richard T. Cella

December 8, 1943

Hello, Darling,

Perry pulled a fast one last night. He was sure he could be here today. He didn't stay with me last night, and that kind of messed things up. My pictures turned out better than expected. The one of you and I standing on the steps of the nurses quarters is especially good. I will bring the negatives when I come. It's raining like hell outside, so I guess I won't be flying today. I don't really care because I have gotten so I enjoy flying this "crate." However, flying and fighting are two different things. We have been having fun just playing around as we haven't been able to do since we've been here.

As ever—

Love,

George

December 10, 1943

The training flights in the 47s was all we had today, too. Lt. (John C.) Price, one of the newer pilots, made a crash landing at 12 Mile. The plane was a total wreck. The pilot was injured somewhat. He had to make a dead-stick landing at the Berry Field, when circling here (14 Mile) for a landing.

December 10, 1943

Dear Mary,

"Jump" must have gotten home very quick. Andy's mother said he called her while he was in

San Francisco. I'm glad to hear Patty has made her trip home okay. From what Jack told me, they should be together again soon. Have you received a letter from her yet? I'm sending you a picture we took of Capt. Sullivan when he returned after 24 days in the jungle. He had lost over 30 pounds. He has returned to the States now. His story would make a good motion picture. Fights with headhunters and whatnot.

Love,

George

U.S. Army 105th General Hospital
Gatton, Queensland, Australia
1943

"The Scrapbooks"

Lieutenants: Jack C. Mankin, 9th FS, 49th FG; Patricia (Knapp) Mankin, 105th; George E. Morgan, 39th FS, 35th FG; and Mary L. Scott, 105th.

Mrs. Jack C. Mankin (the former 2nd Lt. Patricia M. Knapp), wrote the following letter to George's mother, bringing her up to date on her son's activities in Australia.

> *December 11, 1943*
>
> *Dear Mrs. Morgan,*
>
> *I have just returned from Australia where I knew George very well. He was down on leave when I left and asked me to write and tell you a number of things. I assured George I would be very glad to do it. When George first came over, he joined my husband's squadron for a couple of months. At that time they were stationed at Amberley Field, Ipswich, which is just 30 miles west of Brisbane. George came up to one of our dances, and that is how we met him. He started coming up often with Jack after that, and by the time the boys left, George and Mary, Perry and Fitzie, and Jack and I were thick as thieves. It has been that way ever since. After the first of the year, the squadron (17th FS (P)) was broken up and the boys scattered to the four winds. George joined the 39th Squadron that was at Port Moresby and has been there until just recently. When I left, George had been on 96 missions and by now must be over 100. They usually escort the medium bombers on the raids. But there are several P-38 squadrons up there so you can't tell if it is George or not that is along, and every once in a while they have a day off. So it is practically impossible to be sure they are on a particular raid—unless it is a very big one, and*

then everyone goes along.

George was along on both the Big Wewak and Rabaul raids. George sailed over Rabaul at 29,000 feet, and Jack at 1,000 feet, and us gals are uncertain as to just which one was the most scared. Apparently height doesn't make much difference. George's little episode of being listed as missing was a picnic to him—and to him only—according to the way we felt, and I know that you felt the same way—to a greater degree. He had a bit of motor trouble and landed on a sandy beach. It is rumored that the missionary and his wife took exceptionally good care of him. The wife fed him roast duck, let him sleep in her feather bed, and even went so far as to draw hot baths for him. Needless to say, the boys all have that particular spot plainly marked on their maps. So from then on, if any of the boys turn up missing, we are sure they are there taking a vacation. Who could blame them!

George was very upset about your being sent a cablegram, but it has all worked out as it should. Another thing George wanted me to be sure to tell you was that he has flown every day with the exception of two—at which time he had a cold. That is a better record than most of the boys have. Jay was at (Port) Moresby with George for quite a while, and then was transferred to Brisbane. George introduced Jack and I to him one day in August and in October, Jack and I met Jay on the street. He looked well and seems happy in his work. George also looks very well—better than Perry and Jack. He is deeply tanned and has lost very little weight. He is immensely proud of his squadron and loves his flying—as all the boys do. I understand he is now a flight leader. When George went back from this last leave, he expected his squadron to have already moved to the new strip. It is a place called "Nadzab" and is up near Lae. I don't believe it has as much jungle around and will probably be very pleasant compared to some of the places he could be. I seem to have covered everything George wanted me to—at least I can't seem to think of anything else. If there is anything else you would like to know, I shall be only too glad to write you. Of course, I would appreciate it if you didn't tell anyone where you received all this information. It could cause complications—I'm sure you understand. In the meantime—I wouldn't worry too much about George. He is a very capable pilot—"Hot"—as the boys would say—and he can take care of himself. I hope you have a very pleasant Holiday Season and that the new year will find George at home with you.

Sincerely,

Patricia Mankin

December 13, 1943

Training flights continue. Late in the day word was received that the 39th Fighter Squadron was Nadzab bound at once. Everyone worked the entire night packing and loading transports.

39th FS moved to Nadzab, New Guinea, APO 713, Unit 1

December 14, 1943

Pilots flew all our P-47s to Nadzab. The first group of transports landed at Nadzab.

December 16, 1943

Dear Mary,

Our loafing days are over. I started working yesterday and hated it. I guess you know why. It's starting to rain. Our tent is in a low spot, and we'll probably have to swim to chow the first big rain we have. We hope to get a floor in it soon. Four of the older fellows are going home. They were really surprised. (Edward W.) Randall was down at the flight line—he had just returned from a mission. The Operation Officer told him he was grounded, and the guy wanted to know what the hell the idea was. Then they told him he was going home. His face lit up like a searchlight! I did some washing today—all my pretty socks and some other stuff. We might have to do all our own washing from now on. Snowball isn't with us any longer.

As always—

Love,

George

In a letter to his father, George explains the miraculous return of his friend, Captain George "Sully" Sullivan, who had been missing for 24 days.

December 18, 1943

Dear Dad,

Today was out cutting logs to get lumber in a hurry for our tent floor. Have to cut the logs and bring them in to our sawmill and creosote them. To get the logs, we had to go into the jungle. What a place! Every bush a briar, ants, mosquitoes, and other unknown insects that bite. Will have to get some more logs to make the frame for the tent. I hated to leave my old tent. It was very cozy. We had plenty of shelves and tables—also a couple of chairs. Now we start over again. What a life. I sent home a picture we took of Capt. Sullivan when he returned after 24 days in the jungle. He had lost over 30 lbs. He's returned to the States now. His story would make a good motion picture. Fights with headhunters and whatnot. We are hard at work again. The rest was really nice. It will be a long time before we get another.

Love,

George

December 23, 1943

Dear Mary,

How was Christmas? New Years? I hope you had a big time. I'm fairly certain after the first of the month, I can arrange my leave to within 3 days of yours. I passed my hundredth combat mission the other day. I was the first of my bunch here to do so. Between flying and working on the tent, I have been keeping pretty busy this last week. Andy messed up the tent's foundation when he put it down so the last couple of days off I have spent taking it up and doing it over. I really cussed him when I discovered his measurements were off so far that we had no lumber long enough. It's slow work working by yourself. I've been taking my time and trying to do it right. I've already found enough screen to screen it in. It should be nice when we finish. Things are pretty dull around here at night except for the mosquitoes—they are vicious. We have our mess hall screened-in so everyone comes here to write. Christmas will probably be pretty dull. Everyone has opened their packages. Good night, Mary. Have a good time at the dance tomorrow night. I'll be thinking of you. Beware the scotch.

As ever—

Love,

George

During the month of December, George flew several patrols from Lae to Finschhafen and Kiaipit, over Cape Gloucester covering the withdrawal of shipping, weather recons to Madang and Alexishafen areas, strafed targets of opportunity along the north coast of New Guinea, and escorted B-24s to Madang.

UNIT OPERATIONS REPORT, JANUARY 1944

The month of January commenced with a strength of 44 officers and 280 enlisted men.

Members of the squadron were luxuriating a camp that was turning out to be the best setup so far. It had taken 3 months to build, was well laid out, and pleasantly located. The various buildings featured cement floors, recessed lighting fixtures, and were fully screened.

The pleasure was not unmitigated, however, for the climate had its bad points. Hot, dusty days were followed by warm nights. Furthermore, a large ack-ack gun position located nearby provided disconcerting eruption.

The Termite Lumber Company of New Guinea continued to make good lumber easily available. Quite a few men were making trips to Lae to see and be photographed in the Japanese wreckage there, it being the first we had seen in any quantity.

The flocks of cockatoos flitting thru the tall trees were both raucous and colorful.

More than one person lay shivering in his sack wondering if that tree he heard cracking was falling on his tent.

January 1, 1944

Dear Mary,

Christmas was nice. Had the day off and didn't do anything but sleep and read. I'm starting on the second chapter of Rears and Roebuck that Dad sent. Everyone has gotten a big kick out of it. (Our toilet paper is about the same as this paper I am writing on.) I received peanuts and pecans, razor blades, little cigarette lighters, and a camera with a light meter. Hope Dad can find some film for it. Been out strafing Jap land positions today. This strafing is a tricky game. There's a hell of a lot you have to watch out for. Have been averaging about a mission a day for the last couple of weeks. It's hard work—especially on the fanny. Just heard a broadcast from the States as it's around two a.m., Jan. 1st there now. The program was all the best orchestras all over the States. It was very good. Heard "Pistol Packin Mama" for the first time about a week ago. Some song!

Love,

George

UNIT OPERATIONS REPORT

Replacement pilots were assigned and joined on the 3rd in the persons of 2nd Lts. Maurice M. Boland, Telesphore M. Gruber, John M. Lockhart, and Billy E. Richards.

They were P-39 pilots with combat experience in the 40th and 41st squadrons so their first duty was to check out in the Thundermugs.

January 3, 1944

Dear Mary,

I will leave for down south on the fifth. Grice was here last night, and I heard about Jack going home—Jeakle, too. Jack and Patty couldn't have timed it better. Lucky fellows. In a letter from my mother today, she told of Mrs. Mankin writing her. She was tickled to death to receive the letter and said that, "she (Patty) must be a lovely girl to write such a nice letter." Well, she's right about that. That bunch that Jack, Perry, and Grice are in (475th FG) are being taken care of very well by higher-ups. We don't understand it. I haven't the slightest idea why Miss Pickett thinks I am your "darling." Is it possible she has noticed something you haven't? Thanks for putting my name on the Christmas present to Mrs. Fields, Peg, and Edna. I think a lot of them. Good night, Mary.

As always,

Love

George

More replacements were added on the 4th when 2nd Lts. James C. Steele, Robert Thorpe, Fredrick S. Tobi, and Marcus Trout joined up. Fresh from the States they took pride in about 80 hours' time flying in the P-47.

UNIT OPERATIONS REPORT

HEADQUARTERS THIRTY-FIFTH FIGHTER GROUP, UNITED STATES ARMY AIR FORCE, APO 713, Unit 1, 2 January, 1944.

Special Orders No. 1: Under the auth contained in AR 605-115 and 5AF Reg. 35-31, dtd 5 Aug/43, the foll named O, A/C, orgn indicated, are granted seven (7) days lv of abs excl of trav time to and fr APO 927, eff o/a 4 Jan/44, and immediately upon arrival thereat and upon termination of lv, will rpt to the Red Cross Service Bureau, David Jones Building:

1st LT. WAYNE P. ROTHGEB, 39th Fi Sq
1st LT. GEORGE E. MORGAN, 39th Fi Sq

Sydney, Australia
January 10, 1944

2nd Lt. Mary L. Scott and 1st Lt. George E.
Morgan in Sydney sitting near the railroad
station.

2nd Lt. Mary Louise Scott
U.S. Army Nurse Corps
155th Station Hospital, Camp Roberts, California
1941

George and Mary had leave at the same time for a few days in Sydney, Australia. Mary flew to Sydney as an honorary copilot of a B-26 arriving a few days before George's leave started and George had a few days after Mary left to return to Gatton.

Mary stayed at the Red Cross place for nurses. George stayed at the apartment that the 39th squadron had for its pilots on leave.

They spent days at Bondi Beach and went dancing at the Roosevelt Club at night. That's when Mary met Wayne Rothgeb, fellow pilot of George's. George met Neil Wyatt—a fellow he knew in school in Memphis. Mary saw Chuck Rathe from Sauk Centre, Minnesota, who was on the staff of "YANK Down Under."

Sauk Centre People Met in Australia—
Special to the Herald (By Chuck Rathe)

Southwest Pacific—Lt. Mary Scott, ANC, nurse in a mainland stationed hospital unit, and I had probably the most exciting old home session since the Sauk Centre high school marked its fiftieth year with a gathering of the clan and getting its basketball pants knocked off by Melrose. Only ours was in a corner of the office of YANK Down Under, some 12,000 miles from home with a Pacific Ocean stretched between us and the topic of our conversation.

Miss Scott is probably the first Sauk Centreite to reach the SWPA. She arrived nearly 2 years ago at a southern Australian port when things were hot and the Jap was sweeping down over the islands, hopping from one to another with greater alacrity than any of us liked.

It's an oddity that the only one who might have beat her to the punch on arriving here was the first home towner Miss Scott saw. He's Jim Forsberg who was with the division that did the Buna job. He met Mary when he became a patient in her hospital.

Our meeting was one of those surprise affairs. She had seen my name in the masthead of YANK, and when she got leave she bounced into the office. She was wearing dark glasses, but I knew her. "That's the guy I want to see," she said, pointing in my direction. "Mary," I said while she fumbled with her glove. "I wrote you a letter. It's still in my desk." Only a week or two before I had found her address.

It happens that Don Brewer, YANK's promotion man, is out of her outfit. He gave me the address, and one night all fluttered with ambition I had written. Then we launched into talk of what we had been doing and a whole procession of people, places, and things passed in review.

This was her first leave in service. "And Dad," she grinned, "is having a 30-day one—and at home." "Dad" is Lt. Col. Roy L. Scott. For her family at home I can say she looks swell with her perky nurse's cap saucily crowning her dark hair. She talked about them, her mother, and Betty and Jim whose wedding she hated missing.

But a war and a Pacific Ocean don't allow a GI nurse to be a guest at her brother's wedding. That is, she talked of them when I wasn't race-horsing my tongue telling about my wife and my folks. It was fun. When she had asked for YANK Down Under, someone in headquarters said laughingly, "No publicity, Lieutenant."

She promised. But I didn't.

UNIT OPERATIONS REPORT

Lieutenant Clymer broke the ice during a fighter sweep over Wewak on the 8th. The squadron had dropped its belly tanks preparatory to peeling off on 16 enemy fighters below, when 16 more peeled off on us from a 6,000 feet advantage. A Zeke latched on to Lieutenant Colonel Doss's tail, who was unable to drop his belly tank. It was then Clymer broke away and shot down the Zeke. This Zeke crashed in the water. It was the 39th's first victory in the P-47 with no damage suffered because of the plane's ability to dive rapidly.

The social event of the summer season took place on the 13th when four unusually lovely airborne nurses accepted an invitation to dine with the officers. Captain Dake created a romantic atmosphere in candlelight and served a scrumptious feast preceded by eggnogs that lacked none of the necessary ingredients. The boys went to work quickly, but found the competition pretty rough.

The Nips threw a surprise punch at 0705 of the 15th when eight Tonies strafed the Nadzab strips. The damage to the 39th was a plane destroyed and another ship with a few holes.

Charles S. Collins (sergeant) became the involuntary recipient of the Purple Heart as a result of being grazed by a .30-cal. bullet. To those in camp the raid was an exciting display of fireworks.

The pilots and men on the line were caught flat-footed, but didn't remain that way long. The first inmate of the operations' slit trench was a mongrel dog who would, despite unbelievers, hit the handiest trench at the sound of "Air Raid" and remain until "All clear" was called.

January 17, 1944

Back from leave—went to Sydney—very nice place. Our mail hasn't been coming through very good in the last month, and we still have a lot of mail they won't deliver. They say we have to come and get it, but we can't get transportation for it. Asked my sister to write Patty but told her not to say much about my love life— she's a friend of Mary's.

Love,

George

January 19, 1944

Hello, Darling,

I had such a good time on this leave. I'm glad I could get to see you on my way back. I enjoyed helping you girls cook. They had a little excitement around here the morning before I got back. It's funny to hear the different guys tell about it—especially Andy's version.

Love,

George

January 20, 1944

This afternoon word was received that the outfit was ordered to move to Gusap immediately, ordered by General Whitehead. It was explained that the entire outfit would move tomorrow and be ready for operations that same night. Only a rear detail would be left behind. Late at night word was received that the outfit would not move tomorrow, but that an advance detail would leave early in the morning; the outfit to follow within a few days.

January 21, 1944

No missions today. The advance detail left this morning for Gusap, the outfit to follow within a few days.

UNIT OPERATIONS REPORT

A batch of well earned decorations were presented on the 26th by Gen. Wurtsmith:

Captain Denton received 2 OLC to the DFC, 1 OLC to the AM;

Captain Bills 1 OLC to the DFC, 3 OLC to the AM;
Captain Cella the DFC,
Captain Flood 1 OLC each to the DFC and the AM;
Captain Rogers 1 OLC to the AM;
Lt. Anderson 1 OLC each to the DFC and AM;
Lt. Clymer 1 OLC each to the DFC and AM;
Lt. Duncan 1 OLC each to the DFC and the AM;
Lt. Kish 1 OLC to the DFC and 2 OLC to the AM;
Lt. Lockhart the AM;
Lt. Morgan the DFC;
Lt. Smith 1 OLC each to the DFC and AM;
Lt. Urquhart the AM;
Lt. Vining the DFC and AM;
M/Sgt Martini the Legion of Merit.

Lt. Sander, a former member of the 39th, received the AM at the same ceremony.

M/Sgt Diehl received an engraved watch in recognition of his service to the squadron.

Master Sergeant Martini was transferred to OCS on the 27th. During his tour of duty with the 39th, Martini had distinguished himself in the Armament section. His first coup was the designing of a supporting bracket for the .50-cal. guns, thus preventing the guns from jumping their mounts. Later, he invented a device that by controlling the feeding of the machine guns, eliminated the major source of stoppage. Both these improvements were widely adopted in the air force. For these accomplishments, Martini was awarded the Legion of Merit by General Wurtsmith.

Likewise, on the 27th, 25 planes cross-countried to Gusap, thereby completing the movement of the squadron. Construction of the camp was well under way and within a day, the squadron was in full operation at Strip No. 5.

January 27, 1944

24 P-47s were ferried to our new base at Gusap. All the activity comes from camp where everyone is busy setting up our new camp.

January 28, 1943

Darling,

Things have been in a mess the last few days, and Andy and I start to work tomorrow. We brought our lumber with us so we should have a nice place someday. We put in a hard day working on our tent. Another day's work and we should be able to move in. The sun here is really rugged. Andy had his shirt off for about 30 minutes and he is now beet red. The nights are very cool. Two blankets feel good every night. In the early mornings, we have to wear our jackets. I saw Perry 5 or 6 days ago. We talked for about an hour before he had to leave. He was really envious of my leave—he should be. Jan. 29, I got in a "bull-session" last night and didn't finish. I've seen Neil Wyatt, the boy from Memphis I ran into at the Roosevelt, a couple of times. Both times we had a nice party—scotch, beer, and Cokes. He plans to drop in and see us if he gets the chance. Take care of yourself.

As always—

Love,

George

UNIT OPERATIONS REPORT

A mild epidemic of respiratory diseases affecting approximately 10 percent of the personnel, five cases of malaria and four cases of dengue fever, due to moving the squadron to a highly malarious area, constituted the health record for the month.

19 planes were received, 16 planes being transferred, and two planes each destroyed and damaged, including the losses on the ground from enemy action. 285 escort, 90 fighter sweep, 9 interception, 244 patrol, and 7 strafing sorties were made, totaling 635 sorties and 1,490 combat hours.

Most offensive missions were directed against Alexishafen-Bogadjim areas, Hansa Bay, and Wewak. 50 snafus gave us an average of 89.8 percent planes completing their missions.

The squadron acclimated itself to the new surroundings as the month ended. Historical Data, 1 January to 31 January 1944.

January 31, 1944

Dear Mary,

Spent the day working on our tent. Another day and we should be able to move in. This is the nicest place I've been in New Guinea. The elevation is pretty high, so it's always cool, if not cold, at night. I have my jacket on at the present. We have the nicest stream for fishing or swimming a few feet from my tent. It's almost clear and always cool. The current is very swift but not too deep. Saw a bird of paradise the other day flying very low—it was beautiful.

Love,

George

During the month of January, George participated in missions of escorting bombers to Bili-Bili, Erima Plantation, Madang, Hansa Bay, Bogadjim, Wewak, patrolling Alexishafen, Gusap, Dumpu, areas north of Madang, and a fighter sweep over Hansa Bay.

UNIT OPERATIONS REPORT, February 1944

The strength of the squadron on the 1st of February was 51 officers and 279 enlisted men.

The squadron was in the process of settling down at the new station, Gusap, APO 715-Unit 2.

Lieutenant McGettigan was in charge of the primary construction, as acting adjutant. The members of the squadron quickly grew to prefer this location to any that they had occupied overseas.

The camp was located on the east bank of the Ramu River, which, at that point, runs down the west side of the valley 10–12 miles wide, bordered by mountains 4,000 feet high. An altitude of 1,579 feet, very cool nights, warm days, and sufficient rain to keep the dust down, combined to make life unusually comfortable.

The pilots found the strip quite satisfactory in its length, smooth metal surface, asphalt taxiways, and revetments and open approaches. The alert hut and mess shack on the line were conceded to be the best yet.

Recreation started rapidly, the various sports including baseball, basketball, volleyball, and badminton. The enlisted men built a baseball diamond, and with Sgts. Leo Brooks and Willard Thompson on the mound, became the valley champions. The officers didn't do so bad either.

February 3, 1944

Hello, Darling,

I'm in our new tent tonight. It's much better than our old one. Perry should be getting his promotion to captain soon. I have at least 4 months to wait for mine. I'm glad Jay seemed in such good spirits. I've seen Neil three or four times since my leave. He was up near here the other day and dropped in to see me, but I was working. He couldn't stay but for a minute, so I missed him. It will be at least a month before I can get down there. They are working the new boys in on their leaves. It seems an awful long time since I have seen you. It's getting late so I better turn in. Good night, darling.

All my love,

George

February 8, 1944

Dear Mary,

I've seen my share of Japs. I've seen them going down in flames, bailing out, crashing into land and sea, had them shooting at me both from their planes, from boats (ack-ack), and ground (ack-ack). In fights, I've had tracers flying all around me and seen my shells hitting their planes. We received official notice that a large number of bags of packages were lost due to enemy action—packages mailed between the 1st and 31st of October. Packages are still arriving here, though. Have about 130 missions. Most missions are shorter now. Today was another big washday. Washed five shirts and eight pants besides shorts, socks, and handkerchiefs. Had to use water from the stream for boiling and rinsing. Was kind of muddy but got the sweat smell out. Have quite a number of pictures to send home in the next few days.

As always—

Love,

George

UNIT OPERATIONS REPORT—February 1944

New blood was added on February 9 by the assignment of 2nd Lt. Kenneth M. Dunn, 2nd Lt. James J. Querns, and F/O Robert W. Querns, the latter two being brothers, together since the start of their flying career. They had about 60–70 hours each in the Thundermug.

One of the most hysterically funny incidents in the life of the 39th was a paratroop alert that was sounded at 0200 hours on the 9th of February and lasted till 0310 hours. A suspicion of a parachute raid had started when a large force of Jap bombers came into We-wak shortly before.

For once, confusion reigned supreme in the squadron. Gradually, the ordnance tent was mobbed by officers and enlisted men clamoring for guns and ammo.

Lieutenant Deedy was in a dither, with everyone demanding nothing less than a machine gun and getting pistol rounds for their carbines, machine-gun clips for pistols, and none knowing how to load his weapon. Of course, Lieutenant Clymer was completely equipped, machine gun, two pistols, and assorted knives.

Orders were issued to hold the riverbank as a defense line; no one to fire his gun until attacked. A few shots were heard, but the alert was called off fortunately before the squadron succeeded in committing mass murder upon itself. A second alert was sounded at 0530 hours.

Naturally, work was started that day on a coordinated defense plan. A victory was credited to the squadron on the 10th by Major T. J. Lynch, operating out of Fifth Fighter Command, when he shot down a twin-engine bomber over Wewak. This gave Major Lynch 17 victories.

HEADQUARTERS, V FIGHTER COMMAND, APO 73, Unit 1, 15 February 1944, Special Orders No. 46: The fol named O are o/a 15 Feb 44, placed on TD for the purpose of ferrying mil acft as the CG may direct, WP by mil acft $6 per diem atzd for trav fr port of entry in Australia to APO 925, CGMD, and to port of departure fr Australia, and for TD.

Capt. RICHARD T. CELLA, 39th Fi Sq
1st Lt. GEORGE E. MORGAN, 39th Fi Sq
1st Lt. LEWIS LOCKHART, 39th Fi Sq
2nd Lt. ROBERT A. HUSSA, 39th Fi Sq

February 24, 1944

The first thing this morning we were awakened by the sound of sirens and gunshots. It was another red alert. It was about the same thing as yesterday morning, the enemy plane was overhead before the alert was sounded. There were no bombs dropped, but he must have got a good view of Gusap while all of the lights were on. Again at 2200 hours there was another red alert which sent many fellows hurrying away from the show. John Garfield was playing in the *Fallen Sparrow*—pretty good too.

UNIT OPERATIONS REPORT—February 1944

A freak accident occurred on the 24th when Lt. Lee P. Vining, testing a P-38, got into a dogfight with a P-47, piloted by Lieutenant Morton of the 40th Fighter Squadron.

A head-on pass resulted in a midair collision that rendered both planes uncontrollable. The planes crashed in flames, but Lieutenant Vining and Morton both parachuted safely to the ground.

It was a great relief to see two parachutes blossom and float to the ground just 5 miles south of the strip.

In March, George, with other pilots, was in Australia for a few days—ferrying planes back to New Guinea. He did get out to Gatton to see Mary.

The Post Record, Australia's Biggest American newspaper, 105th unit newsletter, February 25, 1944—Among those seen tripping the light fantastic at our recent costume party was that handsome fellow, George Morgan, who escorted a vision in red. Yes, our little Mary Scott.

In one of his first missions with the 39th, Lieutenant Thorpe's P-47 developed engine problems, forcing him to bail out at a very low altitude.

UNIT OPERATIONS REPORT—February 1944

Lt. Robert E. Thorpe was returning from valley patrol with mechanical trouble when his engine froze over the dispersal area at a very low altitude.

Bailing out, he hit the ground the instant after he felt the jerk of his chute. The onlookers were not sure whether his fall had been broken, so close was his escape.

Minor bruises and scratches were his only injuries.

UNIT OPERATIONS REPORT—February 1944

By the end of the month the construction of the camp was almost completed, including portable buildings for the mess, squadron supply, and the dispensary, all this in spite of 14 red alerts.

During the month, malaria and dengue were under control following the initiation of a strictly supervised antibrine roster and instruction and enforcement of individual protective measures.

A number of cases of sinusitis and arthritis had been activated which could be attributed to the climate of the present location. The mail and chow had one of their poorest months.

Five new planes were received during the month for the loss of the one whose engine froze, an accident record that the squadron was proud of.

The operations for the month consisted of 153 escort, 99 fighter sweep, and 389 patrol sorties, a total of 641 combat sorties, 1,497 combat hours. 38 planes snafued, making an average of 94.1 percent of the planes having completed their missions.

The missions were in the main to Wewak, Hansa Bay, Bogadjim, and Madang areas. Nine pilots had over 400 combat hours as of the last day of the month. February ended with the morale of the enlisted men at an all-time high in anticipation of going home.

George Morgan participated in various squadron missions throughout the month of February. One mission was flown from Nadzab escorting bombers to Alexishafen. There were several patrols from Gusap to Dumpu to Kaiapit, a fighter sweep to Wewak, an escort of A-20s to Murik Lagoon, a weather recon to Madang and Hansa Bay, and an escort of B-24s to Wewak.

March 6, 1944

The squadron was given permission to carry out a search mission for Lt. Col. Kirby (Neel E. Kearby) who went down. The search was in vain. They did make some sightings, though, along shore of Manam Island.

March 8, 1944

Major Lynch is gone. He was our squadron leader for 6 months and Captain Bong used to fly with us. Major

Lynch was the best squadron leader we ever had—a great man.

March 14, 1944

This morning at 0950 Captain Denton, Lieutenants Hodge, Tansing, Price, Widmann, Haws, Urquhart, Dunn, Baker, Rymer, Kramme, Querns, R., Duncan, Grosshuesch, Mettler, Querns, J. took off to escort B-25s to Wewak. Over the mouth of the Sepik River Lieutenant Duncan's motor cut out on him, and he made a forced landing into the sea. There was to be a Cat there to pick anyone up that should go down, but because of a lack of gas they could not be there. He was covered by the squadron for a while, then all but Lieutenants Grosshuesch and Querns, J. returned at 1325. Querns returned at 1425. Lieutenant Grosshuesch staying over Lieutenant Duncan until relieved by Tubby White. He landed at Saidor. Refueled. When he arrived at this field Captain Widmann and Lieutenant Grosshuesch took off at 1700. They went up to try to find Lieutenant Duncan who was not picked up by the third relief. They returned at 1930. When last seen, Lieutenant Duncan was floating around on his life raft. He was drifting at a rate of from 3 to 4 miles per hour in a northeasterly direction. As yet, he is still on the water.

March 14, 1944

Dear Mary,

It will probably be sometime in April before I get to see you. On my next leave, we have a lot of things to talk over. I really enjoyed the party we had, but there is a lot I don't remember too well. What all did I drink that night? I do re-

member that I didn't want to leave, but then I never do. I've started playing bridge. I've had to or go nuts. We start early in the morning and play until late at night. I hope to see you soon.

All my love,

George

March 16, 1944

Still no word of Lieutenant Duncan so Col. (Furlo S.) Wagner, Captains Denton, Bills, Widmann, and Lieutenant Grosshuesch took off on a search mission at 0752. No success.

March 17, 1944

One flight remained in the target area of where Lieutenant Duncan was last seen but were unable to see anything of him. Very early this morning everyone was scrambled from their beds by three bomb bursts from an enemy plane that had slipped in. There was no damage from the bombs, but several mosquito nets, screen doors, and tent ropes were seriously damaged from the half-asleep fellows attempting to make the slit trench before the echo of the bombs had left the valley.

March 21, 1944

A flight of three planes took off on a search for Lieutenant Duncan in the Schouten Island area. They sighted a small fire but no one around it.

March 22, 1944

Hello, Darling,

I finally got home and learned I'm a flight leader now. Also, Jay is back and up near here. My sister wrote Patty and received a letter from her. She sent Patty some foot warmers for the baby from me. I know Patty will get a kick out of it, but that's my sister—a pretty swell gal. I think you remember Duncan. We have been in the same outfits for the last year and a half, ever since receiving our wings. You met him when we heard about Perry. He's now in T. D. Price's outfit. I hated to see him go. I had better close, and I will try to write a better letter next time.

Love,

George

HEADQUARTERS, FIFTH AIR FORCE, 23 March 1944.
<u>AWARDS OF THE OAK-LEAF CLUSTER (A.M.).</u>

By direction of the President— In addition to the Air Medal awarded to First Lieutenant GEORGE E. MORGAN by the Commanding General, Fifth Air Force, a Bronze Oak-Leaf Cluster is awarded to him by the Commanding General, Fifth Air Force. The citation is as follows:

First Lieutenant GEORGE E. MORGAN, Air Corps, United States Army. For meritorious achievement while participating in sustained operational flight missions in the Southwest Pacific area from 27 September 1943 to 24 December 1943, during which hostile contact was probable and expected.

These operations included escorting bombers and transport aircraft, interception and attack missions, and patrol and reconnaissance flights.

In the course of these operations, strafing and bombing attacks were made from dangerously low altitudes, destroying and damaging enemy installations and equipment.

March 26, 1944

Hello, Darling,

I had today off for the first time in six days. I lead the squadron for the first time, believe it or not. Tell Fitz it is a date for the three of us to cook dinner. Anderson just went to bed and is playing the harmonica and says he won't stop until I turn the lantern off and go to bed. What a threat! He's playing, "How Drunk I Am." I had better close before he drives me nuts. He is now murdering "White Christmas."

Good night—

All my love,

George

During the month of March in addition to his other duties, George participated in several patrol missions from Gusap to Dumpu, four missions escorting bombers to Wewak, and one mission escorting B-24s back from Hollandia.

April 3, 1944

Dear Mary,

They have been working the hell out of me since I've returned. I've had only three days

*off in about the last fifteen and on one of them,
I was the O.D. I like it this way. A lot is going on, and I don't want to miss it. I thought
I would see Perry today, but the plane "snafued." I haven't seen him since the middle of
January. Andy and I are both writing while
listening to a radio program. We have a loud-
speaker hooked on to one of the fellow's radio.
The programs are damn good. We have radio
stations up here that have a good collection of
records and good announcers, too. I have to get
up at four forty-five in the morning— so pleasant dreams, my dear.*

All my love,

George

HEADQUARTERS, FIFTH AIR FORCE, APO 925, 4 April 1944.

Special Orders No. 95: Announcement is made of the temp promotion of the following named O to the gr indicated in the AUS
(AC) with rank from the date of this order.

<u>1st LT to CAPT</u>

ANDERSON, WILLIAM W. JR
MORGAN, GEORGE E.
TANSING, RICHARD M.

April 5, 1944

*The third mission was a most disastrous one. Lieutenant
Lane crashed into base operations while taking off and
was burned up in the plane, as was the operator in the
shack. Lieutenant Rothgeb's tire blew out on landing and
his plane nosed up. He came out of it smiling.*

April 7, 1944

Dear Mary,

I'm afraid it will be about the 25th of April before I can get down. Our operations officer is on leave, and I am taking his place while he's gone. I won't get my leave until he returns. I'm doing more work than I've done before up here. When I ask the CO (Major Denton) something about flying, he tells me I'm boss down at the line, so do what I think best. Hell, when I was a wingman, I didn't have any worries. I didn't know when I was well off. I saw Grice the other day but not Perry. They are being kept very busy, but I guess you know that. Well, dear, I have a poker game to break up here in the tent so I can go to bed. Happy dreams, darling.

All my love,

George

April 11, 1944

The first mission today was carried out by 18 P-47s of this Sq. Major Denton, F/O Fallier, Lieutenants Hodge, Tobi, Rothgeb, Foster, Richards, Steele, Mettler, Graber, Rogers, Schopka, Kramme, Neumann, Boland, F/O Querns, and Captain Cella and Lieutenant L. Lockhart. Takeoff time at 0930 and the B-24s were escorted to Hansa Bay and returned. The bombing of the B-24s was excellent. There were no enemy sightings, and they returned back here at 1230. Lieutenant Foster is still missing from this mission. Just above station 5 he broke away from the formation and headed home. He appeared all right but didn't contact the squadron by radio. A search is being made for him by all planes going up the valley and also by L-5s.

April 11, 1944

Dear Mary,

I am now a captain, and they are working the hell out of me. I fly every other day on the usual stuff, but now I fly about every day doing other jobs such as testing planes and taking new pilots up to look over the area and teach them combat flying. My job now is operations officer, which means I have charge of all flying and pilots. It's a full-time job. Usually have to put in a couple of hours every night making out the list of pilots for the next day's missions and look over reports, etc. On my next day off, I'm going down to see Jay. As I have charge of all flying, I'll just ask myself if I can, and that's that. It's nice to have a few privileges. It's the first time in the army that I've been in such a position.

Love,

George

April 13, 1944

The mission was a search mission by Captain Tansing and Lieutenant Ross. There were no sightings of interest on this mission. They were looking for our Lieutenant Foster.

April 14, 1944

No flying except Captains Morgan, Anderson, and Cella.
They all returned back here in the late afternoon.

THIRTY-NINTH FIGHTER SQUADRON, THIRTY-FIFTH FIGHT-ER GROUP, 15 April, 1944. Squadron Orders No. 7:

The verbal orders, 9 April 1944, designating Captain George E. Morgan, A.C., Assistant Operations Officer, Principal Duty, are hereby confirmed and made a matter of record.

George had an opportunity to visit his brother, Staff Sgt. Jay Morgan, who was stationed at Port Moresby.

Dear Mom,

Flew down to see Jay yesterday. We got to talk for about an hour. He's looking very good and seems to be enjoying his work. Saw Grice, "Perry," and Ehlinger. Anderson and Cella flew down with me. We all are captains now. Except for Cella, they are a few of the guys I came overseas with. Jay and Billy Jones are going to try and visit me one of these days. Have been working very hard the last 3 or 4 weeks. Sent home a photo of the mural in our old officer's club at Port Moresby. It was painted by one of the pilots, Henry Turlick.

Love,

George

Dear Mary,

Hello, Darling.

Here it is the middle of the month and I am still up here. I miss you very much. Went down to see Jay, Perry, Grice, Ehlinger, and Jeakel. Andy, Cella, and I went down about noon and stayed until four. Had a nice bull session, especially Perry and I. Perry was very nice, all of them were; they didn't try to rack us back once. I've been working pretty hard since I returned from my little "jaunt." Be good and take care.

All my love,

George

April 16, 1944

16 ships took off at 1222 to escort B-25s return from a strike on Hollandia. They didn't get very far for the weather was closed in, and then they returned. Major Denton led the flight with Captain Morgan and Lieutenants Johnson, Rothgeb, Tobi, Lynn, Lockhart L., Thorpe, Vining, Frost, Ross, Steele, Mettler, Robertson, Rogers, Jones flying with him. They returned at 1330. The pilots sat alert from the time of landing until 5:30.

April 17, 1944

The only mission for today was an 8-ship search mission for missing planes of the day before. The target area was searched from the altitude of 8,000 feet. The only sightings were the sighting of an A-20 down on the beach and was afire. The crew had been picked up previous to the sighting.

April 17, 1944

Hello, Dear,

It has been very cool the last couple of days. I sure do envy you your hot showers. I don't see how our water gets so cold—the water we drink never seems that way. You are a "lazy cuss"—breakfast in bed. Mrs. Field has spoiled you, hasn't she? I hope you are feeling all right. There must be more to getting your new job than what you told me. We had the show Girl Crazy with Mickey Rooney tonight, but I didn't go to see it. It looked like rain, and I wanted to finish this letter. Jay and a friend of ours came up to see me yesterday. They were here about 2 hours—we had a nice talk. Perry dropped in late yesterday afternoon and spent the night. It's the first time he's come to see me when I was here. Well, he didn't exactly stop just to see me. He was supposed to start out to see Fitz today. I hope he got off okay. Wayne (Rothgeb) just stopped by and told me to tell you "hello." He is a peach of a kid. I've heard there are nurses up here, but as yet, I haven't seen one. The idea of a picnic with Dr. Hartwell and the bunch sounds very good to me. I hope I can be with you when you celebrate your fourth year in the army. Tell Hartwell, Charley, Bill, Fitz, the two Jeans, and my other girlfriends "hello" for me. Good night, dear.

All my love,

George

April 20, 1944

Hello, My Darling,

Guess what I'm drinking—no, you are wrong—it's orange juice—canned orange juice. I had enough rye last night to last me until next time. We had a USO show near our camp last night. After the show, they came over to our club. There were a couple of girls that weren't bad looking (there were only two). It sure was drunk out and everyone seemed to have a good time. Just found out two fellows are going home. They came over after I did. They are going as first lieutenants—hope I don't have to. I want to see that letter of mine, the one the gin affected so much. It's nice that you like it anyway—was it really that bad? Darling, I'm going to have to finish this tomorrow night. Guys have been coming and going in the tent, and I had to stop and talk with them all. I have about 15 minutes before lights out, and I have to make my bed. Sent my sheets to be washed this morning and haven't remade my bed as yet. Good night, darling, and sweet dreams.

Love,

George

April 23, 1944

Sorry, darling,

I haven't had time to write in the last 2 days. I have only 15 minutes to write tonight. I guess it's safe to tell you now, as I'll probably be there by the time you receive this that I have finally made captain and am the squadron operations officer. The last is the reason I haven't had time to write. I have work to do every night, plus work on my days off. The last 3 days, I have been in the process of moving over to the CO's tent. He wants me to move in. We have a number of new pilots, and that means extra work. I'll bet Perry and Fitz are enjoying themselves. I hope so anyway.

As always,

Love.

George

April 24, 1944

Hello, Again,

I couldn't finish last night's letter. I know you would like it better if I wrote separate letters, but this seems to be the only way I can write. I like doing it this way because I can talk to you every night. Andy is driving me crazy trying to find out something I know but can't tell him. He is asking one question after another. I've been almost an hour writing this and that is an hour since lights out. My faithful lantern is assisting me. I don't want to stop writing but I have to be up early in the morning. Andy is now *calling me names.*

Good night, Sweetheart.

Love,

George

THIRTY-NINTH FIGHTER SQUADRON, THIRTY-FIFTH FIGHTER GROUP, APO 713, Unit #2, 25 April, 1944. Squadron Orders No. 8:

Capt. George E. Morgan, A.C. is hereby designated Operations Officer, Principal Duty.

George's next leave was late April 1944. He had made captain. That's when they started talking marriage someday.

During the month of April, George participated in missions escorting B-24s to Kairiru Island, Hansa Bay, returning B-24s from Hollandia, and DC-3s to Momote. He also conducted a strafing mission from Ramu River to Kronprinz Harbor, a fighter sweep over Wewak, and provided cover for a downed P-38 pilot.

HEADQUARTERS, ADVANCE ECHELON, FIFTH AIR FORCE, APO 713 u#1, 28 April 1944. Special Orders No. 119:

The fol AC O & EM are reld fr asmt to orgns and stas indicated, are asgd and trfd in gr to 268th Repl Co, APO 929 and WP o/a 29 Apr 44 by mil acft rptg on arrival to the CO for further instructions.

Captain WILLIAM W. ANDERSON JR., 39th Ftr Sq, 35th Ftr Gp
Captain GEORGE E. MORGAN, 39th Ftr Sq, 35th Ftr Gp
Captain RICHARD M. TANSING, 39th Ftr Sq, 35th Ftr Gp

On April 29, 1944, 2nd Lt. Mary L. Scott was promoted to first lieutenant.

THIRTY-NINTH FIGHTER SQUADRON, OFFICE OF THE OPERA-
TIONS OFFICER, APO3 713, Unit 2, May 2, 1944.

CERTIFICATE

I certify that George E. Morgan, Captain, AAF, A.S.N. – 0-662970
has flown 149 combat missions and 362:45 combat hours with
this squadron. The above time was flown in accordance with General Orders, Headquarters, Fifth Air Force, APO #925. LELAND P.
VINING, 1st LIEUT., AAF, Operations Officer

HEADQUARTERS, UNITED STATES ARMY FORCES IN THE FAR
EAST, OFFICE OF THE COMMANDING GENERAL, APO 501, 3 May,
1944.

SUBJECT: Orders to officers concerned, 268th Repl Co, 91st Repl
Bn, APO 929. Following-named O reld present asgmt and further dy in SWPA, effective date of departure. WP to U.S. reporting upon arrival to Air or Water Port of Debarkation for further
disposition.

Travel by mil, Naval or commercial aircraft, Army or Naval T, bel-
ligerent vessel or aircraft, commercial steamship or any other
means of T to U.S. is authorized. Personal baggage not to exceed
65 pounds authorized while traveling by air. Per diem $7 autho-
rized while traveling by air only.

CAPTAIN RICHARD M. TANSING
CAPTAIN GEORGE E. MORGAN
CAPTAIN WILLIAM W. ANDERSON JR.

May 11, 1944

My Dearest,

*This is one letter I hate to write; I think you
know why. My orders to go home were here
when I arrived. I tried to get down there, but*

I couldn't get in touch with any of the fellows that could have helped me. I reported in thinking I might still be able to get down, but they tell me I catch a plane tonight. If I refused it, I don't know what would happen. I can't help but hope you will be home soon. There are times that I think I was wrong in not marrying you over here. I hope our plans for the future do come true. Jay will be going down on leave soon, and he will see you about my clothes. I should have brought them back with me, but I was so sure I could get down again before I left. Mary, I want you to know and remember, I love you very much. I told you how I felt when I was down there—as if I was coming home and it was a wonderful feeling. Darling, there is very little light so I'm going to have to close. I'll write first chance I get. Take care of yourself.

All my love and I love you,

George

After 15 months and 149 missions, Captain George Morgan arrived back in the States on May 13, 1944.

AIR TRANSPORT COMMAND, STATION NUMBER 11, PACIFIC WING, AIRPORT OF EMBARKATION, HAMILTON FIELD, CALIFORNIA, 14 MAY 1944. SPECIAL ORDERS NO. 135:

The following named O's, auth shown after their respective names, are asgd to AAFRS #2, Miami Beach, Fla. Delays en route of 22 days are authorized to proper sta to which O's will report 13 June 1944. O's will be reasgd upon completion of processing at AAFRS #2.

CAPT (1056) GEORGE E. MORGAN, AC, Ltr O, Hq USAFFE, APO 501, 3 May 1944

Authorized Leave of Absence: May 22, 44 – June 12, 44 – 22 days.

May 22, 1944

Hello, My Darling,

I'm sitting in my bedroom and have just finished "brunch"—steak and eggs. My sis and mother think the combination is crazy. I stayed with Andy one night in Frisco. We played poker with his folks and friends. We did have fun. The censor was very nice. He let me bring pictures through that I never expected. I think you remember me telling you about Leo Akridge, bombardier on a B-26 in North Africa, anyway he is missing in action over Italy. His little brother" Babe" is missing on a flight here in the States. I ate dinner with Leo's mother and father yesterday. They let me have one of the cars, 1940 Ford, to use while on leave. The ration board gave me 15 gallons of gas. Since getting home, I have been very nervous for some reason. I haven't been able to eat much either. Darling, if you should get back before I get overseas again, I want to get married. I'd rather be married to you and be apart than not. I know I won't be happy with anyone else. I hope you feel the same as I. I have to stop. I'm having dinner with some friends, and I want to get this in the mail. Remember, darling, I love you more than I thought possible. Good night, dear. I will write every chance I get, and I hope to see you soon.

I love you, Mary,

George

May 30, 1944

Hello, My Darling,

My dad has been home the last few days and we have eaten out about once every day, and I have gotten damn tired of it. No matter what I plan, I usually have to change it. I am getting anxious to get down to Miami. I'll probably see Grice down there. Perry will probably go to Atlanta, GA. I would like to buy you things. It would help ease my conscience for having to leave you. As you know, anything weighing over 8 ounces has to have been requested, and then one can send up to 5 pounds. That's why I want you to ask for things. If you don't ask, I will be disappointed. One of mother's friends just dropped in for a few minutes, and, of course, I had to stop writing while she was here. Mother just informed me that Friday she is having some of her friends over for dinner, and, of course, she expects me to be here, so that's that. We haven't heard from Patty the last few days so I imagine the baby has arrived. Be sure and tell everyone "hello" for me.

As always, I love you,

George

SPECIAL ORDER, NUMBER 165: 14 June 1944—Following-named O will proceed by first available water transport to U.S. reporting upon arrival to CG, SFPE Ft Mason, Calif., for further disposition.

1st Lt. Mary L Scott, ANC

From May 1942 to July 1944, the 105th General Hospital treated nearly 19,000 patients. The vast majority were battle casualties from New Guinea, New Britain, and the Admiralty Islands.

HEADQUARTERS, AF REDISTRIBUTION STATION NO. 2, Miami Beach, Fla, 14 June 44. PERSONNEL MEMORANDUM No. 65: Following O AC unless otherwise designated having reported this sta 13 June 44 are eff 13 June 44 asgd qrs or shelter as indicated and asgd to Sec "C" Dept & Flt indicated:

CAPTAIN (1056) GEORGE E. MORGAN Asgd qrs 6B-210

June 14, 1944

My Dearest Darling,

I am now at Miami, Florida, at the redistribution center. I arrived here yesterday. I have never received better treatment from the army as I am receiving here. We are treated the same as civilians in one of the nicest hotels on Miami Beach. It couldn't be better in peacetime because they have entertainment going on all the time for us. No ties are worn during the day. Enlisted men are in the hotel next door—men from overseas. They receive the same kind of treatment we do. The men are allowed to have their wives with them. The wives live in the hotel with their husbands and have the same priv-

ileges as everyone else. Grice is here. I ran into him yesterday. We are in hotels next to each other. This afternoon we went on a picnic given by the Red Cross. We went boat riding and some rode horses. Later, we played softball, then had a weenie roast. The Red Cross is really doing a swell job here—having something for us to do all the time. They have three boats for deep sea fishing. I wish you were with me. I will only be here a couple of weeks so please send your letters to my home address. Jay wrote that he couldn't get his furlough, so I guess you won't see him for a while. He is one guy that wants you for a sister-in-law. In every letter to Mother, he says what a swell girl you are. As for my clothes, you can send them or wait until Jay gets down. I don't know if they will let you send the boots or not. If you wish, you can keep them, and I will claim them when I claim you. While I was home, I fixed up an album of the pictures I took overseas. I left home day before yesterday, and was I glad to leave. I bet I was asked a million questions, and they were all the same. Then when you would answer, they usually believed whatever they wanted. I made enough enemies to last me the rest of my life. Everyone wanted me to have dinner with them, and when I didn't, they would get mad as hell. I didn't call up half the people I should have, and I know what they are thinking. I'm ashamed to put the date down as it is 4 days ago that I started this letter. Grice left yesterday for Chico, California, where he is to be stationed. He is driving out in the red convertible (1941) that he paid $1,300 for.

*In peacetime, he could have bought it for $500.
Grice didn't know what kind of place Chico will
be—not even if it's a P-38 field. I am going to try
to be stationed in California and P-38s, if possible. I had better get this in the mailbox. Have
fun, darling, and remember,*

I love you,

George

On June 20, 1944, Mary departed from the 105th and moved to the
42nd General Hospital at Stuartholme, Brisbane, Australia, to await transportation back to the States.

June 21, 1944

Dear Mary,

*It is now midnight, and I just got a call through
to Mother a few minutes ago, and she told me I
have some letters there from you. It was the best
news I've received since being home. My chances of getting a P-38 unit are very slim as they
need P-47 pilots. I might have a slim chance to
be near Jack and Patty. Did Willie tell you, he
saw me over at Eagle Farm the morning I left
to go back up to New Guinea? We had to stop
at Eagle Farm to let a couple of pilots out to
ferry some planes up north, and by the time we
got to Townsville, it was too late to go on that
day. When we reached Nadzab the next day, it
was too late to go on to Gusap so I stayed there
that night. It was there I found out about going
home. I was looking at the orders of a fellow
who was going home to see if there was anyone
on it I knew, and Anderson's, Tansing's, and my*

name was on it. While I was home, Bill, Eva's husband, came down for 4 days. It was the first time I had seen him in about 4½ years. I went out with them one night and really had a swell party. I told Eva about our plan to have her take care of the children when we get together with Jack and Patty. She said she wouldn't mind but had rather go with us. I guess it's cold as hell there now. Have you used the pajamas I gave you? I wore them when I was in cadet training in Oklahoma. Wish I were there instead of the pajamas. There isn't more to tell you so I had better close. Don't work too hard and have fun.

Love,

George

HEADQUARTERS, AAF REDISTRIBUTION STATION NO. 2, Miami Beach, Florida, 28 June 44:

ADVANCE NOTICE OF ASSIGNMENT

TO: OIC, Department No. 6B. Captain George E. Morgan, 6B 210, will be assigned to 4th AF Ephrata AAB, Ephrata, Wash. on or about 30 June 44.

Officer will report to OIC Shipping & Receiving Section, Lobby Copley Plaza Hotel, immediately after receipt of this notice regardless of method of travel upon change of station. This post must be cleared on or before the date shown in paragraph one. Inability to secure transportation will be the only acceptable reason for remaining after clearance date.

HEADQUARTERS, AAF REDISTRIBUTION STATION NO. 2, Miami Beach, Fla, 28 June 44. SPECIAL ORDERS NO. 179: Following O AC are reld from asgmt and dy 1020th AAF Base Unit (Sec "C" Dept & Flt indicated) this sta are asgd to sta indicated eff o/a 30 June 44.

CAPT (1056) GEORGE E. MORGAN (Dept & Flt 6B-210), 4th AF Ephrata AAB, Ephrata, Wash. 23 June 44

WESTERN UNION, 1944 JUN 30, EPHRATA WASH.

CAPT GEORGE E. MORGAN CROYDON ARMS HOTL MIAMI BEACH FLO

REQUEST FOR TEN DELAY EN ROUTE APPROVED PROVIDED YOU HAVE SUFFICIENT ACCRUED DAYS TO JUSTIFY DELAY EN ROUTE. THORNE CO EAAB

On July 19, 1944, transportation became available for 1st Lt. Mary Scott and several other nurses in the form of a Dutch merchant ship. Hidden under her raincoat, Mary carried George's boots aboard.

After several days at sea, the ship's engine ceases to function and the rest of the convoy moves on. Alone and adrift without power for 3 days, the nurses decide to remain aboard ship should the order to "Abandon Ship" be given.

They are not comfortable with the looks they have been receiving from the ship's crew and believe it would be safer to remain aboard an abandoned drifting ship than to join the crew in lifeboats.

Fortunately, the ship's engine is finally repaired, and they are, once again, on their way home.

Authorized Leave of Absence: July 5, 44–July 14, 44–9 days.

430th AAF Base Unit, Squadron T, Ephrata AAB, Ephrata, WA

15 July 1944–SUBJECT: assignment of Quarters in BOQ

TO: Club Officer, AAB, Ephrata, Washington.

Assign quarters to Capt George E. Morgan, quarters No. 20 in Building No. 3451.

Ephrata Army Airfield, Ephrata, Washington.

July 16, 1944

Dear Mary,

I got here all right. Had a little trouble with my ticket in Chicago, but got it straightened out in time to catch my train. Everyone on our car was very nice, just like a big family. We played cards and talked. Those that had food passed it around, and we swapped reading material. The food service on the train was very good and not too expensive. Ran into a bunch of fellows here that I knew overseas, but none that I knew real well. I will be instructing in P-39s and P-63s (a much better version of the P-39) and start flying in the next couple of days. The town of Ephrata has a population of about a thousand. The closest town of any size is Spokane—about a hundred and forty miles from here. We will fly half of each day with one day off every 4. They have some basic trainers, dive-bombers, and a few other types of planes that we can use on our days off to fly to Seattle, Spokane, or Portland and spend the night. Some of the fellows go fishing on their day off. The fishing around here is very good with lots of places to go. The post itself is kind of barren, not any grass, just rocks. It's a large post counting the trainees. The Officers Club is one of the nicest I've seen, and they have dances fairly often.

Love,

George

HQ EPHRATA AAB, Ephrata, Wash, 17 July 44. Special Orders Number 108:

CAPT GEORGE E. MORGAN, AC, aptd Inst C Flt Sec (prin duty).

1st Lt. Mary L. Scott reported in to Letterman General Hospital in San Francisco, California, on July 20, 1944—as a patient. She had become very anemic and would require hospitalization before resuming her military duties.

July 24, 1944

Dear Mom,

I have been flying a little since I arrived. Checked out in a P-39 and a P-63 the other day. Have been leading flights the last few days. Practiced laying smoke screens yesterday. Took four other pilots along to do the same thing. To lay a smoke screen, one flies about 200 feet above the ground and releases the smoke so it will drift over the target. Just finished supper a little while ago. I'm back down at the line now. Our trainees are night flying, and we have to be here although we don't have to fly. We are getting a number of P-38s in soon so I'll get to fly them occasionally. Have been off post here only once, and that was to a picnic given by our flight section. Had a steak fry after swimming. It was a stag affair, but everyone had a good time. There must have been 50 or 60 guys there. This week we are flying in the afternoons so can sleep late in the mornings now.

George

July 27, 1944

Dear Mom,

Today is my day off, and I am going out to a lake with another fellow to fish and swim. I flew over to Tacoma, Wash., a couple days ago and spent the night. Came back here the next afternoon. I took three fellows over and came back by myself. Used a C-78 for the trip. A C-78 is a twin-engine advanced trainer, the same as the AT-17 I flew about 2 years ago. This place has really been hot the last few days. There isn't a single tree for miles of this place. Today seems as if it will be another hot one. Hebert and I started to get a plane and fly to Seattle today and spend the night, but we decided we had rather go to the lake. We go to work tomorrow afternoon, and we would be pretty tired if we went to Seattle. Received letters from Mary, and she was still in Brisbane July 8th. Our CO told me that I might be sent down to Matagorda Island, Texas, for a 6-weeks course in gunnery. He said it wasn't definite, and I hope it doesn't turn out. The idea of sending us to gunnery school is to make us better instructors.

George

July 31, 1944

My Dearest,

I was so glad to hear your voice tonight. I had wondered how long it would be before you came home. It's hard to believe that you are actually here in the States, and I wish I could see you. I can't help but worry about you—I wish I could be there to take care of you. Do you have any idea how long you will be in the hospital? I hope you will be sent someplace where you will be near home until you receive your leave. I asked at Miami Replacement Center to be sent to some base in the South, but as you can see, it did no good. Let me tell you about Ephrata. It is a town of about a thousand population, only a mile or so from the air base. There is very little more there than there was at Gatton. Soap Lake is the next nearest town—about 800 population—15 miles from here. This country is as barren as can be—nothing but rocky ground and rolling hills. Not a very pleasant picture, is it? Since I started this letter, some funny things have happened. One is—we have to have all the trainees finished by September 15th instead of one bunch by the first of September and another around the first of November, as planned. There is also talk of our getting all P-38s soon instead of the P-39s and P-63s we have now. Some think we might move out for the winter since the weather is bad for flying. You said in your letter you wanted a simple wedding. Well, that's what I want. We will have to wait until we can find out more about our leaves. All I can find out so far about the hospital here is that it's a base hospital. They take care of hospital cases from different fields near here. Another thing I found out was there is a 3-day wait here before you can be married. It's a state law. I've been asking around about a place to live while I'm here, and we can get a place in Soap Lake where most of the instructors here live. There aren't any places that are real *nice, and everybody is in the same boat, but it is a place to ourselves. There are some lakes not so far from here that are supposed to be very nice. They have cabins, boats, and things like that for rent. From what they say, the places are very nice. I think I would like that. I'm putting in for my leave September 4th. That's about the latest I can get it. No one knows what will happen after the middle of September, but whatever it is, we are supposed to be too busy doing something to get a leave. I can't understand it, and neither can anyone else. I know you must spend some time at home, and I expect you to, so come when you can. Darling, I have to fly in a few minutes, so I had better close. I love you very, very much, and I am waiting for the days we can be together. So long for now.*

I love you,

George

1st Lt. Mary L. Scott, having arrived safely in San Francisco, was transferred by hospital train to Schick General Hospital, Clinton, Iowa, on August 5th for continuation of treatment. While at Schick, she received 10 days leave (August 10–21, 1944) allowing her to visit her family in Minnesota.

August 15, 1944

My Dearest Darling,

I just got in from town where I saw a show with one of the fellows. That's about all I've been doing the last few nights. Your letter written from home arrived this afternoon, and I know just how you feel—lost and restless—I felt the same. People try to be nice and considerate, but the way I wanted it was to be left alone to do what I wanted to do. Yesterday afternoon, I went into Soap Lake to see about this place I got for us. Captain Mulvay, one of the instructors here, found the place and took me in to see it. It's worse than you can imagine, I know. It's very small. The bedroom is just large enough to have the bed in it. The living room is smaller, I believe, and the ceiling is not much higher than my head. The kitchen has a wood stove for cooking and heating the hot water, but I will get a hot plate for the cooking. The icebox is an actual icebox, if you know what I mean. I know you don't care what kind of a place it is, and I don't either—for myself, but it's you I'm thinking of. I hope I can find a better place before you arrive, and if I can't, maybe we can spend a large part of your leave away from here. I believe we can get a waver on the 3-day wait to get married, but I'll find out for sure, and we can be married here at the post. I think going to Seattle would be a good idea as there is a lot more to do there, and other places nearby to go—so I'm told. We can decide definitely when you get here. Darling, I do want you to be happy, especially while you are here with me. Mother thought your letter was wonderful, and she says Jay still writes about how much he likes you. I don't believe you have to worry about the rest of the Morgan family either. It's getting late, and I have to fly in the morning, so I had better close. I hope it won't be too much longer before I can have you with me. I've missed you an awful lot.

I love you, Mary,

George

Captain and Mrs. George E. Morgan
Ephrata AAB, Washington
September 6, 1944

"I met Mary in Tacoma and flew her back to Ephrata. She sat in the co-pilot's seat and is the first person in the family to fly with me. We were married in the Base Chapel with Chaplain Charles B. Smith officiating.

September 7, 1944

Dear Mom,

I expect you received our telegram sent this morning of your youngest son getting married.

The wedding was in the chapel out at the air base by the Protestant chaplain. We were in uniform, of course, and friends of mine from the base were there.

The wedding took place at 7:30 p.m. last night, and we sent the wire this morning. We are going up to Lake Chelan in the mountains for a 7-day honeymoon starting tomorrow.

We have a nice little place at Soap Lake where we will stay while I am working. Mary has until the end of the month before having to report to Santa Barbara, California, redistribution center. We believe that Mary will be stationed near Ephrata, and that is what we want.

I met Mary in Tacoma Monday, where she had to report to Fort Lewis for her leave, and then flew her back to Ephrata.

It was the first time she had flown with me, and I believe she enjoyed it very much. I took a twin-engine trainer over, a cabin plane, so she was able to sit in the copilot's chair for the trip. The reason I was allowed to let her fly with me was because she is in the army.

It's a funny thing—she is the first one in our family that ever flew with me.

Mother, I am quite sure you will love Mary. She is the type that can go fishing in the afternoon, and then go dancing that night. She doesn't worry so much about her looks that she doesn't have a good time whether it's swimming, picnicking, fishing, or any of the things we used to do at Apalachicola.

I am sorry I worried you when I didn't write for so long, but I have been very busy. I have so many students that I have to finish up by a certain time, and I have to fly with them all.

We are flying all the time in P-63s now, but within the next months it will be P-38s again. The P-63 is a very good plane and cruises about 250 miles per hour. That's about 15 miles per hour faster than the P-38.

Mom, I'll write more often than I have, but I had better close for now.

We both send our love.

Your favorite youngest son,

George

Chapter 12
Losing the P-38s

At first, Lt. Lew Lockhart thought it was a rumor. The P-38s were being pulled from the Pacific area and sent to Europe. Why, after the 39ths' extraordinary performance with the Lightning—including 109 kills of Japanese planes in 3 months—would the High Command replace the Lightning with any other plane? Why monkey with success?

The answer was in the mixed priorities of the two-theater war. Victory in Europe had a higher priority than victory in Asia, as it had since the war began. The superb performance of Lightnings in aerial combat was just the point. They were needed to combat the Luftwaffe and escort bombers over occupied Europe, which was considered far more important than defeating the Imperial Japanese air force.

Germany's scientific and technological prowess was the cause of tremendous concern for the Allies. What if a new and improved V-2 rocket became capable of delivering the first atomic bomb to be developed and used in combat? A mushroom cloud over London could end World War II right then and there. And the possibility was not that farfetched in the minds of the Allied chiefs. While it was determined after the war that the Germans were still years away from achieving nuclear fission and nuclear weapons, that fact was not known in 1943.

What was known was that the Germans, after rapid advances in nuclear research in the 1930s, had deemphasized these research projects in 1937 in the belief that they would not help end the coming war quickly. Then, in 1939, a new nuclear weapons research program began, but in

1942, it was cancelled and most of the researchers and staff were scattered to other military projects or drafted into the Wehrmacht. Nuclear research was transferred to the Reich Research Council, and work continued at nine major universities.

On March 4, 1945, a purported eyewitness named Clare Werner claimed to have been standing on a hillside in the eastern German state of Thuringia at the time of a nuclear explosion test. "Not too far away was the military training base near the town of Ohrdruf. Unexpectedly, there was a flash of light. I suddenly saw something. It was as bright as hundreds of bolts of lightning, red on the inside and yellow on the outside, so bright you could've read the newspaper. It all happened so quickly, and then we couldn't see anything at all. We just noticed there was a powerful wind."

Rumors like this, combined with the known capabilities of Germany's supersonic V-2 rocket, in use since mid-1944 and for which there was no effective defense, created a perfect nightmare for the Allied leaders. The V-2 carried a 1-ton payload, but if a German atomic bomb could be reduced from the size of the American atomic bombs under development and the rocket enlarged, that dreaded mushroom cloud over London could become a horrifying possibility.

There was also intelligence that the Germans were developing a submarine-towed launch platform. Already tested successfully and code-named *Prüfstand XII* (Test stand XII), it was also called the rocket U-boat. If deployed, it would have allowed a U-boat to launch V-2 missiles against United States cities. Hitler, in July 1944, and Speer, in January 1945, made speeches alluding to the scheme.

Adding these fears to the urgency of keeping the Soviet Union in the war and the stubborn might of the Wehrmacht, it was clear that Germany had to be defeated first. Then there would be time to take care of the Japanese.

But these priorities were far more apparent in Washington and London than in New Guinea. The men of the 39th, sweating and dying in an equatorial hell, had seen enough of inferior equipment. They had gone on to experience the satisfaction and elation of besting their enemies with the Lightning. Now they would have to do battle with an ugly plane, the P-47, known as the Thunderbolt, in which pilots had little confidence. Worse yet, the Thunderbolts they were getting to replace the Lightnings were second rate. They had extensive wear and tear from long use by other squadrons.

Gusap Airfield Complex, Gusap, New Guinea
January 1944

Kenneth W. Honeycutt sitting in the cockpit and Joseph L. Fallon standing by the wing of "Modena VI", a P-47, serial number 42-75285, squadron #21.

"They called it a new airplane, but for us, it was a new type of airplane," says Frank Royal, explaining that the white-painted tail of these so-called Jugs tipped them off that they had come from another highly active fighter squadron. "It was unfair to have these tired old birds foisted off on us. Later on, we were supplied with 'fresh' planes. As with most injuries, the pain eased with time."

Also easing the pain for the squadron was a new chemistry emerging between the men, both pilots and ground crews. As veteran pilots, still very young but having flown many missions, were cycled out, new pilots and ground crews were coming in. These new men, like Bob Thorpe, had never flown or serviced a Lightning. All of their fighter-plane training had been with the Thunderbolt.

Schwimmer Air Drome
Port Moresby, New Guinea
July 9, 1943

After painting "Dumbo" on the nose of #37, Lt. John C. Dunbar stands beside his P-38.

Lt. Lew Lockhart had a good reason for his attachment to the P-38. While flying a mission against Rabaul on Oct. 29, 1943, one of the engines in his P-38 was hit by ground fire. He was able to land at Kiriwini on one engine.

There were other reasons why pilots of the 39th were reluctant to give up their P-38s. A fighter plane had just room enough for the supplies and equipment needed to get off the ground, find and engage the enemy, and get home. Anything else had to be small enough to fit in the pilot's pockets.

The pilots of the 39th were an ingenious lot, and, when they needed to bring something along, they would find a way. Lt. John Dunbar was a volleyball addict. No matter what the pressures of war, he and his young friends could find relaxation in batting the ball back and forth over the net for hours. So when the squadron relocated from Port Moresby to Gusap, he had to bring the volleyball gear along. But where could he put it?

His solution was the weapons compartment in the nose of his P-38. The guns stayed, but, by removing all of the ammunition, he was able to fit in the ball, net, and other volleyball paraphernalia.

Playing volleyball in the equatorial heat at Gusap worked up a sweat. Players were able to cool off with a few cold beers, thanks to Lew Lockhart's equally ingenious use of his plane's weapons compartment. Assigned to ferry P-38s from Australia to Port Moresby, he substituted beer for ammo. Just as he was looking forward to other beer runs, the squadron transitioned to the P-47. No weapons compartment, no beer.

Both the Lightning and the Airacobra were sleek airplanes. Straight or gently curving lines ran back from their pointed noses or nacelles to their tails. Their tricycle landing gears leveled them so they appeared to be in flight even when standing on the ground.

The P-47 Thunderbolt, quickly nicknamed the Jug because of its bottlelike appearance, was anything but sleek. The bulbous nose and massive radial engine towered in front, the rest of the fuselage dropping steeply back down to the tail-dragging rear wheel. In fact, the nose was so high that the pilot's sightline straight-ahead was blocked on takeoff. And, with its wing-mounted guns, the pilots lost the treasured straight-ahead firing capability they had had with the Lightning, and even with the Airacobra's often-temperamental cannon.

1st Lt. Lewis Lockhart
Gusap, New Guinea
1944

But the Jug did have some formidable strengths. When bullets pouring out of the eight .50-caliber wing-mounted machine guns reached their set convergence point, 100 to 250 yards ahead, their concentrated wallop turned targets into mangled, smoldering wrecks if it did not vaporize them altogether. Once off the ground, the stubby plane's flight performance was remarkable.

Someone, probably a Jug hater, suggested a flight contest between a Lightning and a Jug one day in Gusap, soon after the Jugs had arrived. "The Jug and the Lightning came in at a shallow dive, crossed our runway side by side, and buzzed low over the Ramu Valley toward what appeared to be a cinder cone sticking up in the valley maybe 3 or 4 miles away," recalls crew chief Sgt. Roy Seher. "Both planes turned behind the cinder cone and disappeared.

"Having turned shorter than the Lightning, the Jug came into view on the other side in the lead. Both planes climbed a bit, then again made their shallow side-by-side dive across our runway, this time pulling up into a near vertical climb.

"In disbelief, I watched the Lightning slow and level off before stalling as the bellowing Jug just kept right on climbing. Slowly and reluctantly, I had to admit to myself (but never to anyone else) that the Jug was a pretty good airplane."

But the controversy over replacing Lightings with Thunderbolts would not go away. The veterans remaining with the squadron had many hours of combat experience, but few, if any, flying a Thunderbolt. So there developed a mutually beneficial exchange of ideas and experience. Unlike typical rookies, the Thunderbolt-trained men had skills that the veterans needed and appreciated.

On takeoff, the Lightning emitted a deep-throated purr and levitated into the sky like it belonged there. In contrast, complains Royal, the Thunderbolt, with its big radial engine, "bellowed loud and long, protesting all the way until it finally clawed its way into the air. Then, miracle of miracles, once up and clean, the ugly duckling turned into a swan. This transformation was amazing. It took us a long while to put aside our prejudice and admit that this Jug was a formidable weapon and really could do everything that the Lightning could do."

While the 39th was acclimating to the Jug in Australia, in New Guinea, the Japanese had been driven back from Solomons, Buna, and Lae, and U.S. and Australian ground forces had occupied Markham Valley. Flat and enormous, the valley was ideal for airfields, so after having operated out of Port Moresby for more than a year, on returning to New Guinea, the squadron was moved up to an old Japanese fighter strip at Lae. While that substantially reduced the distance to targets, it also introduced some new hazards.

A strong prevailing crosswind forced pilots to come in far to the windward side of the runway. One pilot who came in too far to the windward side smashed into three P-40s. Two of these were too badly damaged to be repaired, but the Jug needed only a wing replacement, demonstrating to the men that the Jug was "one tough bird."

The crosswind problem was solved when a long, smooth fighter strip was finished at Nadzab, several miles up the Markham Valley. Engineers had also completed two other fighter strips and two bomber strips in the valley, moving the Fifth Air Force to better striking distance. Eight Thunderbolts from the 39th flew their first operating mission from Nadzab on December 15, 1943.

On January 27, 1944, the squadron moved 100 miles further north to Gusap in the Ramu Valley. The forward most of all Allied bases, Gusap, was bombed and strafed regularly, but not with the intensity the squadron endured at Port Moresby. Wewak was still a Japanese stronghold, and squadron Thunderbirds both escorted bombers and made strafing attacks intended to destroy everything on the ground there.

On March 4, the entire squadron had front-row seats at an unusual fighter contest right over the airstrip. A Thunderbolt flown by Major Tom McDonough was making a landing approach with wheels and flaps down when four Japanese Tonys roared in for a strafing attack. The Tony, which got its nickname when it was mistaken for an Italian design, was light, fast, and maneuverable like the Japanese Zeke, and even had a self-sealing fuel tank. But that was not going to do the Japanese much good in this action.

Apparently not having seen MacDonough approaching, the Tonys cut in front of him to make their strafing pass. McDonough hit full throttle, picked up his wheels and flaps, and went after them. He destroyed one of the planes with a burst of fire. Unfortunately, however, they were all so low that part of the burst hit the base's hospital tent up on high ground above the field. Lt. Frank Royal happened to be a hospital patient at the time, racked with dengue fever.

"Luckily, no one was hit," he remembers. "I staggered on wobbly, weak legs to a foxhole, fell in it, and righted myself just in time to see Mc-Donough bring his guns to bear on another plane. The Jap plane smoked and dove into the ground, resulting in a huge ball of flame. We cheered loud and long, and then we struggled back to our beds."

The Thunderbolt's radial engine was exceptionally rugged, but, like any other machine, it could malfunction, and on March 14, it failed Lt. Gene Duncan at the worst possible time. His flight was passing over the mouth of the Sepik River in Japanese-controlled territory when he had to ditch in the sea. His flight mates circled around him and called for an amphibious rescue plane to pick him up. Duncan managed to get into this life raft as a Japanese patrol boat set out from shore to pick him up. Pilots of the 39th strafed the patrol boat, but an onshore wind was blowing Duncan in despite his desperate efforts to paddle out. Pilots stayed as long as their remaining fuel permitted, hoping for the rescue plane to show up. It never came.

Returning to base, Lt. Lee Grosshuesch and Captain Widman quickly refueled and flew back, but Lieutenant Duncan was nowhere to be found. Years later, at the war crimes trials at Yokohama, it was learned that Duncan had been captured and beheaded.

Back at Gusap, the squadron was wrestling with another problem that had nothing to do with the Thunderbolt's engine or design. The planes were experiencing frequent tire blowouts on takeoffs and landings, the result of defective inner tubes.

"There is no doubt that slipshod product cost lives," Royal declares. All planes were grounded while every tire was dismantled and inspected. Prior to the inspections, he had noticed a deep gash in one plane's tire and had it replaced with a "premounted shiny new tire and wheel." But when that plane returned from its next mission, the same tire blew out. The plane pulled to the right, left the runway, dug into the soft soil, and flipped over onto its back. "The pilot was drenched with fuel, but thankfully, there was no fire," Royal said. "Flipping onto the dirt rather than the steel runway saved the pilot's life."

Chapter 13
Black Sunday

On Easter Sunday, April 16, 1944, a force of more than 300 Fifth Air Force aircraft attacked the major Japanese base at Hollandia, a name indicating a Dutch presence in the East Indies. Their bombing mission complete, the planes were returning south when they encountered an enormous weather front between the mountains and the sea. The returning pilots had no option but to take on the storm. The day would come to be remembered as Black Sunday, as 37 planes were lost, the biggest noncombat loss ever suffered by the U.S. Air Force.

Based at Gusap, 16 pilots of the 39th FS had taken off to escort the B-24s as they returned from Hollandia. Major Harrison Denton led the squadron, accompanied by Captain Morgan and Lieutenants Johnson, Rothgerb, Tobi, Lynn, Lockhart, Thorpe, Vining, Frost, Ross, Steele, Mettler, Robertson, Rogers, and Jones.

As the squadron flew down the Ramu Valley to greet the returning bombers, the storm front had clearly consolidated ahead. To keep clear of the clouds, they were forced lower and lower. Denton had to decide whether to try to climb up over the turbulent weather or to simply abort the mission. He made his decision by swinging his P-47 around in a wide 180-degree turn and heading the squadron back to Gusap. His decision was met favorably by some of his subordinates, but not by all of them. How could a squadron leader turn his back on such an important mission? The heavy bombers were depending on the cover the pilots of the 39th would provide.

When one of the officers challenged him at the debriefing, Denton let him have it. "Have you ever seen weather like that this early in the morning?" Denton demanded. "Do you have any idea what it will be like a few hours from now?" The argument ended a few minutes later when word came from Fifth Fighter Command that all planes were now grounded. By noon, the solid overcast had reached as far east as Gusap, home of the 39th Fighter Squadron, and bases at Nadzab, Saidor, and Finschaven were also closed.

Radio signals reflected total confusion. Gas was low, and the returning pilots were deciding whether to bail out or let down below the level of the mountains, hoping to gain some visibility.

Lt. Lew Lockhart recalls the atmosphere in the debriefing room. "Some of them practically called Major Denton a coward for aborting the mission. But he didn't take any crap from them. It was his decision and responsibility, and he 'wasn't going to listen to any second-guessing,' he announced in a loud voice."

Lt. John J. "Jack" Frost
39th FS, 35th FG, 5th AF
Gusap, New Guinea
1944

Lt. Jack Frost remembers the incident vividly. "We were a little past Dumpu when Major Harris called an abort, explaining that the weather would block us out of the Ramu Valley if we continued.

"The response from some of the pilots was mutinous, openly accusing Denton of cowardice. They got to eat those words when we got back to operations, and the radio began to crackle. Incoming pilots called each other, asking about options as they calculated their fuel supply and tried to guess their location," Frost added.

Within the next few hours, 11 aircraft would disappear: four ditched, three crashed, four crews bailed out over remote areas, and nine would be destroyed in landing accidents. Survivors would return from the jungle for the next several weeks. Black Sunday eventually claimed the lives of 54 airmen.

Denton wasn't the only CO to abort his mission that day. As it turned out, the sister 40th Squadron made an identical decision with their Thunderbolts and returned all 16 safely to Gusap.

"We went on a search mission the next day, trying to locate survivors," Frost said. "If Major Denton hadn't made the right decision, other pilots would have been out looking for us. We didn't lose one plane or pilot thanks to his courageous decision."

Each year, the 39th Fighter Squadron holds a reunion at a city in the United States. During the 1993 reunion at the USAF Air Academy at Colorado Springs, Colorado, the subject of "Black Sunday" was introduced. The former Harris Denton sat in the audience as the Reverend William Rogers recalled the time when he flew behind Denton when the mission was aborted.

Rogers admitted that he had been one of the more critical pilots when questioning the decision that day. He apologized to Denton for himself and any of the other pilots who reacted poorly. "If we had ventured to the other side of that weather, it was certain that at least some of us would have lost our lives."

It was a touching moment, since it came at a time when Harris Denton was dying of cancer. The final cost of "Black Sunday" was:

- 11 aircraft force-landed
- Four aircraft ditched
- Three aircraft abandoned
- 11 aircraft missing
- Two aircraft crashed

Fifteen additional aircraft were damaged beyond repair. Black Sunday claimed a total of 37 Fifth aircraft damaged or lost. Years later, General Kenney wrote in his memoirs, "That night there was gloom in the Fifth Air Force. It was the worst blow I took in the whole war."

The weeks following Black Sunday were the busiest in the history of the Air-Sea Rescue Service. Catalina flying boats rescued some of the men floating in yellow rubber boats. Many more who went down at sea were never found. Crew members walked out of the jungles for weeks, but many more simply disappeared. Burned wreckage of crashed planes was spotted on mountainsides from Lae to Wewak.

Representatives of the American Graves Registration Service and the Australian Philippine-Ryukyus Command searched New Guinea in 1948 for missing Allied aircraft from "Black Sunday." Eyewitnesses to crashes including natives and Japanese POWs held at Manus Island and Rabaul were interrogated. Two Liberators, one Mitchell, and seven Lightnings and their crews remain missing from that fateful day.

The reason that both 39th and the 40th Fighter Squadron were assigned to escort the bombers on their "return" from Hollandia was the limited range of the Jug. It was this range problem more than any other issue— the ungainly shape, the wing-mounted guns, the deafening engine—that limited its combat effectiveness and frustrated the pilots.

"We didn't come here to watch the war," complained Jack Frost. "We came to fight." The fighting spirit of these pilots was to be unleashed just weeks later when the Jug's range was almost doubled by a flight endurance system devised by the American aeronautical genius Charles Lindbergh, who had been a leading opponent of American intervention in World War II prior to the attack on Pearl Harbor.

Black Sunday - April 16, 1944

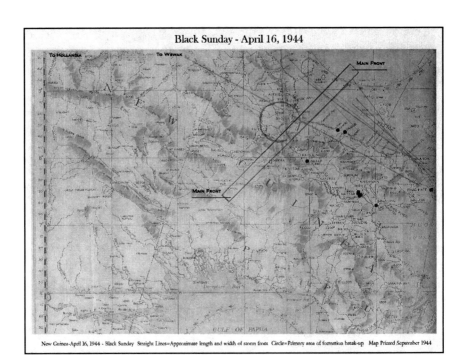

New Guinea-April 16, 1944 - Black Sunday Straight Lines=Approximate length and width of storm front Circle=Primary area of formation break-up Map Printed September 1944

Chapter 14
Pushing North

Relations between the veteran P-39 pilots of the 39th and the new men who joined the squadron in January 1944 were good, but not perfect. "All of us newcomers were referred to as 'New Boys,' although some of us had significantly more flying time in the P-47 than any of the veterans," Jack Frost said in an interview in 2009.

Frost had joined the squadron along with Lts. James Steele, Fred Tobi, Bob Thorpe, and Marcus Trout. "We had just completed our last stop at Guadalcanal. The marines were doing a mop-up action, but the island was pretty well secure so that refueling could occur without concern. Our destination was Brisbane, Australia. We saw the city and the broad beach from the air, but that was all. We went through the usual accounting of issued equipment and medical exams, including STDs. I wonder just where one would pick up an STD on a flight where the passengers were treated with less respect than the freight.

"We made a quick stop at Townsville, Australia, on our way north and stayed at the Queens Hotel. Now that was more like it. The beer was great, and our spirits revived with each sip. Now off to Port Moresby in an old Gooney Bird (C-47) over the Coral Sea. A number of tin shacks huddled on one street in Port Moresby, straight out of Somerset Maugham. We didn't stay long and were soon on our way over the snow-topped Owen Stanley Mountains and into Nadzab, the distribution point for all pilots. Thorpe, Trout, Tobi, and I were assigned to the 39th Fighter Squadron that was at Gusap, up a way in the Ramu Valley.

Nadzab, New Guinea
December 1943 - January 1944

Entrance to the 39th FS encampment

"We were again in a C-47, this time perched on 50-gallon drums of aviation gas. We would learn that Gusap was the precursor to the Berlin airlift, because everything had to be flown in by air. We were totally familiar with the P-47, but we had flown newer birds in training than what we had to fly in combat."

On Jan. 1, 1944, the 39th Fighter Squadron consisted of 44 officers and 280 enlisted men. Other pilots joined the 39th in early January, included Lts. Maurice Bolund, Telesphore Gruber, John Lockhart, and Billy Richards. They were P-39 pilots with combat experience in the 40th and 41st squadrons, so their first duty was to check out in the P-47s.

The 39th Fighter Squadron moved from Nadzab to Gusap on Jan. 27, 1944, and established itself in one large camp along the banks of the Ramu River. The new camp had taken 3 months to build, was well laid out, and the various buildings featured cement floors and full screening. Gusap, like Taili Taili, was only accessible by air. At that time, it was the most forward of Allied bases and was subject to enemy bombing and strafing runs from Wewak, a Japanese stronghold.

P-47s from the 39th covered bombing runs and conducted strafing sweeps to destroy everything possible on the ground. At the war crimes trials at Yokohama in 1948, it was revealed that Japanese soldiers at Wewak actually painted chickens green to protect them from destruction at the hands of American pilots.

Moving to Gusap gave the P-47s a better chance to escort the bombers on their missions against Wewak. Hollandia, further up the coast from Wewak, was still beyond the range of the P-47.

All pilots of the 39th could do was to meet the bombers on their way back, which offered little protection for bombers over the targets.

Men of the 39th had other challenges to consider.

"We could never be sure of the natives in the area," Fred Tobi said in an interview in 2007. "Some of them were friendly, but we had to always be on guard. Before the war, missionaries had persuaded some headhunters and cannibals to abandon their gruesome occupations. It didn't work with all of them.

39th Encampment Area
Gusap Airfield Complex, New Guinea

February 1944

"Home Sweet Home" a few feet from the Ramu River.

"Among the headhunters, a man is judged by the number of heads he has in his collection. No headhunter reaches manhood until he has at least one head in his collection. We carried our sidearms at all times when natives prowled the camps," Tobi said.

"Most of January 1944 was devoted to transition and training flights for the new pilots. Our first flight was an orientation flight to give us an idea where we were and a little look at the jungle, a first-time sight," Frost said. "The flight took us up the Ramu Valley to the deltas of the Sepik and Ramu rivers. We deployed in flights of four. Outcast Red was leader with White, Blue, and Green designations for the other flights. Our first mission was to Wewak, a Japanese air base on the north coast of New Guinea."

Gusap, New Guinea
39th FS, 35th FG, 5th AF
March 1944

Fifteen Pilots of the 39th Fighter Squadron

Front row - L to R: Idon M. Hodge, Gene Haws, William W. Anderson, William L. Urquhart, Gene Duncan, Richard T. Cella with his saxophone and Lloyd P. Shipley with his holstered .45.

Second row: Frederick G. Tobi, Robert P. Harvey, and George E. Morgan.

Third row: Edward J. Deedy, Richard E. Smith, Benjamin M. Widmann, Robert A. Hussa, and Wayne P. Rothgeb.

The 39th FS participated in operations when the Sixth Army landed at Saidor on January 2, 1944. After the initial landing, the squadron's operational activity consisted of fighter sweeps over the peninsula as the ground forces pushed forward toward Bogadjim and Madang.

Lieutenant Clymer scored the 39th's first victory in a P-47 when he shot down a Zeke during a fighter sweep over Wewak on Jan. 8. The squadron had dropped its belly tanks while engaging 16 enemy fighters. When Lieutenant Colonel Doss was unable to drop his belly tank, a Zeke latched on to his tail. Clymer gave the Zeke a short burst, and the plane exploded and crashed into the sea.

By the end January 1944, construction at Gusap was completed, including portable buildings for the mess, operations, and the dispensary. The mail and chow had one of their best months, according to squadron reports. The operations for January 1944 consisted of 155 escort fighter sweeps and 389 patrol sorties, a total of 1,487 combat hours.

On Feb. 9, 1944, the quiet of a peaceful evening was disturbed by the "parachute scare" as members of the 39th now refer to the occasion. Intelligence reports received that day stated that possible enemy paratroop units had been identified at northern New Guinea bases. When low-flying planes approached Gusap, it was assumed that the base was about to be attacked by the air.

Confusion reigned supreme in the 39th as officers and enlisted men screaming for guns and ammunitions mobbed the ordinance tent. Most of them did not even know how to arm the guns they were demanding. Orders were issued to hold the riverbank as a defensive line, and no one was to fire his weapon until attacked. The official log states: "The alert was called off, fortunately, before the squadron succeeded in committing mass murder upon itself."

On Feb. 10, Major Thomas Lynch shot down a twin-engine bomber over Wewak, his 17th victory. A freak accident occurred on Feb. 24 when Lt. Lee Vining, testing a P-38, had a midair collision with a P-47 piloted by Lieutenant Norton of the 40th Fighter Squadron. The planes crashed in flames, but both pilots parachuted safely to the ground.

On Feb. 25, 1944, Lt. Robert Thorpe was returning from a valley patrol when his engine froze over the dispersal area at a very low altitude. Bailing out, he hit the ground the instant after he felt the jerk of his chute. Onlookers were not sure whether his fall had been broken, so close was his escape. Minor bruises and scratches were his only injuries, and Lieutenant Thorpe was flying missions the following day.

During a meeting with Gill Thorpe and Ken Dooley in 2007, Fred Tobi told the story about Bob's bailout. It was the first time Gill had ever heard it. Tobi wasn't surprised. "A couple of weeks after his bailout incident, Bob was reading a letter from home when I walked into our tent," Tobi said. "I asked him how the family reacted to his near-miss. Bob said they didn't know anything about it. 'No sense in worrying them,' he said."

March 16, 1944

Still no word of Lieutenant Duncan, so Colonel Wagner and Captains Denton, Bills, Widmann, and Grosshuesch took off on a search mission at 0752. Wagner and Bills returned at 1230, and the rest at 1320 without success. We had 11 planes left so they took off at 0855 to escort B-24s to Wewak. Landing at 1222, they said they were over the target from 1050 to 1105 and flew at an altitude of 18,000 feet. The bombing was excellent.

March 17, 1944

The mission for today was a 16-ship escort for the B-24s to Wewak. One flight remained in the target area where Lieutenant Duncan was last seen, but was unable to see anything of him.

On April 5, 1944, there was a fiery P-47 crash that took the life of Lt. Albert Lane and an enlisted man working in the operations shack. When Lane started his takeoff, his plane left the runway and ran full throttle into the base operations shack. Two of the men working there escaped by diving over the back railing, but the third man was trapped.

April 11, 1944

The first mission today was carried out by 18 P-47s, including Major Denton, Captain Cella, Lieutenants

Hodge, Thorpe, Tobi, Roghgab, Foster, Richards, Steele, Mettlier, Uraben, Rogers, Schopka, Kramme, Neumann, Boland, Querns, and Lockhart. Takeoff time at 0930 and the B-24s were escorted to Hansa Bay and returned. The bombing of the B-24s was excellent. There were no enemy sightings, and they returned at 1230. Lt. Dewey Foster is still missing from this mission. Just above station 5, he broke away from the formation and headed home. He appeared all right but didn't contact the squadron by radio. A search is being made for him by all planes going up the valley and also by L-5s.

April 13, 1944

A search mission for Lieutenant Foster was conducted by Lieutenants Lockhart, Johnson, Thorpe, Rohrs, Ross, and Captain Tansing. No sightings of interest were reported. Foster was never found, and he is listed as killed in action on 4/11/44.

May 3, 1944

Captain Rothgeb and Lieutenants Frost, Richards, and Rohrs took off this morning at 1030 on a strafing mission to Wewak. The results were generally observed, with just a few fires. The next mission was a patrol of Wewak. Grosshuesch, Johnson, Hodge, Querns, and Thorpe were the pilots. Takeoff time was at 1155, and landing time was 1520. No enemy sightings.

May 25, 1944

The mission for today was strafing runs over Wewak. Takeoff time for Major Denton, Lieutenants Kramme,

Lockhart, and Mittlestadt was at 1020. Some small fires were observed in the area. Captain Vining and Lieutenants Perkins, Thorpe, and Tobi were off at 1022. Captain Prentice, Lieutenants Linn, Trout, and Querns were off at 1040. Green flight with Lieutenants Grosshuesch, Robertson, Steele, and Schupka took off at 1043.

May 26, 1944

Vining, Johnson, Steele, Schopka, Kramme, Mittlestadt, Lockhart, and Querns took off on a strafing mission against Wewak at 1415. Several fires were started, and a small bridge was set afire.

Unfortunately, the flight log for May 27, 1944, the mission on which Lt. Robert Thorpe was shot down, captured, and beheaded, is missing. Thorpe is mentioned in two subsequent reports.

The squadron was grounded by bad weather the day after Thorpe was reported missing. Fred Tobi and Lew Lockhart broke regulations and went in search of their missing friend. Things were never the same for Tobi, who had gone through flight training with Thorpe and was his tent mate at Gusap.

June 2, 1944

The squadron conducted a search mission for Lt. Robert Thorpe. Lieutenants Prentice, Aycock, Ross, and Lynn searched the target area around Wewak and had to return because of bad weather.

June 3, 1944

Major Denton, Captains Bills and Vining, and Lieutenant Trout were off this morning at 0850 on a search mission for our missing Lieutenant Thorpe. There were no sightings of him, and they returned back here at 1125.

Lt. Jack Frost, who kept his own daily diary, was also missing an entry for the mission on May 27. "I was on that mission with Bob Thorpe," Frost said in a 2013 interview. "I have no idea why this mission is a blank. I flew on a number of missions with Bob Thorpe, and he had a good record. No record of aborted missions for Thorpe."

On June 8, 1944, word was received that the 39th Fighter Squadron was to move back to Nadzab. "We had word that Charles Lindbergh, who had been at Guadalcanal teaching marine pilots to reduce their gas consumption and increase their flight range, was coming to the 39th to train us," Fred Tobi said.

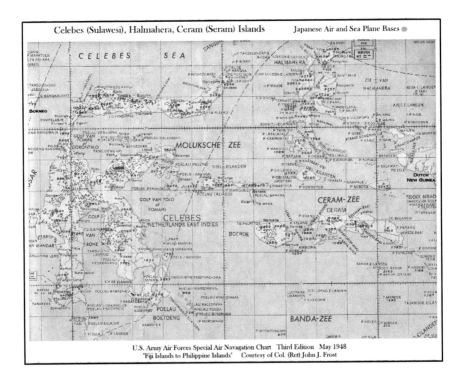

U.S. Army Air Forces Special Air Navagation Chart   Third Edition   May 1948
'Fiji Islands to Philippine Islands'   Courtesy of Col. (Ret) John J. Frost

Chapter 15
Lucky Lindy and the 39th

Lt. Fred Tobi never forgot his first combat mission. He and Bob Thorpe were given an orientation flight with Lt. Lew Lockhart, and then sent out the next day on an escort mission to protect U.S. ships from Japanese air attacks. The mission was under the command of Major Billy Anderson, who had "Nasty" for a nickname. His name had nothing to do with his disposition or combat experiences. He earned the "Nasty" title over a strategy he used in a game of Hearts.

The mission flew over the Owen Stanley Mountains with Tobi in "wing" position, the usual spot for new pilots. Tobi used his 200-gallon belly tank before switching to his main fuel supply. He called Anderson and reported his gas situation was getting low. Anderson merely told him "You're all right." When Tobi landed, he was totally out of gas and had to climb out of his plane and run off the runway to avoid being hit by landing planes.

"When Bob Thorpe, Jack Frost, and I joined the 39th, veteran pilots like Lew Lockhart were still complaining about losing their beloved 38s," Tobi said. "Bob, Jack, and I had been thoroughly trained in the P47s, so we were really comfortable with the aircraft. But there was one argument we couldn't win. They were gas-guzzlers, which kept us from taking part in a lot of critical missions—until Charles Lindbergh got involved."

"We heard that Lindbergh had been at Guadalcanal working with the P-38 and Marine F4U squadrons there, teaching them how to reduce gas consumption and increase their flight range," Lt. Jack Frost recalls. "He first briefed a large meeting in Nadzab, and then came back for individual briefings with the 39th. He did not fly any missions with us, because General Kenney issued orders that he was not to take part in combat," Frost said.

"He returned to duty with the marines who were more liberal and allowed him to fly missions against Rabaul. We heard later that he shot down an enemy plane. What he did for us was a lot more important than any role he could have supplied in combat," Frost said. In 1944, Lindbergh was 42 years old.

The Lindbergh method was to open the throttle wide, and then reduce RPMs by increasing the pitch of the propeller, which would leave the engine laboring heavily. Then the pilot would lean the fuel mixture, starving the engine for fuel and greatly reducing its power output. Leaning the mixture too much would produce vibration, which was corrected by making the mixture a little richer. At the correct setting, this would result in a 180-mph cruise speed at a very low altitude.

Lindbergh combined his teaching with combat flying, mostly unknown to the Fifth Air Force brass. On May 21, 1944, he flew a strafing mission at Rabaul, and, a few days later, a bomber escort mission from the marine air base at Bougainville. One pilot flying on the second mission refused to go with him again, explaining he did not want to be known as the guy who killed Lindbergh.

In his 6 months in the Pacific, he flew 50 combat missions, including one on July 28, 1944, when he shot down a Sonia observation plane. General MacArthur once said that Charles Lindbergh was the unsung hero of the war in the Pacific. There was a good reason why his role was not publicized during the war.

When he proposed that a neutrality pact be negotiated with Germany during testimony before the U.S. House Committee on Foreign Affairs on January 23, 1941, he had gone too far for the Roosevelt administration. The president described him as a "defeatist and an appeaser" at a White House press conference on April 25, 1941.

"When I read Lindbergh's speech, I felt that it could not have been better put than if it had been written by Joseph Goebbels himself," Secretary of War Henry Stimson said. "What a pity that this youngster has completely abandoned his belief in our form of government and has accepted Nazi methods because apparently they are more efficient." Treasury Secretary Henry Morgenthau added, "If I should die tomorrow, I want you to know this. I am absolutely convinced that Lindbergh is a Nazi."

On April 28, 1941, Lindbergh resigned his commission as an Air Corps colonel, claiming he had no honorable alternative. The Japanese attack on Pearl Harbor shocked Lindbergh, although he had previously predicted that America's "wavering policy in the Philippines" would invite war there. In one speech, he warned, "We should either fortify these islands adequately or get out of them entirely." He had consistently advocated alertness and military strength, while maintaining that defending the country from attack was the U.S. military's sole purpose. Now, the country had been attacked, and its best-known aviator wanted to rally to its defense . . . but would the defense establishment welcome his help?

When Stimson declined his request for a commission in what was now the United States Army Air Corps, he approached several aviation companies to offer his services as a consultant. Lindbergh was welcomed at Ford Motor Company, where Henry Ford shared many of his views and contributed to troubleshooting early problems on the B-24 production line. Then he joined United Aircraft in 1943, first as an engineering consultant and later as a technical representative in the Pacific Theater to study aircraft performances under combat conditions.

So much had changed in the 16 years since Charles Lindbergh took off from Roosevelt Field, Long Island, at 7:52 a.m. on Friday, May 20, 1927, burdened with a record load of gasoline and hampered by a muddy, rain-soaked runway. He was not the best-known aviator attempting a nonstop transatlantic flight. Five others had attempted . . . and failed before him. But 33½ hours later, when he landed at Le Bourget Airport, 7 miles northeast of Paris, he became a worldwide hero who had transformed aviation.

"Before that, people seemed to think we aviators were from outer space or something," wrote Eleanor Smith Sullivan, winner of the 1930 Best Woman Aviator of the Year Award. "But after Charles Lindbergh's flight, we could do no wrong. It's hard to describe the impact Lindbergh had on people. Even the first walk on the moon doesn't come close. The '20s was such an innocent time, and people were still so religious—I think they felt like this man was sent by God to do this. And it changed aviation forever because all of a sudden, the Wall Streeters were banging on our doors looking for airplanes to invest in. We'd been standing on our heads trying to get them to notice us, but after Lindbergh, suddenly *everyone* wanted to fly, and there weren't enough planes to carry them."

He arrived back in the United States aboard the United States navy cruiser *Memphis*. On June 11, 1924, a fleet of warships and multiple flights of military aircraft, including pursuit planes, bombers, and a rigid airship, escorted him up the Potomac River to the Washington Navy Yard where President Calvin Coolidge awarded him the Distinguished Flying Cross.

Two days later, a ticker tape parade was held for him before enthralled crowds down New York's Fifth Avenue, and the next night he was honored with a grand banquet at the Hotel Commodore attended by some 3,700 people. On December 14, the Medal of Honor, normally only awarded for heroism in combat, was awarded to him by a special act of Congress. He was selected as the first *Time* magazine "Man of the Year," appearing on its cover on January 2, 1928. At age 25, Lindbergh remains the youngest individual to receive the designation.

The massive publicity transformed the public's skepticism about air travel. By 1928, applications for pilots' licenses had tripled, and the number of licensed aircraft quadrupled. Between 1926 and 1929, the number of U.S. airline passengers grew from 5,782 to 173,405.

Lindbergh's connections with the Army Air Corps began in 1924 with a year of military flight training with the U.S. Army Air Service. On March 5, 1925, he experienced his most serious flying accident. Just 8 days before graduation, he was involved in a midair collision while practicing aerial combat maneuvers and was forced to bail out. He graduated first in his class of 104 cadets and earned his pilot's wings and a commission as a 2nd lieutenant in the Air Service Reserve Corps.

Years later, he attributed that year of training to his development as a focused, goal-oriented individual, and a skillful and resourceful aviator. At the time, the army did not need any more active-duty pilots so he returned to civilian aviation as a barnstormer and flight instructor. As a reserve officer, he continued to do some part-time military flying by joining the Missouri National Guard's observation squadron, where he was promoted to 1st lieutenant.

Fame has its price, and in his case it was the kidnapping and murder of his baby son. The circus atmosphere surrounding the trial of the century when the kidnapper was sentenced to execution so disgusted Lindbergh that he moved to Europe in 1930.

In December 1937, after years of living abroad, the Lindbergh family returned to the U.S. at the personal request of General "Hap" Arnold, chief of the United States Army Air Corps in which Lindbergh had risen to the rank of colonel in the reserves. He accepted a temporary call-up to active duty to help estimate that service's readiness for a potential war. This included evaluating new aircraft types being developed, recruitment procedures, and finding a site for a new air force research institute and other potential air bases.

Assigned a Curtiss P-36 fighter, he toured various facilities in the U.S., and made several trips to Germany to report on the German air force, the Luftwaffe. Touring German aviation facilities, sometimes in the company of Luftwaffe Chief Hermann Goring, Lindbergh became convinced that the Luftwaffe was the most advanced air force in the world. He was the first American permitted to examine the Luftwaffe's newest bomber, the Junkers 88, and the frontline fighter, the Messerschmitt 109. Of the 109, he said that he knew "of no other pursuit plane which combines simplicity of construction with such excellent performance characteristics."

In Berlin, Lindbergh was lionized much as he had been in Washington 9 years before. At a dinner held in his honor, Goring presented him with the Commander Cross of the Order of the German Eagle. The medal became controversial a few weeks later with the anti-Jewish rioting and violence of Kristallnacht, but Lindbergh declined to return it. "If I were to return the German medal, it seems to me that it would be an unnecessary insult. Even if war develops between us, I can see no gain in indulging in a spitting contest before that war begins."

Lindbergh warned in a secret memo that it would be "suicide" for

Britain and France to oppose Hitler's violation of the 1938 Munich treaty. He contended that the French army was incapable of stopping Hitler, and that Britain's military, overly reliant on naval power, was outdated. Lindbergh apologists have argued that he was not so much pro-German as anti-Soviet. In an issue of the *Reader's Digest* in 1939, Lindbergh wrote, "Our civilization depends on peace among Western nations and, therefore, on united strength." Deploring the rivalry between Germany and Britain, he favored conflict between Germany and Russia.

By late 1940, he was serving as a spokesman for the antiwar American First Committee, addressing large crowds at Madison Square Garden and Soldiers' Field in Chicago. Rather than opposing Germany, he insisted America's focus should be on upholding the Monroe Doctrine, preserving the Western Hemisphere from European conflicts.

Lindbergh's growing rift with Washington may have had much to do with his stubbornness in his convictions and his inexperience in political maneuvering as with his convictions themselves. A. Scott Berg, his Pulitzer Prize–winning biographer, points out that Lindbergh's acceptance of the German Eagle medal had been approved by the American embassy and that his nonintervention message and participation in the America First Committee had broad-based popular support.

What probably hurt him most in the public eye, according to Berg, was his willingness to make excuses for Hitler. Lindbergh had written in his diary on April 2, 1939, "I believe she [Germany] has pursued the only consistent policy in Europe in recent years. I cannot support her broken promises, but she has only moved a little faster than other nations in breaking promises. The question of right and wrong is one thing by law and another thing by history."

Chapter 16
The Philippines Campaign

On October 20, 1944, General MacArthur kept his famous promise to return to the Philippines, wading ashore among the flashing cameras of the assembled press corps at Palo, Leyte. On January 18, the ground crews of the 39th Fighter Squadron made a far less conspicuous landing at Lingayen, Luzon, 400 miles north of Palo.

The 3 months between those two landings were filled with momentous events in the Philippines Campaign. Three days after MacArthur's landing, one of history's biggest naval battles raged across Leyte Gulf, with Japan making a last-ditch effort to stop the Allied onslaught, and instead, suffering a shattering defeat. Japan lost six aircraft carriers, most of them without aircraft and used only as decoys. Kamikazes did inflict severe damage on the American invasion fleet, sinking 20 ships, damaging 68, and causing thousands of casualties. Battles raged ashore, with the Japanese losing all but 5,000 out of its 55,000-man force on Leyte.

At Lingayen, the men of the 39th, arriving by landing craft, managed to reach camp without incident or casualties.

"Our troops had landed just 4 days before we arrived, and this was a very busy place," remembers Jack Frost. It was busier, in fact, than Normandy had been the previous June. In a strategy General George Marshall described as "brilliant," MacArthur tricked the Japanese command into expecting landings well to the south on Luzon, and then poured 175,000 troops onto a 20-mile wide beachhead, without meeting any opposition other than a few ineffective attacks from a rapidly diminishing Japanese air force.

The Japanese army, still estimated at 200,000 strong, was dug in across the island preparing to try to stop the advance toward Manila. They were about to find out how devastating concentrated air attacks from Allied planes could be.

Sgt. Roy Seher, Crew Chief
39th FS, 35th FG, 5th AF
Schwimmer Air Drome, Port Moresby, New Guinea
September 1943

The 39th FS airplanes were scheduled to fly in a week later, and engineers threw themselves into preparing their airstrip. The sandy runway the Japanese had been using on the beach was too short and soft for the Jugs. Without tractors or graders, the men leveled the sand while Filipino volunteers laid down a layer of palm fronds. That layer was then covered with perforated steel plank, creating an almost instant runway. "We learned far more than we wanted to about linking and locking those steel panels together," says Sgt. Roy Seyer.

Their camp was in town, so the men had a lot of contact with the local population. They were shocked to see the protruding stomachs and spindly arms and legs of so many people, sure signs of malnutrition. "The whole population was starved," says Seyer. "Those damned Japs. Those brutal bastards."

At chow time we went through the food line, filled our mess kits and ate. Leftovers were taken outside to a garbage can to dump, and Filipinos were there begging for every scrap of food.

"Many of us went back through the line a second time and simply emptied the food into their pots and pans. The Filipinos, young and old alike, would look you in the eye, smile and nod their appreciation. There was never a more thankful people on the face of the earth. Obviously, it was impossible to feed all of those people, and very soon, a fence was set up, just a rope strung on stakes with a sign telling the public that they must stay back. And they did. They understood."

After 2 years in the New Guinea jungles, the Philippines was a culture shock for the men—a readjustment to civilization. New Guinea was sparsely populated by a near-Stone Age people. Battered and deprived by 3 years of Japanese occupation, the Filipinos could not have been more different.

"Traveling by the very narrow Luzon roads, there was always an unbroken line of refugees," says Seyer. "As our infantry pushed the Japs back, they were following close behind, apparently anxious to find separated family and to claim property held before the occupation. There were ox carts and wagons pulled by the most emaciated horses I had ever seen, all piled high with the family's meager belongings. And everyone walked. Men, women, and children walked, except for infants carried by their mothers. They had endured 3 years of hell, and now they had hope. They smiled!"

The P-47s of the 39th arrived on January 22, 1945, passing low over Lingayen before landing. The town turned out en masse. As the first planes taxied in and shut down, crowds rushed out to greet their heroes. With so many people on the landing strip, there was great danger that someone would walk into a whirling propeller, but thankfully, that did not happen. As our pilots crawled out of their airplanes, the crowds mobbed them, smiling, laughing, and thanking them for their freedom.

If troops from General Walter Kreuger's 1st and 14th Corps had been there, they would have been celebrating. In the brutal fighting to come at areas like Villa Verde Trail, Balete Pass, and Igo Dam, as the army pushed back stubborn Japanese resistance in their advance across Luzon, pilots of the 39th FS mauled defensive positions and destroyed supply and communication networks to the rear.

It was here that the P-47 came into its own, with tremendous strafing power and big bomb loads, just as it had been doing against German forces since June of 1944 in Europe. Between January and June, the 39th would carry out these attacks relentlessly.

In the Luzon Campaign, pilots of the 39th FS began an extended period of dive-bombing in close support of ground operations. At this time, the United States Sixth Army was driving northward from the plain of central Luzon to Balete Pass, just south of Santa Fe. This narrow, winding mountain pass was the entrance to the Cagayan Valley, and Japanese forces defended it with everything they had. In order to neutralize the enemy's dug-in position and minimize American casualties, air power was called in to destroy those defenses.

Capt. Leroy V. Grosshuesch, CO of the 39th at the time, said, "In conducting close support missions, our pilots were briefed on the ground situation in the sector they were supporting, terrain features, enemy dispositions, antiaircraft, and the location of friendly forces. In most instances, the target was marked either with white phosphorous smoke shells or by an L-5 aircraft dropping colored parachutes. The most essential factor governing the successful accomplishment of support operations are always weather conditions and close coordination with the ground controller," Grosshuesch added.

"If poor visibility over the target causes any uncertainty as to the location of friendly forces or we experienced poor radio contact with the ground controller, our flight went to a secondary target. Close support of ground forces is meticulous work, and extreme caution was necessary at all times to avoid mistakes that would endanger friendly forces. Many of our support strikes were conducted as close as 200 yards from our own front lines," Grosshuesch said.

The Jug's capability of absorbing punishing ground fire, returning to its airstrips, and then getting back into the fight with minimal repairs, was tested again and again. One loss did occur on January 26, 1945, when Lt. Paul Foster's engine failed and he crash-landed 50 miles behind enemy lines. His flight mates saw him get out of the plane safely and circled over him protectively until fading light and low fuel forced them to leave. This was well before the day of helicopter rescues, so it was not until the next morning that they could return to the scene. They found that the plane had been dragged away and assumed he had been captured or worse. He was listed as missing in action.

But Foster was lucky. He had been "adopted" by Filipino villagers and hidden from the Japanese. A small, dark man, he was able to walk right past Japanese checkpoints and patrols as he was escorted by groups of villagers back toward U.S. lines. Three weeks later, he walked into the 39th camp. No starving POW, he had gained 10 pounds and was flying missions 3 days later.

Two days after Foster was reported missing, the squadron's mission was to bomb and strafe a village reportedly occupied by the Japanese. Lt. William Rogers was in command and leading the flight. As he dove in toward the village, he spotted women's and children's garments on the clotheslines. Instantly, he radioed an order to abort the attack. When the flight returned to base, Rogers had no sooner landed then he, along with the squadron commander and the operations officer, were summoned to the office of the colonel commanding the group.

Furious, the colonel demanded to know why a direct order to attack the village was disobeyed. Rogers told him that it was his judgment, and his judgment alone, to abort the attack.

He explained that the village was obviously occupied by innocent civilians, not Japanese troops. That wasn't good enough for the colonel. He said he was ready to convene a court-martial to try Rogers for insubordination and subversion in time of war and do his very best to send him to the federal prison at Leavenworth.

Rogers did not back down. He reminded the colonel that, in a notice every pilot had been required to read and sign, General MacArthur had ordered that no Filipinos should be injured or killed by American forces, and that every effort should be made to protect them.

Rogers insisted that this is what he had done. He had obeyed General MacArthur's order, not the colonel's. Rogers asserted that if he were court-martialed, the colonel should also be tried for disobeying the general's order.

"Dismissed!" the colonel screamed at him. "Get out! I don't want to see your face here ever again!"

The aborted attack sums up the conflicting dimensions of Lieutenant Rogers. He had been a divinity student when the war broke out. If he had finished divinity school, he probably would have entered the service as a chaplain.

Instead, he volunteered, went through flight training, and chose to become a fighter pilot. He turned out to be not only one of the most skillful pilots in his squadron, but among the most aggressive.

Without ever departing from his career aim of becoming a minister, Lieutenant Rogers spent nearly 4 years attacking enemy planes, ships, and ground positions, causing inevitable loss of life. He even extended his combat tours to teach his extraordinary skills to new pilots joining the squadron. When the war ended, he returned to divinity school and spent a 50-year career in the ministry.

A quiet, private man, Reverend Rogers died in 2002 without ever making any public explanation of how he managed to combine these two radically different careers.

Ground support and bomber escort missions afforded minimal opportunities for aerial combat. Since the squadron had given up the Lightnings for the Jugs, only one pilot had achieved the coveted ace status. On January 30, 1945, Capt. Lee Grosshuesch was leading a flight of eight P-47s over the island of Formosa when they encountered a swarm of Japanese planes over the Taichu Airdrome. In the melee that followed, Grosshuesch shot down two biplanes, Lt. Charles Posey, flying the tail-end position, shot down three Zeros, and four other pilots shot down one each for a total of nine Japanese planes destroyed.

The 39th suffered no losses.

The following day, while escorting a formation of B-25s, pilots of the 39th encountered Zeros 15 miles south of Formosa. Lt. Albert Wiget, flying his first combat mission, shot down two, and Lt. Marcus Trout downed one.

At this late stage of the war, aerial encounters were few and far between. But once contact was made, it was not difficult for pilots of the 39th to gain the upper hand.

The Japanese never lacked for numbers of planes, ending the war with more than 6,000 of all types. During the war, the Japanese continued to develop more capable planes, especially fighters. The Nakajima Ki-84 Hayate, referred to by U.S. pilots as the "Frank," was developed as a replacement for the Oscar and was the best Japanese fighter to see action. Heavily armed and extremely maneuverable, it was considered a match for any Allied fighter. Pacific Theater commanders worried that the Frank would be extremely effective at intercepting high-flying B-29 Superfortresses now arriving in large numbers to bomb the home islands.

No war plane is better than its pilot, and it was the shortage of trained and experienced pilots that cancelled out any advantage in the numbers and capabilities of Japanese planes. This was immediately apparent on February 12, 1945, when a fighter sweep over Formosa, led by Rogers, encountered nine Franks and a Sally bomber. Rogers led the flight down on the Japanese formation and was surprised to see their pilots took no evasive action.

He shot one down without difficulty, and then pulled up when his vision was obstructed by oil on his canopy. In spite of obstructed vision, however, he was able to shoot down another. Then he watched his flight mates shoot down four more.

On Feb. 15, 1945, a five-plane flight led by Grosshuesch spotted an estimated 25 training planes over Kobi Airdrome on Formosa. Grossheusch led a diving attack on the trainers, destroying five of them himself. One of those was the Fifth Air Force's 2,500th victory of the war.

By April 1945, Manila had been liberated for over a month, and the 39th had relocated to Clark Field. Stubborn Japanese resistance continued north of the city. There were daily ground-support strafing and bombing missions for which the P-47 was so well-suited. But the P-47 was not the ideal plane for long-range bomber escorts and search-and-destroy fighter sweeps to Formosa and even on the south coast of China. Although the Lindbergh fuel-enhancement method gave the plane the necessary 1,000-mile range, the required low cruising speed was a problem. Fortunately, the Jug was rapidly being replaced by the P-51 Mustang.

William G. Adair's P-51 Mustang - Squadron #26
39th FS, 35th FG, 5th AF
1945

With sleek lines reminiscent of the Airacobra and the Lightning, the Mustang was the curious progeny of British defense needs and American aircraft design and manufacturing capabilities. In 1940, the RAF wanted a fighter with combat capabilities comparable to the Spitfire but with far greater range. The obvious mission for such a fighter would be long-range bomber escort. According to strategic bombing doctrine at the time, heavy bombers bristling with guns and flying in large formations were considered to be capable of fighting off enemy fighters on their own.

The fallacy of this doctrine was not completely obvious until 3 years later when, on just two missions, Luftwaffe fighters shot down 137 B-17s over Germany. Fortunately, the Mustang, designed and developed by North American Aviation and already battle tested by both the RAF and the American air force, was ready. With a cruising speed of 275 mph and top speed of 437 mph and armed with six .50-caliber, wing-mounted machine guns, it, along with the Lightning, had blasted enemy fighters out of the European skies and now was being redeployed in large numbers to the Pacific.

Curiously, some of the pilots who were so angry when their Lightnings were replaced with Jugs were now reluctant to give up the Jug. The Mustang was fast and sleek, and its Merlin engine purred like a kitten. But the engine was liquid-cooled and one bullet could knock it out. Pilots felt they were giving up the security of the Jug's roaring radial engine that could get them home with cylinders shot off.

The vulnerability of the Mustang engine was tragically demonstrated on May 31, 1945, during a 12-plane mission to Balete Pass by the 40th FS. Capt. George Morgan, who, by rights, should not have been there at all, led the Red Flight, having completed a full tour, flying 149 missions with the 39th FS from March 1943 to May 1944. He had been sent back to the United States. He married Mary Scott, an American nurse he had met in Australia.

Mary was now pregnant, and they were setting up housekeeping in California when a "request" arrived that he report to the commanding general, Fifth Air Force in the Pacific.

"They call it a request, but it's an order," he explained to his father. "I've got 5 days leave, and then I go back."

Assigned to the 40th in the Philippines, Morgan's many letters home praised the living conditions and minimized the risks in his new assignment. After all those months in tents and rude huts at the New Guinea air bases, he could scarcely believe the spacious housing, with attentive houseboys, and the excellent food he was now enjoying. And he assured his family that his combat assignments were not much to worry about. "It's nearly all ground support, which is interesting but not dangerous," he wrote to Mary.

"I really like my P-51. It's my idea of a fighter—it's light and plenty fast but tricky on landing."

Ground support was the squadron's mission on May 31, 1945. They were to strafe and bomb Japanese positions near the town of Santa Fe, which were holding up the American advance. As Morgan made his strafing run, his plane was hit by small arms fire. He immediately pulled up and headed for home, radioing his flight mates that he would land at Lingayen, which was closer than Clark, their home base.

When his damaged engine began running better, he radioed that he would try to get back to Clark.

His wingman saw him suddenly verge off toward Lingayen again. He radioed that the plane was not running right, and he had to get down. A few minutes later, he said he would be bailing out at 5,000 feet. His wingman watched him release the canopy, but never saw his chute open.

When Morgan's body was recovered, the squadron doctor reported that large cuts on the side of his body indicated that he had been hit by the stabilizer on bailing out. Fifteen days later a telegram reached Mary:

THE SECRETARY OF WAR DESIRES ME TO EXPRESS HIS DEEP REGRET THAT YOUR HUSBAND CAPT MORGAN GEORGE E WAS KILLED IN ACTION ON LUZON 31 MAY 45 CONFIRMING LETTER FOLLOWS.

The starkness of the telegram stands in strange contrast to the poignant tragedy of Morgan's death. His many letters to Mary and his family celebrate his joy at being an expectant father and of the life he and Mary planned together. His death, coming less than 3 months before the war ended, devastated them all.

After her mother died, Mary Martin, daughter of George and Mary Morgan, found a poem in her mother's desk.

Yellowed with age, it had been cut out of a newspaper. The title is "Missing Him," and the author is listed as anonymous.

Missing him is all the time
Weeping
Ranting
Raving
Screaming
Shaking fist at God
Are less.
But missing him is all the time.
Tears fall more gently now
From time to time
Dripping one after other
From eyes to chin.
A torrent, now and then
But missing him is all the time.
The wishes, prayers and fervent hope
That this might not be true
Come still,
But not as often now.
And with deep knowledge of the truth
Despite the wrong.
And missing him is all the time.
Life now, is altered
Very changed from what it was
No going backward, only forward.
Missing him and moving toward the future all alone
But not alone
Remembering him is all the time.

—Author Unknown

George Morgan's death confirmed the pilots' concerns about the Mustang, but the transition from the rugged P-47 was made. New pilots coming into the squadron were Mustang trained, and veteran pilots were there to teach them combat skills. The redoubtable William Rogers extended his tour by 6 months to make sure the new pilots knew what they were doing. Their strafing and bombing attacks on Japanese positions in northern Luzon continued throughout May, but in early June a major breakthrough in the Cagayan Valley essentially ended Japanese defensive efforts.

Luzon was secured except for mopping-up operations.

Preparations to move north went on for several weeks, and on June 29, 1945, the 39th moved to Okinawa, the squadron's final base for the war. Only 400 miles from the southernmost Japanese main islands, the squadron's Mustangs could now escort the Iwo Jima-based B-29s to their targets, and, after the bombers turned for home, have plenty of fuel to engage in search and destroy sweeps over the southern Japanese islands.

One of those sweeps, on July 30, 1945, was particularly memorable. Capt. Lee Grossheusch was leading a four-plane flight through heavy overcast looking for targets of opportunity. They found and attacked some targets but were looking for more, so they headed west toward Goto Retto, a Japanese naval base. The mountaintops were up in the overcast, but there was a valley between the peaks, and they could see water on the other side.

"As we approached, we saw two destroyers," he says. "We were not carrying bombs that day, but we decided to make a strafing pass, not expecting to do much damage except to personnel. Because of the narrow opening, we had to go in single file."

They took the destroyers by surprise. "I gave a machine-gun burst on the first destroyer and turned left because the harbor was not very wide, and on the other side there was a range of mountains, their tops all in cloud cover. It was a fateful turn. The other three planes turned right, which was a stroke of luck because it let them exit the harbor. If all four of us had been inside, like I was, the destroyers would surely have shot some of us down."

When he turned left, he saw the naval base directly in front of him and the destroyers unleashed some of the heaviest antiaircraft fire he had ever seen. He quickly turned right, hugging the far side of the harbor, which was not far enough away to keep him out of range of the two destroyers.

"I'd seen ack-ack many times before, but nothing compared to this. The sky was filled with tracers and explosions, and they were all aimed at me. I don't know what was behind me, but it was awesome in front of me. They seemed to be shooting above me, so I couldn't pull up above all of that flack into the clouds.

"I had to dive, but there wasn't much space to do that. I decided that if I was going to get it, I'd do as much damage as I could before they hit me. I dove and turned to the nearest destroyer. I let go a long burst aimed at the waterline. I must have hit the ammo magazine because the destroyer exploded. It was a terrific explosion—a huge ball of fire that I had to fly through because I was too close to avoid it. As I burst out of the fireball, I headed for the notch between the mountains, under the clouds, and I exited the way I came in."

The flight reformed and returned to base. "I'd sunk a destroyer," Grossheusch says, "but my poor P-51 was so riddled with shrapnel and debris that it had to be scrapped."

Ten days later, Lt. Jack Frost was on a flight making a fighter sweep over South Korea and southern Japan. The flight was diverted to established coordinates south of Nagasaki and told to hold its position until relieved.

There was a slight under-cast in the vicinity of Nagasaki, and Frost saw the mushroom cloud forming.

"What the hell is that?" Frost remembers saying. It was the end of World War II. Emperor Hirohito announced the unconditional surrender of Japan on August 15, 1945.

It was not the end of the war for one pilot from the 39th who had to crash-land his plane a week after the cease-fire. Oil fumes permeated the cockpit and oil spray covered the windshield of a P-51 being flown by Lt. Henry Chick who was on a patrol mission over Japanese territory. Below him was Tokuno Shima, in the Ryukyus Chain, which was still in Japanese hands. Japan had accepted surrender, but the occupation had not yet begun, and the surrender mood of the Japanese was uncertain.

Rather than crash-land in the sea, Lieutenant Chick decided to land on the island airstrip. He called his wingman and asked him to buzz the strip. Sending his Mustang down over the strip, the wingman drew no fire. As he made his final approach, Lieutenant Chick noticed the strip was cratered and gas drums were set all over the runway. His Mustang plowed right through the obstacles and came to a stop facing a cliff.

For about 15 minutes, nothing happened. Then from out of a cave came four Japanese soldiers, each carrying a rifle. Lieutenant Chick called on his wingman again, and a buzz job sent the soldiers scurrying back to their cave. Two enemy officers came out next and started toward the plane. Chick got out of the plane and placed his life raft on the wing. He called his wingman and told him that if the life raft was kicked off the plane he should come down shooting.

After exchanging salutes, an officer introduced himself in English. Chick asked that the runway be cleared of all obstacles. The officer barked out some orders and about 100 soldiers emerged from the cave and cleared the runway. Meanwhile, a U.S. destroyer had pulled into the bay and sent a boat to shore. Lieutenant Chick was escorted to the beach with enemy soldiers carrying his equipment.

As a parting request, the officer asked Lieutenant Chick to tell his superiors how well he had been treated; this from the same barbarians who had tortured and executed three pilots from the 39th, including Lt. Gene Duncan, Lt. James C. Steele, and Lt. Robert Thorpe!

Chapter 17
They Also Serve
Who Only Stand and Wait
(John Milton)

"The 39th Fighter Squadron was truly a band of brothers. Pilots, crew chiefs, ordinance, administration, medical, and cooks turned it into a premier fighting force," Lt. Jack Frost said in an interview on Feb. 3, 2009.

"We pilots got airplanes that performed, our guns and bombs worked, and our cooks made our food palatable, even though they had little to work with," Frost added.

The closeness between enlisted personnel and officers of the 39th FS started with an incident aboard the SS *Ancon*, the ship that took the squadron to Australia in April of 1942. The ship had accommodations for about 200 people, but it was now loaded with 1,500 officers and enlisted personnel. Everyone was scrambling for bunk space and food arrangements.

Lt. Frank Royal, new CO of the 39th, called his pilots together and delivered a message that sustained the squadron through good and bad times. "We all need a place to sleep and food to eat, but our enlisted troops are lodged in the hold of this ship and their accommodations are far worse than ours. From this point on, we will put the welfare of our enlisted crewmen first and see to it that they have a bed and food before we seek our own comfort. After all, we are headed for combat in this war, and the dedication of these men will do much to keep us alive."

"The enlisted men got the message loud and clear, and a bond, already strong, was strengthened," according to Sgt. Roy Seher, one of those untrained, warm bodies who joined the 39th when the squadron was put together in Townville, Australia, in April 1942. "I was not a member of the 39th when Colonel Royal delivered that message, but I was told about it the first day I reported for duty. The influence of that message had a ripple effect and stayed with the squadron long after Colonel Royal and those early P-39 pilots completed their tour and were sent home," Seher said.

"I always felt that Lady Luck smiled on me that first day with the 39th," Seher said in an interview on July 9, 2008. "We were loaded into a truck and hauled to the flight line. Orders were given that at each revetment stop, one of us was to unload and contact the crew chief of that airplane. When my turn came, I hopped over the tailgate, walked toward the P-39 Airacobra, and came face-to-face with Sgt. Otto Neumann, crew chief of the CO's plane. Otto was one of those people with a firm opinion on just about everything. He could be abrasive, but he was a well trained airplane mechanic and was willing to teach me.

"Otto really hammered me with the finer points. He emphasized that you must look and analyze what you see. There's a scuffed tire, but how serious is it? That fluid streak—Is it coolant or oil? Where is it coming from? You have to know!

"During early morning run-up, the instrument readings tell you much about the health of the plane. Know what they are supposed to read and what they read now. Any deviation is a warning, and you must know why. You are entrusted with a man's life here. There is no room for screw-ups or being slipshod with any work," Neumann warned.

Neumann was typical of the crew chiefs in those early days of the 39th. They watched with pride as their planes took off in the early-morning sun, then waited nervously for them to return.

Lt. Lew Lockhart explained those feelings during a 2008 interview. "It was particularly difficult when we lost a plane. The crew would stand waiting for the missing plane, hoping to see or hear a distant engine. When the plane did not appear, they waited for the debriefing. It was one thing to lose a pilot to enemy aircraft or ground fire. When the plane simply went missing, it had an effect on his ground crew," Lockhart said.

Schwimmer Drome
39th FS, 35th, FG, 5th AF
Port Moresby, New Guinea
July 1943

1st Lt. George E. Morgan with his Crew Chief, Sgt William F. Loy, and their assigned P-38 #20.

"I remember the flight on May 27, 1944, when Bob Thorpe was listed as missing. Fifteen other P-47s returned from that mission. Not one of them reported seeing Bob's plane in trouble. That's when a ground crew starts second-guessing itself. Did they overlook a possible mechanical problem? Was an error made in arming the plane? Did the gun jam or a fuel tank fail to release?"

The pilots never lost faith or confidence in the men who kept their planes running in all sorts of weather and flying conditions. A decision by Capt. Lee Grosshuesch, CO of the 39th in 1944, illustrates this trust.

"In all of our flight training, we were taught to run up the engine before takeoff, check each magneto, and only then go onto the runway and take off. We were on Morotai Island, flying missions over the Philippines and Borneo, sometime stretching our range to the limit. We would come back with only 15 minutes of fuel and sometimes dangerously less. Every gallon of fuel was precious, and it bothered me that we used so much fuel in the magnetos check. We had a meeting of all the pilots and crew chiefs and put a new rule in place. Starting the next morning, the crew chiefs would be responsible for the run-up and mag checks. They would then shut down and top off the tank.

"The pilots would taxi out to the takeoff position. There was no hesitation by either the pilots or the crew chief to accept this transfer of responsibility. I felt that we trusted our crews with every other vital procedure. We knew when we turned on the gun switch and pulled the trigger, all eight cuts would fire. When we dropped our auxiliary gas tanks prior to going into a dogfight, we had faith they would release. So why shouldn't the ground crew be entrusted to check the mags? We were never let down. Our trust paid off big," Grosshuesch said.

"The runway on Morotai was on sand and the pierced planking tended to roll up in front of the wheels, so takeoff was touchy. During the next 1-month period, the other two squadrons lost a total of 25 airplanes, almost all on takeoff. During that same period, we never even had an engine falter. We also extended our range to targets over 800 miles away, allowing ourselves more time for bombing and strafing," he said.

The change in the preflight protocol was seen as a great compliment and a morale builder to the ground crews.

The perfect record was broken when Lt. Fred Tobi crashed on takeoff in November of 1944. There were 15 planes on the mission, and Tobi was taking off last and alone. He was in immediate trouble with his wing wobbling, first to the left, then to the right. Fighting it all the way, Tobi dropped both mounted fuel tanks, relieving his plane of nearly 2,000 pounds of weight. It did not help. Nearing the end of the runway, the plane mushed down, the prop hit, and the plane bellied in, tearing through stumps and piles of dirt left from the building of the runway.

The two fuel tanks slid along the ground following the wreckage, and there was a huge explosion. Everyone thought the pilot had to be dead, except Tobi's crew chief, Bucky Schneider, who was sitting in a Jeep watching the takeoff. Schneider drove right into the ring of fire surrounding Tobi and got him into the Jeep. Lieutenant Tobi was hospitalized with severe burns on his face, neck, and hands, and was sent home to recover. He was not released from the hospital until 1947, after undergoing multiple operations on his face and hands.

That was not the end of the connection between Tobi and his crew chief. Tobi married in 1947 and lived in Tampa where he started his own apple distribution firm. Schneider started a mom-and-pop store in Buchanan, Michigan, and later turned it into a successful chain.

Bucky bought a home in Sarasota, Florida, close to Tobi's home in Tampa. They developed a warm friendship and shared enthusiasm for the game of golf. Bucky Schneider died in 2002, and Fred Tobi followed 6 years later.

The best example of the feelings between the officers of the 39th and enlisted personnel occurred after the squadron moved to Clark Field in the Philippines. Lt. Jack Frost tells the story in his own words:

"I had just returned from temporary duty as a forward air controller up in the Balete Pass, the main road to Baguio, Luzon, headquarters of the Japanese commanding general. It was a hectic week, with Banzai raids every night. I had just unloaded my field gear and was getting ready to clean up when I got a visit from four sergeants who said they had an urgent problem.

"When the 39th moved from Lyngayen to Clark Field, space was provided for operations and for recreational areas. The officers and the noncoms were each issued a building to be used for recreational clubs. The officers were successful in scrounging for furniture and appliances, but the cupboards were bare when the noncoms went looking for material. This was the first time the 39th was located in a civilized area, and the men needed a break from the bugs, sweat, and mud.

"I was known as 'Trader Jack' because of my reputation for putting deals together. My initial efforts were fruitless, but I got a tip that a huge load of lumber had been delivered to a supply warehouse. I drove up to the gate and asked the lieutenant in charge to let me check out the material in storage. He was most helpful as I surveyed clear grain Douglas fir in dimensional sizes and marine-grade plywood. I told the lieutenant that I would be back the next day to pick up what I needed.

"I showed up the next day with some enlisted men on three 2½ ton trucks. I stopped the convoy about a half-mile from the gate and told all the enlisted men that all questions had to be directed to me. The lieutenant saluted as we drove into the supply area. Some Filipino workers loaded the lumber on all three trucks. I had to suppress a giggle when the lieutenant asked me if I needed any nails. I told him a couple of kegs would be fine. I also loaded an 18-foot boat with a 25-hp Johnson Seahorse outboard motor. We were fully loaded and on our way, making sure no one signed for anything and leaving no recognizable identity behind.

"The noncoms unloaded everything into their empty building. About a week later, I was invited to see what was now the NCO Club. The lumber had been turned into tables and benches and a long bar with a metal top painted in aircraft enamel. About a month later, we received a visit from a team of investigators looking for lumber and various items taken from a depot without authority. Did anyone in the 39th know anything about this? Fortunately, the one who answered the questions did not have to lie, since he knew nothing. No one asked me anything.

"The interview was conducted in the NCO club and, as we sat there, I had the feeling that the senior agent, sitting in one of the chairs made from the stolen lumber, knew what had happened, and he seemed to approve. 'That lumber was for General MacArthur's headquarters,' he said as he left the club with a smile. That departing grin, really a faint smile, let us know he understood where the lumber had gone, and it served its purpose well. It provided for an improved lifestyle that had been denied our men through circumstances and geography.

"Many people think this war was fought in leather jackets with white scarves in an area with watering places populated by luscious beauties. The fact is we departed civilization the day we left Townsville, Australia, for Port Moresby, New Guinea. Thick mud, unique wildlife, life-threatening diseases, and Stone Age human beings awaited us. I didn't mention the enemy yet, because as a threat, they come lower than overloaded airplanes and capricious weather.

"This observation is not to denigrate our contribution in stopping the enemy in his tracks. The determination of the enemy was constant and unremitting. The ground fire was deadly. We flew missions in P-47s that equated to a flight to Berlin, and after 7 or 8 hours, came back sweat-soaked and fatigued.

"While we were away the ground crews filled the time with worry and concern, addressing the chores that guaranteed a safe return of their pilots. The challenge to build a real recreation facility for these men was an itch I had to scratch."

SSgt Hugh T. Couch
39th FS, 35th FG, 5th AF
Clark Army Air Field, Luzon, Philippines
May 1945

Chapter 18
If Taken Prisoner

The Geneva Convention, held in Switzerland in 1929, supposedly governed the treatment of prisoners of war. It was signed by the major Western powers, including Britain, Italy, the U.S., and Germany, but not by Japan.

Germany and Italy generally treated prisoners from France, the U.S., and the British Commonwealth in accordance with the Convention. About 99 percent of French, American, British, and Australian prisoners, captured by the Germans, survived the war. Soviet prisoners did not fare as well. The Nazis killed about 2.8 million Soviet POWs during the course of the war.

In refusing to adhere to the terms put forth by the Geneva Convention, Japan argued that since their martial code did not permit surrender, there was no reason why they should follow European standards. Japanese war criminals tried to use this argument during the trials at Tokyo and Yokohama. They were not able to explain why prisoners taken during the Russo-Japanese War (1904–1905) and World War I were not subjected to the same atrocities.

About 27 percent of American, English, Dutch, Australian, and Philippine prisoners died in Japanese captivity. Chinese prisoners fared far worse, with only a small percentage of the millions of prisoners taken surviving the war.

On Dec. 18, 1941, Washington contacted Tokyo and expressed hope that the Japanese government would subscribe to the Geneva Convention.

In his response, Foreign Minister Togo assured American authorities that his country would observe the Geneva Red Cross Convention in the treatment of all prisoners. However, a steady stream of reports about Japan's inhumane treatment of prisoners of war and civilian populations in the occupied countries caused the Allies to send detailed protests to Tokyo.

In one of its few replies, the Japanese government claimed "conditions applied to them (prisoners of war) are more favorable than contemplated by Convention."

On April 5, 1943, Washington warned Tokyo, "The American government will visit upon the officers of the Japanese government responsible for such uncivilized and inhumane acts, the punishment they deserve."

Allied prisoners of war and Asian slave laborers built the Siam-Burma Railway during 1942 and 1943. With primitive tools, the prisoners were forced to remove 3 million cubic yards of earth and 230,000 cubic yards of rock along the route. Conditions were so vile that 27 percent of the Allied prisoners and more than 80 percent of the Asian laborers perished. Work on the railroad varied from 12 to 20 hours a day, depending on the monsoon rain.

Killings were conducted in many ways, including shooting, bayonetting, beheading, live burial, and medical experimentation. Sanitation conditions were also poor, leading to cholera, dengue fever, diphtheria, and dysentery.

David Lean's film, *The Bridge on the River Kwai,* tells a glamorized and not particularly accurate story of the horrors POWs faced while building what is now known as the Siam-Burma Death Railway.

Other POWs were used as slave laborers working in brutal conditions in Japanese coal and copper mines. They were subjected to savage treatment by the camp guards. Beatings with sticks and wire mesh took place every day. Lighted cigarette butts were pressed to flesh and stuck into noses and ears. Men were forced to swallow gallons of water, and then a guard kicked or jumped on their stomachs. Some Allied POWs were even used for medical experiments, including live vivisections and assessments of biological weapons.

Japanese treatment of Asian slave workers was worse than the treatment of European and American prisoners. Between April and July of 1943, about 30,000 Burmese from the Rangoon area were rounded up and marched to the railway site. Since the Japanese kept no records of their coolie laborers, the number and names of Asians who perished along the Siam-Burma track are not known. As many as 200,000 Indonesians forced into slave labor died in a 2-year period.

In his book, *Flyboys,* James Bradley describes the torture and execution of seven American airmen: Jimmy Dye, Glenn Frazier, Floyd Hall, Marvin Mershon, Warren Earl Vaughn, Dick Woellhof, and Grady York. All seven airmen were beaten, tortured, and beheaded, and their bodies were desecrated in the same manner as Bob Thorpe's. In *Unbroken,* Laura Hillenbrand recounts the incredible story of the capture and brutal treatment of Lt. Louis Zamperini as a Japanese prisoner of war.

Rumors of the beheading of American pilots by the Japanese were discussed openly, according to Lt. Fred Tobi when he and Bob Thorpe joined the 39th Fighter Squadron in January 1944. "Thorpe and I were still in flight training when we heard that three members of Gen. Doolittle's raid on Tokyo had been executed. We didn't dwell on the subject, but we knew it was there. Treatment of American POWs in the Bataan Death March had also leaked out," according to Tobi.

All pilots of the 39th Fighter Squadron were given a copy of the following document before going into combat for the first time:

TO ALL MEMBERS UNITED STATES ARMY FORCES IN THE FAR EAST

WHAT TO DO IF TAKEN PRISONER OF WAR

Every member of the U.S. Army whose duties place him in danger of being captured by the enemy will study a copy of this booklet. This publication must NOT be taken into the air or into the combat zone.

HEADQUARTERS
USAFFE
March, 1943

PART I.

If you should be captured, give the enemy only your NAME, RANK, AND SERIAL NUMBER. You are required to give these by International Law. DON'T GIVE ANY OTHER INFORMATION.

You are a source of valuable information to the enemy, which they can use against your country, your buddies, and your family. DON'T HELP THE ENEMY!

PART II.

WHAT THE ENEMY WANTS TO KNOW.

The unit you belong to.
Its strengths.
Where it is stationed.
Where other units are located.
What the recent movements of your unit have been.
Your knowledge of future movements.
Your knowledge of casualties suffered.
The type of weapons or aircraft of your unit, and
What they can do.
New details now used or to be used.
Details of armament.
Location of air bases and landing fields.
Positions of air bases and landing fields.
Position and technical details of antiaircraft and other defenses.
Past weather conditions and weather forecasts.
Training methods in use at training units.
Allied tactics.
Allied knowledge of enemy tactics, plans, strengths, etc.
Allied Defense Organization and raid warning system.
Home conditions: politics, food, clothing supplies, and morale of the people and of the fighting forces.
Relations existing between Allies. Information on these matters can be of great value to the enemy. Do Not Help Him by answering questions.

HE IS YOUR ENEMY.

KEEP QUIET

PART III.

Those notes are based on fact. They are made from the experience of men who have been Prisoners of War and who have first-hand knowledge.

DIRECT QUESTIONING

The enemy may interrogate you.

If he does, DO NOT ANSWER except to give your NAME, RANK, and SERIAL NUMBER.

DO not try to bluff your questioner. He is far more experienced at the game than you are. He is an expert at getting information.

KEEP SILENT!

DO NOT ARGUE with him. He will outwit you.

DO NOT GIVE HIM FALSE INFORMATION. You will not succeed in misleading him, and he will punish you.

DO NOT TRY TO APPEASE HIM. If you do, he will persist in questioning you for weeks and give you no respite.

DO NOT BELIEVE HIM if he tells you that another prisoner (perhaps a high-ranking officer) has given him information.

Lieutenant Thorpe followed the rules to the letter, supplying only his name, rank, and serial number. He was beaten, used for target practice, and then beheaded. Two other members of the 39th Fighter Squadron, Lt. James C. Steele and Lt. Gene Duncan, suffered similar fates after they were taken prisoner.

Steele shared a tent with Tobi, Thorpe, and Lt. Marcus Trout. "He was a real Texan, outspoken and a little on the loud side," Tobi recalled. "He carried his 45-pistol all the time, vowing never to be taken alive." Jack Frost remembers Steele as a "good ole boy Texan whose bluster was a cover for a good-natured guy."

Jack Frost was on a fighter sweep and strafing mission out of Morotai to Davao on Nov. 6, 1944, when Steele reported a "sick" bird and decided he could not make it back to Morotai, so he decided to belly it in. We were short of fuel so we had to continue. But we saw Jim make it to the shore of Kabaruan Island.

Nothing was known about Steele's fate until Japanese soldiers were questioned about him and three Australian airmen. Captain Takahashi, of the Japanese 32nd Division, made the following statement on September 9, 1945: "Lt. James C. Steele, age 22, of the 39th Fighter Squadron, landed 1 km SW of Burude village on Kabaruan Island on Nov. 6, 1944, in a P-47. He was apprehended by Burude villagers and turned over to the Japanese on Nov. 9, 1944."

Sgt. Kempei Koboto reported interviewing the three Allied airmen in December of 1944. Koboto claims he interrogated the prisoners according to the book of rules, called *Sakashen Yamure.*

The fate of the three airmen was the subject of varied reports. Theophilus Joera, a Dutchman employed by the Dutch Civil Administration, was the first to volunteer information. He reported that he had seen the airmen in the civil jail and had taken them food. Later, he said, they were beheaded at the edge of a large bomb crater at the side of the prison.

When a war graves representative visited the site at the end of the war, no remains were found in the crater. After Japanese soldiers were continually interrogated, the true story of what happened to the three prisoners surfaced. All three had been executed by bayoneting on March 25, 1945.

The order for the execution was given by Colonel Koba, commander of Japanese forces in the Talaud area.

On Oct. 31, 1945, five Japanese soldiers made the following confession:

We, the undersigned, members of the Japanese army, were ordered by our superior officers to deliberately stab four Allied airmen on the day of presentation of colors, which took place on March 23, 1945, at BEO. This we did with our bayonets, and the airmen bravely succumbed.

The reason why we were chosen is because we are young and had never had a chance to kill anyone, and they wanted to test our bravery.

Signed Suxuki Asamasassa
Signed Oishi Tuichi
Signed Sistaro Goto
Signed Takeo Tamaka
Signed Seiji Uchino
Signed Lt. Asaoka (witness)
Signed Sgt. Kubota (witness)

Three of the bodies recovered on Talaud Island on March 7, 1947, were the missing Australian airmen. The fourth was later identified as lst. Lt. James Steele.

The "confessions" signed by the five men who butchered four helpless prisoners was typical of the "spirit warriors" who carried out similar crimes. They always made sure that the line "acting in accordance with orders from superiors" preceded their confessions. The men involved in the murder of Lieutenant Steele were never charged at the war crimes trials in Yokohama after the war.

During the war crimes trials in Tokyo in 1948, Prime Minister Hideki Tojo attempted to explain his country's brutal treatment of POWs with the following statement: "The Japanese idea about prisoners is different from that in Europe and America. In Japan, it is regarded as a disgrace to be captured. Under Japanese criminal law, anyone who becomes a prisoner while still able to resist has committed a criminal offense, the maximum punishment for which is the death penalty."

Japan still does not accept the idea that the men who planned, launched, and prosecuted the bloody war in the Pacific are war criminals. All of them have been honored at the Yasukuni Shrine, Japan's most revered Shinto temple dedicated to the war dead. In November 2014, Prime Minister Shinzō Abe labeled the war crimes trials at Tokyo and Yokohama after World War II as illegal and retaliatory, since no war crimes ever took place. "I want to establish the existence of a new Japan that would not be an embarrassment to the spirit of the war dead," Abe said.

The Japanese government refuses to compensate the "comfort women," young Korean girls forced into prostitution for the enjoyment of Japanese soldiers during the war. Pearl Harbor was a defensive measure to stop American imperialism in the Pacific. The draft of slave laborers in Korea is described as a "mobilization" of labor.

The cover-up extends to the classroom. In textbooks prepared by the Japanese Ministry of Education, all of World War II is covered in one chapter, mostly taken up by photographs of Hiroshima and Nagasaki after atomic bombs were dropped on them. The invasion of China is described as an "advance," and the "Rape of Nanking" is attributed to the resistance of the Chinese army.

Not all Japanese people accept the government whitewash. The *Asahi Shimbun*, one of Tokyo's mass-circulation dailies, observed: "Japan sent a large army to China, killed ten million Chinese and caused great damage. If this is not aggression, what is? What happened in those countries, which Japan invaded during World War II, has been put on the record. Historical facts should never be abolished by a play on words."

Chapter 19
The Cover-up

On December 13, 1937, a photograph of two smiling young Japanese officers, Toshiaki Mukai and Tsuyoshi Noda, appeared on the front page of the Tokyo newspaper *Tokyo Nichi Nichi Shimbun* (Tokyo Daily News). The headline read: "Incredible Record to Cut Down 100 People—Mukia 106 and Noda 105—both 2nd Lieutenants Go Into Extra Innings."

The "people" were defenseless Chinese POWs. What is so monstrous about this story, beyond all the murders, was the acceptance—indeed the celebration—of this horror by the Japanese people. So it was to be expected that the Japanese military's savage treatment of civilians and POWs was not to be limited to the butchery of 30 million Chinese—whom they regarded as an inferior race—but would be inflicted on all of the populations and militaries they battled and conquered in Asia and the South Pacific.

After the war, the newspaper article about Mukai and Noda attracted the attention of the International Military Tribunal for the Far East. The two soldiers were extradited to China, tried by the Nanjing War Crimes Tribunal, and convicted of atrocities committed during the Battle of Nanking. They were executed by the Chinese government on January, 28, 1948.

Meanwhile, the Allies prepared to investigate war crimes and bring the perpetrators to justice well before the end of the war. One of the most tenacious and effective of these investigators was Captain John D. Steed, a member of the Australian Board of Inquiry. An attorney, he had a reputation for toughness and thoroughness. He never raised his voice or lost his composure, but simply asked question after question, recording all the answers in a notebook that never left his side.

Steed was part of a team that investigated the Bataan Death March that took place in the Philippines in 1942. Approximately 75,000 Filipino and U.S. soldiers surrendered to the Japanese, under the command of General Masaharu Homma. Captives were forced to walk 60 miles north to Camp O'Donnell and were denied food and water for several days. Those who could not keep up were shot, beheaded, or bayoneted. Based on evidence Steed helped uncover, Homma was convicted and executed on April 3, 1946.

Steed also investigated the 1942 Parit Sulong Massacre in Malaysia. Captured Australian and Indian POWs were murdered by Japanese soldiers under the command of Lt. General Takuma Nishimura, who was convicted and hanged on July 11, 1951.

Steed's next assignment was the 1942 Laha Massacre. After the Battle of Ambron, more than 300 Australian and Dutch soldiers were chosen at random and summarily executed near Laha Airfield. Steed uncovered evidence that led to the hanging of Captain Kunito Hatakeyama, who was in command of the 1946 massacre.

Steed then investigated the Alexandra Hospital Massacre that took place during the Battle of Singapore. Japanese soldiers shot or bayoneted hospital staff members on Feb. 14, 1942. Lt. General Saburo Kawamura and Lieutenant Colonel Masayuki were hanged and five other Japanese soldiers received life sentences for their role in this atrocity.

Steed obviously had a great deal of experience interviewing Japanese officers and soldiers suspected of war crimes when he arrived in New Guinea in 1945 to find out what happened to two Australian soldiers and an American pilot captured in May of 1944. He began his investigation by interviewing Kazuo Maruyama, the surgeon in charge of the hospital on Kairiru Island, who gave him the following account:

"In May or June 1944, I attended a captured fighter pilot at naval headquarters at Sansaria. I heard he was an American. He had come ashore near Jagur. Captain Noto sent him to live at the hospital because there was no other accommodation available. He was quite healthy when I first saw him.

"During the first month he was there, he had fever once. Then he developed malaria. I gave him quinine by mouth for 5 days, and when he became too ill to take it, I gave him three intravenous injections. He went into a coma, however, and his brain was affected. He died about a week after he fell sick.

"Two Australian prisoners were treated at the hospital around the same time. One of them had been severely injured at the time of his capture and died shortly after he was hospitalized. The other, like the American prisoner, died of malaria. We had been treating him with quinine, but the disease had progressed too rapidly, and he never fully regained consciousness."

If Maruyama thought his statement would satisfy Steed, he was utterly mistaken. "You showed such compassion for these prisoners, giving them medicine while you had little for your own troops?" Steed challenged Maruyama. "Meanwhile, your countrymen were murdering captured prisoners throughout the South Pacific."

Maruyama tried to stick to his story, but under Steed's relentless questioning, he began to contradict himself. Steed noted the inconsistencies in his notebook before turning his attention to Kiyohisa Noto, chief of staff of the 27th Special Base Force.

Noto gave Steed a prepared statement before the first interview.

"I was chief of staff, 27th Special Base Force. I first went to Kairiru on March 15, 1944, and remained there until the surrender. We captured an American on Kairiru about the middle of May 1944. He was an airman, and I heard he was lieutenant. He died about 20 days after he was brought in. I think that the cause of death was malaria. I was sick with malaria myself about that time, and I do not remember details about this prisoner. I do think that he came ashore on the north side of Kairiru."

Noto's explanation of the death of the two Australian prisoners matched, almost word-for-word, the story offered by Maruyama. Despite intense scrutiny by Steed, Noto stuck to his story.

The case took a different turn after Steed grilled Tsunehiko Yamamoto on the disposition of the three captured fliers and received the following sworn statement: "About that time the Australians had come to receive the remains of the prisoners and had been guided by Chief Petty Officer Kanzo Bunya to a cemetery on Kairiru Island where a grave was opened up and the remains of three Japanese who had been killed in action were handed over as being the remains of the two Australians and one American who had been executed." Steed later confirmed that the remains were Japanese, not Australian or American.

If allowed to continue the investigation, there is little doubt that he would have uncovered enough evidence to convict Kenro Sato, Yutaka Odazawa, Waichi Ogawa, Naotada Fujihira, Kaoru Okuma, and Tsunehido Yamamoto for the torture and murder of Bob Thorpe. But there were bigger fish to fry, and Steed was reassigned to the Manila Massacre, during which over 100,000 Filipino citizens were murdered.

General Tomoyku Yamashita argued that he knew nothing about the atrocities, so he could not be held accountable. Steed helped establish the "Yamashita Standard," which holds that those who do not make meaningful efforts to uncover and stop atrocities are just as culpable as those who commit them. Yamashita was found guilty and executed.

Before leaving New Guinea, Steed uncovered enough evidence to try Noto as a war criminal. The man who relayed the order to execute Thorpe was found guilty of executing two Australian prisoners of war and sentenced to 20 years at hard labor at Rabaul Prison. Steed was also able to identify Waichi Ogawa as the man who actually beheaded the two Australian prisoners. When he tried to arrest Ogawa, Steed learned that the man who beheaded two of his countrymen and desecrated the body of Bob Thorpe had been allowed to return to Japan.

Steed turned over his files proving that Thorpe had also been tortured and executed by Okuma, Odazawa, Fujihira, Noto, and Yamamoto under a direct order from Admiral Sato. The Americans took no action and the suspects, with the exception of Noto, were allowed to return to Japan and resume civilian life. Meanwhile, Bob Thorpe remained buried in a shallow grave near the beach where he had been tortured, used for target practice, and beheaded.

Three years later at the war crimes trial held in Yokohama, Koji Kawada told the commission that in September of 1945, about a month after the war ended, Captain Kiyohisa Noto called a meeting on Kairiru Island and all company commanders attended.

"I was present, as was Admiral Sato. Noto did all of the talking. He said that if Australian or American authorities asked any questions about the disposition of two Australian pilots and one American, we were to say that we knew nothing about it. If perchance one of us had seen the flyer, we were to say that we had seen him and that he had been taken away and we didn't know where. We were forbidden to mention the execution.

"From Kairiru Island we were taken to Muschu Island where two meetings were held regarding two Australian and one American POW. Noto repeated what he had said at the first meeting. At a second meeting at Muschu Island, I was present when Sato explained that after the war, Chief Petty Officer Kanzo Bunya turned over some Japanese remains to the Australian army at Kairiru Island, representing them to be the bodies of one American and two Australian prisoners of war. We were ordered to say that the prisoners had died of disease and had been buried with full military honors. Noto was not present at this meeting, because he was being questioned by the Australians."

Lt. Isamu Amenomori submitted the following statement concerning the cover-up:

"In October or November of 1945, Admiral Sato held a conference in which he said that the Australian military authorities would conduct an investigation in the case of two Australian soldiers who were executed in 1945 and an American flier who was beheaded in 1944. He told us to tell them that the soldiers died of malaria and that services were conducted over their bodies. He also told us that even after returning to Japan we must remain quiet."

Chapter 20
Judgment at Tokyo

A United Nations War Crimes Commission (UNWCC) recommended that suspected Japanese war criminals be tried before an International Military Tribunal for the Far East (IMTFE) at the conclusion of the war.

The responsibility for forming the IMTFE was given to the Supreme Commander for the Allied Powers (SCAP) General Douglas MacArthur. By September of 1945, 39 "Class A" suspects were about to be arrested and imprisoned at Sugamo Prison. General MacArthur ignored an order to keep the names secret until they were in custody and gave each suspect 10 days to report to Sugamo Prison.

As a result of his decision, Hideki Tojo, former prime minister of Japan, attempted suicide by shooting himself in the chest. The bullet missed Tojo's heart, and he was saved, ironically, by transfusion from a GI blood supply. Eight other "Class A" criminals escaped prosecution by taking their own lives, including:

- Vice Adm. Takijiro Onishi, creator of the kamikaze forces.
- Prince Fumimaro Konoye, trusted advisor to the emperor.
- Shigero Hondo, leader of the Kwantung army clique that started the war with China.
- War Minister Korechika Anami.
- Field Marshal Hajime Sugiyama.
- Shizuichi Tanaka, Eastern Army commander.
- Kumihiko Hashida, former minister of education, and

- Chikahiko Koizumi, army surgeon general, responsible for medical experiments on live prisoners and civilians.

An estimated two to three thousand former members of the Japanese military are believed to have committed suicide at the end of the war to escape trials as war criminals.

The IMTFE convened on April 29, 1946, to try the "Class A" war criminals imprisoned at Sugamo Prison early in the occupation. Like the Nuremberg trials held to punish German war criminals, the Japanese trials were intended to set an example. The defendants were charged with crimes against peace and crimes against humanity, including:

- Waging unprovoked war against China.
- Waging aggressive war against the United States.
- Waging aggressive war against the British Commonwealth.
- Waging aggressive was against the Netherlands.
- Waging aggressive war against France.
- Waging war against Russia.
- Ordering, authorizing, and permitting inhumane treatment of prisoners of war and others.
- Deliberately and recklessly disregarding their duty to take adequate steps to prevent atrocities.

They were also charged with murdering, maiming, and mistreating prisoners of war and civilians, plundering and destroying cities and towns far beyond any military necessity, with mass murder, rape, and torture.

Australia, Russia, and several other Allied countries pushed to add another war criminal to the trial—Emperor Hirohito. MacArthur had warned President Harry S. Truman that it would be necessary to bring another one million troops to Japan if the emperor were tried as a war criminal. Truman and Winston Churchill were in full agreement with MacArthur's position, so no charges were filed against the worst war criminal in the Far East. In a 250-page affidavit, Tojo accepted full blame for the Pacific War, claiming that Hirohito was totally innocent.

There were other war crimes trials before 1946. In 1945, a U.S. Military Commission executed General Sai Yamashita, commander of all Japanese in the Philippines, and General Nubua Homma, responsible for the Bataan Death March in 1945. The U.S. Navy also tried a number of war criminals on Kwajalein in the Marshall Islands and on Guam. Other nations convicting war criminals included Nationalist China (504), Britain (811), Australia (66), The Netherlands (969), France (198), and the Philippines (169).

The IMTFE defined three types of war crimes. "Class A" crimes were reserved for those who participated in a joint conspiracy to start and wage war and were brought against those in the highest decision-making bodies. "Class B" crimes were reserved for those who committed "conventional" atrocities or crimes against humanity. (The five officers charged with torturing and executing Bob Thorpe were classified as "Class B" War Criminals.) "Class C" crimes were reserved for those who planned, ordered, authorized, or failed to prevent such transgressions.

The "Class A" war criminals were tried in the former auditorium of the Japanese War College at the center of Tokyo. The 11 judges sat at a long mahogany bench which had been elevated to a commanding level. A three-tier compartment directly across from the judges held the prisoners. The witness box was set in the center of the 110-by-80-foot room, with long benches for court attendants and lawyers. English and Japanese were the principal languages spoken and translated, but Chinese and Russian were also used.

President Harry S. Truman appointed Joseph Keenan, U.S. asst. attorney general, chief prosecutor for the United States. He opened the trial by warning that the proceedings would have a far-reaching effect on the peace and security of the world.

"The accused declared war upon civilization. They made the rules and defined the issues. The orderly administration of justice for these war criminals may prevent aggressive war in the future," Keenan told the tribunal.

> *"All governments are operated by human agents, and all crimes are committed by human beings. A man's official position cannot rob him of his identity as an individual*

nor relieve him from responsibility for his individual of-
fenses. Every person is liable for the natural and prob-
able consequences of his criminal acts. We find that these
men, who held positions of power and influence in the
Japanese government, planned, prepared, initiated, and
waged illegal wars."

Judges included Sir William Webb, Australia; Edward McDougall, Canada; Major-General Mei Juao, China; Henri Bernard, France; Radhabinod Pal, British India; Bert Roling, Netherlands; Erima Northcroft, New Zealand; Delfin Jaranilla, Philippines; Lord Patrick, United Kingdom; John P. Higgins, United States; General Myron C. Cramer, United States; and Major General I. M. Zaryanov, USSR.

Defendants charged with "Class A" war crimes, included:

- Koki Hirota, prime minister (1937)
- Baron Kiichiro Hiranuma, prime minister (1939), president of the privy council
- Naoki Hoshino, chief cabinet secretary
- Marquis Koichi Kido, Lord keeper of the Privy Seal
- Toshio Shiratori, ambassador to Italy
- Shigenori Togo, foreign minister (1941–1942)
- Mamoru Shigemitsu, foreign minister (1943–1944)
- Okinori Kaya, finance minister
- Yosuke Matsuoka, foreign minister (1940–1941)
- General Hideki Tōjō, prime minister (1941–1944), war minister (1940–1941)
- General Seishirō Itagaki, war minister (1938–1939)
- General Sadao Araki, war minister (1931–1934)
- Field Marshal Shunroku Hata, war minister (1939–1940)
- Admiral Shigetarō Shimada, navy minister (1941–1944)
- General Kenryō Satō, chief of the Military Affairs Bureau
- General Kuniaki Koiso, prime minister (1944–1945), governor-general of Korea (1942–1944)
- Admiral Takazumi Oka, chief of the Bureau of Naval Affairs

- Lieutenant General Hiroshi Ōshima, ambassador to Germany
- Admiral Nagano Osami, navy minister (1936–1937), chief of the Imperial Japanese Navy General staff (1941–1944)
- General Jirō Minami, governor-general of Korea (1936–1942)
- General Kenji Doihara, chief of the intelligence service in Manchukuo
- General Heitarō Kimura, commander of the Burma Area Army
- General Iwane Matsui, commander of the Shanghai Expeditionary Force and Central China Area Army
- Lieutenant General Akira Mutō, chief of staff of the 14th Area Army
- Colonel Kingorō Hashimoto, founder of Sakurakai
- General Yoshijirō Umezu, commander of the Kwantung army, chief of the Imperial Japanese Army General Staff Office (1944–1945)
- Lieutenant General Teiichi Suzuki, chief of the Cabinet Planning Board
- Shūmei Ōkawa, a political philosopher

Three Japanese attorneys played major roles in organizing the defense. They included Ichiro Kiyose, Kenzo Takayanagi, a Harvard Law School graduate, and Somei Uzawa, president of Meidi University. The three argued that no single individual or group of individuals could be responsible for a conflict of the magnitude of the Pacific War.

Despite their efforts, the defense was totally disorganized as the trial was about to open. Keenan appealed to Washington for help, and 15 American attorneys were sent to join six other American attorneys who were already in Japan. Captain Beverly Coleman, a U.S. naval officer and a lawyer in civilian life, was appointed chief of the defense team with John W. Guilder, another navy man, as his assistant. They resigned shortly after they were appointed, claiming they were not given the logistic support by General MacArthur to organize the defense. George Yamaoka, a Japanese American bilingual attorney, replaced Coleman as chief of the defense team.

When the trial opened on May 3, 1946, all 28 defendants pleaded not guilty to the charges against them. The tone of the defense was set when U.S. Army Major Benjamin Blakney charged that the defendants could not get a fair trial since all of the judges were Allied nationals. His suggestion that the defendants should be tried by judges from neutral nations was dismissed as impossible by Keenan.

An immediate problem surfaced: Japanese was a difficult language to translate into English. Attorneys argued over the meaning of a single word or phrase, making interchanges among witnesses, lawyers, and justices difficult to follow. The defense's interpreters, translators, typists, and clerks were in short supply. They had to work on weekends and holidays and still fell behind.

The trial continued for more than 2½ years, with testimony from 419 witnesses and admitting 4,336 exhibits of evidence, including depositions and affidavits from 779 individuals. As the Japanese witnesses testified interminably, it became evident that the defense was deliberately trying to prolong the trial. A Russian reporter wrote in Moscow's *New Times:*

> The major Japanese war criminals will die a natural death long before the International Military tribunal passes its verdict. The defense has literally showered the Tribunal with documents of all kinds with the idea of confusing and protracting the trial, yet Sir William Webb, who does not miss an opportunity to complain of delays, is himself in a large measure responsible for the dilatoriness of the proceedings. Instead of ruling out statements of the defense counsel which are extraneous to the trial, he willingly allows them on the floor.

Finally, the IMTFE announced the sentences on Nov. 12, 1948. One by one, the prisoners arose to hear their fate. Doihara, Hirota, Itagahi, Kimura, Matsui, Muto, and Tojo were sentenced to death. Shigemitsu received a 7-year sentence, while Togo got 20 years. The rest received life sentences.

On Nov. 29, 1948, defense attorneys filed motions with the United States Supreme Court on behalf of the seven condemned prisoners. They argued that MacArthur had exceeded his authority in convening the trials. On Dec. 7, Pearl Harbor Day, the Supreme Court voted five to four to hear the case. After 3 days of deliberation, the Court voted six to three that "the courts of the United States have no power or authority to review, affirm, set aside, or annul the judgments or sentences the IMTFE."

All of the guilty were sent to Sugamo Prison for execution or to serve their sentences. The Eighth Army provided 500 troops to staff Sugamo when it took over the prison in 1946. By mid-1947, approximately 2,000 war criminals were imprisoned at Sugamo.

Built in the early 1920s, Sugamo was initially used for holding political prisoners, including Communists, dissenters, and spies. Publishers and journalists who wrote articles the military considered detrimental to the war effort also spent time at Sugamo before and during the war. The prison was a single compound covering 6 acres and enclosed by a 12-foot-high concrete wall. It was untouched by the war, but almost all of the buildings surrounding it had been destroyed.

Two Russian spies, Richard Sorge and Hotsumi Ozaki, were executed at Sugamo in 1944. They provided the Soviet Union with thousands of coded messages, keeping Russia informed of Japanese military planning. Five Japanese/American agents were executed there in 1944. Members of a six-man team, they had been parachuted from a B-29, equipped with transmitters, rations, weapons, and Japanese currency. Through their efforts, Japan lost five ships in one convoy and four troop transports in another. The sixth agent remained free throughout the war and sent valuable troop movements on a weekly basis. His identity remains secret.

Improvements to the prison were made immediately after the Americans took over the prison. Heating, cooling, and ventilation systems were installed and the first bowling alley built in Japan was constructed for the entertainment of GIs who were assigned as prison guards. A 10-foot-high wire fence was installed around the outer compound to keep starving Japanese from stealing food and coal from prison supplies.

Each prison cell contained a table and chair, electric light, straw floor mat, and a covered lavatory. Prisoners were given clean uniforms that were washed and ironed at a prison laundry. They were also provided with 24-hour medical attention and a healthy diet. Buddhist and Christian services were made available to all prisoners.

When the war crimes trials started, security was strengthened with Jeep patrols, guard towers, and a main gate manned 24 hours a day. Security details were assigned to take the "Class A" prisoners to the Japanese War College in Tokyo and "Class B" and "C" prisoners to stand trial at a Yokohama courthouse.

"Class A" war criminals were isolated from those charged with "B" or "C" crimes. No one ever escaped from Sugamo while it was under U.S. military jurisdiction, but several suicides occurred there, including CWO Ogawa, the man who jumped into Thorpe's grave and desecrated the body. Probably for that reason, a suicide watch was established for the seven who were sentenced to hang at Sugamo.

The teeth of the condemned were X-rayed for poison implants, probably influenced by the suicide of Hermann Goring who ingested potassium cyanide 2 hours before his execution. The prisoners were also forced to stand naked, facing a wall, while their cells were searched. They were watched at all times while shaving or showering. They could not go anywhere unless handcuffed to a guard.

General MacArthur upheld the sentences without change and barred all photographs of the executions because they "would violate all sense of decency."

Immediately after the trial of the "A" war criminals concluded, "B" and "C" war criminals went on trial at Yokohama, including Yutaka Odazawa, Kaoru Okuma, Naotada Fujihira, Kiyohisa Noto, and Tsunehiko Yamamoto.

Rear Admiral Sato, who allegedly issued the order to execute Thorpe, committed suicide before the war crimes trial began.

Chapter 21
Meet the Accused

By January 1948, the war had been over for 2½ years, and Bob Thorpe's executioners had been mustered out of the Imperial Navy and returned to their homes in Japan. Living conditions were grim in the war-ravaged county. Shortages of food, fuel, and most other necessities intensified the hardship of a bitter cold winter with snow deep in the rural communities and northern cities.

Mitigating all of these hardships, however, was the astonishment of the people at the mild, almost benevolent attitude and behavior of the arriving Americans. Conditioned by years of propaganda by the wartime government to expect savage, murderous occupation, the Japanese were confounded and relieved by the highly successful efforts of the occupation government under General Douglas MacArthur to establish civic and social order, and then to work toward economic stability and development.

The Japanese did realize, however, that some retribution would be coming. They had witnessed the trials and punishment of the senior military officials who had been judged to be war criminals. Justice for lower-ranking military personnel who had been discovered to have violated the rules of war had begun in the fall of 1947.

About this time, Captain Richard Chedester, a member of the U.S. War Crimes Investigation Division in Tokyo, opened a file that had been compiled by Captain John Steed shortly after the end of the war. After examining the contents, Chedester issued arrest warrants for the men responsible for the beating, torture, beheading, and desecration of Lt. Robert Thorpe.

It was on January 22, 1948, that notice of charges for the torture and murder of Lt. Robert Thorpe arrived at the home of Yutaka Odazawa in Shirasawamura, a farming community in hill country 150 miles northwest of Tokyo. Crops in the area had been devastated in September by flooding from typhoon rains. Residents who had feared a hard, hungry winter were now threatened with actual starvation.

Odazawa had begun farming a 3-acre plot of family-owned land when he had arrived back in the community in the summer of 1946. He was supporting a family consisting of his wife and 7-year old son and his bedridden mother. His mother had been severely ill since 1924, and Odazawa, then 14 years old, had begun farming to support her and a younger brother. Two older sisters had married and left the area and were unable to help.

In 1929, Odazawa had joined the navy, apparently motivated by the promise of a somewhat better income than he was able to earn by farming. His civilian education had ended with primary schooling, but in the navy he'd been able to go to gunnery school. There he learned a specialty that eventually led to his promotion to the rank of lieutenant junior grade.

Along with the income, officer status gained Odazawa some prestige when he returned on leave to Shirasawamura. "He would tell me about his navy life," recalled his uncle, Juzaboro Matsui, proudly. "He was always performing patriotic duties honestly and conscientiously. I used to feel secure in his thorough, military spirit."

Since his return, Odazawa had earned community respect and gratitude working as a volunteer in the village office. This work apparently consisted mainly of distributing the meager relief supplies that were then arriving in the countryside for the poorest of the villagers and repatriates from overseas.

The January summons startled and terrified the Odazawa household. Since the crop failure 4 months before they didn't know how they would get through the winter. What would they do now with their breadwinner in prison?

Although he was aware of his impending arrest, Tsunehiko Yamamoto continued at his teaching duties at the Inatori Higher School in Shizuoka until the day before he was imprisoned. Today, Inatori is a modern five-story facility serving some 3,000 teenagers. In 1948, it was a far smaller school, located in an old but well maintained building, dedicated to vocational and some college preparatory training.

Like Odazawa, Yamamoto's interests were in agriculture but as an educator rather than a farmer. He had earned his degree and teaching credentials before the war at the Tokyo Agricultural College. His choice of a teaching career was no surprise to his family, since both of his parents were educators. His father had taught English at a middle school for 20 years until his retirement just before the war.

After returning to Japan in late 1946, Yamamoto worked as a temporary employee for the Nippon Agricultural Association in Tokyo, where he apparently made a good enough impression on Shiro Mori, the association director, to be recommended as an agriculture teacher at Inatori. He went to Shizuoka with his friend and colleague Tomoo Ameriya, who remembered that he not only taught on the day prior to his confinement but went around all of the farms where his students had been doing their practical work to make sure that their instruction would continue.

Mori also recalled that Yamamoto's curriculum for his students ranged well beyond agriculture into politics and political philosophy. "I'd often see books on his desk with titles like *What Is Democracy?* and *Protection of Liberalism*," he said.

Kaoru Okuma's arrest startled the employees at the Satake Works in Hiroshima where he had been working as an engineering manager for more than a year. This company, now the Dalian Satake Chemical Equipment Co., Ltd., manufactures chemical production equipment in China, Taiwan, and Korea, as well as in Japan. In 1947, Satake was a struggling one-plant operation like most Japanese manufacturers at the time, and the employees believed that they owed a lot of what was being accomplished to Okuma's "strenuous services."

He had been well prepared for the position. After graduating from middle school at age 17, he had gone directly to the Imperial Navy's rigorous engineering school. Graduating high in his class, he was fast-tracked to the rank of lt. commander at age 28.

Okuma was clearly a brilliant engineer. Why he had entered the military rather than attending a prestigious private university, for which he was certainly qualified, is unclear. The record mentions "family reasons," which probably means financial problems. But just prior to the Pacific war, he cemented his connections with the educated classes by his marriage to a graduate of the Hiroshima College for Women.

At age 46 and a captain, Kiyohisa Noto was the oldest and the highest ranking of the accused men. He was a career naval officer, having graduated from the Officers' Training School in 1920. His service had been both at sea and ashore and had included several years at the Imperial Navy headquarters in Tokyo.

Noto had already been sentenced to 20 years at hard labor by an Australian military tribunal for the execution of two Australian fliers on Kairiru Island in 1945. He was released from prison in Rabaul to stand trial for Thorpe's execution with the other four defendants on June 22, 1948.

Waichi Ogawa was arrested at the Takeshibabashi Hospital in Tokyo, working as an orderly. The man who opened Bob Thorpe's chest and removed an organ denied ever being in the military, telling the arresting officers they had the wrong person. He was also suspected of beheading two Australian pilots while stationed at Wewak. Ogawa was dragged from the hospital kicking, screaming, and protesting his innocence.

Naotada Fujihira returned to his job at the Far East Trading Co., in Osaka, Japan, after the war. He had only been married for a few months at the time of his arrest. He expressed bewilderment, claiming he was only following orders in his treatment of Bob Thorpe.

Fujihira and Ogawa were transported directly to Sugamo Prison to join the other three suspects.

The men had been imprisoned for only a few days when impassioned petitions for clemency began arriving at the War Crimes Administration Division of the U.S. Eighth Army's Judge Advocate Section. They came from families, friends, and entire communities and organization staffs.

Most acknowledged the heinousness of the alleged crimes. "Japan unreservedly deserves to be blamed for her acts of atrocity during the war," wrote one of Kaoru Okuma's family members. "I have profound sympathy for the victims of the atrocities, as well as to the bereaved families," wrote another. Many referred to what they learned about what had happened to Bob Thorpe as "a horrible war crime."

Some expressed their disbelief that their loved one could have done such a thing. "Although I cannot convince myself that he committed such a crime," wrote Noto's wife, "it must have been a condition of inevitability in the whirlpool of war."

"I cannot persuade myself to believe that such a democratic person, who had been loved and respected by his fellow teachers, students, students' parents, and others committed such a horrible crime," insisted a teacher colleague of Yamamoto.

Their arguments for leniency often centered on the rigidity of the Imperial military command structure. They cited tradition of emperor worship and the consequent requirement that every order from a military superior had to be obeyed without question because, logically within this system, every order came down directly from, and cloaked in the divinity of, the emperor. They noted how this requirement was repeated every morning at the roll call of every military unit in the so-called recitation of regulations.

Odazawa, the swinger of the sword, had no alternative, according to his uncle Jusaboro: "He had a strong sense of responsibility toward his duty. This brought about a bad result only because he carried it out in a misled war. But this was a natural obligation of a Japanese subject. Therefore, I do not hesitate to say that he had no option but to take that course at that time."

Jusaboro and all the rest pleaded that the War Crimes Administration look beyond these robotic actions of the accused and take into account their humane and often self-sacrificing behavior before and after the war.

For Odazawa, these involved his selfless dedication to meeting the special needs of his family and his volunteer services in community charities.

For the highly educated Yamamoto and Okuma, the defenders cited interests and activities that suggested or even proved that, far from being brutal military robots, they embodied qualities that could lead to a better Japan and a better world.

Yamamoto sought to educate his students on democracy and personal freedom as well as agriculture. His friend, Mori, suggested that he had taken considerable risks in questioning Imperial authority.

Okuma came across in his defenders' petitions as a man struggling with his military obligation while strongly at odds with the system. An aunt of his wife recalled an incident when Okuma was at home on leave. Somehow he had met a common sailor from his unit who was in the city and had nowhere to stay. Okuma insisted the man use a spare bedroom in his home. What makes this remarkable is vast separation between officers and enlisted personnel throughout the Japanese military. This kind of fraternization was unheard of.

And Okuma went well beyond this token democratization. He was also on occasion—especially for an officer of his rank—dangerously outspoken in his questioning of the wartime government. "He said that he realized that this 'reckless war' would be won by the Allied Powers," recalled one petitioner, "but that he would have to go to the front and carry out his mission."

Okuma's petitioners also stressed that, on the eve of his arrest, he was about to convert to Christianity. His wife's aunt, a graduate of Rumbus College, had become a Christian minister, and several other relatives had graduated from the Hiroshima Mission School.

"We all, therefore, were intending to induce Kaoru to become a Christian," wrote Fusae Tsuabe, an aunt. "And by having faith in God, we desired him to become a warrior of Christianity and render his service to the rehabilitation of Japan, as well as for the peace of the world. However, this divine project in which he was to share some part was totally destroyed by his arrest. I deeply regret that he was detained before he had a chance to learn the meaning of the scripture: 'Repent ye, and ye shall be forgiven.'"

Several of the petitions asserted that they, like the accused, had experienced an "awakening" of liberal, democratic values because of the peaceful and progressive American occupation. "I don't think it is necessary to stress the fact that we actually witnessed the strict order and discipline of your army," wrote one. "At the same time, we personally encountered their lenient attitudes which deepened our confidence in your country. Thus, we are now aware of the fact that the propaganda spread throughout our country during the war was irresponsible and even nonsense."

The greatest irony of these petitions was the assertion, implied and expressed, that if Japan was to free itself from its aggressive, warlike past and join the community of progressive, peace-loving nations, it would need men like those who had tortured and murdered Bob Thorpe.

Chapter 22
Judgment at Yokohama

Guards at Sugamo Prison were startled to find CWO Waichi Ogawa hanging from the bars of his prison cell in a noose fashioned from his underwear.

Ogawa was charged with desecrating Bob Thorpe's body after he was beheaded. Security was stepped up because of his suicide, and he became the first prisoner to take his life at Sugamo.

The trial of the other five officers accused of murdering Bob Thorpe opened on June 22, 1948, under the direction of Leonard M. Rand, prosecutor for the Legal Section of the War Crimes Board. An American attorney, Edmund W. Peters, assisted by two Japanese lawyers, Mr. Nakamua and Mr. Ono, represented the defendants. The five-member court-martial panel was chaired by Lt. Col. Francis Place.

Place ordered each defendant to stand as he read the charges. "Yutaka Odazawa, you are charged with violating the Laws and Customs of War. Specifications are that on or about May 28, 1944, you did willfully and unlawfully kill 2nd Lt. Robert E. Thorpe. How do you plead: Guilty or not guilty?"

"I was merely following my orders," Odazawa said. "I cannot determine if I'm guilty or not."

Place ordered the court reporter to enter a plea of not guilty on both counts.

He then turned to Kaoru Okuma. "You are charged with five specifications:

Spec. 1—That on or about May 28, 1944, at Kairiru Island, New Guinea, you did willfully and unlawfully mistreat 2nd Lieutenant Thorpe, an American prisoner of war, by beating him.

Spec. 2—Did willfully and unlawfully caused the beating of Lieutenant Thorpe by enlisted personnel.

Spec. 3—Did with others participate in firing sidearms at Lieutenant Thorpe.

Spec. 4—Did with others participate in the execution of Lieutenant Thorpe.

Spec. 5—Did willfully and unlawfully order, cause, direct, and permit the unlawful desecration of the body of 2nd Lieutenant Thorpe.

"How do you plead?"

Okuma pleaded guilty to mistreating and allowing others to beat the prisoner. He also pleaded guilty to firing sidearms at the prisoner. He pleaded not guilty to the unlawful killing and desecration of the prisoner's body.

"Captain Kiyohisa Noto, you are charged with violating the Laws and Customs of War and ordering the unlawful execution of Lieutenant Thorpe. How do you plead?" Place asked.

Noto pleaded guilty to both charges. Naotada Fujihira and Tsunehiko Yamamoto both pleaded innocent to beating Lieutenant Thorpe and firing pistols at him.

Rand went after the five defendants in his opening remarks:

"On April 27, 1944, an American fighter pilot named 2nd Lt. Robert E. Thorpe took part in a fighter mission over Wewak Island, New Guinea. His plane was hit by antiaircraft fire, and he was forced to ditch off the north side of Kairiru Island. He was captured by Formosan soldiers and turned over to members of the 27th Special Naval Base Force.

"When word reached headquarters that an American flier had been captured, Captain Noto instructed Okuma and another officer by the name of Amemori, both of whom could speak some English, to interrogate the flier. We will prove that the accused literally had a field day with Lieutenant Thorpe. This case has four atrocity phases: the beating of Thorpe, using him as a living target for pistol practice, his beheading, and the desecration of his body.

"Admiral Sato, commanding officer of the 27th Naval Unit, who allegedly gave the order to execute Thorpe, committed suicide shortly before he was to be arrested. Recently, CWO Ogawa, the man who desecrated Thorpe's body, committed suicide at Sugamo Prison. At the end of the war, Sato and Noto took great pains to conceal the death of Lieutenant Thorpe, coming up with an elaborate plan to prove he died from malaria. Sato warned that all officers under his command should never say anything about the execution of Lieutenant Thorpe.

"These are the facts of the case, and they are undisputed, as you already know, from the confessions you have read. Now, Mr. Peters is going to try to distract you with stories about 'Bushido' and the Japanese code of military justice.

"His defense will be based on the 'I was only following orders' routine. Good. It did not work for Goring who committed suicide the night before he was to hang. Other German war criminals who used that same defense were hanged at Nuremberg. So far, it has not worked for any Japanese war criminals either."

"Objection," Peters cried. "Prosecution has no right to project the defense's case."

"Sustained," Place said. "Move on, Mr. Rand."

"We have studied the facts closely and looked for mitigating circumstances that would allow us to avoid asking for the supreme penalty. There are none. Therefore, the prosecution asks for the death penalty for each of the accused." A hush fell over the courtroom as Rand returned to his seat while his remarks were translated and Edmund Peters addressed the commission.

Peters established the defense theme in his opening remarks: "I think the facts of this case are relatively clear. An American flier by the name of Robert E. Thorpe was executed on Kiriru Island. He was executed by one fell swoop of the sword. There can be no doubt in the mind of any reasonable person about what caused his death.

"Odazawa didn't order his death. Neither did Okuma. They were both following the orders of Captain Noto who had been ordered by Admiral Sato to execute the prisoner. Sato admitted his guilt by taking his own life. There is also no evidence that Okuma permitted or even knew about the desecration of Thorpe's body. Ogawa desecrated the body on his own and has tacitly admitted it by committing suicide.

"The five accused acted under superior orders and had no choice but to obey such commands. Perhaps Emperor Hirohito, the person who issued orders that fliers were to be executed, should stand trial instead of these officers who merely followed his orders," Peters concluded.

"That is not something that this court or you should address, Mr. Peters," Place warned Peters, making it clear that Hirohito's name should not be mentioned in the trial again.

"I apologize to the court," Peters said. "As a civilian, it may seem inappropriate for me to point out the differences between Japanese and American military custom. We Americans follow the chain of command rigidly. We specify exactly who is to do what and on whose orders. We even have provisions when a subordinate may refuse to follow a superior's orders.

"That luxury does not exist in the Japanese military. The simple suggestion that a superior wants something done is enough. Our penalties for disobeying orders result in stockade time or loss of rank. Japanese insubordination always results in loss of life. The officers on trial here today were all acting under orders delivered by a superior officer. They had two choices: Carry out the orders or refuse to do so and be subject to immediate execution."

Peters sat as Rand called his first witness, CWO Naotada Fujihira, to the stand. "When did you first meet 2nd Lieutenant Robert Thorpe?" Rand asked.

"On the night before the capture of the prisoner, I left Muschu Island in a canoe and went to 27th Special Base Headquarters on Kiriru Island for the purpose of liaison," Fujihira said. "I spent the night on the island,

and, right after breakfast, I went to see Tobei Baba, the commanding officer of the Takasago Volunteer Unit. He was formally a member of the Eighth Naval Construction Unit and was accorded the rank of an officer.

"Baba introduced me to the American prisoner. His plane had crashed into the sea on the Northern Coast of Kairiru Island. He had swum ashore and was captured by a member of the Takasago Unit. The prisoner was about 21 years of age, about 5 foot 8 and weighed about 59 kilograms (126 pounds). He wore short trousers, his hands were bound, and he was tied to a post. His body was sunburned, but he didn't have any wounds."

"What happened next?" Rand asked.

"After lunch, Baba asked me to take the prisoner to headquarters. I was assigned two members of the Takasago Unit to act as guards, and I held the rope, and I led the prisoner to headquarters."

"Did the prisoner say anything during the trip?" Rand asked.

"I don't speak any English, and he had no Japanese. He nodded and smiled at me when I gave him some biscuits and water. We tied him to a post outside of the bomb shelter, about 25 meters from headquarters. I went inside and reported the capture to Captain Noto. He went to Admiral Sato and had a conversation. I could not overhear what was said. When he returned, he ordered Okuma and Amemori to interrogate the prisoner."

"Did you leave the scene then?" Rand asked.

"No. I watched as Okuma began to question the prisoner. I don't know what was being asked. But it was clear that Okuma was not pleased with the information he was getting."

"Objection," Peters said. "If the witness could not understand English, how could he judge whether or not Okuma was upset?"

"The witness will explain if he is allowed to," Rand said.

"Objection overruled. Proceed, Mr. Rand," Place said.

"Tell the court why you felt that Okuma was upset," Rand said.

"Okuma's face became red, and he began to shout. Then he started to strike the prisoner on the head and neck," Fujihira said.

"How did the prisoner respond?" Rand asked.

"He never changed his expression, even when he was being beaten.

Okuma became very upset at one of the prisoner's answers. I was told later that he had insulted the emperor. Okuma invited the enlisted personnel to beat the prisoner while he reported to Captain Noto. They took turns beating him with their fists and sticks."

"What was the condition of Lieutenant Thorpe when Okuma returned to the scene?"

"He was bleeding from cuts on his face, back, and shoulders," Fujihira said.

"What did Okuma say when he returned to the scene?" Rand asked.

"He said the prisoner was to be executed on the beach."

"Did he issue any other orders?" Rand asked.

"Yes. He ordered Lieutenant Yamamoto and myself to return to our quarters and get our sidearms."

"Did he explain why?"

"No. He just told us to get our sidearms and join the group at the execution scene."

"No further questions for this witness, but I will recall him later," Rand said to Place.

"Your witness, Mr. Peters," Place said.

"Who ordered Okuma to interrogate the prisoner?" Peters asked Fujihira.

"Captain Noto," Fujihira replied.

"When Okuma said that Lieutenant Thorpe was to be executed, did he say on whose orders?"

"He said he was acting under the orders of Captain Noto."

"No further questions," Peters said.

"Redirect, Mr. Rand?" Place asked.

"Not at this time," Rand answered.

"Call your next witness, Mr. Rand."

"Will Captain Noto take the stand," Rand asked.

"When did you first arrive in New Guinea?" Rand asked.

"I arrived in Wewak on Oct. 4, 1943. My rank at the time was commander, and I was attached to the 2nd Special Base Force at Wewak as Staff Officer. On Oct. 10, 1943, I replaced Captain Tadano. I was moved to Kairiru Island on March 15, 1944. The commanding officer was Rear Admiral Ogata, and I was the Senior Staff Officer under him. Rear Admiral Ogata was replaced by Rear Admiral Sato on April 12, 1944."

"When did you first meet Lieutenant Thorpe?" Rand asked.

"I never did meet Lieutenant Thorpe," Noto replied.

"When did you first learn that Lieutenant Thorpe had been captured?" Rand asked.

"Lieutenant Fujihira reported that a prisoner had been brought in and was being guarded outside the air raid shelter. I relayed this information to Admiral Sato, and he ordered me to have the prisoner interrogated. I ordered Okuma and Amemori to conduct the interrogation."

"Did you instruct Okuma to beat the prisoner or invite others to torture him?"

"Objection," Peters said. "Captain Noto has not been charged with torturing the prisoner or participating in his execution."

"Sustained," Place said. "This is not the time to bring additional charges against Captain Noto," Place warned.

"What happened next?" Rand asked.

"Okuma left to interrogate the prisoner and was gone for quite a while. I sent my orderly to find out the progress of the interrogation. Okuma returned to headquarters and said the prisoner was not cooperative and gave no useful military information."

"Were you aware of what was going on not more than 40 feet from your headquarters tent? This monster [he points to Okuma] had invited the enlisted personnel to beat the prisoner while he made his report at headquarters."

"I heard nothing."

"It seems likely that the noise would carry for that distance."

"Objection. Conjecture," Peters said. "The witness said he didn't hear the noise. We have no evidence to prove otherwise. Captain Noto is not charged with ordering the prisoner to be beaten."

"If it would please the court, it's vital for our case to establish the character—or lack of it—of Captain Noto," Rand said. "He made many contradictory statements in his written reports and was responsible for the attempted cover-up of the murder of Robert Thorpe."

"Mr. Rand," Place warned, "you are to avoid language such as 'monster.' Meanwhile, the objection is overruled. Answer the question, Captain Noto."

"I told Admiral Sato that Okuma failed to get any useful information. Sato ordered that the prisoner be executed. I objected by saying that it was not right to execute the prisoner, since he was not a spy. Sato explained that he had been in the mainland of Japan until recently and had the latest knowledge on the handling of prisoners. Those American fliers who took part in air raids were to be executed."

"Was there anyone else present during your conversation with Admiral Sato?" Rand asked.

"No."

"Did Admiral Sato issue orders on how the prisoner was to be executed?"

"No. He left it up to Okuma," Noto replied.

"I will be recalling this witness. Your witness, Mr. Peters," Rand said.

"Captain Noto, what would have happened to you if you continued to argue with Admiral Sato about the execution of the prisoner?" Peters asked.

"I would have been sentenced to death under the Article of 'Failure to Comply with Orders,' in the Naval Penal Code. Insubordination is the heaviest offense for Japanese military personnel," Noto replied.

"Admiral Sato told you about an order that all captured enemy pilots were to be executed. Do you know who issued this order?"

"Yes. It came from the emperor himself when he had several American pilots executed who took part on the raid in Tokyo."

"The emperor is not being tried by this court-martial," Place warned. "His name is not to be mentioned again."

"I have nothing further for the witness at this time," Peters said.

"Please call your next witness," Place said to Rand.

"Would Kaoru Okuma please take the stand."

"Tell us about your service on Kiriru Island," Rand asked Okuma.

"I was a member of the Imperial Japanese Naval Force. In March 1944, I was posted as staff officer to No. 2 Special Naval Base Force on Kairiru Island."

"I understand you speak English," Rand said.

"Yes. I learned it in middle school and at the Naval Engineering School where we had an English teacher."

"Tell us about the capture of Lieutenant Thorpe in May of 1944."

"I was working when Fujihira came to headquarters and reported to Admiral Sato and Captain Noto that an American flier had been captured and was outside the air raid shelter."

"Could you overhear what was being said?" Rand asked.

"I heard Fujihira make his report. But Noto and Sato lowered their voices, and I couldn't hear them."

"Did you sense any disagreement in their conversation?" Rand asked.

"In the Japanese navy one does not disagree with a superior officer," Okuma replied.

"What officers were present at this time?"

"Sato, Noto, Yamamoto, and myself. Fujihira went back outside to guard the prisoner."

"What happened next?"

"Captain Noto ordered me to interrogate the prisoner since I could speak English."

"Did he specify what information he wanted you to obtain?"

"Any useful military information possible: unit, location, number of planes, and type of planes."

"Did he indicate what was to become of the prisoner after the interrogation?"

"Not at that time. I was to interrogate the prisoner and report back to Captain Noto."

"Describe the scene when you first saw Lieutenant Thorpe."

"I was surprised by his appearance. He didn't look to be more than 20 years old. He was tall, slender build, brown hair, brown eyes. He had no wounds that I could see. I asked him for his name and rank. He said he was Robert E. Thorpe, second lieutenant, U.S. Army Air Corps."

"Was he cooperative?"

"In the beginning, he told me he was from a small town near Boston, Massachusetts. He said he had a sister and a brother and his parents were still living. He also said he was the only member of his family in the military, because his father was too old and his brother too young."

"Did he explain the circumstances of his crash?"

"He said his plane was hit by ground fire, and he had to ditch in the ocean. The plane sank almost immediately, and he wasn't able to inflate the life raft. He said he would have drowned if a tree trunk hadn't floated by and helped him get to shore."

"When did he stop being cooperative?"

"I asked him what type of plane he was flying and the location of his base. He said he could only give me his name, rank, and serial number."

"How did you respond?" Rand asked.

"I slapped him across the face."

"Lieutenant Fujihira testified that you became angry when Lieutenant Thorpe insulted the emperor. Please explain."

"I asked him if he thought the United States would win the war. He told me that his country had many resources and would not lose."

"You interpreted this as an insult and used it to encourage enlisted personnel to beat the prisoner."

"Yes. I suppose that's true."

"Had Captain Noto given you orders to beat the prisoner or to allow enlisted men to do so?"

"He did not. The only instruction I received from Captain Noto was to interrogate the prisoner and report back to him."

"Did you report back to Sato and Noto together?"

"No. I reported only to Noto. I told him the prisoner did not cooperate, and I didn't get anything of value from him."

"What did Noto say about your report?"

"He listened, then told me to execute the prisoner in any manner I wished. I walked with Yamamoto and Fujihira to the site of the execution on the beach. CWO Odazawa walked beside the prisoner with his ceremonial sword."

"Had you ordered Odazawa to act as executioner?"

"I had not."

"You are leaving out an important point that is included in your confession. Tell us about an order you issued to Fujihira and Yamamoto prior to going to the execution scene."

"I told them to return to their quarters and get their sidearms."

"Objection," Peters said. "Counsel belabors the point. Okuma's confession clearly states the reason he ordered the two officers to get their sidearms."

"We have the right to hear the accused relate, in his own words, a barbaric act to torment Lieutenant Thorpe's last minute on this earth."

"Objection overruled," Place said. "Answer the question."

"I told them we would use the prisoner for target practice prior to his execution," Okuma said.

"No further questions at this point," Rand said. "This witness will be recalled."

"Your witness, Mr. Peters," Place said.

"Did Captain Noto tell you on whose authority you were to execute Lieutenant Thorpe?" Peters asked Okuma.

"Yes. He said on the orders of Admiral Sato the prisoner was to be executed."

"No further questions," Peters said.

"Call your next witness," Place said to Rand.

"Yamamoto to the stand," Rand ordered.

"Tell us about your role in the execution of Lieutenant Thorpe."

"Lieutenant Commander Okuma ordered Fujihira and me to bring our sidearms to the execution scene."

"Describe it for us."

"Okuma, Odazawa, the prisoner, and about 20 enlisted soldiers were already there when Fujihira and I arrived. Okuma told Odazawa that we needed a few minutes before the execution to use the prisoner for target practice. Odazawa warned us not to shoot him above the waist, because any wounds in the stomach or head would make it difficult to behead him."

"How did Okuma respond?"

"He told us to listen to what Odazawa had to say."

"Take us through the firing."

"I believe Okuma fired first, and the prisoner staggered slightly as a bullet struck his leg. He did not fall, however. Fujihira fired next and the enlisted men laughed as his bullet struck sand well in front of the prisoner. I fired next and hit the prisoner in the other leg. He remained standing."

"You left out an important point that is recorded in your confession. What did you say to the prisoner before you shot?"

"I don't remember exactly," Yamamoto said.

"Let me help," Rand said, as he removed papers from his briefcase. "This is what Yamamoto said in his signed confession," he said to Place. "I said to Fujihira, 'You have not done a good job, and I will show you how to do it, as I am an expert. I told the prisoner that I will kill you with my pistol.'"

Rand paused for a moment to let the statement sink in. Place and members of the commission reacted visibly.

"No further questions," Rand said.

"Mr. Peters?" Place asked.

"Why did you fire at the prisoner?"

"Because Lieutenant Commander Okuma ordered me to do so," Yamamoto answered.

"No further questions," Peters said.

"Next witness," Place said to Rand.

"The prosecution calls Yutaka Odazawa," Rand said.

"Describe the circumstances when you first saw Lieutenant Thorpe," Rand said.

"I was on my way to headquarters when I heard some soldiers talking about an American prisoner who was tied outside the air raid shelter," Odazawa said.

"When did you learn that you were going to be part of the execution team?"

"Okuma told me that the prisoner was going to be executed by order of the commanding officer. I understood from his remarks that I was to be the executioner."

"Did Okuma order you to behead the prisoner?"

"I don't recall his exact words. But he led me to believe that I was to do so."

"Tell the court the exact words from Okuma that prompted you to get your sword and behead the prisoner!"

"Objection," Peters said. "He is badgering the witness."

"Sustained," Place said. "Yelling at the witness is not going to refresh his memory," Mr. Rand.

"I apologize. But other witnesses contradict what this witness has said in his written statements. I'm simply trying to get to the truth. No one ordered Odazawa to behead Lieutenant Thorpe. He was a willing volunteer."

Rand turned back to Odazawa. "What did you say to Okuma after he allegedly told you that you were to behead the prisoner?"

"I don't recall saying anything. I went back to my quarters for my ceremonial sword."

"Take us through the execution."

"Okuma was the senior officer, and he was giving all the orders. He said that prior to the prisoner being beheaded, he was to be used for target practice."

"What did you say to the three officers prior to their shooting at Lieutenant Thorpe?"

"I told them not to shoot him above the waist."

"Did they heed your warning?"

"Yes. Fujihira fired and missed, but shots from Okuma and Yamamoto hit the prisoner in the legs. Some enlisted men dragged him to the grave, and I beheaded him."

"In his confession, Okuma described a theatrical ceremony you performed prior to beheading Lieutenant Thorpe. He said it made enlisted personnel laugh."

"I performed the ceremony of Bushido. It is a sign of great respect for an enemy soldier."

"Did Lieutenant Thorpe say anything before you beheaded him?"

"Yes. He asked me what time it was."

"Were you aware that Ogawa was going to desecrate Lieutenant Thorpe's body after the execution?"

"I had no knowledge that he was going to commit such a disgusting act."

"No further questions," Rand said.

"Did you say anything to Lieutenant Thorpe prior to his execution?" Peters asked.

"I told him, 'Due to the war, it cannot be helped. I must dispose of you on orders.'"

"Was Lieutenant Thorpe worthy of the Bushido ceremony he received?"

"He refused to give any military information, even when he was beaten. He stood silently as three officers fired at him. Even after he was struck by bullets, he never cried. Yes, Lieutenant Thorpe was most worthy of Bushido."

"No further questions," Peter said.

"At this point, I would like to recall Lieutenant Commander Okuma," Rand said.

"Did you order Odazawa to behead Lieutenant Thorpe?" Rand asked Okuma.

"I did not. As far as I know, neither Admiral Sato or Captain Noto gave Odazawa an order to be the executioner. I feel certain that he volunteered."

"CWO Odazawa claims he performed the Bushido ceremony to honor the prisoner. Do you agree?"

"No. Odazawa performed the act as if it was from a play. He did it in a contemptuous manner, and everybody laughed. He made a soldier fill a bottle with water, poured it on the prisoner's neck, and then on his sword. He then beheaded the prisoner with one blow."

"No further questions," Rand said. "The prosecution rests."

Chapter 23
For the Defense

After the prosecution rested, the defense immediately made motions for findings of not guilty for all five defendants.

"I think the facts of this case are relatively clear," Peters argued. "An American flier by the name of Thorpe was executed on this island. He was executed by one fell swoop of the sword. There can be no doubt in the mind of any reasonable person about what caused his death.

"That being true, it is impossible for anybody else to have participated in his death. Therefore, Okuma could not possibly be guilty of Specification 3, because his directing and ordering the death are covered by Specification 4. His mistreatment of the flier is covered by Specifications 1 and 2, and there is no evidence before this commission on Specification 3.

"The evidence is so confusing as to who fired what shots, who fired first, who fired second, and which bullets hit him. We concede there is evidence that Ogawa desecrated this body, but there is no evidence that Okuma was even present at the time. All of the prosecution's evidence shows that Ogawa desecrated the body. Ogawa has tacitly admitted it by committing suicide.

"The defense asks that a finding of Not Guilty be entered for Yamamoto and Fujihira. Yamamoto did shoot him, but it was the blow by Odazawa that killed him. Fujihira shot at him, but the evidence is so confusing as to who shot first, second, or third, which bullets struck him and which didn't. There is also no evidence that Fujihira beat the prisoner.

"Odazawa willfully killed this flier, yet the testimony of the prosecution's own witness is that when Odazawa was about to behead the prisoner, he said, 'I am doing it under orders.' Odazawa had absolutely no control over what he was doing. He was ordered by Okuma on the orders of Admiral Sato and Captain Noto to execute this flier.

"It is considered appropriate to mention that in all cases where there is conflicting testimony, it is within the province of the commission deciding the facts to weigh the testimony according to its value, accept that part which it considers of value, and reject the remainder," Peters said.

Peters also cited a ruling that a Japanese lance corporal and sergeant major did not violate the customs of war because they were following the order of their commanding officer (*United States of America v Minoru Kato, 2nd Lt., et al.*, Dec. 28, 1946).

Peters also reminded the commission of the conditions on Kairiru Island in May and June of 1944.

"They were being bombed daily. They had an air raid while discussing Lieutenant Thorpe's capture. Their communications were entirely cut off, and the defenses were so bad that Fujihira had to come across there at night in a canoe from the other island. They were afraid to come out in a rowboat during the daytime.

"The Japanese were licked, and they knew it. They were fighting a rear action, a defense action. These few men remained on Wewak to keep it from falling into Allied hands. Suppose you had been one of those men on that island at that time. Do you think you could reason things out as you are reasoning them out here today and will tomorrow? This is war. They had to do what they thought best at that time.

"Noto, in his statement, tells you about the food conditions. They were having a hard time feeding themselves, let alone feeding another prisoner of war who had been absolutely of no benefit to them. This is probably the reason why Admiral Sato gave the order to have him executed."

Peters also accused the prosecution of "blowing hot and cold" throughout the trial.

"They have not advanced one theory and stuck to one theory. They have persistently said no, Noto didn't get an order from Sato. Then they turned right around and say, 'Noto is guilty for having transmitted Sato's order to Okuma.'

"Since Noto pleaded guilty to the charges against him, the commission has no choice but to sentence him. He is already under a sentence of 20 years. I am asking you when you return your verdict that you specify the sentence shall run concurrently and not consecutively."

Peters acknowledged that Okuma struck the prisoner during the interrogation. He also agreed that Okuma gave permission for others to beat the prisoner.

"Captain Noto ordered Okuma to take the prisoner down to the cemetery and have him executed. He had no choice about it.

"There was one act and one act alone which caused the death of this flier, and that was the beheading by Odazawa. All of the testimony is to the effect that the flier was shot below the knee by somebody. The prosecution says that Fujihira shot him and hit him. Other prosecution witnesses say both Okuma and Yamamoto shot and hit him.

"There is no question about the order in which the shots were fired. Fujihira fired the first shot, Yamamoto fired the second shot, and Okuma fired the third shot. Then, Odazawa, who was ordered by Okuma to perform the execution, placed the flier in a kneeling position, gave him a drink of water, and washed off his sword and the prisoner's neck.

"Odazawa honored the flier by saying, 'I have no choice. This is war. I must behead you.'

"There was no animosity shown by Odazawa for this flier. He was simply following out an order and doing it in the true Bushido spirit that is the Japanese spirit of chivalry. He was honoring this man because he was a good fighter, had been shot down, and refused to give strategic information. When Okuma ordered him to go out and execute the flier and make all of the arrangements, he had no choice," Peters argued.

"Yamamoto got his pistol because Okuma ordered him to do so. He thought the execution was to be by pistol. He fired because Okuma ordered him to do so, aiming at the prisoner's legs. Fujihira lost his nerve when he fired at the prisoner, striking the ground harmlessly.

"I have tried to summarize the facts in this case and give the commission my interpretation. These men have been given every opportunity to present their defense. They have received as fair a trial as they possibly could. I trust that when you return your verdicts, the accused will be just as thankful for their fair trial and their fair verdicts as they have up until this time," Peters concluded.

"Mr. Peters has a tough case. I wouldn't like to be in his shoes," Rand said in his final remarks. "He did the very best he could. He did try to seize on the facts that would aid the accused. Those facts are damning against each and every accused in this case.

"Did these acts violate the Rules of Land Warfare? Did they violate the general sentiment of humanity? That, I am sure, is plain. Mr. Peters stated that when I asked for the death penalty in this case I couldn't be serious. I would like to conclude by saying that when I asked for a death penalty for all of these accused I was never more serious in all my life."

The commission retired for deliberation on June 30, 1948, and reconvened on July 6, 1948, to announce its findings.

Yutaka Odazawa was found guilty of murder and was sentenced to be confined at hard labor for the rest of his life.

Naotada Fujihira was found guilty of both charges against him and was sentenced to life in prison at hard labor.

Tsunehiko Yamamoto was found guilty of the same charges and also received a life sentence.

Kaoru Okuma was found not guilty of specification 5 (allowing the desecration of Thorpe's body), but he was found guilty of the other four specifications and was sentenced to be hanged.

Kiyohisa Noto was found guilty of both charges against him and sentenced to an additional 20 years, to be served consecutively, not concurrently, to a 20-year sentence imposed by a Netherlands Military Commission for murdering three Australian prisoners of war.

The defense filed a motion for modification of sentences on behalf of all five defendants. Peters claimed that the testimony conclusively shows that the five acted on the orders of Rear Admiral Sato, commanding officer of the Naval Force Garrison at Kairiru Island.

Peters referred to a letter from General Douglas MacArthur stating:

"Action pursuant to order of the accused's superior or of his government shall not constitute a defense, but may be considered in mitigation of punishment if the commission determines that justice so desires."

"Obedience to authority is inbred in the Japanese soldier or sailor to an extent not found in the American military force. A member of the Japanese military, when issued an order, must treat it as if it came from the emperor himself," Peters said.

"Under the supreme command of the emperor, the voice of the officer is the voice of the emperor. The simple soldier is taught that disobedience, even to his immediate superior, is virtually disobedience to His Majesty. The five accused acted under superior orders and had no moral choice but to obey such commands."

Peters went over the sentences, one by one:

Kaoru Okuma

"The accused Okuma was sentenced to death by hanging. He was charged with beating and permitting others to beat Thorpe. Okuma pleaded guilty to these charges and the evidence sustained the findings of the commission as to specifications one and two.

"As to the shooting of Thorpe by Okuma, there is evidence that Okuma fired one shot from his pistol at the legs of Thorpe but missed.

"As to the charge that Okuma ordered, caused, directed, and permitted the unlawful killing of Thorpe, the evidence proves beyond all doubt that Okuma acted in accordance with superior orders.

"Okuma was guilty of slapping the prisoner of war; ordering and permitting others to mistreat the prisoner; assault with a dangerous weapon and being present at the scene of execution. None of these constitute a capital crime.

"The offenses committed do not justify other than imprisonment for a term of years."

Kiyohisa Noto

"Noto pleaded guilty to unlawfully ordering, directing, and permitting the unlawful killing of Thorpe.

"But the evidence proved that Noto was ordered by his commanding officer, Rear Admiral Sato, to have the prisoner of war disposed of.

"Noto knew nothing of the beating of or firing at Thorpe, and he was not present at the execution site. He committed no crime, other than being chief of staff to Admiral Sato. He was a mere channel of communication, just a messenger. He is deserving of no punishment whatsoever.

"Noto had been tried and convicted of a war crime and sentenced to imprisonment for 20 years at hard labor. The conviction was in no way connected with Thorpe's case.

"Should the Reviewing Authority hold that Noto is deserving of some punishment, it is requested that it run concurrently with the sentence he is now serving."

Yutaka Odazawa

"Odazawa was charged with one specification—the unlawful killing of Thorpe by beheading.

"Odazawa was not a volunteer; he was merely complying with an order of his superior officer. There is no evidence in the entire trial record to the contrary. These mitigating circumstances should be taken into consideration.

"Odazawa should receive no punishment or, at most, a token punishment."

Yamamoto and Fujihira

"The evidence sustains the finding of the commission that these accused slapped the prisoner of war.

"Both Fujihira and Yamamoto were present at the execution scene, and there is evidence that they did shoot at the prisoner.

"Fujihira fired but one shot and purposely missed. Yamamoto fired twice, one shot hitting the prisoner below the knees.

"The evidence shows that the two accused fired their pistols because they were ordered to do so by Okuma.

"Okuma was a superior of Fujihira and Yamamoto, and the two were following the order of a superior officer.

"Yamamoto is guilty of assault with intent to do bodily harm.

"Fujihira, having purposely missed, is only guilty of assault.

"Neither of the accused deserved so harsh a sentence as life imprisonment."

In his summary, Peters asked the Reviewing Authority to disapprove and modify the sentences imposed against all of the accused so that they will "receive a just and reasonable sentence commensurate with the degree of guilt."

On Feb. 11, 1949, Lt. Col. F. R. Undritz, the assistant staff judge advocate, U.S. Eighth Army, upheld the guilty verdicts but reduced the penalties of all of the accused with the following explanations:

Okuma

The accused well knew that orders had been issued for the execution of the flier before he interrogated him. He received no orders to beat the prisoner of war, yet at the interrogation he struck him and invited others present to do likewise. He was present and in charge while the prisoner of war was beaten with hands, fists, and wooden clubs about the face and body.

After the interrogation when he took the prisoner of war out to be executed, he further displayed his fiendish nature by personally firing live ammunition at him and permitting and directing others to likewise torture him. Then he ordered the decapitation.

The commission sentenced the accused to death by hanging. Whereas capital punishment might well be justified for the heinous crimes the accused committed, it is believed that as a matter of policy, it should be reserved for those commanders who, at the time of taking the life of another, are in a position to exercise their power of command independently of any compulsion from higher authority.

The accused was ordered to execute the prisoner of war by his superior officer. He had no moral choice but to obey.

For this reason, it is recommended that the death sentence be commuted to confinement at hard labor for life.

Yamamoto and Fujihira

These accused participated in the beating of the prisoner of war at the interrogation. Later they were eager participants in the killing of the prisoner of war by firing their pistols at him before the decapitation. However, neither was in charge of the interrogation or the execution. They were encouraged to participate by Okuma, the officer in charge. Their culpability is not as great as that of Okuma, but nevertheless, justice demands they be severely punished. The commission sentenced each of these accused to confinement at hard labor for life. It is believed a sentence of 20 years each is adequate punishment for the crimes they committed, and it is recommended that their sentences be reduced accordingly.

Odazawa

This accused was ordered to decapitate the flyer.

He had no moral choice but to obey. He felt he had to comply with his orders.

However, his apparent consent to and encouragement of the barbarous acts committed by his associates upon the helpless victim whose life he was about to snuff out disclose a malignant nature.

His culpability is not as great as that of those who actually did the firing.

The commission sentenced the accused to confinement at hard labor for life.

It is believed that a sentence of 10 years is adequate punishment for the crime he committed, and it is recommended that the sentence be reduced accordingly.

Noto

There was no maliciousness on the part of this accused.

He was the chief of staff of Admiral Sato and transmitted the latter's order for the execution to Okuma.

He knew the order was illegal, objected, and was overruled. He had no moral choice but to transmit the order.

The accused was previously tried by an Australian commission and convicted of a similar offense committed at the same place.

For the offense of which the accused was convicted, he should be punished.

However, it is not believed that any good purpose will be served by imposing additional confinement.

It is recommended that the sentence be reduced to 5 years, and the unserved portion of confinement at hard labor be remitted.

Col. Allan R. Browne, judge advocate, U.S. Eighth Army, disagreed with Lieutenant Colonel Undritz's recommendations for the sentence reductions, starting with Captain Noto. He said that Noto's sentence of 20 years for participation in the killing of Lieutenant Thorpe was plainly inadequate. "Noto volunteered to Sato that he would have Okuma dispose of the prisoner, and when Sato remained silent, Noto turned to Okuma and said, 'Take the prisoner somewhere and do away with him any way you want to.'"

Other evidence indicates that Sato more or less permitted Noto to run the headquarters, Browne pointed out. "Even if it were assumed that Noto was only relaying an order of his superior, he had an obligation to see that the execution was carried out in a military manner. The evidence establishes that nothing was done toward this end. Those who tortured Thorpe would not have committed the various acts in the immediate vicinity of the headquarters without knowing that their actions were permitted. The beating and mistreatment of the prisoner at the interrogation, the pistol practice, the exaggerated mimicry of a Bushido execution, and the desecration of the body certainly indicate a field day by the participants," Browne said.

"After the war, Noto was active in cautioning the various participants to conceal the execution," Browne added. "When he was interrogated by the Australians on Dec. 16, 1945, he stated that an airman had been captured and had died about 20 days later of malaria. He told them he was sick with malaria himself at the time and did not remember the details.

"He admitted in this trial that he had lied to the Australians, and he also stated that he had not been ill with malaria at the time. In view of his false statements, we have no reason to believe his unsupported statement that he had protested to Sato about the execution order," Browne added.

Browne said that Noto's sentence, although amounting to a life sentence at his age and life expectancy, was not excessive for his participation in the authorization of the execution. On March 1, 1949, the sentence of 20 years was approved.

Colonel Browne also disagreed with the commutation of Okuma's death sentence to life imprisonment. "Okuma staged the killing, permitting those of vindictive mind to beat the flyer predeath. He asked for volunteers to kill the victim. He authorized shooting at the prisoner for practice. His own father, in a clemency petition, says that the death sentence was justified."

Colonel Browne refused any reduction of Yutaka Odazawa's life sentence. He said that Odazawa volunteered to behead Thorpe, and he was so eager to accomplish the killing that he cautioned the officers who were shooting at the victim to aim below the hips so that a fatal wound would not deprive him of his opportunity. Browne quoted from the testimony of Okuma in describing the execution:

"Then Odazawa took the prisoner by the back of the neck and pushed him to the ground in a kneeling position with his head bowed forward right at the edge of the grave. He then performed an act as though it were from a play. It was done in a contemptuous manner, and everybody laughed. Odazawa withdrew his sword from its sheath and in Japanese stated his own name, age, birthplace, and told the prisoner in a loud voice 'You will go first to Paradise, and I will follow you later on.'

"Odazawa then made a soldier fill a bottle with water from a stream 10 meters away. He poured water first on the prisoner's neck, then on his samurai sword, all in the Bushido spirit of cleansing the soul. The prisoner was not blindfolded. Odazawa then swung his sword and chopped through the neck with one stroke so that the prisoner's head was attached by only a small shred of skin at the throat," Browne said. He recommended that the sentence of life imprisonment be approved.

Superior orders played no part in the action of Naotada Fujihira, Browne charged. "He showed his malice by beating the bound victim. He was sadistic and murderous. The life sentence, thought inadequate, should be approved since it cannot be increased," Browne said.

The actions of Tsunehiko Yamamoto paralleled those of Fujihira, Browne said. "He was an eager volunteer. He announced that he was practicing and told the prisoner he would kill him. He advised the others to shoot below the knees. It is difficult to understand how a sentence less than the extreme penalty could have been adjudged under facts showing such a malignant spirit as that of this man," Brown said. "Since his penalty cannot be increased, it is recommended that his life sentence be upheld."

On March 1, 1949, the commanding general, U.S. Eighth Army, approved the sentences as follows:

Lieutenant Commander Kaoru Okuma, death.
Captain Kiyohisa Noto, 20 years in prison.
CPO Yutaka Odazawa, life in prison.
CPO Naotada Fujihira, life in prison.
Ensign Tsunehiko Yamamoto, life in prison.

Noto was returned to his Australian prison in Rabaul, while Odazawa, Fujihira, and Yamamoto began their life terms at Sugamo Prison. Okuma was sent to the "death row" section of Sugamo Prison to await execution.

Chapter 24
The Asian Green Mile

Sugamo Prison had just one gallows when the Americans took over the prison, but motivated by the hundreds of death sentences meted out to convicted war criminals, the capacity was expanded so that four prisoners could be executed at the same time.

Considering Japan's overall brutality, the Americans were surprised when they learned that the Japanese had come up with a more humane way to hang prisoners. A cone-shaped wooden block fitted above the noose rendered the prisoner unconscious a millisecond before his neck was broken. These blocks were used during the execution of Japanese war criminals at Sugamo Prison.

The first prisoner to be executed by the Americans at Sugamo, Lt. Kei Yuri, was convicted of allowing subordinates to abuse and torture prisoners and for executing prisoners on his own. The procedure used to execute Yuri on April 26, 1946, became standard for all executions at Sugamo. An old formula, developed by the English for use in Ireland, Scotland, India, and other parts of the British Empire, was used at Sugamo. Yuri's weight, height, health, age, and physical condition were considered to determine how far he would have to drop in order for his neck to be broken.

Yuri was informed of the date and time of his execution 24 hours in advance. He was asked if he had any last requests concerning disposition of last letters, will, or personal belongings to his family.

Yuri was allowed to attend services in the chapel which had been provided a Buddhist shrine with a Buddhist priest in attendance. Thirty minutes before the execution, he was cuffed to a body belt that went from front to back and between his legs. Fifteen minutes later, he walked into the chapel and lit incense sticks. The priest held a cup of ceremonial wine to Yuri's lips to conclude the ceremony.

He left the chapel and walked to the gallows with the assistance of two guards chanting Namu-QAmida-Butsu, a Buddhist prayer. Witnesses sat in a low, narrow platform opposite an elevated deck over which hung five ropes, each ending in a noose. Yuri had to be assisted up the 13 steps leading to the execution platform, because the body belt made walking difficult. He walked to the first trapdoor, and a black hood was placed over his head as the ropes were adjusted and aligned with the noose coil and cone on the left side of his head.

The chief executioner called to the officer in charge that the prisoner was prepared for execution. As soon as the officer shouted "proceed," the trapdoor sprung open with a sound similar to a rifle shot.

The body dangled for a few minutes, a doctor listened to a stethoscope and called out, "I declare this man dead." The body was removed immediately, and the corpse was fingerprinted, placed in a wooden coffin, and taken to be cremated. Yuri's ashes were scattered at sea so there could be no enshrinement by the family or the Japanese government.

During the next 6 months, four other prisoners were executed for killing POWs, including Isao Fukuhara on August 9, 1946; Kaichi Hirate, on Aug. 23, 1946; Masadi Mabuchi, on Sept. 6, 1946; and Uichi Ikegami on Feb. 14, 1947. All of the executions were conducted at night, usually just after midnight.

The first multiple executions at Sugamo occurred on July 1, 1948, 1 week before Kaoru Okuma was placed on death row, the north end of the cell block at Sugamo. Hajime Honda, Sadamu Motokawa, Matsukkichi Muta, Sadamu Takeda, Yoschichi Takagi, Iju Sugasawa, Kazumoto Suematsu, and Masakatsui Hozumi were all convicted of murdering or allowing subordinates to murder POWs.

Although the gallows had five trap doors, only four prisoners were executed at a time. They were led to each of the first four trapdoors, the nooses were adjusted and black hoods placed over their heads. The hangman announced that the prisoners were ready for execution, the officer screamed "proceed," and the four traps were sprung. After the four bodies were removed, the next four were led in.

Ten prisoners were awaiting execution when Okuma arrived at Sugamo Prison. First Lieutenant Junsaburo Toshino was convicted of causing the death of more than 30 American and Allied POWs by refusing to restrain military under his control from shooting them. He also ordered subordinates to kill 15 sick prisoners.

Katutane Aihara was convicted of killing and decapitating more than 20 American prisoners while transferring them from Manila to Moji, Japan. Chief Petty Officer Sachio Egawa was found guilty of murdering two prisoners while he was a guard at Fukuoka Prisoner of War Camp in Kyushu, Japan. Captain Sukeo Nakajima was found guilty of allowing subordinates to murder prisoners of war and executing prisoners of war on his own.

Not all the condemned were from the military. Sadahara Hiramatsui, Harumi Kawate, Tonatsu Kimura, Kunio Yoshizawa, Masao Michishita, and Takuji Murakami were all convicted of murdering prisoners while working as civilian guards at POW camps. They were all executed on Aug. 18, 1948.

Perhaps the most notorious of Okuma's cell mates, a medical doctor by the name of Hisakichi Toshida, had his death sentence commuted to life imprisonment. Toshida had been convicted of causing the deaths of four American prisoners of war and contributing to other deaths through medical experimentation.

Toshida injected prisoners with soybean milk resulting in violent and painful deaths. Shortly after being placed on death row, Toshida became catatonic and had to be fed a liquid diet through his nose each day. Days after his sentence was commuted, Toshida regained his appetite and even asked for his medical books. He was paroled in the general amnesty in 1955 and reportedly opened a private medical practice in Tokyo.

Toshida was not the only Japanese doctor convicted of experimenting and killing prisoners of war. Five doctors were sentenced to death after being found guilty of mutilating, dissecting, and removing parts of the bodies of eight American POWs. They included Goichi Hirako, Yoshiol Mori, Yoshinao Sato, Tomoki Tashiro, and Katsuya Yakamura.

The incident, known as the "Kyushu University vivisection case," drew fire from the Japanese medical community, with the head of the leading medical school in Tokyo, Kenji Yoshido, stating, "Before the eyes of the world, I feel thoroughly ashamed for this disgraceful conduct of our countrymen. We desire that they be dealt with severely."

His recommendation was ignored as all five doctors had their sentences commuted to life in prison and all were released within 8 years.

One other condemned prisoner escaped Sugamo's gallows. Colonel Satoshi Oie had been tried in Manila and sentenced to death by firing squad. He had returned to Sugamo to testify at the war crimes trials at Yokohama. On Oct. 23, 1948, he was removed from Sugamo and placed in a bus to be transported to a nearby firing range.

To the amazement of his guards, Oie fell asleep in the bus and had to be awakened upon his arrival at the execution site. He thanked everyone involved, including the six-man firing squad, walked calmly to a post and was executed.

Things changed dramatically on death row with the arrival of the seven "Class A" prisoners on Nov. 28, 1948, including Kenji Doihara, Baron Koki Hirota, Seishiro Itagahi, Heitaro Kimura, Iwane Matsui, Akira Muto, and Shigenori Tojo.

On Dec. 21, 1948, the seven prisoners were brought, one at a time, to the chaplain's office where Colonel Morris C. Handwerk, the prison commandant, informed them they would be executed in 2 days. With the exception of Hirota, the prisoners accepted the news calmly. Tojo was extremely pleased, since he feared that they might be executed in another country.

Tojo also acted as a spokesman for the group concerning their last meal. They dined on rice, miso soup, broiled fish, and rice wine. They spent their final day writing farewell letters and in prayer with Dr. Shinsho Hanayama, the prison's Buddhist priest, who attended most of the executions at Sugamo.

Tojo wrote personal letters to his family, and then wrote a letter asking

Dr. Hanayama to make public after his execution. He, like the other prisoners, gave Hanayama hair, nail clippings, glasses, and even false teeth to be given to his family.

An incident involving the false teeth created serious problems for an American dentist.

Dr. George C. Foster, a naval oral surgeon, was assigned to Sugamo Prison as chief of dental surgery. When he repaired Tojo's dental plate, he engraved the words "Remember Pearl Harbor" in Morse code on the upper dentures. Even Tojo thought the prank was funny, however, the navy brass did not agree and removed Foster from his post.

At 11:30 p.m. on Dec. 22, Tojo, Doihara, Matsui, and Muto were led into the chapel where Hanayama was waiting. They lit candles, burned incense, and chanted Buddhist scripture.

The executions began at 12:01 a.m. on Dec. 23, 1948. Seconds after midnight, Doihara, Tojo, Muto, and Matsui walked to the entrance of the gallows. Tojo asked Matsui to lead them in their final "Banzai." All four men turned in the direction of the Imperial Palace and shouted "Banzai" three times. Then they mounted the platform and walked to each of the four trapdoors. Black hoods were placed over their heads and the four trapdoors sprung open immediately after the chief executioner ordered "Proceed."

Doihara was pronounced dead at 12:07, Tojo at 12:10, Muto at 12:11, and Matsui at 12:13. Immediately after the bodies were removed, Itagaki, Hirota, and Kimura were led to the gallows. This time there was no Banzais. Itagaki was pronounced dead at 12:32, Hirota at 12:34, and Kimura at 12:35.

The bodies were removed to a heavily guarded crematorium where they were reduced to ashes, then scattered to the winds. On Christmas Eve, MacArthur announced the executions of all seven "Class A" war criminals held in Japan.

The next mass execution was held on Feb. 12, 1949, when eight prisoners were hanged for murdering POWs, including: Yasutosi Mizuguchi, Kuratano Hirano, Yoshitako Kawane, Hideo Ishizaki, Kikuo Tomioka, Zentaro Wantanabe, Masao Kataoka, and Shoji Ito.

On May 28, 1949, exactly 5 years to the day when he supervised the execution of Robert Thorpe, Kaoru Okuma was executed at Sugamo. He had spent 10 months on death row, a relatively long time for a "Class B" war criminal. His stay on death row may have been based on the number of petitions filed on his behalf.

Perhaps MacArthur was more impressed by the fact that Kaoru Okuma's father, Ichi Okuma, refused to sign a clemency petition after learning about his son's involvement with the torture and murder of Robert Thorpe. There is no record indicating whether Kaoru Okuma went to his death with a Christian or Buddhist priest at his side.

Akiyama Yonesaku, Masaji Sekihara, Akira Yanagezawa, and Hiroshi Obinata were hanged on Aug. 20, 1949, for torturing and murdering POWs. The last executions at Sugamo were held on April 7, 1950, when Muneo Enomoto, Otohiko Inoue, Katsutaro Inoue, Yasumasa Taguchi, Tadakuni Narisako, Matsuo Fujinaka, and Minoru Makuda were hanged for torturing and murdering POWs.

Sugamo Prison was demolished in 1971 and replaced with a shopping complex named "Sunshine City."

A large stone with an engraved message marks the location of the prison gallows:

"PRAY FOR ETERNAL PEACE."

Chapter 25
Perfect Strangers

Zero pilot Kaname Harada shot down five American Devastator torpedo planes in the Battle of Midway on June 6, 1942. The Devastator's tail gun made it a dangerous target when he attacked directly from behind. But Harada devised a way of tilting his plane and approaching at an angle so he was out of the tail gunner's sight. By the time he opened fire, he was close enough to see the terrified faces of the doomed American aircrew.

Harada's triumph that day was diminished when he found that his carrier, the *Akagi*, and three others in the Japanese fleet had been sunk. With nowhere to land, he had to ditch his plane. Later, he went on to score a total of 19 kills before mangling his arm in a crash landing on Guadalcanal on September 19, 1943. The injury ended his combat career, and he finished the war as a flight instructor.

Seventy years later, those terrified faces still haunt the 98-year-old Harada. "I didn't hate them or even know them," he told a meeting of middle-aged business leaders in Nagano. "That's how war robs you of your humanity, by putting you in a situation where you must either kill perfect strangers or be killed by them."

Harada said that as he and other aging veterans from World War II die, Japan would lose more than just their war stories. It was his generation's bitter experiences, and resulting aversion to war, that have kept Japan firmly on a pacifist path since 1945.

How does he feel about Prime Minister Abe and other conservative politicians advocating revision of Japan's pacifist constitution and the strengthening of the country's military?

"They were born after the war, so they don't understand it must be avoided at all costs," he says. "In this respect, they are like our prewar leaders."

After Japan surrendered, Harada worked for a time on a dairy farm, but found himself plagued by nightmares. He kept seeing the faces of the terrified American pilots he had shot down. "I realized the war had turned me into a killer of men," he said, "and that was not the kind of person I wanted to be."

The nightmares finally ended when he opened a kindergarten in Nagano in 1965. He was able to alleviate feelings of guilt by dedicating himself to teaching young children the value of peace. Now retired, he still visits the school frequently to see the children's smiling faces.

It took many years before he could finally talk about the war itself. The turning point came during the Persian Gulf War in 1991, when he was appalled to overhear young Japanese students describe the bombing as if it were a harmless video game. He resolved to speak out.

He has been talking about his war experiences ever since. "Until I die, I will tell about what I saw," Harada concluded in his speech to the business group. "Never forgetting is the best way to protect our children and our children's children from the horrors of war."

Many Japanese share similar concerns. Crown Prince Naruhito has urged his nation to "correctly pass down tragic experiences and history to the generations who have no direct knowledge of the war, at a time when memories of the horrors are about to fade."

This has not stopped Prime Minister Shinzō Abe from making ceremonial visits to the Yasukuni Shrine where convicted war criminals are honored. The Japanese navy is building ships that can be easily converted into aircraft carriers. North Korean military development may lead to a nuclear-armed Japan.

So Kaname Harada's lament about "perfect strangers" is troubling and even eerie. Japan is probably the least welcoming nation in the world. The country's aversion and hostility to foreigners certainly did not stop with Admiral Perry's visit to Tokyo Bay in 1843. With an estimated 50 million people worldwide seeking political asylum in 2014, Japan, with the world's third-largest economy and a population of over 100 million, welcomed only 11 people.

Indeed, Harada may have hit on something. If war is the crime that robs us of our humanity, that crime may be less difficult to commit if most people in the rest of the world are perfect strangers.

Joseph Grew, America's prewar ambassador to Japan, wrote in his diary in 1947, "There are no finer people in the world than the best type of Japanese. The best type did not rule Japan between 1931 and 1945."

So now the question is . . . What type of Japanese are emerging to rule in the decades ahead?

Chapter 26
Request for Assistance

The coffee shop was packed with the usual summer tourists and some of the Newport regulars as author Ken Dooley greeted Representative Peter Martin. They were there to celebrate the successful pardoning of Irish immigrant John Gordon, a man who had been hanged in 1845 for the murder of Amasa Sprague, a wealthy Cranston, Rhode Island, mill owner.

Dooley had written a play, *The Murder Trial of John Gordon* which Representative Martin attended in 2011 at the Park Theater in Cranston, Rhode Island.

After attending the first performance, Martin introduced himself to Dooley. "You did a good job of proving the unfair treatment of John Gordon," Martin said. "Now what?"

"It's a little late for a stay of execution," Dooley said. "Gordon was executed in 1845."

"It's not too late to clear his name," Martin replied. He then introduced a bill that led to the pardon of John Gordon by Governor Lincoln Chafee 166 years after his execution.

Dooley had invited Martin to the coffee shop to thank him for his efforts. As they were talking about the Gordon case, Dooley asked Martin, "If you could do this for an Irish immigrant, what do you think you could do for a Rhode Island pilot who was shot down, executed by the Japanese in World War II, and buried on a lonely beach in New Guinea where he still lies today?"

"I don't know. Tell me the story," Martin replied.

Dooley went on to tell the story of growing up in Cranston, Rhode Island, as a neighbor of Lt. Robert Thorpe who was captured by the Japanese on May 27, 1944. The Japanese officers involved in his execution were tried at Yokohama in 1948.

Dooley described the attempts by Thorpe's family, especially his brother, Gill, to have Bob Thorpe's remains returned to RI for burial in the family plot.

"Why haven't his remains been returned?" Martin asked.

"Walter Thorpe, Bob's father, was told by military authorities that the remains were unrecoverable and the court-martial records were classified as secret," Dooley said. "In 2007, I got the trial records under the Freedom of Information Act. The records included a detailed map showing Bob Thorpe's burial spot on Kiriru Island, New Guinea."

"Was the grave exhumed then?" Martin asked.

"For the next 6 years officials in charge of locating missing American servicemen came up with a number of excuses, including weather and finances, to explain why no efforts were made to go to the burial site. Two years ago, the grave was finally opened, and no remains were found."

Representative Martin, a member of the Rhode Island House Committee on Veterans Affairs, immediately took interest in this case. While recovery Bob's Thorpe's remains was no longer feasible, he felt it would be appropriate to provide some posthumous recognition of Bob Thorpe's sacrifice for the remaining members of the Thorpe family.

As Martin drove away from the coffee shop, he realized he knew little about military awards and less about proper military protocol. Two years of the Army ROTC at Providence College 50 years earlier hardly qualified him to know where to start. He wondered how he could go about creating such recognition. He immediately thought of his friend, Sgt. Major Ed Kane (U.S. Army Ret). Ed had recently volunteered to serve on the Rhode Island House Veterans Advisory Council. He also knew that Ed had a reputation for getting things done.

The HVAC Committee Meeting

It wasn't long after that meeting that Dooley was invited to make a presentation of the Thorpe case to members of the House of Veterans Advisory Council. At the end of the presentation, the council members agreed to provide a ceremony that would recognize the sacrifice of 2nd Lt. Robert Thorpe.

Planning the House Celebration

Once this project was supported by the HVAC, it did not take long for Sgt. Maj. Ed Kane to take the lead in formulating this celebration. He enlisted the support of the Honors subcommittee of the House Veterans Advisory Council and the United Veterans Council.

Working with Jerry Squatrito and the staff of the House Veterans Advisory Committee, a celebration was scheduled for May 17, 2013, and was announced by the Rhode Island House of Representatives:

Cranston Pilot to be Honored for WWII Heroism

Warwick, RI. A Cranston native, 2nd Lt. Robert E. Thorpe, who was executed by the Japanese in 1944, will be honored at ceremonies in the RI House Chambers, May 17, at 1 p.m.

State Rep. Peter Martin (75th District, Newport) made the announcement at the annual meeting of the DAV at the Crown Prince Hotel in Warwick. Martin was honored by the Disabled American Veterans as "Legislator of the Year" for his work in veteran affairs.

"After 69 years of silence, it's time for us to do something to honor this heroic young man," Martin said.

Martin said he introduced a resolution to honor Thorpe at the request of playwright and author Ken Dooley, who grew up as a close friend of Bob Thorpe's brother, Gill, in Edgewood.

"Dooley and Martin are united again in a good cause," Martin said. After seeing Dooley's play, *The Murder Trial of John Gordon*, Martin introduced legislation that resulted in Gov. Lincoln Chafee signing a pardon for a man who was executed in 1845.

Gill Thorpe asked for Dooley's help in trying to recover the remains of his brother who had to ditch in the waters off of Kairiru Island, New Guinea, after his P-47 was struck by small arms fire during a strafing run on Wewak, a Japanese naval base.

Dooley got access to 1,200 pages of court-martial testimony and was able to reconstruct the events that led to Thorpe's torture and execution. Thorpe was interrogated by Lt. Commander Kaoru Okuma who became enraged when the prisoner refused to provide any information beyond name, rank, and serial number. Okuma struck Thorpe unmercifully, then invited Japanese personnel to join in the beatings.

An execution detail under the direction of Okuma led Thorpe to a nearby beach where he was used for target practice prior to his execution. Thorpe remained standing even as he was struck in both legs.

He was then dragged to a shallow grave, forced to kneel, and, after enduring an elaborate "Bushido" ceremony, was beheaded by Warrant Officer Yutaka Odazawa. Lt. Naotada Fujihira, one of the officers who shot the prisoner in the leg, described Thorpe's behavior as "magnificent" during court-martial testimony.

The five Japanese officers involved in the execution went on trial on June 22, 1948, at Yokohama, Japan. Four of the officers received life sentences, while Kaoru Okuma was hanged at Sugamo Prison. All four men were paroled within 5 years.

Captain Lewis Lockhart, a P-47 fighter pilot and close friend of Bob Thorpe, will attend the ceremony on May 17. Lockhart was on the mission when Thorpe was shot down during a strafing mission at Wewak, New Guinea, a Japanese naval base during WWII.

Lockhart and the late 2nd Lt. Fred Tobi broke orders and went looking for Thorpe when he failed to return. Now 93, Lockhart will journey from Franklin, TN, to honor his friend and comrade. Bob Thorpe's brother, Gill, and his sister, Nancy, will also attend. "The ceremony is open to the public, and I urge everyone to attend and honor this man who gave his life for his country," Martin said.

Resolution Honoring Robert Thorpe

In preparation for this event, Representative Martin and others introduced a resolution honoring 2nd Lt. Robert Thorpe for his sacrifice. It resulted in Rhode Island House of Representatives Resolution 6114.

HOUSE RESOLUTION—HONORING 2nd LT. ROBERT E. THORPE FOR HIS HEROISM DURING WWII

2013 - H 6114 - 5/14/2013 Introduced By: Representatives Martin, Gallison, Abney, Newberry, and Fox

Date Introduced: May 14, 2013

WHEREAS, In the words of famed newscaster Tom Brokaw, "When the United States entered World War II, the U.S. government turned to ordinary Americans and asked of them extraordinary service, sacrifice, and heroics"; and

WHEREAS, World War II was the most destructive conflict in history. It cost more money, damaged more property, killed more people, and caused more far-reaching changes than any other war in history; and

WHEREAS, A resident of Cranston, 2nd Lt. Robert E. Thorpe enlisted in September of 1942, shortly after graduating from Cranston High School. He was commissioned on August 30th of 1943, and became a World War II pilot. He had flown 17 missions during his first month in action before being captured when his P-47D Thunderbolt was hit by small arms fire during a strafing run on the Japanese garrison at Wewak on May 27, 1944; and

WHEREAS, Managing to survive by using a drifting log to get to shore after ditching his failing plane in the waters off Kairiru Island, New Guinea, 2nd Lt. Thorpe was captured by a Formosan civilian unit and marched across the island to the 27th Japanese Special Naval Base Force, which was under the command of Rear Admiral Kenro Sato; and

WHEREAS, The unit commander ordered his senior staff officer, Captain Kiyohisa Noto, to take charge of the prisoner, who, in turn, instructed Lt. Commander Kaoru Okuma to interrogate 2nd Lt. Thorpe: and

WHEREAS, Despite the 1929 Geneva Convention agreement, which provided for humane treatment of prisoners of war, atrocities still occurred. Prisoners were instructed to give captors only their name, rank, and military serial number. According to the Geneva Convention agreement, captors were allowed to question prisoners but were not allowed to use force or brutality to extract military information; and

WHEREAS, Following Military Law to the letter, 2nd Lt. Thorpe refused to provide his captors with any information beyond his name, rank, and service number. This infuriated Lt. Commander Okuma; and

WHEREAS, 2nd Lt. Robert E. Thorpe endured multiple beatings, physical and mental torture, and multiple gunshots, and was finally beheaded and mutilated by his captors. Months later the *Providence Journal* described the execution of 2nd Lt. Thorpe as "one of the most revolting crimes uncovered by the war crimes investigators." The article further stated that "Assassins of Local Flyer Now on Trial in Japan"; and

WHEREAS, After the war had ended, the five officers involved in the execution of 2nd Lt. Thorpe went on trial on June 22, 1948, in Yokohama, Japan. Four of the officers were sentenced to life in prison while Lt. Commander Okuma was sentenced to hang. Only one of the original sentences received by the five convicted war criminals, Lt. Commander Okuma's execution, was ever carried out; and

WHEREAS, In the aftermath of the trial, transcripts describing the horrible truth about the brutalities surrounding the death and the location of the burial site of 2nd Lt. Robert E. Thorpe were sealed and remained secret as Walter Thorpe, his father, began a campaign to have his son's remains returned to Rhode Island; and

WHEREAS, Sadly, wars often necessitate the unnatural act of a parent burying their child. Even more heart wrenching is when a parent cannot carry out or find any peace through this final act of closure and love. Walter and Nora Thorpe, 2nd Lt. Robert E. Thorpe's parents, died believing that their son's remains were unrecoverable and all records pertaining to the search and recovery of their son were closed; and

WHEREAS, Through the Freedom of Information Act in 2007, Ken Dooley, an author, and a close friend of 2nd Lt. Thorpe's brother, Gill, obtained a record of the court-martial. Although the facts brought out during the trial of 2nd Lt. Thorpe's captors produced descriptive details of where the 2nd lieutenant was buried, to this day, his remains lie unclaimed in an unmarked grave site on Kairiru Island; and

WHEREAS, Throughout American history our nation has been propitiously blessed with so many of her citizenry willing to serve their country at moments of great peril. These brave soldiers were and are prepared to risk all and many have made the ultimate sacrifice in order to protect our precious freedoms and liberties; and

WHEREAS, The heroism of the World War II generation embodies the personification of what makes our country so glorious. In return for their honorable service, we, as individuals and as a country, have a debt and an obligation to fulfill to the men and women serving in our military. We owe this young man, 2nd Lt. Robert E. Thorpe, who gave so much to his country and received so little in return, our gratitude, our acknowledgment of his sacrifice, and our best efforts to bring him home to his family and his country; now, therefore be it

RESOLVED, That this House of Representatives of the State of Rhode Island and Providence Plantations hereby respectfully

requests the Governor to honor 2nd Lt. Robert E. Thorpe posthumously with the Rhode Island Star for his extraordinary
heroism in the service of our nation during WWII; and be it
further

RESOLVED, That this House hereby urges the Graves Record Administration to reinvestigate and bring the remains of 2nd Lt.
Robert E. Thorpe home; and be it further

RESOLVED, That the Secretary of State be and hereby is authorized and directed to transmit duly certified copies of this resolution to The Honorable Lincoln Chafee, the Rhode Island Congressional Delegation, Maj. Gen. Kelly K. McKeague, Commander
of the Joint/POW/MIA Accounting Command, the Providence
Regional Office of the U.S. Department of Veterans Affairs, and
Nancy and Gill Thorpe.

Captain Lew Lockhart

Representative Martin was proud of the resolution that had been prepared for the House of Representatives ceremony. He met with Dooley to
show him a copy of it and the press release.

Dooley told Martin there would be a "special guest" at the ceremo-
ny—Captain Lewis Lockhart, a then 93-year-old resident of Franklin,
Tennessee, who had flown with Bob Thorpe as a member of the 39th
Fighter Squadron in New Guinea.

Captain Lockhart was at his home in Tennessee when he received a
call from Ken Dooley. Dooley told him about the plans to recognize the
ultimate sacrifice of Robert Thorpe.

Lockhart agreed to honor his friend by coming to Rhode Island and
speaking at the commemoration ceremony. Doug Hale, his nephew and a
Franklin attorney, escorted him.

The ceremony had special meaning for Lew Lockhart, who had flown
149 combat missions with the 39th FS in New Guinea. He was in charge of
the orientation flight when Bob Thorpe joined the 39th Fighter Squadron
at Gusap, New Guinea, in January of 1944.

Lockhart also flew on Bob Thorpe's last mission on May 27, 1944.

The 39th FS was grounded for weather the day after Bob Thorpe was listed as missing. That was when Lockhart broke regulations and took off in search of his friend.

Although they had only flown together as pilots for a short time, Lew Lockhart had never forgotten his friend Robert Thorpe and the mission on which he was lost.

It was only a few years earlier that Lockhart has learned about Thorpe having been murdered by his Japanese captors.

A related article published in the *Tennessean* quoted Lockhart as saying "Bob Thorpe was an excellent pilot and a real hero, as far as I'm concerned."

The article provided some background information:

An East Tennessee native, Lockhart was a student at Middle Tennessee State College when Pearl Harbor was attacked on Dec. 7, 1941. On Jan. 2, 1942, he became an aviation cadet at Berry Field and went through pilot training in Florida and Alabama. On Oct. 9, Lockhart, who didn't have any flight experience prior to enlisting, earned his wings in Dothan, Ala.

From there, Lockhart shipped overseas to Australia, and then Papua New Guinea, where he joined the squadron on March 23, 1943, flying his P-38 to escort other planes such as B-24s and B-25s. By December of that year, he began flying a P-47 on dive-bombing and strafing missions.

"I flew many missions and had a lot of close calls," he said. Going by the call sign "Blue 2," Lockhart completed 171 combat missions.

Resolution in Honor of Captain Lew Lockhart

In preparation for Lockhart's visit, Martin introduced a resolution on the House floor honoring Captain Lew Lockhart for his efforts to locate 2nd Lt. Thorpe at the time of his loss and his ongoing efforts to keep Thorpe's memory alive.

HOUSE RESOLUTION—HONORING CAPTAIN LEWIS LOCK-HART FOR HIS HEROISM DURING World War II 2013—H 6118 5/15/2013

WHEREAS, Captain Lewis Lockhart joined the 39th Fighter Squadron in New Guinea, a group that was formed in WWI by flyers such as Jimmy Doolittle and Eddie Rickenbacker; and

WHEREAS, Captain Lockhart endangered his life daily by flying through the 13,000 foot peaks of the Owen Stanley Mountains in New Guinea to bomb and strafe the Japanese 9th Fleet headquarters on Kairiru Island; and,

WHEREAS, the 39th Fighter Squadron cut off transport ships from mainland Japan and totally destroyed Japanese planes and ships at Wewak, New Guinea; and

WHEREAS, conditions became so bad for Japanese soldiers and sailors stationed on Kairiru Island that they fantasized about food and painted chickens green to camouflage them from the repeated air attacks by the 39th Fighter Squadron; and

WHEREAS, Captain Lockhart flew combat cover missions to Hollandia and Rabaul; and,

WHEREAS, Captain Lockhart had to make an emergency landing in his P-38 after one of his engines was destroyed in a combat mission over Rabaul; and

WHEREAS, Captain Lockhart flew as flight leader when the 39th covered a major parachute drop in the Markham Valley, New Guinea; and

WHEREAS, Captain Lockhart led the bombing and strafing mission on May 27, 1944, when 2nd Lt. Robert E. Thorpe was reported missing; and

WHEREAS, Captain Lockhart and 2nd Lt. Fred Tobi went looking for Lt. Thorpe in hazardous flying conditions when the entire squadron was grounded; and

WHEREAS, Captain Lockhart flew as wingman when his squadron leader had to bail out and escape from hostile natives in New Guinea, a story that was captured in a documentary *Injury Slight*; and

WHEREAS, Captain Lockhart flew a total of 171 combat missions in the P-38 and the P-47; and

WHEREAS, the 39th Fighter Squadron, together with other units of the Fifth Air Force, is credited with preventing New Guinea, and probably Australia, from falling into Japanese hands during the early years of the war in the Pacific; and be it further

RESOLVED, That his House of Representatives of the State of Rhode Island and Providence Plantations hereby respectfully requests the governor to honor Captain Lewis Lockhart for his extraordinary heroism in the service of our nation during WWII and in particular for his efforts to save 2nd Lt. Robert E. Thorpe, a Rhode Island hero who lost his life after flying a combat mission for the 39th Fighter Squadron.

Chapter 27
The Ceremonies

On May 17, 2013, 2nd Lt. Robert Thorpe was finally given recognition at a ceremony that was held in the House of Representatives chamber in the Rhode Island State House.

Family members attending included Thorpe's brother, Gill; Gill's daughter and son-in-law, Susan and Richard Waterman; Gill's grandsons, Richard and Sam Waterman; Gill's daughter Janet Thorpe; daughter Gill's cousin Neil Ganz and his wife, Caroline.

Representative Raymond Gallison, the then chairman of the House Committee on Veterans Affairs, hosted the ceremony and recognized all of the family, military, and elected officials in attendance.

Governor Lincoln B. Chafee acknowledged Robert Thorpe's sacrifice by saying "despite brutal treatment he did not cower, he went to his death bravely and defiantly."

Brigadier General Petrarca, RI Army National Guard, spoke in tribute to Thorpe and the members of the American World War II armed forces.

WHEREAS, Despite the 1929 Geneva Convention agreement, which provided for humane treatment of prisoners of war, atrocities still occurred. Prisoners were instructed to give captors only their name, rank, and military serial number. According to the Geneva Convention agreement, captors were allowed to question prisoners but were not allowed to use force or brutality to extract military information; and

WHEREAS, Following Military Law to the letter, 2nd Lieutenant Thorpe refused to provide his captors with any information beyond his name, rank, and service number. This infuriated Lieutenant Commander Okuma; and

WHEREAS, 2nd Lt. Robert E. Thorpe endured multiple beatings, physical and mental torture, and multiple gunshots, and was finally beheaded and mutilated by his captors. Months later the *Providence Journal* described the execution of 2nd Lieutenant Thorpe as "one of the most revolting crimes uncovered by the war crimes investigators." The article further stated that "Assassins of Local Flyer Now on Trial in Japan"; and

WHEREAS, After the war had ended, the five officers involved in the execution of 2nd Lieutenant Thorpe went on trial on June 22, 1948, in Yokohama, Japan. Four of the officers were sentenced to life in prison while Lieutenant Commander Okuma was sentenced to hang. Only one of the original sentences received by the five convicted war criminals, Lieutenant Commander Okuma's execution, was ever carried out; and

WHEREAS, In the aftermath of the trial, transcripts describing the horrible truth about the brutalities surrounding the death and the location of the burial site of 2nd Lt. Robert E. Thorpe were sealed and remained secret as Walter Thorpe, his father, began a campaign to have his son's remains returned to Rhode Island; and

WHEREAS, Sadly, wars often necessitate the unnatural act of a parent burying their child. Even more heart wrenching is when a parent cannot carry out or find any peace through this final act of closure and love. Walter and Nora Thorpe, 2nd Lt. Robert E. Thorpe's parents, died believing that their son's remains were unrecoverable and all records pertaining to the search and recovery of their son were closed; and

WHEREAS, Through the Freedom of Information Act in 2007, Ken Dooley, an author, and a close friend of 2nd Lieutenant Thorpe's brother, Gill, obtained a record of the court-martial. Although the facts brought out during the trial of 2nd Lieutenant Thorpe's captors produced descriptive details of where the 2nd lieutenant was buried, to this day, his remains lie unclaimed in an unmarked grave site on Kairiru Island; and

WHEREAS, Throughout American history our nation has been propitiously blessed with so many of her citizenry willing to serve their country at moments of great peril. These brave soldiers were and are prepared to risk all and many have made the ultimate sacrifice in order to protect our precious freedoms and liberties; and

WHEREAS, The heroism of the World War II generation embodies the personification of what makes our country so glorious. In return for their honorable service, we, as individuals and as a country, have a debt and an obligation to fulfill to the men and women serving in our military. We owe this young man, 2nd Lt. Robert E. Thorpe, who gave so much to his country and received so little in return, our gratitude, our acknowledgment of his sacrifice, and our best efforts to bring him home to his family and his country; now, therefore be it

RESOLVED, That this House of Representatives of the State of Rhode Island and Providence Plantations hereby respectfully requests the Governor to honor 2nd Lt. Robert E. Thorpe posthumously with the Rhode Island Star for his extraordinary heroism in the service of our nation during WWII; and be it further

RESOLVED, That this House hereby urges the Graves Record Administration to reinvestigate and bring the remains of 2nd Lt. Robert E. Thorpe home; and be it further

RESOLVED, That the Secretary of State be and hereby is authorized and directed to transmit duly certified copies of this resolution to The Honorable Lincoln Chafee, the Rhode Island Congressional Delegation, Maj. Gen. Kelly K. McKeague, Commander of the Joint/POW/MIA Accounting Command, the Providence Regional Office of the U.S. Department of Veterans Affairs, and Nancy and Gill Thorpe.

Captain Lockhart was introduced and escorted to the dais. The audience was very moved that this 92-year-old veteran, who had traveled from Tennessee, was able to express his memories of Thorpe with a speech that was short and to the point.

> *I think it is a great privilege for me to be here in order to honor Bob. I flew with Bob on many missions before the one where he went down. Although I was on a flight that same day, Bob was on another flight.*
>
> *We didn't know what happened to him when he didn't return to the base the next day for the debriefing. Bob's closest friend and tent mate, Fred Tobi, and I were on a search mission for him the next day. Of course, we found no remains.*
>
> *It was only many, many years later that we found out what happened to him through the efforts of Ken Dooley. I think it is only proper that Bob gets the recognition today that he deserves as a true American hero.*

Author Ken Dooley spoke about his attempts over many years of researching what actually happened to Thorpe and the postwar trial of the five Japanese soldiers who were tried and found guilty of Thorpe's murder.

Franklin attorney Doug Hale, Lockhart's nephew by marriage who had accompanied him from Franklin, Tennessee, was introduced. Hale had been quoted in an article that appeared in their local newspaper, *The Tennessean*, 2 days earlier, as saying:

> *That generation is tough as nails, the whole group of them. They didn't wait to get drafted. They are truly great Americans. People don't need to forget what they did. The people of Rhode Island sure didn't.*

Alan Fung, the mayor from the Thorpe hometown of Cranston, read a citation honoring him.

The House reading clerk, Francis McCabe, then read a resolution honoring Captain Lockhart.

HOUSE RESOLUTION—HONORING CAPTAIN LEWIS LOCKHART FOR HIS HEROISM DURING WWII

Introduced By: Representatives Martin, Gallison, Abney, Newberry, and Fox

Date Introduced: May 15, 2013

Referred To: House read and passed

WHEREAS, While in New Guinea during World War II, Captain Lewis Lockhart joined the 39th Fighter Squadron, a group that was formed in WWI by flyers such as Jimmy Doolittle and Eddie Rickenbacker; and

WHEREAS, Captain Lockhart endangered his life daily by flying through the 13,000 foot peaks of the Owen Stanley Mountains in New Guinea to bomb and strafe the Japanese 9th Fleet headquarters on Kairiru Island; and,

WHEREAS, the 39th Fighter Squadron cut off transport ships from mainland Japan and totally destroyed Japanese planes and ships at Wewak, New Guinea; and

WHEREAS, conditions became so bad for Japanese soldiers and sailors stationed on Kairiru Island that they fantasized about food and painted chickens green to camouflage them from the repeated air attacks by the 39th Fighter Squadron; and

WHEREAS, Captain Lockhart flew combat cover missions to Hollandia and Rabaul; and,

WHEREAS, Captain Lockhart had to make an emergency landing in his P-38 after one of his engines was destroyed in a combat mission over Rabaul; and

WHEREAS, Captain Lockhart flew as flight leader when the 39th covered a major parachute drop in the Markham Valley, New Guinea; and

WHEREAS, Captain Lockhart led the bombing and strafing mission on May 27, 1944, when 2nd Lt. Robert E. Thorpe was reported missing; and

WHEREAS, Captain Lockhart and 2nd Lt. Fred Tobi went looking for Lt. Thorpe in hazardous flying conditions when the entire squadron was grounded; and

WHEREAS, Captain Lockhart flew as wingman when his squadron leader had to bail out and escape from hostile natives in New Guinea, a story that was captured in a documentary *Injury Slight*; and

WHEREAS, Captain Lockhart flew a total of 171 combat missions in the P-38 and the P-47; and

WHEREAS, As a testimony to Captain Lockhart's heroic service to our nation during World War II, he received the Air Medal with Two Oak Leaf Clusters; and

WHEREAS, the 39th Fighter Squadron, together with other units of the Fifth Air Force, is credited with preventing New Guinea, and probably Australia, from falling into Japanese hands during the early years of the war in the Pacific; and be it further

RESOLVED, That this House of Representatives of the State of Rhode Island and Providence Plantations hereby expresses our gratitude to Captain Lewis Lockhart for his service to our nation during the darkest days of World War II; and be it further

RESOLVED, That this House respectfully requests the Governor to honor Captain Lewis Lockhart for his extraordinary heroism in the service of our nation, in particular for his efforts to save 2nd Lt. Robert E. Thorpe, a Rhode Island hero who lost his life after flying a combat mission for the 39th Fighter Squadron; and be it further

RESOLVED, That the Secretary of State be and hereby is authorized and directed to transmit duly certified copies of this resolution to Governor Lincoln Chafee and Captain Lewis Lockhart.

John Gallo - Chief Master Sergeant - President of the HVAC - and members were recognized.

Also recognized were the attending veterans' organizations including the Disabled American Veterans, the Rhode Island Veterans Council, and the Patriot Guard Riders.

Chaplain Ron Martin Minnich of the RI Army National Guard gave the closing blessing and Army Sgt. Clifford Soares played "Taps" to end the ceremony.

After the formal ceremony, Capitol TV announcer Dave Barber interviewed Representative Martin, Ken Dooley, Lew Lockhart, and Gill Thorpe. During the interviews, Barber quoted General Patton as saying, "Live for something rather than die for nothing."

As he walked out of the House chamber, Martin, who had never heard that quote before, started to think, *Should it really be "Die for something rather than live for nothing?"*

2nd Lieutenant Robert Thorpe did not die for nothing.

Chapter 28
Memorial Day

The skies were overcast as Martin walked down the driveway to wait for Representative Abney who had offered to drive for the day. He was hoping that the rain would hold off until after the annual Memorial Day ceremony at the Rhode Island Veterans Cemetery in Exeter.

They drove through historic Newport to pick up the man who had introduced them to the Thorpe case, author Ken Dooley.

Dooley was waiting on the corner when the two representatives pulled up, Abney driving and Martin riding shotgun. Abney and Dooley had met many times, however, Dooley was not familiar with Abney's army background. During the 30-minute ride Abney told of his experiences, some of them humorous, about his time as the protocol officer for the U.S. Army in New York City.

As Martin listened to his two friends, he was hoping, for the sake of the Thorpe family, that today's ceremony would go as well.

The sky had started to clear as they crossed the two bridges from Newport heading toward Exeter. Martin was thinking how grateful he was to have been able to return to live in his hometown 11 years earlier and to have become friends with Abney while they were both serving on local city boards. They had come from very diverse backgrounds; Abney from Texas, and Martin from Rhode Island.

Now their paths had not just crossed, but they were partners as state representatives and members of the House Committee on Veterans Affairs. They had found a new bond, that of getting some long overdue recognition for 2nd Lt. Robert Thorpe.

Today was the 69th anniversary of Robert Thorpe being shot down, captured, tortured, and murdered on what was to be his last mission.

Martin thought of all the un-lived years of life that the Japanese had taken from Thorpe and the young men who never had the privilege of the return trip home from the battles of World War II.

As they arrived in Exeter, Martin was feeling somewhat ashamed that he had never been to the Veterans Cemetery before. He was sure that he had ridden past it on his vintage motorcycle—just never took the time to stop by to honor those who had served their country.

He was very surprised to see the large number of cars parked in the field and all of the people next to the ceremonial tent. He realized that this was going to be a much bigger event that he had predicted.

He was wondering how he would find his friend Ed Kane in this crowd. Just as he stepped out of the car, there Kane was—pulling into the parking spot next to him. Another problem solved. It seems like this whole project was coming together that way from the very start!

Fortunately, those who planned the event included the large tent. It must have been planned for the possibility of rain. Now that the skies were clearing, it would provide welcome shade from the bright sun.

As they walked toward the tent, they saw Gill Thorpe standing with members of his family. He seemed also overwhelmed by the preparations for this event.

Then they heard the music. It was the 88th Army Band from nearby Camp Fogarty in East Greenwich, Rhode Island. It was very comforting to see and hear this well trained band.

Martin later learned that this band, part of the Rhode Island Army National Guard, is referred to as "The Governor's Own." Its mission is *"to provide music that promotes troop morale, unit esprit de corps, and support civil and military operations and ceremonies."*

As Martin picked up a copy of the program for the ceremony, he wondered how much recognition Robert Thorpe actually would get from this prestigious group of military officers, congressional representatives, and others. He was happy to see two of his friends, Lisa Rama, the public information officer from Naval Station Newport, and Kim Ripoli, Rhode

Island Associate Director of Veterans Affairs, a retired U.S. Navy medic. He had confidence that these two knew what they were doing.

He was very happy to see that the entire Rhode Island Congressional Delegation, including Senators Sheldon Whitehouse and Jack Reed, as well as Congressmen David Cicilline and Jim Langevin. Martin knew that many of them and their staff members knew about Robert Thorpe. He knew that some of their staff had worked diligently and fruitlessly with Gill Thorpe in the attempt to bring back Robert's remains.

Martin was very impressed not only with the size of the group of attendees, but also with this gathering of individuals whom he had come to know as strong supporters of veterans affairs in Rhode Island.

Following the musical prelude, the welcoming remarks were given by Daniel Evangelista, CSM (Ret), Rhode Island's Chief of Veterans Affairs. John N. Christenson, USN, President of Naval War College in Newport, called for the posting of the colors, the 88th Army Band played the "National Anthem," Lt. Governor Elizabeth H. Roberts led the Pledge of Allegiance, and Father Robert L. Marciano, Chaplain, Colonel, USAF, gave the invocation.

After Associate Director Kim Ripoli introduced the distinguished guests, Governor Lincoln D. Chafee gave the welcoming remarks and John N. Christenson introduced Dr. John Parrish, MD, a Vietnam veteran who shared his personal experiences as a veteran with the audience.

Although Representative Martin enjoyed the speeches and was particularly moved by Dr. Parrish's comments, he was wondering if the program was going to acknowledge Robert Thorpe or were the Thorpe brothers, Robert and Gill, going to once again be forgotten in the midst of "political activity."

Then it happened! Naval Health Clinic N.E. members came to formation in front of the dais while Kim Ripoli started to read the very impressive "Old Glory" poem. Representative Martin and others watched as the sailors in their white uniforms folded the flag and very formally passed it from one to another.

Martin's concerns about the ceremony giving proper respect to Robert Thorpe were soon ended when he realized that the flag was being passed to Robert's brother, Gill.

Most fortunately, Lisa Rama was able to capture this "Old Glory" ceremony on her iPad. Watching that video, which would be posted on Naval Station Newport's Facebook page, provides invaluable memories of the day. Robert Thorpe and his family had finally been given recognition for his ultimate sacrifice.

The ceremony continued with the laying of a wreath and the firing of a volley by the RING Rifle Squad. 1st Sgt. Cliff Soares played "Taps" and the 88th Army Band played "The Battle Hymn of the Republic." and Father Marciano gave the benediction.

Chapter 29
39th Fighter Squadron Association Reunion

During the process of getting recognition for Robert Thorpe, Representative Martin had not realized that his efforts were part of a larger scene. He had focused on this one individual without realizing that Robert Thorpe is representative of many more individuals who had made the ultimate sacrifice and had not been "brought home" by our government.

Martin was very surprised when he received a call from Linne Haddock, the daughter of Frank Royal, a former commanding officer of the 39th Fighter Squadron during World War II. She was calling to ask the representative if he would be willing to speak about the posthumous honors at the 39th Fighter Squadron Association (FSA) 2013 Reunion that was to be held in San Antonio, Texas, in October.

Without hesitation, he called the airline and purchased a ticket to San Antonio. He then asked Representative Abney if he would like to join him. Abney, a native of Texas and one-time resident of San Antonio, immediately agreed.

During the reunion dinner, Representative Martin provided a short overview regarding 2nd Lt. Thorpe's life, death, and the long overdue recognition of his ultimate sacrifice.

He also presented a petition requesting that the U.S. government do everything possible to repatriate the remains of Lieutenant Thorpe so his exemplary service and sacrifice for his country could finally be properly recognized and honored. Twenty-three veteran members of the association signed the petition. The petition was to be sent to the president, vice president, and all members of the U.S. Senate.

At the banquet, Representative Abney presented the 39th Fighter Squadron Association with two citations. The first was from Rhode Island Governor Lincoln D. Chafee recognizing the Cobra Squadron's "steadfast and loyal contribution to the defense of our country since 1939."

The other was from Rhode Island's senior U.S. Senator Jack Reed recognizing the 39th Fighter Squadron for its "steadfast and patriotic contributions to the defense of the United States of America since 1939." Both of these documents are now on display at the 39th Flying Training Squadron Headquarters (FTS) located at Randolph Air Force Base.

To show their appreciation to Representatives Martin and Abney, 39th FSA President Lt. Col. Brian "Bluto" Haines presented each of them a 39th FSA silver medallion.

The 39th Fighter Squadron Association wrote in their 2013 reunion report:

> *"The 39th FSA was honored to have Rhode Island State Representatives Peter Martin and Marvin Abney attend the 2013 Reunion. Martin was the force behind the May 2013 Memorial Service held in the Rhode Island House of Representatives for 2nd Lt. Robert Thorpe, a member of the 39th Pursuit Squadron who lost his life in WWII."*

The previous 39th FSA newsletter had an article about Lieutenant Thorpe, the Memorial Service, and the involvement of Lew Lockhart.

Shortly after returning from Texas, Representative Abney sent the following message to Ken Dooley and Gill Thorpe expressing his appreciation for having been able to attend the reunion.

> *It was amazing, but not surprising to witness firsthand, the camaraderie which existed that day between sky warriors of the past and present. The age spans of some approached 50 years. There was talk of magnificent flying machines which took these aviators on combat missions*

and brought them back safely from enemy action over enemy airspace far away from home. The enthusiasm of fighting to preserve freedom, as they knew it, was clearly evident. For anyone to take part in such historic conversations would be incredibly emotional, as it was for me.

Though the bulk of the conversations revolved around the technical abilities of man and machines, a very human side of these multigenerational aviators came through. Jokes were told about early members being able to still get into the same flying uniforms they wore decades ago. There was no doubt of the camaraderie that existed between active members of the 39th FS, former members, and their families.

Most notably was how involved and informed the early members were of present-day social, economic, and political events and their willingness to come to the defense of their country again.

Chapter 30
Finally a Marker

During the 2014 Christmas season, Gill Thorpe, Ken Dooley, Rep. Marvin Abney, Sgt. Major Ed Kane [U.S. Army Ret], and Representative Martin met with CPO Jonathan Rascoe [U.S. Navy Ret] to discuss the placement of a stone at the RI Veterans Memorial Cemetery in memory of 2nd Lt. Thorpe.

The stone will be placed in the section of the cemetery dedicated to those who are missing in action and/or those whose remains could not be brought home. While the stone commemorates the sacrifice of Lt. Robert Thorpe, it stands in silent testimony to the sacrifices made by all of the World War II members of the 39th Fighter Squadron who also gave their lives for their country.

Gill Thorpe agreed to abandon his lifelong search for his brother's remains in order to have this commemorative stone placed at the Veterans Cemetery. As he signed those documents, his lifelong friend, Ken Dooley looked on.

On June 12th, 2015, a ceremony was held at Veterans Memorial Cemetery during which a marker was dedicated to the memory of Lt. Robert E. Thorpe.

After the ceremony, Gill Thorpe sent the following message to all those who had been involved in honoring his brother, Robert Thorpe.

In 2002, I started the venture to find out about Bob. I had no idea where it was going to lead me, however, my guilt trip of not doing anything was getting to me in a big way. By now, you know all there is to know about the journey and thanks to you in the biggest way the journey was more successful having you on board than it would have been without you.

My closure with Bob only came to me, and gratefully so, when Ken Dooley got us involved with Peter Martin and the group at the State House.

Then there was the beautiful day at the Veterans Cemetery. That was the icing on the cake.

I can't express to you my feeling of Bob's case now being completed and that finally after all these years, the state of RI and the Veterans Association have finally recognized Bob.

I have just begun to realize that my mind and body have come to terms with Bob, Mom, and Dad. Now it is time to end the journey.

Nothing will surpass the recognition given to the Thorpes at the State House and the Veterans Cemetery.

My journey is now complete.

I can never thank you enough.

Gill

Closure

Gill Thorpe, Ken Dooley and Peter Martin stand by the memorial stone dedicated to Lt. Robert E. Thorpe at Veterans Memorial Cemetery on June 12, 2015.

Epilogue

"Leapfrogging," the strategy of bypassing heavily fortified Japanese positions and concentrating on strategically important islands that were not well defended, was one of the keys to Japan's unconditional surrender on the USS *Missouri* on September 2, 1945.

This strategy allowed United States forces to reach Japan more quickly without expending the time, manpower, and supplies to capture every Japanese-held island on the way. The troops on islands that had been bypassed, such as major Japanese bases at Rabaul and Wewak, were left to wither on the vine.

The overall leapfrogging strategy involved two prongs: Admiral Chester Nimitz, with a smaller land force and larger fleet, advanced north and captured the Gilbert and Marshall islands and the Marianas. The southern prong, led by General Douglas MacArthur, with larger land forces and pilots from the Fifth Air Force, took the Solomons, New Guinea, the Bismarck Archipelago, and the Philippines.

The best strategy is only as good as the men trained and motivated to implement it.

The 39th Fighter Squadron of the Fifth Air Force demonstrated this remarkable effort and achievement in microcosm. Many of its pilots were youngsters who had never been off the ground, much less flown an airplane, on December 7, 1941. Rushed through training and initially assigned airplanes seriously inferior to those they would meet in combat, they never faltered in their determination to win this war—or in their belief that, no matter how many setbacks they suffered, they would win it.

What is astonishing about their determination and performance are the challenges they faced daily. Weather was frequently a greater peril than the enemy, as the pilots faced a solid front of fog and clouds hovering over the eastern coast of New Guinea. This front might be 1,000 miles long and 100 miles deep, and our planes had difficulty getting under it, over it, through it, or around it.

War and danger are synonymous. But each time these men climbed into the cockpits of their fighter planes, they had to be keenly aware that death—and particularly grisly death—might well await them. Beyond the high probability of crashing on takeoff, being lost in weather, or exploding in aerial combat, they knew that capture by the enemy would almost certainly result in torture and execution.

It was a particularly ghastly aspect of their peril that they would be beheaded, not only by out of control Japanese soldiers, but also under Japanese Imperial policy. It was one of the travesties of the war that execution by beheading would be imposed on captured pilots by this supposedly civilized government as some kind of sick system of honor.

When the war ended, these beheadings and other atrocities were discovered and investigated, and the perpetrators were tried and, when convicted, punished. It is one of the great strengths of this book that these crucial postwar events are recounted in detail. More than an epilogue, it is a detailed exploration of the minds and motivations of the men on both sides of this terrible conflict.

I arrived in the Pacific as a young naval officer on a landing craft in late 1945. While I was too late to see action, I was able to view, firsthand, the results of their heroism.

The course of history in World War II would have been altered greatly if it had not been for the determination and sacrifice of the men of the 39th Fighter Squadron, who, together with other members of the Fifth Air Force, stopped the Japanese onslaught dead in its tracks.

Author Ken Dooley takes us on a crusade, island by island, as men of the 39th Fighter Squadron meet and defeat a determined and brutal enemy. His writing is well paced, and you can feel his enthusiasm as he recounts the stories of remarkable young men who gave so much under the most difficult circumstances. He does an excellent job of weaving the stories—ranging from a future ace apologizing to a housewife for buzzing her clothesline to ferocious air battles during which some pilots of the 39th paid the ultimate price.

The photography and maps are well captioned and help immeasurably in understanding the brilliant island-hopping strategy of General Douglas MacArthur and Admiral Chester Nimitz.

When young men go to war, their families are with them in love, spirit, and often wrenching anxiety. When a warrior fails to return, the loss is suffered by his loved ones for years to come. What are the obligations of the officials, both civilian and military, to these young men?

In the popular imagination, they are depicted in elaborate funeral ceremonies at Arlington National Cemetery. But the reality can be far different. The bodies of battle casualties often stay where they fell—the harsh realities of warfare preventing their recovery. Even when physical recovery is not possible, however, there is a solemn obligation for responsible officials to treat the families both compassionately and truthfully.

Ken Dooley describes a different kind of treatment given to the family of Robert Thorpe. This fallen hero's family was victimized by a deliberate pattern of official deceit stretching over a period of more than 60 years.

Although the exact location of Thorpe's remains were documented in a map drawn in 1948 during the war crimes trials in Yokohama, the Thorpe family was told his remains were "unrecoverable."

The records of the court-martial were also listed as "secret" until Ken Dooley got copies of them in 2007 under the Freedom of Information Act. While his heroism remains a secret to most of the nation, Thorpe's home state of Rhode Island has not forgotten.

When Representative Peter Martin, a member of the Rhode Island House Committee on Veterans Affairs, learned about the sacrifice of Lieutenant Robert Thorpe from Dooley, he initiated the steps which led to posthumous recognition for the Thorpe family.

Martin introduced resolutions honoring 2nd Lt. Robert E. Thorpe, as well as Captain Lewis Lockhart, Thorpe's wingman on his last flight.

A ceremony was held in the RI House Chamber on May 17, 2013.

Thanks to the efforts of Martin and Sgt. Major Edward Kane, the Thorpe family is now able to visit the monument honoring Robert E. Thorpe at the Rhode Island Veterans Cemetery in Exeter, Rhode Island.

J. William Middendorf
Former Secretary of the Navy

Acknowledgments

It was an exciting time to be 13 years old in 1944, especially for Gill Thorpe and myself, living one street apart in Edgewood, Rhode Island. My brother Jack was fighting in the Pacific with the 1st Division of the USMC, and my brother Bill was in Europe with the 88th Infantry Fighting Blue Devils Division. Gill had a brother, Bob, a P-47 pilot with the 39th Fighter Squadron flying combat missions in New Guinea.

What army censors took away, Gill and I were able to replace with imagination, as we exchanged stories about the exploits of our brothers. Neither one of us was the least bit worried about their safety. John Wayne was winning the war in the Pacific and Errol Flynn, when he was not playing Robin Hood or General Custer, was handling the Nazis in Europe.

Only the bad guys got wounded or killed in war. Nothing happened to the good guys, right? That thinking all changed one day in early June of 1944 when an army vehicle stopped in front of the Thorpe home. Gill was home with his sister, Nancy, when two army officers came to the door and asked to speak to the parents of Lt. Robert Thorpe. Gill explained that his mother and father, Walter and Nora Thorpe, were playing bridge at a cousin's home.

One of the officers told Gill that his brother had been missing since May 27th and handed him a telegram to deliver to his parents. Gill called his father immediately. "Bob's missing in action," he said to his father. Gill still remembers his parents returning to the house, his mother crying softly. His father didn't say anything as he read the telegram. Word spread through the neighborhood quickly.

A few days after the official visit, an article from the AP appeared in the *Providence Journal* reporting that Lt. Robert Thorpe was missing after a strafing mission against an enemy air strip near Wewak, New Guinea. His plane was last seen as it went into a dive and was hit by enemy ground fire. The target was close to the ocean, so it was presumed that his plane had fallen into the sea. No trace was found of him or his plane, and he was officially listed as missing in action.

The news about Bob Thorpe served as a wake-up call for all of the young boys who had previously felt that war was so exciting. Gill and I suddenly realized good guys do get hurt in wars. We never again looked at John Wayne or Errol Flynn the same way.

Four years later, on June 21, 1948, Nora Thorpe received a phone call from a woman in California offering her condolences on the death of Bob Thorpe. She had a son who was also killed in action and wanted to share her grief with another Gold Star mother. When Nora explained that Bob was "missing" and the family still had hopes that he would be found, the woman read her an article that appeared in her local newspaper. It named five Japanese officers who were going on trial for torturing and beheading Robert E. Thorpe in May of 1944.

Nora called her husband at the drugstore, and Walter made inquiries about the story. Before he received any formal notification from the military, an article appeared in *The Providence Journal* on June 22, 1948, describing what was called one of the most revolting crimes uncovered by war crimes investigators. Five Japanese officers admitted beating Lieutenant Thorpe, using him for target practice, beheading him, and desecrating his body at a beach on Kairiru Island, New Guinea.

Admiral Kenro Sato, the officer who gave the order to execute Thorpe, committed suicide in 1948 after learning that he was about to be arrested and charged in the war crimes trials at Yokohama. CWO Waichi Ogawa, who was charged with desecrating Lieutenant Thorpe's body, hanged himself at Sugamo Prison shortly before the trial began.

On July 6, 1948, three Japanese officers were sentenced to life imprisonment, while a fourth received a 20-year sentence. Lt. Commander Kaoru Okuma, the officer in charge of the execution, was sentenced to death. On May 27, 1949, 5 years to the day of Bob Thorpe's last mission, Okuma was hanged at Sugamo Prison in Japan.

The Thorpe family accepted the news quietly and made no public comment, even after the sentences were announced and Okuma was hanged. Nora Thorpe never fully recovered from her son's brutal execution. Friends say her beautiful smile disappeared right after she learned about Bob's death, and she became withdrawn and quiet. She died prematurely in 1956 at the age of 56.

Behind the scenes, Walter Thorpe never stopped in his efforts to have his son's remains returned to Rhode Island, even though he was told repeatedly they were unrecoverable. The trial records of the officers found guilty were classified as "secret," under the direct orders of General Douglas MacArthur, the supreme commander of Allied Powers in Japan.

Walter Thorpe never accepted the "unrecoverable" explanation, reasoning that if his son had been executed on a beach, his remains had to be buried somewhere. He enlisted the aid of several elected officials to get some answers. All inquiries continued to be answered with a one-word comment from the military—"unrecoverable."

Walter Thorpe died in 1977 at the age of 82. He had never fully escaped the nagging feeling that his son's remains were out there somewhere near the beach where he had been tortured and buried. His goal of burying Bob's remains in the family plot was never achieved.

Gill followed in his father's footsteps, becoming a pharmacist and, with his sister Nancy, took over the family business. Almost 60 years later, Gill decided that he had not done enough on his brother's behalf.

He began to make inquiries in 2003. He was given the name of Michael Claringbould, a historian and author of several books on the Fifth Air Force, which included the 39th Fighter Squadron, Bob's unit in New Guinea. Claringbould grew up in Papua New Guinea and became an expert at locating missing planes and aircraft downed in the Pacific in World War II.

Claringbould gave Gill a "Missing Air Crew Report" containing critical information about Bob's capture and execution, including two sketches of his burial site, only yards from the beach where he had been beheaded.

Thorpe immediately contacted Sen. Jack Reed's office with the detailed maps of his brother's grave.

Bob Kerr, a columnist for *The Providence Journal*, wrote a column about Gill's efforts that attracted my attention. I had left Rhode Island in 1960 and spent the next 40 years as a writer, working in Connecticut, New York, New Jersey, and Pennsylvania. I assumed Bob's remains had been returned after the trials in 1948.

I called Gill, and we had our first conversation in 30 years. Gill sent me a copy of the "Missing Air Crew Report" Claringbould had given him. After reading the report, I called Gill and advised him to get copies of the records from the trials in Yokohama in 1948.

When Gill said he did not know how to go about it, I decided to take action under the "Freedom of Information Act." After a number of letters, phone calls, and trips to Washington, D.C., I finally obtained official transcripts of the trials of the five officers convicted of torturing and beheading Bob Thorpe. I read the transcripts in a hotel room, finishing at 3 a.m.

The actual details of what Bob Thorpe had endured kept me up for the rest of that night and for many nights to come. I decided that morning to write a book about Bob Thorpe and the courage, conviction, and dignity he displayed on that lonely beach where he made the ultimate sacrifice for his country so many years before.

I began with a search for former pilots of the 39th Fighter Squadron who flew with Bob Thorpe in New Guinea. I hit gold with my first contact, John Dunbar, a pilot who remembered flying with Bob at Gusap Air Base, New Guinea. John had kept a diary of his time with the 39th, which provided critical information for this book. It was John who gave me the contact information for Fred Tobi, Bob Thorpe's closest friend in the 39th Fighter Squadron. I was living in Sarasota, Florida, at the time, about 45 minutes from Fred Tobi's home in Tampa.

Fred had gone through flight training with Bob Thorpe at Dove Field in Arcadia, Florida. He remembered meeting Bob's mother, Nora, when the two pilots got their wings in 1943. After I had several interviews with Fred, Gill Thorpe flew to Tampa to meet with his brother's best friend. Now a retired fruit broker, Fred had almost total recall of his time in New Guinea.

He still remembers his first combat mission with Bob Thorpe. "Bob and I were sent in a fighter sweep against Wewak, a Japanese air base," Tobi said. "We were deployed in four flights of four. Outcast Red was leader, with White, Blue, and Green the other flights. The air and sky were clear. We flew over Wewak and observed that it was pretty beat up with wrecked aircraft and craters on the runways." Tobi said that he and Bob always made it to their target, which was usually Wewak. When they weren't escorting bombers, they were strafing the fields at Wewak.

Fred shared a tent in Gusap, New Guinea, with Bob Thorpe, Marques Trout, and James C. Steele. Like Bob Thorpe, James C. Steele was captured by the Japanese and executed. After flying 97 missions, Fred Tobi was horribly burned when his P-47 crashed on takeoff in New Guinea in 1944. He spent the next 3 years undergoing extensive surgery and did not leave the hospital until 1947.

Fred made arrangements for me to meet with Captain Lew Lockhart at his home in Brentwood, Tennessee. I learned that Lockhart had flown 149 combat missions with the 39th FS in New Guinea. He and Tobi were both on what was to be Thorpe's last combat mission on May 27, 1944.

"I was leading Blue Flight, and Fred Tobi was my wingman," Lockhart said. "Bob Thorpe was the wingman for Lt. Raymond Kramme in Green Flight. Lt. James Robertson was also on Green Flight. Major Denton, the squadron commander, was leading Red Flight.

"Overall, it was a successful mission, with one big negative. Bob didn't return. At the debriefing, Robertson said he saw Bob just before he made his final run, and his aircraft was in good shape. Kramme said ground fire was heavier than usual, and Bob may have been hit. Weather grounded the squadron the next morning, but Fred Tobi and I broke orders and went looking for Bob," Lockhart said. "No trace of him or the plane."

It was through Fred Tobi and John Dunbar that I made contact with Frank Royal, two-time CO of the 39th FS and probably its most beloved leader; S/Sgt. Roy Seher; Jack Frost; and Chuck O'Sullivan. They patiently answered questions posed by me, a former staff sergeant who fought the Korean War in Europe and Africa with a typewriter.

The memories of these men are astounding. Every time I checked their accounts of missions, squadron records, lost pilots, and planes, their recollections were extremely accurate.

Lew Lockhart spent many hours on the telephone with me, reliving his days with the 39th when his plane crashed on takeoff, and he escaped with a few minor bruises and was flying the next day. I will always remember his laughter when he told me about a trick he had discovered while ferrying P-38s from Australia to New Guinea. "I would remove the ammunition and replace it with beer for my thirsty friends in New Guinea."

Jack Frost was able to make a not particularly technical person understand the Lindbergh method of extending the range of bombers and pursuit aircraft. His story about confiscating Gen. Douglas MacArthur's lumber provides one of the light moments in the book.

Lew Lockhart introduced me to a very special person by the name of Mary Morgan Martin, daughter of Captain George Morgan who was killed in the Battle of the Philippines in 1945.

Mary's mother, Lt. Mary Scott Morgan, met Captain George Morgan while serving as a nurse in Australia. They fell in love, returned to the States, and were married in Washington State. Even though he had already flown 149 missions with the 39th Fighter Squadron in New Guinea, he was recalled for the battle of the Philippines.

Mary's mother was 3 months pregnant with Mary when Captain Morgan was killed. His plane was hit by ground fire, and he was struck by the fuselage while bailing out.

Mary sent me her father's wartime love letters to her mother, photos, clippings, and daily squadron reports I never would have been able to find on my own. She painstakingly restored all of the photos in this book, many of them taken by her father. Without Mary Morgan Martin, there would not be a book.

Mary also answered a question that had bothered me early in my research. Fred Tobi became quite emotional when I told him about the brutality of Bob Thorpe's death. He had never contacted the Thorpe family after the war to find out what happened to his best friend. He knew nothing about the trial of the Japanese officers who had murdered Bob Thorpe.

"Silence seemed to be the accepted practice," Mary Martin said.

"These men were uncomfortable in discussing death, having been so close to it themselves. They did not know how their visits or telephone calls would be received. There were reports of grieving relatives verbally attacking survivors by saying things like, 'Why did he die and not you?'" So Mary understands why even close friends like Fred did not try to find out what happened to Bob.

After meeting these incredible people and listening to their fascinating stories, I changed the focus of the book from Bob Thorpe to the entire 39th Fighter Squadron. I began an 8-year journey through squadron mission reports, letters, diaries, photographs, telegrams, telephone interviews, e-mails, and records of war crimes trials.

The journey was not always easy, especially when reading about the deaths of these outstanding young men and the families they left behind.

Fred Tobi, John Dunbar, Roy Seher, and Chuck O'Sullivan died while I was still writing this book. Lew Lockhart and Jack Frost are both 94, and Frank Royal will turn 100 this summer.

I want to send special thanks to Linne Haddock for a treasure trove of information that was so invaluable in telling this story. Linne is the daughter of Col. Frank Royal, the man who put the 39th FS together in Brisbane, Australia, in 1942.

It is always dangerous for an author to choose brighter and better writers for the foreword and epilogue of his book. I took that risk by asking Dr. Patrick T. Conley and former Secretary of the Navy J. William Middendorf to fill those roles.

As expected, Dr. Conley proved to be a tough act to follow. As Historian Laureate for the state of Rhode Island, I am not at all surprised by his legendary knowledge of Rhode Island history. I was impressed, however, by his total command of world history, including World War II.

Secretary Middendorf takes special pains to explain his arrival in the Pacific Theater as a young naval officer after the fighting had ceased. He does not mention that it was under his watch as the secretary of the navy that the Ohio-class ballistic missile submarine and the companion Trident missile, the Aegis surface-launched missile system, and the F/A18 carrier-based fighter aircraft were all introduced.

I am deeply indebted to one man who acted as my personal alarm clock in restarting this book that had slowed to a crawl until he became involved. As chief motivator and graphic designer, former State Representative Peter Martin deserves special recognition. His experience as a software development project manager and his technical skills played a huge role in keeping this book on schedule and bringing it to a successful conclusion.

I owe special thanks to several people, starting with Louise Casavant, my chief proofreader. Louise's diligence and enthusiasm in checking facts were invaluable. I am also grateful to my other proofreader, Dr. Donald Deignan, who made several important contributions.

I would like to recognize my special researchers, Wayne N. Muller and Steve Petrides, for assembling more than 2,000 separate pieces of information into one cohesive unit.

I am especially grateful to my childhood friend, Gill Thorpe, for allowing me to tell the story of his brother's tragic capture and death.

Finally, I want to thank all of the men of the 39th Fighter Squadron, living and dead, who served in World War II.

They were, indeed, the greatest generation.

Ken Dooley
Newport, RI
April 2015

Notes

All interviews were conducted by the author either in-person, by e-mail or telephone.

Introduction

Interviews with Gill Thorpe, John Dunbar, Fred Tobi, Lew Lockhart, Frank Royal, Jack Frost, and Roy Seher

Letters of Captain George Morgan

A History of the 39th Pursuit Squadron by Col. Frank R. Royal and S/Sgt. Roy Seher

Chapter 1: Bob Thorpe's Last Flight

Missing Aircraft Combat Report (MACR) 5754, Dec. 20, 1945

Interviews with Fred Tobi, Lew Lockhart, Jack Frost, John Dunbar, Frank Royal, and Roy Seher

A History of the 39th Pursuit Squadron by Col. Frank R. Royal and S/Sgt. Roy Seher

39th FS Squadron Diary recorded by Sgt. Donald Thomas

Yutaka Odazawa, Kaoru Okuma, Naotada Fujihira, Kiyohisa Noto, Tsunehiko Yamamoto, et al.: Record of Trial, National Archives 343112

Yutaka Odazawa, Kaoru Okuma, Naotada Fujihira, Kiyohisa Noto, Tsunehiko Yamamoto, et al.: Record of Trial, National Archives 343113

Chapter 2. Meet the Thorpes

Interviews with Gill Thorpe, Fred Tobi, Jack Frost, Lew Lockhart

A History of the 39th Pursuit Squadron by Col. Frank R. Royal and S/Sgt. Roy Seher

Chapter 4. The Battle of the Coral Sea

Interviews with Frank Royal, John Dunbar, Lew Lockhart, Jack Frost, and Roy Seher

Diary of John Dunbar

39th Fighter Squadron Combat Diary for the following dates:

May 17, 1942
May 18, 1942
May 20, 1942
May 26, 1942

A History of the 39th Pursuit Squadron by Col. Frank R. Royal and S/Sgt. Roy Seher

Chapter 5. The P-38 Arrives

Interviews with Lew Lockhart, John Dunbar, Frank Royal, and Roy Seher

A History of the 39th Pursuit Squadron by Col. Frank R. Royal and S/Sgt. Roy Seher

Chapter 6. Gaining Air Supremacy

Interviews with Jack Frost, Lew Lockhart, Fred Tobi, Frank Royal, and Charles Sullivan

A History of the 39th Pursuit Squadron by Col. Frank R. Royal and S/Sgt. Roy Seher

39th Fighter Squadron Combat diary for the following dates:

July 19, 1943
October 19, 1943

Chapter 7: The Battle of Bismarck Sea

A History of the 39th Pursuit Squadron by Col. Frank Royal and S/Sgt. Roy Seher

The Diary of John Dunbar

Flight report of Lt. Danny Roberts, April 12, 1943

Mission reports of the 39th Fighter Squadron during the Battle of Bismarck Sea

39th FS Squadron Diary recorded by Sgt. Donald Thomas

Chapter 8: The Flying Circus

Interviews with Lew Lockhart, Fred Tobi, Frank Royal, John Dunbar, and Roy Seher

39th Fighter Squadron Combat diary for the following dates:

May 17, 1942
May 18, 1942
May 20, 1942
Dec. 27, 1942

Flight report of Lt. Richard Bong, March 8, 1944

Chapter 9: Faith, Determination and a Bit of Irish Luck

A History of the 39th Pursuit Squadron by Col. Frank Royal and S/Sgt. Roy Seher

Diary of John Dunbar

Chapter 15: Lucky Lindy and the 39th Fighter Squadron

Interviews with Jack Frost, Lew Lockhart, Fred Tobi, John Dunbar, Roy Seher, and Frank Royal

A History of the 39th Pursuit Squadron by Col. Frank Royal and S/Sgt. Roy Seher

Diary of John Dunbar

39th FS Squadron Diary recorded by Sgt. Donald Thomas

Chapter 16: The Philippines Campaign

Interviews with Jack Frost, John Dunbar, Lew Lockhart, Frank Royal, Fred Tobi, and Roy Seher

A History of the 39th Pursuit Squadron by Col. Frank Royal and S/Sgt. Roy Seher

Diary of John Dunbar

Letters from Captain George Morgan

Flight Log of Lt. William Rogers, Jan. 26, 1945

Flight log of May 31, 1945

Flight log for Capt. Lee Grosshuesch on July 30, 1945

Flight log of Lt. Henry Chick, Aug. 10, 1945

Chapter 17: They Also Serve Who Only Stand and Wait

Interviews with Jack Frost, Fred Tobi, John Dunbar, Lew Lockhart, Roy Seher, and Frank Royal

A History of the 39th Pursuit Squadron by Col. Frank Royal and S/Sgt. Roy Seher

Chapter 18: If Taken Prisoner

Handbook for POWs given to all pilots of the Fifth Air Force

Confession of five Japanese soldiers who took part in the execution of Lt. James Steele on March 23, 1945

A History of the 39th Pursuit Squadron by Col. Frank R. Royal and S/Sgt. Roy Seher

Chapter 19: The Cover-up

Report of an Australian Board of Inquiry conducted on Dec. 20, 1945, by Captain John Steed, concerning three missing pilots, two Australians and one American

Report of Investigation by Legal Section, U.S. Army, by Captain Richard Chedester

Chapter 20: Judgment at Tokyo

The Other Nuremberg: The Untold Story of the Tokyo War Crimes Trials by Arnold Brackman

Defending the Enemy: Justice for World War II Japanese War Criminals by Elaine Fischel

Chapter 21: Meet the Accused

Yutaka Odazawa, et al.: Clemency Petitions, 1945–1949, National Archives Identifier 34314

Yutaka Odazawa et al.: Clemency Papers, National Archives Identifier 505471

Case Docket No. 329: Yutaka Odazawa, et al. Record of Trial, National Archives Identifier 505470

Chapter 22: Judgment at Yokohama

Yutaka Odazawa, et al.: Record of Trial, National Archives 505471

Case Docket No. 329: Yutaka Odazawa, et al. Record of Trial, National Archives Identifier 505834

Case Docket No. 329: Yutaka Odazawa, et al. Record of Trial, National Archives Identifier 506442

Chapter 23: For the Defense

Case Docket No. 329: Yutaka Odazawa, et al. Record of Trial, National Archives Identifier 506442

Case Docket No. 329: Yutaka Odazawa, et al., National Archives Identifier 507059

Case Docket No. 329: Yutaka Odazawa, et al. (Appeal Office File) National Archives Identifier: 507468

Chapter 24: The Asian Green Mile

Odazawa, Yutaka, et al., National Archives Identifier A1 144

Case Docket No. 329: Yutaka Odazawa, et al. (Clemency Papers) National Archives Identifier 505471

Bibliography

A History of the 39th Pursuit Squadron, by Col. Frank R. Royal and S/Sgt. Roy Seher

A War to be Won: Fighting the Second World War, by Williamson Murray

Ace of Aces, by Carol Bony and Mike O'Conner

Air War Against Japan 1943–1945, by George Odgers

Airacobra Advantage: The Flying Cannon, by Rick Mitchell

Black Sunday, by Michael J. Claringbould

Cobra! Bell Aircraft Corporation, by Birch Matthews

MacArthur's ULTRA: Codebreaking and the War Against Japan, by Edward Drea

Defending the Enemy, by Elaine Fischel

Fighter Tactics and Strategy, by Edward Sims

Flyboys, by James Bradley

Fork-tailed Devil, by Martin Caidin

Fortress Rabaul: The Battle for the Southwest Pacific, by Bruce Gamble

General Kenney Reports: A Personal History of the Pacific War, by Duell, Sloan, and Pearce

Into Darkness, by Edward Imparato

Japanese Naval Air Force Fighter Units and Their Aces, by Ikuhiko Hata

Lindbergh, by A. Scott Berg

Lockheed P-38 Lightning, by Edward Maloney

MacArthur's Airman: General George C. Kenney and the War in the Southwest Pacific, by Thomas Griffith

Magnificent Mustang: A Production History of the North American P-51, by Ken Wixey

Operations of the Imperial Japanese Armed Forces in the Papua New Guinea Theater During World War II, by Steve Thompson

Operations of the Imperial Japanese Armed Forces in the Papua New Guinea theater During World War II, by Kengoro Tanaka

Outcast Red, by William Rogers

P-38 Lightning Aces of the Pacific, by John Stanaway

P-38 Lightning: The Great Book of World War II Airplanes, by Jeffrey Ethell

P-39 Airacobra Aces of World War 2, by George Mellinger and John Stanaway

P-39 Airacobra in Action, by Ernest McFarland

P-47 Thunderbolt at War, by Cory Graff

P-47 Thunderbolt in Action, by Larry Davis

Piercing the Fog: Intelligence and Army Air Forces Operations in World War II, by John Kreis

Retaking the Philippines, by William Breuer

Royal Australian Air Force 1939–1943, by Douglas Gillison

The Battle Against Intervention in World War II, by Wayne S. Cole

The Battle of the Bismarck Sea, by Lex McAuley

The Bell P-39 Airacobra, by Jay Dial

The Codebreakers, by David Kahn

The Diary of John Dunbar by Lt. John Dunbar

The Eagle and the Rising Sun: The Japanese-American War, by Alan Schom

The Forgotten Fifth, by Michael J. Claringbould

The Japanese Army in the Pacific War, by Saburo Hayashi

The Last Zero Fighter, by Dan King

The Modeller's Guide to the Bell P-39 Airacobra in RAAF Service, by Gary Byck

The New Guinea Offensives, by John David

The New York Times Book of WW II, by Richard Overy

The North American Mustang, by Leonard Bridgman

The Other Nuremberg: The Untold Story of the Tokyo War Crimes Trials, by Arnold Brackman

The Papuan Campaign, by Richard Watson

The Republic P-47 Thunderbolt, by Greg Goebel

The Wartime Journals of Charles A. Lindbergh, by Charles Lindbergh

Unbroken, by Laura Hillenbrand

War Pilot: True Tales of Combat and Adventure, by Richard Kirk-
land

*We Shall Return! MacArthur's Commanders and the Defeat of Ja-
pan,* by William Leary

We, by Charles A. Lindbergh

Who Shot Down Yamamoto? by Douglas Canning

Glossary

A-20G – Douglas Havoc twin-engine bomber

ADVON – Advanced, Fifth Air Force, located at Nadzab

Betty – The Japanese twin-engine bomber

Bogey – Unidentified plane in a combat situation, assumed to be the enemy

B-17 – Boeing Flying Fortress four-engine bomber

Bully beef – Australian corned beef, the standard diet for the American army in the Southwest Pacific

B-24 – Consolidated Liberator 4-engine bomber

B-25 – North American Mitchell twin-engine bomber

B-26 – Martin Marauder twin-engine bomber

Cat – The Catalina flying boat, the PBY

C-47 – Twin-engine cargo plane

Daisy Cutter – Antipersonnel fragmentation bombs

Deflection – The angle of lead required when aiming the plane with its fixed forward-firing guns

Dive-bombing – Aiming the plane directly from above at the targets

DNG – Dutch New Guinea, now part of Indonesia

Element leader – Number three man in a flight formation, with the Tail End Charlie as his wingman

E&F report – Escape and evasion report submitted by aircrews

Five by five – Loud and clear indicating the radio transmission was heard and understood

Form I – The plane's flight report, which always had to be filled out by the pilot before leaving the plane

FG – Fighter Group

FS – Fighter Squadron

Frank – The Nakajima Ki-84 Hayate, the top-performing Japanese fighter of the war

Immelmann – A half-loop at the top of which the pilot half-rolls the plane to come out straight and level in the opposite direction from the start

Japs – Abbreviation for Japanese used by the Allies to refer to their enemy

KIA – Killed in Action

Lazy eight – The training maneuver of pulling the plane up in a near-stall turn repeatedly, then falling off on a wing to come back and repeat the process in the other direction, completing the figure eight

MACR – Missing Air Crew Report

MIA – Missing in Action

Mae West – The bright yellow life vest worn on all flights over water

Napalm – An inflammable jellylike substance which, when added to gasoline, burned long and intensely

Nip – the term used by most American pilots when referring to their Japanese enemy

Oscar – The Nakajima Ki-43, the most maneuverable Japanese fighter plane used in World War II

Outcast – The call name of the 39th Fighter Squadron throughout most of its combat history

Paddlefoot – The term used by pilots to describe anyone who was not an air crew member

P-38 – Lockheed Lightning twin-engine fighter

P-30 – Bell Airacobra single-engine fighter

P-47 – Republic Thunderbolt single-engine fighter

POW – Prisoner of War

PRG – Photographic Reconnaissance Group

PSP – Pierced Steel Planking

RAAF – Royal Australian Air Force

Red Flight – The lead flight of a squadron formation with its leader also being the squadron leader

Roger – I hear and understand

RPM – Propeller revolutions per minute

Skip bombing – A low-flying aircraft releases a bomb that skips along the ocean surface before striking its target

Snafu – A universal World War II term indicating either an aborted mission, or the pilot aborts and returns home before completing the mission

Split-S – A half-roll with the plane, then pulled through for a vertical dive, as in dive-bombing or to escape an enemy plane on its tail

Strafing – Firing the fixed forward guns of a fighter at ground targets

Stateside pallor – Referred to new arrivals in New Guinea who had not yet developed a yellow-brown complexion resulting from the use of quinine in the treatment of malaria

Strategic bombing – It meant the destruction of cities, railways, factories, dock areas, and human habitations to destroy production, human lives, and morale

Tony – Kawasaki Ki-61, the only liquid-cooled Japanese fighter in World War II

USAAF – United States Army Air Force

Wing loading – the ratio of the area of the plane's wings to the total weight of the plane. The P-47 had the highest wing loading of any fighter plane in World War II

Zeke – Mitsubishi A6M Zero-Sen, the most famous of Japanese fighters and the most successful. It could outturn and outclimb any American fighter in the early part of the war. American pilots turned the air war around when they were given the P-38 and the P-.

CPSIA information can be obtained at www.ICGtesting.com
Printed in the USA
BVOW02*1902270715

409989BV00001BA/1/P

9 780578 165424